Economics of International Business

To Janet
On Our Twenty-fifth Anniversary

Economics of International Business

A New Research Agenda

Mark Casson

Professor of Economics, University of Reading, UK

Edward Elgar

Cheltenham, UK • Northampton, MA, USA

Published by
Edward Elgar Publishing Limited
Glensanda House
Montpellier Parade
Cheltenham
Glos GL50 1UA
UK

Edward Elgar Publishing, Inc.
136 West Street
Suite 202
Northampton
Massachusetts 01060
USA

A catalogue record for this book is available from the British Library

Library of Congress Cataloguing in Publication Data

Casson, Mark, 1945–
 Economics of international business : a new research agenda / Mark Casson.
 Includes bibliographical references and index.
  1. International business enterprises—Research—Methodology. 2. International trade—Research—Methodology. 3. Industrial organization (Economic theory).
 4. Competition, International. 5. Industrial policy. 6. Economics. I. Title.

HD2755.5 C3916 2000
338.8'8—dc21

99–045194

ISBN 1 84064 355 2

Typeset by Manton Typesetters, Louth, Lincolnshire, UK.
Printed and bound in Great Britain by Biddles Ltd, *www.biddles.co.uk*.

Contents

Figures

Tables

Preface and acknowledgements

There are several different ways of explaining how this book came to be written and – more important – why it should be read. I could say that it is a manifesto for international business research in the New Millennium. I am sure that some authors will be 'hyping up' their books in this way. The truth is, however, that the book would have been written whether there was a New Millennium to celebrate or not. Alternatively, I could say that it is the sequel to my book on *The Organization of International Business*, published five years ago. That would be half-true. Unfortunately, though, sequels are rarely as good as the originals, as they tend to be produced by people who are running out of fresh ideas. I hope that this isn't true in the present case, but the reader can judge for themselves.

The whole truth is, I think, that I wrote this book for my own benefit, which is possibly one of the worst reasons there is for writing a book. Certainly, I have enjoyed writing the book – apart from the tedious though essential task of polishing up the final drafts and chasing up missing references. Writing is a form of therapy, as far as I am concerned – though not so far as my family are concerned, who find that it only exaggerates my antisocial tendencies. I would not wish to claim, however, as one rather arrogant economist once did, that 'I wrote this book because I like writing books'. Apart from the need for therapy, I wrote this book because I felt that the various papers and articles I had written over the past five years reflected a reasonably coherent view of recent trends in international business. This view, I felt, could not be fully articulated within the constraints of a single paper. The full expression and development of the view required the space permitted by a book.

The book is based mostly, though not entirely, on this previously published work. This material has been thoroughly revised and rewritten during the preparation of the book. A number of the original papers were co-authored, and I would like to thank my co-authors for their substantial intellectual contributions, and also for agreeing to their work being revised and published in its present form. The co-authors' names are listed on the Contents page and in the headings of the individual chapters of the book. I should also like to acknowledge the co-operation of the publishers of the original material.

None of the material in Chapters 3 and 7 has appeared in print before, but Chapters 1, 2, 4, 5, 6, 8, 9 are based on previously published work. Many professional colleagues have contributed comments on the drafts. I would like to thank the following people in particular for their support and encouragement, as well for as their advice and criticism: Tom Brewer, John Cantwell, John Dunning, Jose Paulo Esperanca, Peter Gray, Stephen Guisinger, Bruce Kogut, Ram Mudambi, Bob Pearce, Filipe Ravara, Alan Rugman, Ana Tavares, Christine Weisfelder, Eleanor Westney, Bernard Wolf and Bernard Yeung. I should also like to record my appreciation of the intellectual contribution of the late Gunnar Hedlund, whose untimely death has been such a loss to the profession. He and I shared a strong interest in the internal organization of the multinational enterprise and, although we approached the subject from very different methodological standpoints, we always found plenty to talk about when we met. He is sadly missed by his many friends.

All the previous papers that form the basis for chapters in this book have been radically revised and rewritten.

Chapter 1 is derived from Peter J. Buckley and Mark C. Casson (1998) 'Models of the multinational enterprise', *Journal of International Business Studies*, **29**(1), 21–44.

Chapter 2 is derived from Peter J. Buckley and Mark C. Casson (1998) 'Analysing foreign market entry strategies: extending the internalisation approach', *Journal of International Business Studies*, **29**(3), 539–61.

Chapter 3 is entirely original.

Chapter 4 is loosely based on Mark Casson and Nigel Wadeson (1999) 'Bounded rationality, meta-rationality and the theory of international business', in Fred Burton, Malcolm Chapman and Adam Cross (eds), *International Business Organization: Subsidiary Management, Entry Strategies and Emerging Markets*, London: Macmillan, 119–40.

Chapter 5 is a revised version of 'The organisation and evolution of the multinational enterprise: an information cost approach', *Management International Review*, **39**(1), 1999, 77–121.

Chapter 6 is based on Peter J. Buckley and Mark C. Casson (1996) 'An economic model of international joint venture strategy', *Journal of International Business Studies*, **27**(5), 849–76.

Chapter 7 is a revised version of Mark Casson and Mohamed Azzim Gulamhussen (1998) 'Foreign direct investment and real options: implications for globalisation and regionalism', paper presented to the Annual Conference of the ESRC International Economics Study Group, St. Anthony's College, Oxford, September.

Chapter 8 is a revised version of a paper presented to the Annual Conference of the Academy of International Business, Vienna, October 7–10, 1998. Another version of this paper forms the basis for the Introduction to Mark

Casson (ed.) (1999) *The Emergence of International Business*, London: Routledge/Thoemmes Press.

Chapter 9 is a revised and much extended version of 'Entrepreneurial networks in international business', *Business and Economic History*, **26**(2), 1997, 1–13.

Chapter 10 is loosely based on Mark Casson and Sarianna M. Lundan (1999) 'Explaining international differences in economic institutions: a critique of the "national business system" as an analytical tool', *International Studies of Management and Organization*, **29**, Special Issue.

Mark Casson

1. Models of multinational enterprise: a new research agenda

with Peter J. Buckley

1.1 INTRODUCTION

International business (IB) is a discipline that has reached maturity. It has a professional body – the Academy of International Business – with over three thousand members. The academy publishes a journal – the *Journal of International Business Studies* – which is widely cited by other social scientists, and several other reputable journals have been established in the field. A major work of survey and synthesis (Caves, 1996) has gone into a second substantial edition. At the end of the millennium, the scholarly study of IB appears to be in very good shape.

Maturity can sometimes indicate stagnation, however. This is certainly true of technological development in some industries. Is it also true of intellectual development in the 'industry' of IB research? There is some evidence to support this view. Many of the key concepts in IB date back to the 1960s and 1970s. This was a time when social and political concerns about the spread of multinational enterprises (MNEs) were running high. A large amount of data was collected in order to address issues about national sovereignty, imbalances in international capital flows, foreign dependence on US technology, and so on (see for example United Nations, 1973; United States Tariff Commission, 1973; Vaupel and Curhan, 1974). The need to interpret this data was a considerable stimulus to theoretical research. Internalization theory was applied to the MNE about this time (McManus, 1972; Rugman, 1981; Hennart, 1982). In particular, Buckley and Casson (1976) used internalization theory to explain why foreign direct investment by US manufacturing MNEs was concentrated in high technology industries. Shortly afterwards, Dunning (1977, 1981) launched his eclectic theory, in an attempt to synthesize internalization theory with the Hymer–Kindleberger approach, which had dominated the field up till then (Hymer, 1960; Kindleberger, 1969).

A great strength of all these theories was that they focused on explaining newly discovered facts on a topic of considerable political significance. They exemplified theory that was not only logically rigorous but also extremely relevant. The theories were so well focused on facts that they were of considerable practical value to managers.

A great deal has changed since that time. The social and political impact of MNEs is no longer so controversial; governments that previously rushed to defend the threat to their national sovereignty now compete to attract MNEs with tax concessions and subsidies. The rate of growth of US MNEs has levelled off since the 1970s, and fears of global domination have consequently abated. The MNE has become a commonplace institution within the world economy.

The declining passion aroused by MNEs seems to have caused a decline in theoretical innovation too. Theoretical advances continue to occur, but they tend to be of an incremental rather than a radical nature. Most recent advances in MNE theory have been imported from other disciplines, such as economics and management studies, rather than developed from within the discipline itself.

MNEs continue to change, however, and to pose new challenges for theoretical work. This chapter charts some of the most important changes since the 1970s. It looks behind the facts at the fundamental drivers of change. It identifies new types of model that are required to analyse these changes in a rigorous and relevant way.

These new models must build on the foundations laid in the 1960s and 1970s. These foundations have proved remarkably secure. But the models of the 1960s and 1970s, though well grounded, are limited in the range of issues they can address. A new research agenda is required, which combines a commitment to advance existing models with a commitment to theoretical innovation. The major innovations required to address emergent issues are described in this book.

This book sets out a substantial research agenda for IB, which may take ten years or more to complete. The agenda is summarized in Sections 1.2 and 1.3 below. The new agenda is a response to the economic forces unleashed by globalization. These forces are examined in Sections 1.4–1.6, and their wider implications for public policy are discussed. Their specific implications for the corporate strategies and structures of MNEs are examined in Sections 1.7–1.13. Section 1.14 provides a simple example of how the new agenda works in practice, and Section 1.15 summarizes and concludes the chapter.

1.2   A NEW RESEARCH AGENDA

The new research agenda comprises four main items. These are:

1. to move from a firm-specific view of the MNE to a general systems view of the MNE;
2. to analyse the impact of volatility and information cost on the organizational structure of the MNE;
3. to link the theory of the MNE with the theory of entrepreneurship; and
4. to embed these theories within a broader social and political context.

The first item in the agenda involves completing the theoretical edifice whose construction was begun in the 1960s and 1970s. This fundamental body of theory was concerned with the boundaries of the firm. An MNE is a firm whose boundaries of ownership and control transcend the geopolitical boundaries of any single nation state. The modern world economy is dominated by a constellation of MNEs that compete and co-operate with each other in a range of different markets. Buckley and Casson's original research agenda was to explain where the boundaries between these MNEs were drawn. Their long-run objective was to explain the entire configuration of MNEs within the world economy. To simplify this task, they focused on the short-run objective of establishing where the boundaries of a single firm were drawn. Along with other scholars they quickly became absorbed in this specific issue. Subsequent research was side-tracked by controversy between different schools of thought (see for example, Casson, 1986). The broader question became lost from sight. It is now time to return to the original agenda, and pick up from where the broader issue was dropped.

To address the broader issue it is necessary to embed the theory of the MNE within a general systems view of the global economy. The behaviour of systems can be very complex. To analyse the behaviour of the global system with logical transparency it is necessary to formalize the theory of the MNE in a rigorous way. A suitable approach is to analyse multinational corporate strategy as a rational choice between discrete alternatives. This approach is set out in Chapter 2. The chapter focuses on one particular aspect of corporate strategy which is crucial to the expansion of the MNE: the foreign market entry decision.

The global systems view itself is set out in Chapter 3. Instead of the MNE, this chapter takes the global economy as the unit of analysis. From this perspective, the MNE emerges as an institutional product of the global system. More precisely, families of MNEs emerge in which each MNE both co-operates and competes with the other MNEs in the system. The system also contains many uninational firms. These firms co-operate and compete with each other, and with the MNEs. This global perspective generates a range of predictions which cannot be obtained when focusing purely on a single MNE.

The second item of the research agenda is to understand the changes in the organization of the MNE that began in the late 1970s. Like many other organizations, MNEs have adopted much 'flatter' pyramids of authority in order to be more responsive to local needs. They have decentralized decision-making, and de-layered their organizations by removing levels of middle management. Why should flatter organizations have become so fashionable at this particular time? There is a problem in addressing this question for, while the boundaries of the firm are normally discussed in terms of their economic logic, it has become customary in IB to analyse organizational questions in sociological terms (see for example the survey by Boyacigiller and Adler, 1998). This difference in approach is unfortunate, because it makes it difficult to synthesize the results obtained from the two approaches into a coherent body of knowledge.

One way of addressing this problem is to integrate sociological insight into economics. This is not as difficult as it seems, as is pointed out in Chapter 4. The principles of economic analysis are far more versatile than most critics of economics appear to believe. Many sociological insights can be included in economic models by recognizing two important facts: decision-makers pursue non-pecuniary objectives as well as pecuniary ones, and they also incur costs in obtaining the information they need for their decisions. Organizations allow individuals to gratify their non-pecuniary desires, and they provide information to individual members who require it. Once information costs and non-pecuniary rewards are incorporated into economic models, it becomes straightforward to construct an economic theory of organization.

A major insight of the economic theory of organization is that the pattern of volatility in the environment of an organization holds the key to its structure. When organizational structure adapts efficiently to changes in the pattern of volatility, an increase in volatility will induce a 'flatter' structure. Within this flatter structure, individuals will be 'empowered' to act upon information they have collected for themselves. Because they do not have to consult a superior, fewer superiors are required. This response is efficient because an increase in volatility increases information costs. Flattening the structure reduces information costs by economizing on internal information flow. This is explained in detail in Chapter 5, where it is shown that volatility has different implications for different functional areas within the MNE.

Volatility has other implications too. In a volatile environment it pays to be flexible. The ability to respond to new information is constrained by previous decisions. Valuable resources that are required to tackle a problem or exploit a market opportunity may already have been committed as a result of previous decisions. It may be advisable to defer decisions until uncertainties have been resolved. This has obvious implications for an MNE entering a new market, for example. Joint ventures provide flexibility through the nature of the contract with the partner firm. In the absence of volatility it would be difficult to explain why joint ventures are preferred to alternative arrange-

ments, such as outright ownership, except in cases where governments pro-
hibit foreign acquisitions. The role of joint ventures in the expansion of the
MNE is discussed in Chapter 6.

The value of a joint venture reflects its role as a 'real option'. Real options
are created when decisions are deferred until additional information has
become available, or where decisions are made in a way that makes their
reversal easier. Chapter 7 explains how volatility increases the potential value
of real options. This is reflected in the way that firms pursue flexibility, not
only in the way they structure their organizations, but also in the nature of the
decisions that they take. In particular, incremental 'toe in the water' investment decisions are an appropriate response to volatility, while large-scale,
pre-emptive investments are not. This provides important insights into the
scale and timing of foreign investments.

The analysis of real options takes the theory of the MNE out of the realm
of statics and into dynamics. The long-run dynamics of the MNE form the
third aspect of the new research agenda. From a long-run perspective the
evolution and growth of MNEs are linked to the accumulation of natural
scientific knowledge and its commercial exploitation, the emergence of civil
society and the refinement of the legal system, advances in transport and
communication, and political integration at the national and supranational
level. The analysis of long-run dynamic issues pushes social science theory
to its limits – and beyond. For example, unfulfilled prophecies about a crisis
of capitalism continue to abound while, at the opposite extreme, there are
heroic claims that the modern global market economy represents the 'end of
history' (Fukuyama, 1992).

The analytical tools of economics make it possible to improve on such
sweeping generalizations, however. The key is to link the rigorous economic
modelling of the kind described above to reliable sources of evidence. This
can be achieved by applying IB theory to business and economic history. It
was noted above that the rich data sets compiled in the 1960s were a major
stimulus to theoretical research in IB. The business archives of MNEs provide an even richer potential source of evidence. Some writers claim to have
traced back the MNE for several millennia (Moore and Lewis, 1999). Others
have identified antecedents of the modern MNE in the chartered trading
companies of the seventeenth century (Carlos and Nicholas, 1988). These
historical episodes have only tenuous links with the modern form of MNE,
however, which emerged from the managerial revolution that gained momen-
tum in the US at the end of the nineteenth century (Chandler, 1977). The
archival evidence on the evolution of the modern MNE has been interpreted
in the monumental works of Wilkins (1970, 1974, 1989).

A link between theory and history is established in Chapter 8. There are
many ways of linking theory and history, and this chapter focuses on just one

of them. Historical research into the growth of firms has always accorded a leading role to the entrepreneur. This emphasis on entrepreneurship has often been associated with an anti-theoretical stance, in which the particularities of entrepreneurial personality have been held to be more important than any systematic economic effects. However, once the significance of non-pecuniary motivation and information costs is recognized, it becomes evident that many of these apparently idiosyncratic factors reflect systematic underlying forces. Non-pecuniary motivation can stimulate entrepreneurs to commit themselves to risky innovations (Schumpeter, 1934), while the entrepreneur's ability to economize on information costs is reflected in his or her 'foresight' – which is a recognized quality of the leader of industry (Marshall, 1919; Knight, 1921).

The long-run dynamics of the world economy can be modelled by integrating the theory of entrepreneurship with the systems view described above. The resultant model highlights a striking contrast between the localized nature of an individual entrepreneurial project and the complex interdependent economic system of which each project forms a very tiny part. One way of resolving this tension is to recognize that successful entrepreneurs do not operate in social isolation, but as members of networks. These networks feed entrepreneurs with the information they require about developments in related sectors of the economy. Indeed, the value of social networks is so great that entrepreneurs often play a leading role in setting them up. Networking is particularly significant in promoting new channels of international trade. This particular aspect of entrepreneurship is examined from an historical perspective in Chapter 9.

The importance of social networking points to the final aspect of the research agenda, which is to embed the analysis of MNEs within a social and political context. It is often alleged that economic analysis of the MNE 'de-contextualizes' the firm, but this is only true of economic analysis in its narrowest possible form. The type of economics discussed above, based on information costs and non-pecuniary motivations, encompasses both social and political institutions. It affords important insights into the functions that these institutions perform, and the way that their members behave.

It is, therefore, a great mistake to believe that the social and political dimensions of MNE activity can only be analysed fully by rejecting an economic approach. Indeed, the reverse is true: the institutional framework of the MNE cannot be analysed fully without reference to the economic approach, because otherwise important insights will be lost. This is illustrated in Chapter 10, which discusses national business systems. MNEs are rooted in the national business systems of their home countries, and they must learn to operate within the national business systems of their host countries. The chapter examines the costs of analysing national business systems without reference to the economic approach. Ignoring economic insights leads to error, and conversely, avoiding error is possible only by reinventing economic principles under a different name. The chapter demonstrates how the theory of MNEs can be integrated with the national business systems approach.

It would be wrong to claim that the agenda described above has to be pursued from scratch. Various writers have already identified certain aspects of this agenda (see below). The agenda might, indeed, be described as a compilation of their ideas, but this would be wrong. Its unique feature is that the elements are constructively synthesized in a logically coherent form. The agenda is not a mere 'wish list' of theoretical developments, but a feasible programme of work that will make those wishes come true. The various elements of this agenda have surfaced – slowly and separately – within the IB literature over the past fifteen years. It is difficult to recognize them clearly, however, because they have not yet fully coalesced. A major objective of this book is to place these individual contributions within a broad perspective which reveals how these apparently unrelated ideas are linked together.

1.3 THE END OF THE 'GOLDEN AGE'

The initial stimulus for the emergence of the new agenda was the end of the 'golden age' of Western economic growth (Marglin and Schor, 1990). During the 'golden age' of Western economic growth, trade was liberalized through UNCTAD and through customs unions such as the EEC and EFTA. Cheaper consumer durables combined with higher incomes raised aspirations to historically unprecedented levels. The golden age terminated suddenly with the oil price shock of 1973. Imports of manufactured goods from Japan and the newly industrializing countries (NICs) of South East Asia quickly began to replace domestic production in Western markets – including motor vehicles, which had been one of the 'engines' of Western growth up to that point. The West woke up to the fact that for some time Asian firms had been systematically absorbing Western technologies, and adapting them to local conditions. The full consequences of international technology transfer and trade liberalization were finally being felt. However, lags in recognizing and interpreting these changes caused their impact on IB literature to be delayed until the early 1980s.

Traditional IB theory can easily explain how technology transfer to Asia was effected. However, the mechanisms were somewhat more varied than those suggested by the early literature. Transfer was effected on government initiative as well as on the initiative of Western multinationals (Fransman, 1995). Licensing agreements and joint ventures were widely used. The domestic partner was often a 'national champion'. Once it had mastered the technology, the champion diffused it to other firms. Diffusion to other large firms was effected through social networking, factory visits and collaborative research. Diffusion to smaller firms was effected through subcontracting arrangements in which substantial training was often involved. Small firms could also play a direct role in pirating technologies from blueprints, and in 'reverse engineering' products. Product designs were even easier to imitate than technologies, because patent protection was weaker, and 'me too' designs proliferated as a result.

The price advantage of Asian products stemmed from a number of factors. The weakness of trades unions (often as a direct consequence of political measures) maintained wages at competitive, market-clearing levels (Mirza, 1986). The limited scope of social security gave a strong incentive to work. Government expenditure was concentrated on infrastructure investment, such as roads, ports, airports and telecommunications, which reduced the costs of intermediate inputs such as transport. Investment in large container terminals cut the cost of shipping to Western markets. Improved domestic communications facilitated 'just in time' production, which economized on inventory costs. Mass production was initiated from the outset to exploit economies of scale to the full. Temporary protection of the domestic market helped to build up demand quickly, and exporting commenced at the outset. A strong desire by households to save for old age ensured that domestic consumer demand did not crowd out export demand in the long run.

The contrast with the West is clear. During the 'golden age', Western public expenditure was focused on fighting the 'Cold War' and on building a 'Great Society' or 'Welfare State'. Military expenditure, and transfer payments to the poor crowded out productivity-enhancing investment. Rising taxes, it is alleged, discouraged work and risk-taking. The concept of a 'corporate economy' (Marris, 1979) institutionalized collective bargaining and legitimated union strike-threat power. Wage inflation and 'featherbedding' increased costs – particularly the costs of intermediate inputs like transport which were supplied by highly unionized industries.

A similar set of factors explains why technology transfer succeeded in Asia but failed in Africa. (The Latin American experience lies somewhere between these two extremes.) The deficiencies of European governments were mirrored in their former colonies in Africa. Industrial strategy was based on state-of-the-art technology applied to mega-projects rather than on the diffusion and incremental improvement of established techniques (Ergas, 1987). Competition for status between neighbouring nations encouraged lavish public expenditure, financed by foreign borrowing, which could not be repaid when projects failed. Foreign borrowing was also used to finance wars, as well as conspicuous consumption by the political elite. Corruption raised transaction costs. 'Inward looking' protectionist policies distorted domestic prices and inhibited agricultural development. Industry, though protected, failed to reap economies of scale because of the slow growth of the domestic market. When Western MNEs retrenched in the 1970s, they retreated from Africa in order to concentrate on defending their markets at home.

The lessons for international business theory are fairly clear. It is not sufficient to focus exclusively on the choice of appropriate mode when analysing the success of technology transfer. As Dunning (1997) has emphasized, full account must be taken of location factors such as the structure of the host economy, the policies of the host government and the nature of local business culture when explaining the comparative success and failure of foreign operations.

1.4   VOLATILITY AND THE DEMAND FOR FLEXIBILITY

Competition from Asia was a visible symbol of a less apparent but more fundamental change in the business environment – namely a persistent increase in the amount of volatility with which firms have to contend. Volatility is a measure of the size and frequency of the shocks that impinge on a firm. It is reflected in the amplitude and frequency of fluctuations in the profit stream.

Volatility puts a premium on flexibility. Flexibility is the ability to reallocate resources quickly and smoothly in response to change. The greater the volatility of the environment, the greater the significance of flexibility. Low volatility characterized the economic environment during most of the golden age. The old research agenda was dominated by the experiences of this age.

The main reason why volatility has risen since the end of the golden age is that international diffusion of modern production technology has increased the number of industrial powers. It has thereby increased the number of countries in which political and social disturbances can impact significantly on global supplies of manufactured products. The liberalization of trade and capital markets means that the 'ripple' effects of shocks travel farther and wider than before (Casson, 1995, Ch. 4). Ripples are transmitted more quickly too: news travels almost instantaneously, thanks to modern telecommunications. Thus speculative bubbles in stock markets spread quickly around the world. Following the breakdown of the Bretton Woods system, exchange rate fluctuations have created a new dimension of financial volatility too.

As a result, any given national market is now affected by a much wider range of disturbances than ever before. Every national subsidiary of an MNE experiences a multiplicity of shocks from around the world. It is no longer the case that a national subsidiary has to respond to shocks originating in its national market alone. The shocks also come from new sources of import competition and new competitive threats in export markets. Shocks may also reveal themselves in the form of new opportunities for co-operation. The awareness of this sustained increase in volatility has led to a search for more flexible forms of organization.

This search has had a major impact on both the individual firm and the nation-state. The search for flexibility by the nation-state has altered the policy environment in which MNEs operate. The next two sections examine the impact of the search for flexibility on the nation-state. The subsequent sections look at the impact on the MNE.

1.5   THE SEARCH FOR NATIONAL COMPETITIVENESS

Initial Western reaction to de-industrialization and the plight of the 'rust belt' heavy industries was concern over 'competitiveness'. There continues to be considerable debate, however, over what competitiveness really means (Buckley, Pass and Prescott, 1988). Some economists argue, using the Ricardian concept of comparative advantage, that loss of manufacturing competitiveness is a natural consequence of economic maturity (Krugman, 1996). The strength of Western economies no longer lies in manufacturing, but in services. Thanks to jet travel and television broadcasting, an increasing number of services, such as tourism and media entertainment, are readily exportable. Consumer demand for services is income-elastic, moreover, so the long-term prospects for the service sector are good. Furthermore, manufacturing is increasingly capital-intensive, whereas many service industries are inherently labour-intensive, because they are more difficult to automate. To regain competitiveness, therefore, labour must be shifted out of manufacturing and into services. To eliminate frictional and structural unemployment, this process must be expedited by measures to promote labour market flexibility.

According to this view, Asian countries, being at an earlier stage of industrial development, have exploited labour market flexibility to switch labour out of agriculture into industry. First-generation workers who have just left the land are often very hard-working, and so, despite their inexperience, this gives a productivity boost to nascent industry. If flexibility can be sustained, then workers can be switched from one industry to another – from textiles to semi-conductors, for example – as competition increases from other countries following up the ladder of development. As long as Japan remained flexible, it managed to stay ahead of competition from Korea and Taiwan. Such has been the speed of Asian development that several economies, including Singapore, Hong Kong and Japan, have already completed the manufacturing phase, and become major service economies in their own right.

An alternative view of competitiveness emphasizes the firm-specific nature of competitive advantage. There are wide differences in productivity between firms in the same industry, it is claimed. Theories of comparative advantage, framed in terms of a representative firm, ignore this (Thurow, 1992). Some firms have major competitive advantages, and others have none at all. The competitive advantages of leading Western firms have been eroded by internal failings, it is alleged. It is not that Western workers have lost comparative advantage in manufacturing, but that Western firms have lost the ability to manage.

The distinction between *firm-specific competitive advantage* and *nation-specific comparative advantages* is essentially a question of the period of analysis. Firm-specific competitive advantage is essentially a short-run concept. Firm-specific advantages cannot be taken as given in the long run because they continually obsolesce, and have to be regularly renewed (Buckley and Casson, 1976). A nation with a comparative advantage in entrepreneurship will be able to renew firm-specific advantages through sustained innovation, but a nation without such comparative advantage will not. An explanation of loss of competitiveness that emphasizes loss of firm-specific advantages is equivalent, from a long-run perspective, to an argument that local comparative advantage in entrepreneurship has been lost. Countries that systematically generate firms with specific advantages are those that have a nation-specific comparative advantage in entrepreneurship.

From this perspective, it is plausible to argue that the West has lost comparative advantage both in manufacturing and in entrepreneurship. The first is an unavoidable consequence of economic maturity, but the second is an avoidable consequence of institutional failure and inappropriate business culture. The conflict between the nation-specific view and the firm-specific view is actually a disagreement about whether nation-specific comparative advantage has declined more in manufacturing than in entrepreneurship, or less. Those who adhere to the firm-specific view, which probably includes a majority of international business scholars, implicitly believe that entrepreneurial decline is the major problem, and that cultural and institutional changes are required to put it right. The increased volatility of the world economy, and the consequent increase in demand for flexibility, has put Western entrepreneurial failures under the spotlight.

1.6   POLICIES TO RESTORE COMPETITIVENESS

Western governments have attempted to restore labour market flexibility through legislation. In the UK, for example, the legal privileges of trades unions (such as secondary picketing) have been reduced, and minimum wage laws relaxed. Qualifications for the receipt of unemployment benefit have been tightened up. Firms have responded in a predictable way. Greater use is made of temporary labour to accommodate peaks and troughs in demand. Full-time workers are expected to work more flexible hours. Work has been subcontracted out to avoid statutory national insurance premiums. The rise in labour-only subcontracting has brought back the 'putting out' system which was characteristic of the eighteenth-century 'commercial revolution'.

Privatization has been used to promote greater flexibility in the supply of intermediate products to industry. The UK has privatized 'strategic' heavy industries (steel), public transport (railways and airlines), and utilities (telecommunications, electricity, gas and water). Privatization allows peripheral activities to be sold off, and complementary activities to be combined, thereby facilitating significant changes in the scope of the firm. Newly privatized enterprises can acquire other newly-privatized enterprises, or enter into joint venture agreements with them. For the first time in the post-war period, large-scale multinational enterprise is now possible in most of the utility industries.

Steps have also been taken to improve entrepreneurship. Business education has been expanded, top rates of income tax have been reduced to encourage risk-taking, and successful business people have been encouraged to play a more active role in public life in order to raise the status of entrepreneurs. Politicians have increasingly promoted the values of competitive individualism, and downgraded the values of organic solidarity which characterized the welfare state (Casson, 1990, Ch. 4).

Links between universities and business have been strengthened in order to improve the co-ordination of product development and basic research. This may not directly benefit the nation as much as might be expected, however. Products researched in one country can be produced in another country, and even exported back to the country where they were researched to compete with local products there. The decentralization of R&D within large MNEs (Pearce and Singh, 1992) creates internal markets where this kind of transfer can be easily effected. Thus a US MNE could use a wholly-owned research laboratory in the UK to tap into government-funded research in order to develop a product to be made in the US for export to the UK. The profits from the product innovation will also accrue to the US – an effect that has been stressed, in a somewhat different context, by Reich (1990).

Government measures to improve competitiveness seem to have been reasonably successful over the past decade. However, it should not be forgotten that the reason why some MNEs continue to produce in Europe for the European market has more to do with the common external tariff of the European Community, and the threat that it might increase, than with the location advantages of Europe *per se*. Thus tariff considerations and substantial job-creation subsidies have played a major role in the attracting of Asian motor vehicle manufacturers to the UK. Similarly, one of the advantages to foreign firms of producing in the US is that it is easier to adapt product designs to the market using a local production base.

The fact that Asian firms can successfully produce in the West behind a tariff wall suggests that they possess firm-specific advantages of the type generated by sustained entrepreneurship. One of these advantages appears to lie in *internal* labour market flexibility. There is a tendency in the West to see labour market flexibility as something external to the firm. It is reflected simply in low wage rates. There is less emphasis on firm-specific training, and workers are less versatile than in Asian firms. This is apparent on the shop-floor. On-the-job training is weaker, and attention to quality is lower as a result. Machine down-time is greater because workers cannot fix minor repairs, or help each other out when re-tooling a production line.

In general, Asian firms appear to have taken flexibility more seriously as a production issue. Not only have they invested more in labour versatility, but they have also invested more in equipment for flexible manufacturing systems. This is reflected not only in their Asian plants, but also in the operations in the West.

1.7 FLEXIBILITY TO EVADE MONOPOLY

Increased volatility is not the only reason for greater interest in flexibility. Contemporary culture is very much opposed to building organizations around a single source of monopoly power. The nation state, for example, is under threat from advocates of regional government. The traditional role of the state, to supply defence, can in principle be effected through multilateral defence treaties in which politically independent regions club together for this specific purpose. The demise of the Soviet bloc, and the subsequent political realignment between its member states, may be seen as an example of this kind of cultural change at work. This distrust of monopoly power may be linked to an increase in other forms of distrust, as suggested below.

The aversion to internal monopoly is apparent in the organizational restructuring of MNEs. The restructuring movement began in the early 1980s when the powerful central research laboratories of high-technology MNEs were either closed down, shifted to the divisions, or forced to operate as suppliers to 'internal customers' in competition with outside bodies such as universities (Casson, Pearce and Singh, 1991). Bureaucratic corporate headquarters came under attack shortly afterwards, as 'delayering' got underway. The favoured form of firm has become a federal structure of operating divisions drawing on a common source of internal expertise, but where each division belonging to the federation is free to out-source expertise if it so desires. Central services are 'hard charged' to divisions, which consequently reduce their demand. Headquarters staff become redundant as a result. Because of the reduced demand for office space, city-centre office buildings are sold off, and headquarters are relocated to smaller premises on out-of-town business parks.

As with any trend, there has been a tendency for certain advocates to take it to extremes. Just as the 'golden age' was rife with suggestions that oligopolies of hierarchical MNEs would come to dominate world markets, so the 1990s have spawned visions of the 'network firm' and the 'virtual firm'. A factor common to these visions is a 'fuzzy' boundary of the firm, where the firm fades into the market through joint ventures with declining proportional equity stakes. These arguments for fuzzy boundaries are, unfortunately, often based on equally fuzzy reasoning. Fuzzy boundaries can be configured in many different ways, as pointed out in the following chapters. The new research agenda set out in this book places arguments for fuzzy boundaries on a rigorous basis, and predicts the specific form that fuzziness will take in each particular case.

1.8   FLEXIBLE BOUNDARIES OF THE FIRM: NETWORKS AND JOINT VENTURES

The typical US MNE of the 'golden age' was a vertically- as well as horizontally-integrated firm. In consequence, each division of the firm was locked into linkages with other divisions of the same firm. As Asian competition intensified, there was growing recognition of the costs of integration of this kind.

Commitment to a particular source of supply or demand is relatively low-cost in a high-growth scenario, since it is unlikely that any investment will need to be reversed. It is much more costly in a low-growth scenario, where production may need to be switched to a cheaper source of supply, or sales diverted away from a depressed market. The desire for flexibility therefore discourages vertical integration – whether it is backward integration into production, or forward integration into distribution. It is better to subcontract production and to franchise sales instead. The subcontracting of production is similar in principle to the 'putting out' arrangement described above, but differs in the sense that the subcontractor is now a firm rather than just a single worker.

'Dis-integration' was also encouraged by a low-trust atmosphere that developed in many firms. Fear of internal monopoly became rife, as was explained above. Production managers faced with falling demand wished that they did not have to sell all their output through a single sales manager. Sales managers resented the fact that they had to obtain all their supplies from the same small set of plants. Each manager doubted the competence of the others, and ascribed loss of corporate competitiveness to selfishness and inefficiency elsewhere in the firm. Divisions aspired to be spun off so that they could deal with other business units instead. On the other hand, managers were wary of the risks that would be involved if they severed their links with other divisions altogether.

A natural way to restore confidence is to allow each division to deal with external business units as well as internal ones. In terms of internalization theory, internal markets become 'open' rather than 'closed' (Casson, 1990, p. 37). This provides divisional managers with an opportunity to bypass weak or incompetent sections of the company. It also provides a competitive discipline on internal transfer prices, preventing their manipulation for internal political ends, and bringing them more into line with external prices. There are other advantages too. Opening up internal markets severs the link between the capacities operated at adjacent stages of production. The resulting opportunity to supply other firms facilitates the exploitation of scale economies, because it permits the capacity of any individual plant to exceed internal demand. Conversely, it encourages the firm to buy in supplies from other firms that have installed capacity in excess of their own needs.

The alignment of internal prices with external ones increases the objectivity of profit measurement at the divisional level. This allows divisional managers to be rewarded by profit-related pay based on divisional rather than firm-wide profit. Management may even buy out part of the company. Alternatively, the firm may restructure by buying in a part of an independent firm. The net effect is the same in both cases. The firm becomes the hub of a network of interlocking joint ventures (Buckley and Casson, 1988). Each joint venture partner is responsible for the day-to-day management of the venture. The headquarters of the firm co-ordinates the links between the ventures. Internal trade is diverted away from the weaker ventures towards the stronger ones, thereby providing price and profit signals to which the weaker partners need to respond. Unlike a pure external market situation, the partners are able to draw upon expertise at headquarters, which can in turn tap into expertise in other parts of the group.

A network does not have to be built around a single firm, of course. It may instead consist of a group of independent firms. Sometimes these firms are neighbours, as in the regional industrial clusters described by Best (1990), Porter (1990) and Rugman, D'Cruz and Verbeke (1995). Industrial districts, such as 'Toyota city', have been hailed as an Asian innovation in flexible management, although the practice has been common in Europe for centuries (Marshall, 1919). As tariffs and transport costs have fallen, networks have become more international. This is demonstrated by the dramatic growth in intermediate product trade under long-term contracts. For example, an international trading company may operate a network of independent suppliers in different countries, substituting different sources of supply in response to both short-term exchange rate movements and long-term shifts in comparative advantage.

Flexibility is also needed in R&D. A firm cannot afford to become overcommitted to the refinement of any one technology in case innovation elsewhere should render the entire technology obsolete. As technology has diffused in the post-war period, the range of countries with the competence to innovate has significantly increased. The pace of innovation has consequently risen, and the threat of rapid obsolescence is higher as a result. The natural response for firms is to diversify their research portfolios, but the costs of maintaining a range of R&D projects are prohibitive, given the enormous fixed costs involved. The costs of basic R&D have escalated because of the increased range of specialist skills involved, while the costs of applied R&D have risen because of the need to develop global products which meet increasingly stringent consumer protection laws. Joint ventures are an appropriate solution once again. By establishing a network of joint ventures covering alternative technological trajectories, the firm can spread its costs while retaining a measure of proprietary control over new technologies.

The advantage of joint ventures is further reinforced by technological convergence – for example, the integration of computers, telecommunications and photography. This favours the creation of networks of joint ventures based on complementary technologies, rather than on the substitute technologies described above (Cantwell, 1995).

Joint ventures are important because they afford a number of real options (Trigeorgis, 1996) which can be taken up or dropped depending upon how the project turns out. The early phase of a joint venture provides important information which could not be obtained through investigation before the venture began. It affords an opportunity later on to buy more fully into a successful venture – an opportunity which is not available to those who have not taken any stake. It therefore provides greater flexibility than does either outright ownership or an alternative involving no equity stake.

1.9   FLEXIBILITY AND INTERNAL ORGANIZATION

In a very volatile environment the level of uncertainty is likely to be high. Uncertainty can be reduced, however, by collecting information. Flexibility was defined above in terms of the ability to respond to change. The costs of response tend to be smaller when the period of adjustment is long. One way of 'buying time' to adjust is to forecast change. While no-one can foresee the future perfectly, information on the present and the recent past may well improve forecasts by diagnosing underlying long-term trends. Collecting, storing and analysing information therefore enhances flexibility by reducing the costs of change.

Another way of buying time is to recognize change as early as possible. In this respect, continuous monitoring of the business environment is better than intermittent monitoring because the potential lag before a change is recognized is eliminated. Continuous monitoring is more expensive than intermittent monitoring, though, because more management time is tied up.

Investments in better forecasts and speedier recognition of change highlight the trade-off between information cost and adjustment cost. This trade-off is particularly crucial when volatility is high. High volatility implies that more information should be collected to improve flexibility, which in turn implies that more managers need to be employed. This is the reverse of the usual recommendation to downsize management in order to reduce overhead costs.

To improve flexibility while downsizing management, the trade-off between information cost and adjustment cost must be improved. There are two main ways of doing this. The first is to reduce the cost of information processing through new information technology (IT). The second is to reduce adjustment costs by building flexibility into plant and equipment, both through its design and its location. A combination of IT investment and flexible plant can reconcile greater flexibility with lower management overheads in the manner to which many MNEs aspire.

The information required for strategic decision-making is likely to be distributed throughout the organization. It is no longer reasonable to assume that all the key information can be handled by a single chief executive, or even by the entire headquarters management team. It is difficult to know in advance where the really crucial information is likely to be found. Every manager therefore needs to have the competence to process information effectively. Managers need to be able to recognize the significance of strategic information that they acquire by chance, and to have the power of access to senior executives in order to pass it on. In other words, ordinary managers need to become internal entrepreneurs.

Few entrepreneurs have sufficient information to make a good decision without consulting other people, however. In a traditional hierarchical firm the right to consult is the prerogative of top management. If ordinary managers are to have the power to initiate consultation, and act upon the results, then channels of communication within the firm need to be increased. Horizontal communication as well as vertical communication must be easy, so that lower level managers can readily consult with their peers.

A natural response is to 'flatten' the organization and encourage managers to 'network' with each other. This improves the trade-off between local responsiveness and strategic cohesion (Bartlett and Ghoshal, 1987; Hedlund, 1993). Unfortunately there has been some confusion over whether flatter organizations remain hierarchies at all. However, as Casson (1994) shows, the efficient managerial processing of information normally requires a hierarchical structure of some kind. The key point is that the more diverse the sources of volatility, the greater are the advantages of widespread consultation. The less predictable the principal source of volatility on any given occasion, the greater the incentive to allow consultation to be initiated anywhere in the organization. In practice this means that an increased demand for flexibility is best accommodated by flattening the organization while maintaining the basic elements of hierarchy.

1.10   INTERACTION OF FIRM FLEXIBILITY AND LOCATION FLEXIBILITY

The desire for flexibility may encourage the firm to produce the same product in several locations so that it can switch production between them as circumstances change. Multiple internal sourcing may therefore be pursued even where some sacrifice of economies of scale is involved. DeMeza and van der Ploeg (1987), Capel (1992) and Kogut and Kulatilaka (1994) have all emphasized that firms can switch production between alternative locations in response to real exchange rate shocks. The basic idea is that MNEs can use a combination of their superior information on foreign cost conditions and their ability, as owners of plants, to plan rather than negotiate output levels, to switch production more quickly than independent firms can.

This strategy requires, however, that the firm should commit itself in advance to the locations where it believes it will wish to produce. If it is difficult to foresee where the best locations may lie, then flexibility may be enhanced by subcontracting arrangements instead. Speed of response may be slower, but the range of potential locations is greater. Where short-run volatility predominates, multinational integration may well enhance the value of the firm (Allen and Pantzalis, 1996), but long-run volatility may favour the dis-integration of the firm instead.

If a firm is seeking flexibility at one stage of production, then it will experience a derived demand for flexibility at adjacent stages of production. The kind of flexibility required relates, not to production methods, but to shipment of the product. Each plant at an upstream stage must be able to transport product readily to any of the downstream locations that may be used; conversely, each plant at a downstream stage must be accessible from all the upstream locations that may be used. Some locations are inherently more flexible in this respect than others, because they are at nodal points on transport networks. They therefore have low transport costs to a wide range of different destinations. For example, if production is dispersed, then warehousing of finished product should be at an appropriate hub. Greater demand for flexibility concentrates demand for warehousing at such hubs – for example, Singapore (for South-east Asia) and Lille (for North-west Europe).

An MNE that is seeking flexibility in its sources of supply will wish to choose a location where government policy is *laissez faire*, so that there are no import restrictions. It may also be seeking flexibility in the range of products it produces. This encourages it to seek out locations with a versatile labour force. Flexibility is also conferred by supplier networks that operate with a high degree of trust. Local production needs to be embedded in an impartial legal system, and in strong social networks, to ensure that trust is high. An 'invisible infrastructure' of mediating institutions, or equivalently, a large endowment of 'social capital', is therefore a feature of the locations that MNEs committed to flexibility are likely to seek out. Flexibility is not just an element of corporate strategy, but a component of location advantage too. Such location advantage depends crucially on the nature of local institutions and local culture.

1.11   FLEXIBILITY AND FIRM-SPECIFIC COMPETITIVE ADVANTAGE

Flexibility has implications for firm-specific competitive advantage. Skill in recruiting imaginative employees becomes a competitive advantage when internal entrepreneurship is required. Charismatic leadership from the chief executive may promote loyalty and integrity among key staff. A tradition of informal and consultative management will facilitate the sharing of information among employees. One way of expressing this is in terms of the 'capabilities' or 'competencies' of managers (Richardson, 1960; Loasby, 1991). In a volatile environment where flexibility is crucial, the key resources of the firm are those that promote internal entrepreneurship. The firm consists, not of a single autocratic entrepreneur, but a team of entrepreneurs (Wu, 1988), co-ordinated by a leader who promotes high-trust communication between them.

It is worth noting that the need for flexibility does not necessarily support the idea of a 'learning organization'. To be more exact, flexibility has important implications for what people in a learning organization actually need to learn. According to Nelson and Winter (1982), learning supports the refinement of existing routines. This is misleading. It suggests that the firm operates in a basically stable environment, and merely learns how to do even better what it already does well. In a volatile environment, however, much of what has been 'learned' from past experience quickly obsolesces. The truly durable knowledge that needs to be learned in a volatile environment consists of techniques for handling volatility. These techniques include forgetting transitory information about past conditions which are unlikely to recur. But while 'unlearning' or 'forgetting' is important, it is often difficult to do. The difficulty of 'unlearning' helps to explain why so many 'downsizing' and 'delayering' exercises have identified middle-aged middle managers as targets for redundancy or early retirement. Such people are believed to find it too hard to forget. The 'knowledge' they acquired as junior managers was very relevant during the golden age, but has since become obsolete. Some managers have proved sufficiently flexible to be 'retrained', but others have not. Those who were too inflexible to benefit from retraining have been required to leave because their 'knowledge' has become a liability instead of an asset in the more volatile situation of today.

1.12 THE COSTS OF FLEXIBILITY: ENGINEERING TRUST

If flexibility were costless then all organizations could build in unlimited flexibility at the outset. In practice, the greater the flexibility, the higher transactions costs become. For example, the flexibility to switch between different sources of supply and demand, described above, means that relations with customers and suppliers become more transitory than before. Cheating becomes more likely, because the prospect of further transactions between the same two parties is more remote. Direct appeals to the other party's loyalty lose their credibility too.

The same effect occurs when internal entrepreneurship is promoted. Internal entrepreneurs are given more discretion to act upon information that they have collected for themselves, and this increases their opportunity to cheat. Likewise, locational flexibility means that firms become less 'embedded' in the local economy, and that investment in supplier development is discouraged.

Giving managers a direct stake in the business activities they help to build is one solution. The firm incubates new business units in which particular managers, or groups of managers, have equity stakes. An alternative approach is to appeal to the integrity of managers instead. They are treated well, and in return are expected to be open and honest about what they know.

It is one of the ironies of recent years that at a time when personal integrity needed to be high in order to support more flexible organization, it has been allowed to fall to a very low level. The decline of traditional religion, the intellectual cynicism created by two world wars, and the rise of mass consumerism have all been blamed for this state of affairs. Communitarians argue correctly that moral values like integrity are most efficiently engineered at the societal level, through family, church and school. In recent years these institutions have increasingly failed to fulfil their moral role. New mechanisms for promoting morals have had to be found (Casson, 1991; Fukuyama, 1995). Firms have sought to motivate integrity and hard work in their employees through developing and promoting a suitable corporate culture (Kotter, 1996). They have had to do this at their own expense. Thus failings in public and charitable organizations have increased the costs to firms of motivating employees, and thereby served to undermine firms' competitiveness at a time when it desperately needed to be strengthened.

1.13 THE WESTERN MNE AND 'SHAREHOLDER CAPITALISM'

Nowhere is the modern climate of cynicism more evident than in the new form of 'shareholder capitalism' in which pension fund managers, merchant bankers and market analysts pressurize top managers to maximize shareholder value. Takeover raiders monitor firms for signs of managerial underperformance, thereby creating a 'market for management control'. The alleged efficiency gains from the market are sometimes used to legitimate the oft-quoted maxim that 'greed is good'.

This cynicism can be interpreted, like so many other aspects of contemporary culture, as a reaction to the excesses of the golden age. In the 1960s and early 1970s, management in many US MNEs became dynastic. Retiring managers appointed their own successors. Knowing this, subordinates 'toed the line' so that they could step smoothly into their superior's shoes. So long as firms were expanding, there were plenty of top jobs for people to be promoted into but, when demand levelled off, new posts continued to be created in order not to disappoint the expectations of those who were still climbing up the 'promotion ladder'. The consequent proliferation of top management posts not only added to overhead cost – it created conflict and confusion too, as personal responsibilities increasingly overlapped. Internal conflicts distracted management attention from external changes, with the result that leading firms were slow to respond to the emergence of new sources of competition.

The managerial dynasts were also notable philanthropists (Whitman, 1999). They distributed shareholder funds to local community projects and took the credit for themselves. This was their contribution to the contemporary political agenda of the time, which centred on promoting public welfare. They awarded themselves large expense accounts, in order to maintain their status (and the company's reputation) through lavish hospitality. The pensioners who held shares in the company, however, carried a very low priority where managerial patronage was concerned. Jensen and Meckling (1976) were the first to point out the practical difficulty that shareholders faced in making their 'agents' responsible to them, and to analyse this problem in theoretical terms. By assuming self-interest in managers, they gave their analysis of the 'agency problem' a distinctive policy slant. Friedman and Friedman (1980) strengthened this slant by setting out a moral basis for shareholder power. Shareholders should not be denied the opportunity to be philanthropic themselves: managers should maximize profit and distribute it freely, and not pre-empt the shareholders' right to decide upon philanthropic claims for themselves.

Because US MNEs had been growing faster than European MNEs up to this time, the abuse of management discretion seems to have been greater in the US than in Europe. This provided an opening for European takeovers of US firms. European firms were seeking access to US markets and US technology at this time, and they were able to acquire these resources cheaply because US shareholders perceived them as being badly managed. However, the cult of shareholder power quickly crossed the Atlantic, and some of the European managers themselves fell victim to it when their investments in the US did not succeed as well as expected.

In particular, UK shareholders became just as suspicious about the abuse of management discretion as US shareholders had been. They began to favour the introduction of 'downsizing' and 'delayering' in UK firms. Thus measures for driving down costs which had been developed for addressing problems in the US were soon vigorously applied in the UK as well.

The cult of shareholder power has since produced excesses of its own, however. There is growing suspicion that some takeover raids are founded upon dishonest allegations of underperformance. There is also growing concern about the social consequences of the 'downsizing' and 'delayering' that usually follows a takeover. The re-emergence of the concept of 'stakeholder capitalism', and the continuing debate over corporate governance, is a symptom of such concerns. In some European countries the electorate may well prefer protectionism to the loss of jobs that 'downsizing' entails – particularly when it is managers as well as workers whose jobs are at risk. These trends suggest that the 'age of reaction' against the excesses of the golden age may itself be coming to an end. If so, there will be a further wave of national policy changes to which MNEs will have to respond.

1.14   NEW TECHNIQUES OF ANALYSIS: AN EXAMPLE

What does a scholar pursuing the new research agenda actually *do*? How does the formal specification of a dynamic model differ from that of a static one? A simple example may clarify the position.

Consider the problem of modelling the impact of volatility on multinational business strategy. The simplest way to model volatility is to postulate a steady stream of shocks impinging at random on the international business environment. Two types of shock need to be distinguished: exogenous shocks, which are autonomous, and endogenous shocks which are induced as a consequence of the exogenous ones.

The need for simplicity in modelling the global system means that many shocks that are endogenous to the system have to be modelled as though they were exogenous. This is because too many endogenous shocks complicate a model unduly. Increasing the number of endogenous factors in a model considerably increases its complexity, and so makes an explicit solution more difficult to find.

For example, it is often said that economic and political factors within the global system 'co-evolve'. This implies that there are many endogenous factors which change simultaneously in response to the interplay of exogenous shocks. However, the modelling of such complex interdependencies is not always a practical proposition, given the limited range of techniques currently available. Thus political factors may have to be taken as exogenous while economic factors are treated as endogenous, or vice versa. Two partial models therefore replace a single general model because the general model is too difficult to solve.

For example, when analysing MNE behaviour, political realignments and changes in national policy regimes may be treated as exogenous, even though they are, in practice, endogenous responses to economic events in which MNEs were involved. The formation of customs unions and the breakdown of the Soviet system may both be treated as exogenous random shocks impinging on the global economy. These shocks influence the relative rise and decline of individual nations. They also impinge on the growth and decline of various product markets. These changes in national incomes and market sizes then transmit the shocks to MNEs.

The explicit recognition that market decline is just as likely as market growth is one of the distinguishing features of the new research agenda. While the growth of a market encourages firms to enter, its decline encourages firms to exit. Once future scenarios include market decline, divestment and withdrawal must be considered as serious strategies. Static models of MNE strategy assume that the market will be constant, while very simple dynamic models, such as Buckley and Casson (1981) only suppose that the market will grow. In a volatile environment a market may grow to begin with, attracting investment, but then go into decline, requiring divestment instead.

The new agenda also recognizes that switching between strategies is costly. Switching costs depend both on the strategy the firm is switching from and the strategy the firm is switching to. In some cases switching costs decompose neatly into a cost of exit from the old strategy and a cost of setting up the new strategy, while in other cases the costs are different for every pair of strategies involved. Detailed specification of such costs is a key step in the implementation of the new research agenda.

To preserve flexibility, it is important for the firm to choose at the outset strategies whose exit costs are low. Suppose, for example, that the firm is contemplating entering some foreign market for the first time. Producing in the host country incurs sunk costs which cannot be recovered should the firm withdraw from the market later on. Negotiating a licensing contract also incurs sunk costs, although on a smaller scale. Increasing the utilization of domestic facilities to generate exports, on the other hand, may incur no sunk costs at all. In this case the flexibility criterion favours exporting over licensing, and licensing over foreign direct investment (FDI). When decline of the market is a possible scenario, FDI is revealed as a high-risk strategy.

Switching decisions can be mistaken because the information upon which they are based is poor. Expected switching costs are reduced by avoiding unnecessary switches. Different strategies afford different opportunities for capturing information from the host environment and feeding it back to inform subsequent switching decisions. The new agenda involves explicit modelling of how the strategy chosen at one stage affects the information available at following stages.

FDI offers better opportunities for information-capture than either licensing or exporting, since ownership of assets confers ownership of information too. This means, for example, that if volatility caused the market to grow unexpectedly, the foreign investor would recognize this quickly. Since it is often cheaper to expand existing capacity than to build from scratch, the foreign investor also faces lower costs of capacity expansion than an exporter who decides to switch to foreign production at a later stage. While exporting continues to confer more flexibility in response to market decline, therefore, foreign investment confers more flexibility in respect of market growth.

Is it possible to find a strategy with a better combination of characteristics than either exporting, licensing or FDI? An international joint venture (IJV) may provide the answer (Kogut, 1991). Investing in a 50:50 partnership with a host-country producer lays off some of the risks associated with wholly-owned FDI. At the same time information capture remains reasonably good. There is an option to expand capacity if there is unexpected market growth, and a further option to increase commitment by buying the partner out. There is also an easy option to withdraw by selling out to the partner. The partner provides a ready market for divested assets that an ordinary direct investor lacks. There is a downside, of course – an obvious problem is that the partner may themselves become a source of volatility. This is why trust is such an important element in an IJV. In this way the emphasis on risk management within the new research agenda leads to the emergence of new 'compromise strategies' which would be dominated by more conventional strategies were it not for the 'option value' they possess within a volatile environment (see Chapter 6).

IJV options can be exercised only once, of course, unless the investor switches back to an IJV arrangement at a later date. This explains the well-known phenomenon of IJV instability as a rational response to the role that IJVs fulfil. An IJV in which the options are never exercised is probably inferior to a wholly-owned investment, while an IJV where options are exercised at the first available opportunity does not last for very long. When IJVs are chosen because of their option value, it is normally inefficient either to switch out right away or never to switch at all. The optimal timing of a switch is one at which uncertainty about future market growth is dispelled for a reasonable period of time. This implies that the duration of IJVs is, on average, fairly short, and relatively variable. The new research agenda provides a simple means of deriving such hypotheses about the period of time for which a given strategy will be pursued.

The globalization of markets has been a major factor in the growth of volatility, as explained above. A feature of many global markets is the use of regional production and distribution hubs, where several neighbouring countries are serviced from the same location. The regional hub, like the IJV, can be understood as a strategy that offers superior flexibility (see Chapter 7). Just as an IJV offers a compromise ownership strategy, so a regional hub offers a compromise location strategy. Because the hub is nearer to each market than is the home location, it reduces transport costs, and also offers better information capture. Yet because it is close to several markets, it avoids exclusive commitment to any one. If one market declines, production can be switched to other markets instead. Provided the shocks affecting the national markets are independent (or less than perfectly correlated, at any rate), the hub provides gains from diversification. These are real gains that only the firm can achieve, as opposed to the financial gains from unrelated product diversification, which are best exploited through the diversification of individual share portfolios.

The two strategies of IJV and hub can be combined. Since one is an ownership strategy and the other a location strategy, they can, if desired, be combined directly in an IJV production hub. Closer examination of the issues suggests that this is not normally the best approach, however. The model suggests that a combination of a wholly-owned production hub supplying IJV distribution facilities in each national market is a better solution. A hub facility is too critical to global strategy to allow a partner to become involved, because the damage they could do is far too great. Even with a wholly-owned hub facility, the combination still affords considerable flexibility to divest or withdraw from any single market. The advantage of the combination is that, when divesting, the distribution facility can be sold to the partner, while the production capacity can be diverted to markets elsewhere. These options for divestment are combined with useful options for expansion too.

This example illustrates the crucial role that the concepts of flexibility and volatility play in analysing multinational business strategy in the modern global economy. Without these concepts it is impossible fully to understand the rationale for IJVs and production hubs. It is also impossible to understand why these strategies have emerged at this particular historical juncture and not before.

1.15   CONCLUSION

This chapter has set out a new research agenda for IB, focused on four key areas of research. The hallmarks of the new agenda are its dynamic, systemic and interdisciplinary nature. It focuses on:

- the global economic system;
- volatility;
- flexibility and the value of real options;
- entrepreneurship; and
- co-operation through IJVs.

By contrast the traditional agenda, which has dominated research since the 1960s, emphasizes

- initial overseas expansion into a given market;
- the nature of a given short-run, firm-specific competitive advantage; and
- the determination of the boundaries of a single firm.

It is evident that the traditional agenda takes a more static view of IB. It recognizes change, but interprets it as a sequence of independent one-off events rather than as a continuous systemic process.

This does not mean that static analysis is obsolete. Static analysis is much simpler than dynamic analysis, and for this reason the traditional static approach is a natural preliminary to the new dynamic one. For example, the static approach has proved very useful in analysing the mode of entry into newly-liberalized Central and Eastern European markets (Hood and Young, 1994). A dynamic model always contains a static model as a special case, and the properties of this special case provide important clues as to whether the dynamic model is logically sound. Indeed, the development of new dynamic models requires existing static models to be refined, as illustrated in Chapter 2.

The need for a more dynamic approach does not, therefore, arise because the static theory is completely worked out. Far from it. Statics and dynamics are complements, not substitutes. Although certain areas of the static theory may now be encountering diminishing marginal returns to further intellectual effort, the returns remain positive.

The demand for a more dynamic theory is driven by recent changes in the world economy. The key turning point, and the defining moment in the transition from the old research agenda to the new, was the end of the golden age of Western growth. Corporate profitability declined, and strategy switched from entering new foreign markets to defending existing ones. The entry of new multinational producers, and a general commitment to continuous innovation, increased volatility in global markets. MNE operations were restructured to drive down costs and improve supply responsiveness.

Survival in a volatile environment depends upon flexible response. This applies to nation-states, to industrial regions and to individual firms. Flexible firms need to locate in flexible regions of nation-states with flexible economic policies. In this way the forces of flexibility are continuously restructuring the world economy. This is why contemporary conditions call for a more dynamic theory, with flexibility at its core. As Arpan (1997) has noted, international business research must change if it is to retain its relevance and its basic simplicity. The new agenda sets out the way in which this can be done.

REFERENCES

Allen, L. and C. Pantzalis (1996) 'Valuation of the operating flexibility of multinational corporations', *Journal of International Business Studies*, **27**(4), 633–53

Arpan, J.S. (1997) 'Palabras del Presidente', *AIB Newsletter*, **3**(3), 2

Bartlett, C.A. and S. Ghoshal (1987) 'Managing across borders: new strategic requirements', *Sloan Management Review*, Summer, 6–17

Best, M.H. (1990) *The New Competition: Institutions of Industrial Restructuring*, Oxford: Polity Press

Boyacigiller, N.A. and N.J. Adler (1998) 'Insiders and outsiders: bridging the worlds of organizational behaviour and international management', in B. Toyne and D.

Nigh (eds), *International Business: An Emerging Vision,* Columbia, SC: University of South Carolina Press, 396–416

Buckley, P.J. and M.C. Casson (1976) *The Future of the Multinational Enterprise,* London: Macmillan

Buckley, P.J. and M.C. Casson (1981) 'The optimal timing of a foreign direct investment', *Economic Journal,* **91**, 75–87

Buckley, P.J. and M.C. Casson (1988) 'A theory of co-operation in international business', in F.J. Contractor and P. Lorange (eds), *Co-operative Strategies in International Business,* Lexington, MA: Lexington Books, 31–53

Buckley, P.J. and M.C. Casson (1996) 'An economic model of international joint venture strategy', *Journal of International Business Studies,* **27**(5), 849–76

Buckley, P.J., C.L. Pass and K. Prescott (1988) 'Measures of international competitiveness: a critical survey', *Journal of Marketing Management,* **4**(2), 175–200

Cantwell, J. (1995) 'Multinational enterprises and innovatory activities: towards a new evolutionary approach', in J. Molero (ed.), *Technological Innovation, Multinational Corporations and the New International Competitiveness,* Chur: Harwood Academic Publishers, 21–57

Capel, J. (1992) 'How to service a foreign market under uncertainty: a real option approach', *European Journal of Political Economy,* **8**, 455–75

Carlos, A.M. and S.J. Nicholas (1988) 'Giants of an earlier capitalism: the chartered trading companies as modern multinationals', *Business History Review,* **62**, 399–419

Casson, M. (1986), 'General theories of the multinational enterprise: their relevance to business history', in P. Hertner and G. Jones (eds), *Multinationals: Theory and History,* Aldershot: Gower, 42–63

Casson, M. (1990) *Enterprise and Competitiveness,* Oxford: Clarendon Press

Casson, M. (1991) *Economics of Business Culture,* Oxford: Clarendon Press

Casson, M. (1994) 'Why are firms hierarchical?', *International Journal of the Economics of Business,* **1**(1), 3–40

Casson, M. (1995) *Organization of International Business,* Aldershot: Edward Elgar

Casson, M., R.D. Pearce and S. Singh (1991) 'A review of recent trends', in M. Casson (ed.), *Global Research Strategy and International Competitiveness,* Oxford: Blackwell, 250–71

Caves, R.E. (1996) *Multinational Enterprise and Economic Analysis,* 2nd edn, Cambridge: Cambridge University Press

Chandler, A.D., Jr (1977) *The Visible Hand: The Managerial Revolution in American Business,* Cambridge, MA: Belknap Press of Harvard University Press

DeMeza, D. and F. van der Ploeg (1987) 'Production flexibility as a motive for multinationality', *Journal of Industrial Economics,* **35**(3), 343–51

Dunning, J.H. (1977) 'Trade, location of economic activity and the multinational enterprise: a search for an eclectic approach', in B. Ohlin, P.O. Hesselborn and P.M. Wijkman (eds), *The International Allocation of Economic Activity,* London: Macmillan, 395–418

Dunning, J.H. (1981) *International Production and the Multinational Enterprise,* London: Allen & Unwin

Dunning, J.H. (1997) *Alliance Capitalism and Global Business,* London: Routledge

Ergas, H. (1987) 'Does technology policy matter?', in B.R. Guile and H. Brooks (eds), *Technology and Global Industry,* Washington, DC: National Academy Press, 191–245

Fransman, M. (1995) *Japan's Computer and Communications Industry*, Oxford: Oxford University Press

Friedman, M. and R. Friedman (1980) *Free to Choose: A Personal Statement*, New York: Harcourt Brace Jovanovich

Fukuyama, F. (1992) *The End of History and the Last Man*, London: Penguin

Fukuyama, F. (1995) *Trust: The Social Virtues and the Creation of Prosperity*, London: Hamish Hamilton

Hedlund, G. (1993) 'Assumptions of hierarchy and heterarchy: an application to the multinational corporation', in S. Ghoshal and E. Westney (eds), *Organization Theory and the Multinational Corporation*, London: Macmillan, 211–36

Hennart, J.F. (1982) *A Theory of the Multinational Enterprise*, Ann Arbor: University of Michigan Press

Hood, N. and S. Young (1994) 'The internationalization of business and the challenge of East European business', in P.J. Buckley and P.N. Ghauri (eds), *The Economics of Change in East and Central Europe*, London: Academic Press, 320–42

Hymer, S.H. (1960) *The International Operations of National Firms: A Study of Direct Investment*, PhD thesis, MIT, publ. 1976, Cambridge, MA: MIT Press

Jensen, M.C. and W.H. Meckling (1976) 'Theory of the firm: managerial behaviour, agency costs and ownership structure', *Journal of Financial Economics*, **3**, 305–60

Kindleberger, C.A. (1969) *American Business Abroad*, New Haven, CT: Yale University Press

Knight, F.H. (1921) *Risk, Uncertainty and Profit*, Boston: Houghton Mifflin

Kogut, B. (1991) 'Joint ventures and the option to expand and acquire', *Management Science*, **37**(1), 19–33

Kogut, B. and N. Kulatilaka (1994) 'Operating flexibility, global manufacturing, and the option value of a multinational network', *Management Science*, **40**(1), 123–39

Kotter, J. (1996) *Leading Change*, Cambridge, MA: Harvard Business School Press

Krugman, P. (1996), 'The myth of Asia's miracle', in *Pop Internationalism*, Cambridge, MA: MIT Press

Loasby, B.J. (1991) *Equilibrium and Evolution*, Manchester: Manchester University Press

Marglin, S.A. and J.B. Schor (1990), *The Golden Age of Capitalism: Reinterpreting the Post-war Experience*, Oxford: Clarendon Press

Marris, R.L. (1979) *The Theory and Future of the Corporate Economy and Society*, Amsterdam: North-Holland

Marshall, A. (1919) *Industry and Trade*, London: Macmillan

McManus, J.C. (1972) 'The theory of the international firm', in G. Paquet (ed.), *The Multinational Firm and the Nation State*, Toronto: Collier Macmillan, 66–93

Mirza, H. (1986) *Multinationals and the Growth of the Singapore Economy*, London: Croom Helm

Moore, K. and D. Lewis (1999) *Birth of the Multinational: 2000 Years of Ancient Business History – From Ashur to Augustus*, Copenhagen: Copenhagen Business School Press

Nelson, R. and S.G. Winter (1982) *An Evolutionary Theory of Economic Change*, Cambridge, MA: Harvard University Press

Pearce, R.D. and S. Singh (1992) *Globalising Research and Development*, London: Macmillan

Porter, M.E. (1990) *The Competitive Advantage of Nations*, London: Macmillan

Reich, R.B. (1990) 'Who is us?', *Harvard Business Review*, **68**(1), 53–65

Richardson, G.B. (1960) *Information and Investment*, Oxford: Oxford University Press

Rugman, A.M. (1981) *Inside the Multinationals: The Economics of Internal Markets*, London: Croom Helm

Rugman, A.M., J.R. D'Cruz and A. Verbeke (1995) 'Internalisation and deinternalisation: will business networks replace multinationals?' in G. Boyd (ed.), *Competitive and Cooperative Macromanagement. The Challenge of Structural Interdependence*, Aldershot: Edward Elgar, 107–28

Schumpeter, J.A. (1934) *The Theory of Economic Development* (trans. R. Opie), Cambridge, MA: Harvard University Press

Thurow, L.C. (1992) *Head to Head: The Coming Economic Battle Among Japan, Europe and America*, New York: Morrow

Trigeorgis, L. (1996) *Real Options*, Cambridge, MA: MIT Press

United Nations (1973) *Multinational Corporations in World Development*, Washington, DC: United Nations Department of Economic and Social Affairs

United States Tariff Commission (1973) *Report on the Implications of Multinational Firms*, Washington, DC: United States Government Printing Office

Vaupel, J.W. and J.P. Curhan (1974) *The World's Multinational Enterprises: A Sourcebook of Tables based on a Study of the Largest US and Non-US Manufacturing Corporations*, Geneva: Centre d'Etudes Industrielles

Whitman, M. von N. (1999) *New World, New Rules: The Changing Role of the American Corporation*, Cambridge, MA: Harvard Business School Press

Wilkins, M. (1970) *The Emergence of Multinational Enterprise: American Business Abroad from the Colonial Era to 1914*, Cambridge, MA: Harvard University Press

Wilkins, M. (1974) *The Maturing of Multinational Enterprise: American Business Abroad from 1914 to 1970*, Cambridge, MA: Harvard University Press

Wilkins, M. (1989) *The History of Foreign Investment in the United States to 1914*, Cambridge, MA: Harvard University Press

Wu, S.-Y. (1988) *Production, Entrepreneurship and Profits*, Oxford: Blackwell

2. Foreign market entry: a formal extension of internalization theory

with Peter J. Buckley

2.1 INTRODUCTION

Empirical studies of FDI have become much more ambitious in scope over the last 30 years. In the 1960s the main focus of the Hymer–Kindleberger theory (Hymer, 1976; Kindleberger, 1969) and the product cycle theory (Vernon, 1966) was exporting versus FDI. In the 1970s the internalization approach identified licensing, franchising and subcontracting as other strategic options. The resurgence of mergers and acquisitions in the 1980s – often as a 'quick fix' route to globalization – highlighted the choice between greenfield ventures and acquisitions. At the same time, the growing participation of US firms in international joint ventures (IJVs) drew attention to the role of co-operative arrangements.

In the 1990s the role of FDI in 'transitional' or 'emerging' economies (East and Central Europe, China, Vietnam, and so on) has brought back into focus some of the classic issues of the 1960s: the 'costs of doing business abroad' and the importance of 'psychic distance'. It has renewed interest in the general question of why some modes of entry offer lower costs than others, and of why certain circumstances seem to favour certain modes over others.

Linking all these issues together generates a high degree of complexity. Although the eclectic theory has been regularly revised and updated to accommodate the changing *foci* of applied research, it is too much of a 'paradigm' or 'framework' and too little of a 'model' to provide detailed advice on research design and hypothesis testing (Dunning, 1980). Complexity appears to have created a degree of confusion among scholars which only a formal modelling exercise can dispel.

The model presented below has three distinctive features. First, it is based on a detailed schematic analysis that encompasses all the major market entry strategies. In existing literature, most strategies are appraised as alternatives to exporting or to greenfield FDI. It is unusual to see a direct comparison between, say, licensing and joint ventures, or between franchising and subcontracting. The present model permits any strategy to be compared with any other strategy. It is therefore particularly useful when the leading strategies in contention do not include either exporting or conventional FDI.

The second feature of the model is that it distinguishes clearly between production and distribution. Historically, a large proportion of initial FDI relates to foreign warehousing and distribution facilities. Production facilities only come later, if at all. The distinction is obvious in empirical work, but it has not been properly reflected in theory up till now. The result has been some confusion as to how theory should be applied to situations in which investment in distribution has a prominent role.

Finally, the model takes account of the strategic interaction between the foreign entrant and its leading host-country rival after entry has taken place. Following recent developments in industrial organization theory (as summarized, for example, in Tirole, 1988), it is assumed that the entrant can foresee the reaction of its rival and take this into account at the time of entry. It is argued that this theoretical refinement is of the utmost practical importance in explaining the choice between greenfield investment and acquisition as entry modes.

The model concentrates on FDI for market access reasons and excludes resource-orientated FDI and offshore production.

2.2   HISTORICAL DEVELOPMENT OF THE THEORY

Much of the early literature on foreign market entry concerned the choice between exporting and FDI (for previous overviews see Root, 1987; Young *et al.*, 1989; Buckley and Ghauri, 1993). The cost-based view of this decision suggested that the firm must possess a 'compensating advantage' in order to overcome the 'costs of foreignness' (Hymer, 1976; Kindleberger, 1969). This led to the identification of technological and marketing skills as the key elements in successful foreign entry (Hirsh, 1976; Horst, 1972). This tradition of firm-specific advantages (Caves, 1971; Rugman, 1981) connects with the literature on core competencies arising from the Penrosian tradition (Penrose, 1959; Prahalad and Hamel, 1990). Sequential modes of internationalization were introduced by Vernon's 'Product Cycle Hypothesis' (1966), in which firms go through an exporting phase before switching first to market-seeking FDI and then to cost-orientated FDI. Technology and marketing factors combine to explain standardization, which drives location decisions.

Internalization

Buckley and Casson (1976) envisaged the firm as an internalized bundle of resources which can be allocated (1) between product groups and (2) between national markets. Their focus on market-based *versus* firm-based solutions highlighted the strategic significance of licensing in market entry. Entry involves two interdependent decisions – on location and mode of control. Exporting is domestically located and administratively controlled, foreign licensing is foreign-located and contractually controlled and FDI is foreign-located and administratively controlled. This model was formalized by Buckley and Casson (1981) and empirically tested by Buckley and Pearce (1979), Contractor (1984) and others.

Stages Models of Entry

The Scandinavian 'stages' models of entry suggest a sequential pattern of entry into successive foreign markets, coupled with a progressive deepening of commitment to each market. Increasing commitment is particularly important in the thinking of the Uppsala School (Johanson and Wiedersheim-Paul, 1975; Johanson and Vahlne, 1977). Closely associated with stages models is the notion of 'psychic distance', which attempts to conceptualize and, to some degree, to measure the cultural distance between countries and markets (Hallen and Wiedersheim-Paul, 1979). For a more recent view see Casson (1994).

Non-production Activities

In explaining foreign market servicing policies, the role of non-production activities must be made explicit. The location of research activities is widely debated, especially in relation to spatial agglomeration (Kogut and Zander, 1993). There is also an extensive literature on the entry aspects of marketing and distribution (Davidson, 1980), much of it in a transactions cost framework (Anderson and Coughlan, 1987; Anderson and Gatignon, 1986; Hill, Hwang and Kim, 1990; Kim and Hwang, 1992; Agarwal and Ramaswani, 1992).

Mergers and Acquisitions versus Greenfield Ventures

Stopford and Wells (1972) examined takeovers *versus* acquisitions as part of their analysis of the organization of the multinational firm. The predominance of entry *via* takeovers in most advanced economies has stimulated a number of good empirical studies (Dubin, 1975; Wilson, 1980; Zejan, 1990; Hennart and Park, 1993), which have drawn on both the internalization perspective and the strategy literature (Yip, 1982). Particular attention has been paid to the costs of adaptation and cultural integration that are encountered in the case of mergers. The theoretical issues have recently been surveyed by Svensson (1996) and Meyer (1997).

Joint Ventures versus Wholly-owned Subsidiaries

The recent literature on IJVs is immense and has spawned some innovative developments in international business theory and much insightful empirical work based on extensive data sets (Contractor and Lorange, 1988; Beamish and Killing, 1997). Buckley and Casson (1988, 1996) summarize the conditions conducive to IJVs as: (1) the possession of complementary assets, (2) opportunities for collusion, and (3) barriers to full integration – economic, financial, legal or political (see also Beamish, 1985; Beamish and Banks, 1987; Kogut, 1988; Hennart, 1988; and Contractor, 1990).

The IJV literature has focused particularly on partner selection, management strategy and the measurement of performance. Partner selection is examined by Beamish (1987), who relates selection to performance, Harrigan (1988b) who examines partner asymmetries, and Geringer (1991). Kogut and Singh (1987, 1988) relate partner selection to entry method. Management strategy in IJVs is analysed by Killing (1983) and Harrigan (1988a), whilst Gomes-Casseres (1991) relates strategy to ownership preferences.

The performance of IJVs is the subject of much debate. It cannot be assumed that joint venture termination indicates failure – an IJV may end precisely because it has achieved its objectives. Similarly, the restructuring of joint ventures and alliances may indicate the exploitation of the flexibility of the organizational form, rather than a response to underperformance – see Franko (1971), Gomes-Casseres (1987), Kogut (1988, 1989) and Blodgett (1992). Other analyses of IJV performance include Geringer and Hebert (1991), Inkpen and Birkenshaw (1994) and Woodcock, Beamish and Makino (1994). Nitsch, Beamish and Makino (1996) relate entry mode to performance and Gulati (1995) examines the role of repeated ties between partners as contributing to success – an interesting attempt to encompass 'cultural' variables.

Cultural Factors

The relationship between (national) culture and entry strategy is explicitly examined (using a reductionist version of Hofstede's (1980) cultural classification) by Kogut and Singh (1988) (see also Shane, 1994). Cultural barriers are utilized in an examination of foreign market entry by Bakema, Bell and Pennings (1996) and a 'cultural learning process' is invoked by Benito and Gripsrud (1992) to help explain the expansion of FDI.

Market Structure and Entry Strategy

It is one of the contributions of this chapter to introduce market structure issues into the modelling of entry decisions. The relationship between entry behaviour and market structure was emphasized in Knickerbocker's (1973) study of oligopolistic reaction, which set up a crude game-theoretic structure for competitive entry into key national markets. Flowers (1976) and Graham (1978) emphasized 'exchange of threats' in their respective studies of European and Canadian investment in the US, and two-way investment between the US and Europe. Yu and Ito (1988) more recently examined oligopolistic reaction and FDI in the US tyre and textiles industries. Graham (1992) laments the lack of attention to competitive structure in the international business literature, where the entrant is effectively a monopolist (Buckley and Casson, 1981). Indeed, Casson's (1985) study of cartelization versus multinationalization is one of the few economic models of multinational industrial organization available.

Summary

Location costs, internalization factors, financial variables, cultural factors such as trust and psychic distance, market structure and competitive strategy, adaptation costs (to the local environment) and the cost of doing business abroad are all identified in the literature as playing a role in determining firms' foreign market entry decisions. The model which follows includes all these variables and analyses their interactions in a systematic way.

2.3   FORMULATION OF THE MODEL

The model applies the economic theory of FDI presented in Buckley and Casson (1976, 1981), Buckley (1983), Casson (1991) and Buckley and Casson (1996) to the set of issues identified in the literature review above. Although the model involves a number of apparently restrictive assumptions, these assumptions can, if necessary, be relaxed, at the cost of introducing additional complications into the analysis. The assumptions are not so much restrictions upon the relevance of the model as indicators of key contextual issues on which every researcher into foreign market entry must pass judgement before their analysis begins. If some of the assumptions seem unfamiliar, then it is because few researchers have actually made their assumptions sufficiently explicit in the past.

The Entrant

1. A firm based in a home country is seeking to sell for the first time in a foreign market. The emphasis on first-time entry makes it important to distinguish between the one-off set-up costs of an entry mode and the

recurrent costs of subsequent operation in that mode. It is assumed, unless otherwise stated, that recurrent operations take place in a stable environment.

2. Foreign market demand for the product is infinitely elastic at a price p, up to a certain volume at which it becomes totally inelastic. For example, each customer may desire just one unit of the product, which they value at p, and when everyone has bought that unit no more can be sold however far the price is dropped. The volume at which demand becomes inelastic is determined by the size of the foreign market, x.

3. The focus of the model on market entry makes it appropriate to distinguish between production activity (P) and distribution activity (D). Distribution links production to final demand. It comprises warehousing, transport and possibly retailing too. Distribution must be carried out entirely in the foreign market, but production may be located either at home or abroad.

4. The entrant's production draws upon proprietary technology generated by a research and development activity (R). Effective distribution depends upon a marketing activity (M). Marketing involves investigating customers' needs and maintaining the reputation of the product by giving customers the service they require.

5. The entrant has no foreign activity M at the time of entry. It consequently lacks market knowledge. This knowledge can be acquired through experience (learning from mistakes) at the time of entry, incurring a once-for-all cost of entry m. The knowledge can be obtained in other ways as well, as described below. One of the keys to successful entry strategy is to acquire M in the most appropriate way.

6. The flow of technology from R to P defines the first of three 'intermediate products' in the model. The second is a flow of marketing expertise from M to D. The third is a physical flow of wholesale product from the factory or production unit P to the distribution facility D. (The internal flow of information between R and M is not discussed, as it is a fixed cost which is the same for every form of market entry considered in the model.)

7. Production at home means that the product must be exported. Exporting incurs transport costs and tariffs that foreign production avoids. On the other hand, foreign production incurs additional costs of communicating the technology – for example training foreign workers. Foreign production may also result in the loss of economies of scale. Exporting increases the utilization of the domestic plant, and allows it to be extended at low marginal cost. All of these factors are summarized in the net additional cost of home production, z, which is equal to transport costs and tariffs *less* savings on account of training costs and economies of scale.

8. The firm may enter the foreign market either by owning and controlling.

   - *P* and *D*;
   - *P* only;
   - *D* only; or
   - neither *P* nor *D*.

   In the second case it uses an independent distribution facility which is franchised to handle the product. In the third case it either exports from its home production facility or subcontracts to an independent local facility. In the final case the firm licenses an independent local firm to both produce and distribute the product. Because there is only one host-country rival (see (14) below), the possibility that the firm could subcontract to one firm and franchise another is ignored.

9. The transaction cost of operating an external market is normally greater than that of an internal one. The availability of alternative incentive structures in an internal market reduces the costs of haggling and default (Hennart, 1982). Indeed, it is assumed in the present model that the transaction cost of obtaining marketing expertise from an external consultant rather than from the firm's own *M* activity is prohibitive. The entrant can tap into an established *M* activity only by franchising the local rival, forming a joint venture with the rival, or acquiring its distribution facility.

10. The cost of external transfer of technology is also high, but acceptably so. One of the main problems in transferring technology is to monitor the output of the production process to make sure that the contract is being complied with. This is easier to do under a subcontracting agreement, where the product is 'bought back' than under a licensing agreement, where it is not. The transactions costs of a subcontracting agreement exceed the internal costs of technology transfer by t_1, while the costs of licensing exceed internal costs by $t_2 \geq t_1$.

11. When the ownership of *P* differs from that of *D* then the flow of intermediate product between them is effected through an external market. When compared to the alternative of vertical integration of *P* and *D*, this incurs additional transaction costs t_3.

12. Entry of any type can be effected by either greenfield investment or acquisition. Under greenfield investment the firm uses its funds to pay for the construction of a new facility. Under acquisition it uses its funds to purchase the facility second-hand as a going concern instead. This is done by acquiring the equity in the firm which previously owned the facility.

13. An effective internal market requires a high degree of trust within the organization. This trust is not available immediately after an acquisition. It costs q_1 to build trust in technology transfer when a P facility is newly acquired. It costs q_2 to build trust in the transfer of marketing expertise when a D facility is newly acquired, and q_3 to build trust in the transfer of intermediate product when either P or D (but not both) is newly acquired.

The Host-country Rival

14. The firm faces a single local rival which previously monopolized the foreign market. At the time of entry this rival operates as a fully integrated firm. It has the expertise, conferred by an activity M, which the entrant lacks. On the other hand, the local rival has higher costs because of inferior technology, on account of having no activity R.
15. It is assumed that in all bargaining (for example, over acquisition) the local rival plays an essentially passive role. The rival does not bargain for a share of the entrant's profits, but simply ensures that it receives full opportunity earnings for the resources it surrenders to the entrant firm. The rival realizes that the entrant has a superior technology and believes that when confronted with such a competitor its best strategy is to exit the industry by selling the entrant those resources it wishes to buy and redeploying the others to their best alternative use.
16. If the entrant uses the rival's production facility then a cost of adaptation, a, is incurred. This is because the entrant uses a different technology from the rival, and equipment must be modified accordingly. This applies whether the entrant acquires the facility outright, or merely licenses or subcontracts to the rival firm. On the other hand, the rival may have local production expertise, which the entrant lacks, providing savings to offset against the adaptation cost. The net cost of adaptation may therefore be negative. A negative adaptation cost, in this context, signifies that the cost of adapting the entrant's technology to local conditions using a greenfield plant is higher than the cost of adapting an existing local plant to the entrant's technology.
17. By contrast, use of a rival's D facility incurs no adaptation cost. This is because warehouses are normally more versatile than production plants. Use of the rival's D facility always brings with it the marketing expertise associated with M.
18. The rival's P and D facilities are the only existing facilities that can meet the needs of the market. Other local firms cannot enter the market and the rival firm itself cannot invest in additional facilities. Under these conditions acquisition of either a P or D facility gives the entrant

monopoly power: acquisition of a D facility gives the entrant a monopoly of final sales, while acquisition of a P facility gives the entrant a
monopoly of supplies to D. Greenfield investment, on the other hand,
confers no monopoly power because it eliminates no rival facility:
greenfield investment in D creates duopoly in the sourcing of final
demand, whilst greenfield investment in P creates duopoly in the sourcing
of D.

19. When the rival retains ownership of both its P and D facilities then it
remains a potential competitor. Although it may have switched some of
its facilities out of the industry, it can in principle re-enter by switching
them back again. If it has contracted out its P facility under a subcontracting arrangement, or contracted out its D facility under a franchising
arrangement, then it can in principle re-enter competition when the
agreements expire. Under a subcontracting arrangement the entrant and
the rival remain potential competitors in the final product market, since
each has their own distribution facility. Any attempt by the entrant to
charge the full monopoly price would encourage the rival to switch to
producing its own output instead. The entrant must persuade the rival
not to compete by reducing its price to a 'limit price' $p_2 < p_1$, at which it
just pays the rival to keep its distribution facility out of the industry.
Under a franchising arrangement the local rival retains the option of
switching back to supplying its distribution facility from its own production plant. To discourage this, the entrant must set an intermediate
output price which is equivalent (after deduction of distribution costs)
to the same limit price p_2. The final customers pay the monopoly price,
since the franchisee is the sole distributor, but the difference between
the monopoly price and the limit price accrues to the franchisee. In
either case, therefore, the persistence of rivalry costs the entrant $s = (p_1 - p_2)x$ in lost sales revenue.

20. Matters are slightly different in the case of a licensing agreement. It is
assumed that licensing is a long-term agreement, as opposed to short-term
agreements like subcontracting and franchising. A licence, it is supposed, involves either an outright purchase of the right to use the
technology, or a long-term agreement for the whole of the period over
which patent protection is likely to extend. The licence agreement
therefore confers effective monopoly power on the local licensee, but at
the same time allows the entrant to appropriate all the monopoly rents
by negotiating suitable terms for the licence agreement.

21. Apart from licensing, the only way to avoid the competitive threat is
acquisition. Acquisition of either the rival's P or D facility will do. It is
assumed that the costs at which these facilities can be acquired are
equivalent to the cost of new construction under a greenfield strategy

(although acquisition incurs additional conversion costs, as explained above).

Joint Ventures

22. Joint ventures are owned 50:50 by the two firms. Either the P or D plant, or both, can be jointly owned. It is assumed that where an IJV is undertaken the partner is always the local rival. If both P and D are jointly owned, then they are both part of the same IJV and so the market in intermediate output is internalized within the IJV. The IJV does not involve new facilities; it is assumed to be a 'buy in' by the entrant to the local firm. This means that IJV production incurs the costs of adaptation described above. Greenfield IJVs can easily be included in the model, although its complexity increases considerably as a result. Because the local rival contributes its facilities to the IJV, the IJV enjoys monopoly power in the same way that an acquisition does.

23. Where an IJV is linked to one of the entrant's wholly-owned activities, the relevant intermediate product market is only partially internalized. It is assumed, however, that once the appropriate degree of trust has been built up, the market can operate as though it was fully internal. The relevant costs of building trust are j_1 for technology transfer, j_2 for marketing expertise and j_3 for intermediate output flow.

24. Where both entrant and rival possess P facilities with which to source an IJV D facility, they employ the IJV to maintain a monopoly price but compete to supply it. The competition from the rival's P facility forces the entrant to supply the IJV at a limit price, and so allows the rival to obtain half the monopoly rent through its share in the IJV, even though it does not actually supply the IJV itself. If both entrant and rival possess D facilities able to draw upon an IJV P facility, then they can maintain a monopoly price by competing for a franchise to handle all the output. This forces the entrant to bid up the price for IJV output so that the profits are again shared with the rival through its stake in the IJV.

25. Learning costs m, adaptation costs a and trust-building costs j_i, q_i ($i = 1$, 2, 3) are once-for-all set-up costs that are financed by borrowing at the given interest rate r. By contrast, the home location cost premium z and the transaction costs are recurrent costs incurred each period.

2.4 SOLUTION OF THE MODEL

Defining the Strategy Set

The basic approach is to determine the set of all possible market entry strategies, to measure the profitability of each, and to identify the most profitable strategy. The dimensions of the strategy set are defined by the following issues:

1. where production is located;
2. whether production is owned by the entrant;
3. whether distribution is owned by the entrant;
4. whether ownership is outright or shared through an IJV; and
5. whether ownership is obtained through greenfield investment or acquisition.

The first four issues determine twelve main strategies of market entry. These twelve strategies are listed on the left-hand side of Table 2.1, and summarized schematically in Figure 2.1. Six of these strategies have different variants generated by the fifth issue. These variants are indicated on the right-hand side of the table. The figure distinguishes linkages involving the flow of information from R to P and M to D and linkages involving the flow of physical product from P to D and from D to final demand. Location is distinguished by the columns, and ownership by the rows. Ownership by the rival is also identified by shading; facilities owned by the entrant are shown as clear. The strategies associated with each particular linkage are indicated by the numbers 1–12 in the figure.

Deriving the Profit Equations

A profit equation for each variant of each entry strategy can be derived by applying the assumptions given above to the schematic illustrations in Figure 2.1. Certain elements of cost and revenue are common to all the profit equations, and it simplifies matters to net these out. This generates a set of summary profit equations in which profitability is expressed in terms of deviations from a profit norm. An appropriate norm is the profit generated by pursuing strategy 1 under ideal conditions in which the firm is already acquainted with the local market and there is no indigenous rival. The profit norm is the revenue generated by sales at the monopoly price *less* the cost of greenfield foreign production *less* the cost of greenfield foreign distribution, *less* the cost of internal technology transfer to a greenfield foreign plant, *less* the cost of internal transfer of goods from production to distribution.

Table 2.1 Twelve entry strategies and their variants

Ref	Type	Description	Variants	
1.	Normal FDI	Entrant owns foreign production and distribution facilities	1.1	Both facilities are greenfield
			1.2	Both facilities are acquired
			1.3	Production is greenfield and distribution is acquired
			1.4	Distribution is greenfield and production is acquired
2.	FDI in production	Entrant owns foreign production but uses independent distribution facilities	2.1	Production is greenfield
			2.2	Production is acquired
3.	Subcontracting	Entrant owns foreign distribution but uses independent production facilities	3.1	Distribution is greenfield
			3.2	Distribution is acquired
4.	FDI in distribution	Entrant exports to own distribution facility	4.1	Distribution is greenfield
			4.2	Distribution is acquired
5.	Exporting/franchising	Entrant exports to independent distribution facility		
6.	Licensing	Entrant transfers technology to independent integrated firm		
7.	Integrated JV	Entrant jointly owns an integrated set of production and distribution facilities		
8.	JV in production	Entrant jointly owns foreign production but uses an independent distribution facility		
9.	JV in distribution	Entrant jointly owns foreign distribution but subcontracts production to an independent facility		
10.	JV exporting	Entrant exports to a jointly owned distribution facility		
11.	FDI/JV combination	Entrant owns foreign production and jointly owns foreign distribution	11.1	Production is greenfield
			11.2	Production is acquired
12.	JV/FDI combination	Entrant owns foreign distribution and jointly owns foreign production	12.1	Distribution is greenfield
			12.2	Distribution is acquired

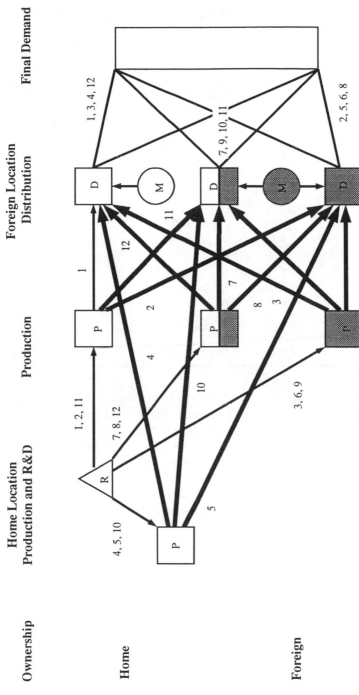

Figure 2.1   Twelve entry strategies and their variants

Table 2.2   Costs of alternative strategies compared with the profit norm

$c_{1.1} =$					$+ s$	$+ rm$
$c_{1.2} =$	rq_1	$+ rq_2$		$+ ra$		
$c_{1.3} =$		rq_2	$+ rq_3$			
$c_{1.4} =$	rq_1		$+ rq_3$	$+ ra$		$+ rm$
$c_{2.1} =$			t_3		$+ s$	
$c_{2.2} =$	rq_1		$+ t_3$	$+ ra$		
$c_{3.1} =$	t_1		$+ t_3$	$+ ra$	$+ s$	$+ rm$
$c_{3.2} =$	t_1	$+ rq_2$	$+ t_3$	$+ ra$		
$c_{4.1} = z$					$+ s$	$+ rm$
$c_{4.2} = z$		$+ rq_2$	$+ rq_3$			
$c_5 = z$			$+ t_3$		$+ s$	
$c_6 =$	t_2			$+ ra$		
$c_7 =$	rj_1	$+ rj_2$		$+ ra$		
$c_8 =$	rj_1		$+ rj_3$	$+ ra$		
$c_9 =$	t_1	$+ rj_2$	$+ rj_3$	$+ ra$		
$c_{10} = z$		$+ rj_2$	$+ rj_3$		$+ s/2$	
$c_{11.1} =$		$+ rj_2$	$+ rj_3$		$+ s/2$	
$c_{11.2} =$	rq_1	$+ rj_2$	$+ rj_3$	$+ ra$		
$c_{12.1} =$	rj_1		$+ rj_3$	$+ ra$	$+ s/2$	$+ rm$
$c_{12.2} =$	rj_1	$+ rj_2$	$+ rj_3$	$+ ra$		

If the actual profits of each strategy are compared with this norm, then every strategy incurs some additional cost. The relevant cost expressions are given in Table 2.2. The subscripts applied to the cost symbol c refer to the strategies and their variants listed in Table 2.1. The variables on the right-hand side have already been explained when introducing the assumptions of the model. Set-up costs are multiplied by the rate of interest to convert a once-for-all cost into a continuous equivalent.

To see how the profit equations are derived, consider strategy 2. This involves FDI in production, with sales being handled by the rival firm. There are two variants of this strategy, depending upon whether or not the production plant is acquired. The only international transfer of resources under this strategy involves technology, which moves across the column boundary from R to P. The transfer is internalized because no change of ownership is involved. Change of ownership only occurs where the flow of intermediate output from P to D crosses the row boundary. From D the product is distributed to the entire foreign market, as indicated by the flow fanning out from D.

The advantages of this particular strategy are twofold. It internalizes the transfer of technology within the entrant firm and the transfer of marketing expertise within the local firm. This can only be achieved, however, by externalizing the flow of intermediate output, which generates the transaction cost premium term t_3 which appears in the expressions for both $c_{2.1}$ and $c_{2.2}$. This is, in fact, the only term that is common to both expressions. The remaining terms are all accounted for by the difference between greenfield and acquisition methods of FDI. The greenfield strategy avoids the cost a of adapting an existing plant to the needs of a new technology. Thus the term ra, which appears in the expression for $c_{2.2}$, does not appear in the expression for $c_{2.1}$. The greenfield strategy also means that the internal transfer of technology is not bedevilled by a lack of trust, which arises when the production facility is acquired instead. The cost of building trust in internal technology transfer, rq_1, therefore appears in $c_{2.2}$ but not in $c_{2.1}$. The compensating advantage of the acquisition strategy is that it does not add to overall capacity in the foreign country. Indeed, because the entrant faces a single local rival, acquisition of the rival's production facility effectively prevents the rival from entering into competition with the entrant firm. Given that under strategy 2 the local firm retains control of distribution, it can threaten to source distribution from its own production plant instead of from the entrant's plant. Although the entrant may be able to constrain this threat in the short term by signing an exclusive franchise contract with its local rival, in the long run this contract will expire and the threat will reappear. Only acquisition of one of the rival's facilities can eliminate this threat altogether. This means that the greenfield strategy incurs a loss of revenue s compared to the acquisition strategy.

Dominance Relations

Theory predicts that the strategy with the lowest cost will be chosen. Which strategy is chosen depends on the relative magnitude of the different variables on the right-hand side of Table 2.2. The easiest way to understand the general properties of the solution is first to eliminate any strategies that are clearly dominated by others and then to compare the remaining ones in terms of the major trade-offs involved.

Whether strategies are dominated or not depends upon what restrictions are imposed upon the right-hand-side variables. So far the only restrictions implied by the assumptions are $m, r, s, j_i, q_i, t_i > 0$ ($i = 1, 2, 3$) and $t_2 \geq t_1$. In particular, the variables a and z are unrestricted in sign. Under these conditions only two of the strategies are dominated, namely the bottom two in the table:

$$c_{12.1} > c_8; \quad c_{12.2} > c_8 \tag{2.1}$$

These strategies involve a production IJV and a wholly-owned sales subsidiary. They are inferior to a production IJV combined with the franchising of sales. This shows that, if the entrant is to partner the IJV in production, then there is no point in buying back the product to distribute it afterwards.

Once additional restrictions are imposed, further dominance relations emerge. For example, if the net cost of home production is positive, $z > 0$, then all the export strategies are dominated by equivalent strategies involving greenfield foreign production:

$$c_{4.1} > c_{1.1}; \quad c_{4.2} > c_{1.3}; \quad c_5 > c_{2.1}; \quad c_{10} > c_{11.1} \tag{2.2}$$

This illustrates the important point that location effects are independent of internalization effects in models of this kind.

If the net cost of technological adaptation of existing production facilities is positive, $a > 0$, then it follows that

$$c_{3.1} > c_{1.1} \tag{2.3}$$

This means that the strategy of investing only in a greenfield distribution facility is inefficient compared to the strategy of investing in a greenfield production facility as well. Put simply, subcontracting production is not a good idea when the net cost of adapting existing plant to the new technology is positive.

So far no use has been made of restrictions on transactions costs. Suppose now that external market costs exceed the costs of building trust in internal markets after acquisition. In the context of production, this means that $t_1 > rq_1$, from whence it follows that

$$c_{3.2} > c_{2.2}; \quad c_9 > c_{11.2} \tag{2.4}$$

The first inequality shows that subcontracting production in conjunction with the acquisition of a distribution facility is more costly than franchising distribution in conjunction with the acquisition of a production facility. The second inequality shows that subcontracting production in conjunction with a jointly-owned distribution facility is more costly than acquiring a production facility in conjunction with a jointly-owned distribution facility. These results underline the fact that high transaction costs in technology markets, combined with easy trust-building post-acquisition, discourage subcontracting and favour acquisition instead.

The process of elimination through dominance can be continued by postulating that the cost of building trust is lower after an acquisition than it is within a joint venture: $q_i < j_i$ ($i = 1, 2, 3$). Not surprisingly, this eliminates several IJV strategies – though not all:

$$c_7 > c_{1.2}; \quad c_{11.1} > c_{1.3}; \quad c_{11.2} > c_{1.3} \tag{2.5}$$

It is inefficient to combine an IJV distribution facility with a production facility that is either wholly or jointly owned. Obviously, if the cost of building trust were thought to be lower in an IJV then the inequalities would be the other way round and the three acquisitions-based strategies would be eliminated instead.

It is not only inequality restrictions that can be used to generate dominance relations: equality restrictions can be used as well. For example, if the costs of building trust after acquisition are the same in each internal market, $q_i, = q$ ($i = 1, 2, 3$), then

$$c_{1.4} > c_{1.2} > c_{1.3} \tag{2.6}$$

This means that it is inefficient to acquire production when distribution is wholly owned; it is better to use greenfield production and acquire distribution instead.

If in addition the costs of building trust within IJVs are also the same in all markets, $j_i = j$ ($i = 1, 2, 3$) then

$$c_8 > c_{1.3} \tag{2.7}$$

It is better to combine greenfield production with the acquisition of a distribution facility than to undertake an IJV in production and franchise distribution to the partner firm.

Finally, consider two further restrictions. The first asserts that the cost of learning about a foreign market through a greenfield distribution facility exceeds the transaction cost of an external intermediate product market; $rm > t_3$. It follows that

$$c_{1.1} > c_{2.1} \tag{2.8}$$

so that it is cheaper to combine greenfield production with an acquired distribution facility rather than a greenfield one.

The second restriction asserts that the transaction cost of the external intermediate product market exceeds the cost of building trust in that market following an acquisition; $t_3 > rq_3$. It follows that (given that $q_1 = q_2$ from an earlier restriction)

$$c_{2.2} > c_{1.3} \tag{2.9}$$

so that it is cheaper to combine greenfield production with acquired distribution than to acquire production and franchise distribution instead.

Properties of the Solution

By carrying the process of elimination so far, only three of the original strategies are left in contention:

- 1.3.   greenfield production combined with acquired distribution;
- 2.1.   greenfield production combined with franchised distribution; and
- 6.   licensing.

The choice between these strategies is governed by six of the original variables: a, q, r, s, t_2, t_3. The solution is to choose

$$
\begin{array}{lll}
1.3. & \text{if } q \le (t_3 + s)/2r, \quad ((t_2/r) + a)/2 & (2.10.1) \\
2.1. & \text{if } t_3 + s \le 2qr, \quad t_2 + ra & (2.10.2) \\
6. & \text{if } t_2 + ra < 2qr, t_3 + s & (2.10.3)
\end{array}
$$

It can be seen that strategy 1.3 is preferred wherever the cost of acquisition q is low. This is reasonable because 1.3 is the only one of the three strategies that involves acquisition. Strategy 2.1 is preferred when the transaction costs of the external market in intermediate output, t_3, are low, and when the loss of monopoly profits from competitive distribution, s, is low. This is reasonable, because strategy 2.1 is the only one to involve an arm's-length sale of intermediate output, and the only one to leave the local rival in a position to compete. Strategy 6 is preferred when the transactions costs of licensing a technology, t_2, and adapting local production facilities, a, are low. This is reasonable because the licensing strategy is the only one of the three to utilize existing production facilities; the other two use only existing distribution facilities instead.

Deriving the Propensity to Adopt a Given Strategy

The logical structure of the model means that a change in any variable that increases the cost of certain strategies tends to inhibit the adoption of these strategies, and to encourage the adoption of alternative strategies instead. These alternative strategies are the ones whose costs are independent of the variable concerned. Indeed, apart from the rate of interest, r, and the cost of competition, s, every variable that enters into several cost functions enters into each of them in the same way. It is therefore impossible for a change in any variable of this kind to induce any switch between the strategies whose costs depend upon it.

In the case of r, however, the impact varies according to the particular set-up costs involved, and the impact of r upon the choice of any strategy cannot be determined unless the relative size of different set-up costs is known. An increase in r reduces the propensity to adopt any strategy that involves a set-up cost compared to any strategy that does not. If a strategy with a positive set-up cost has a lower set-up cost than the best alternative strategy, then an increase in r will increase the propensity to adopt this strategy. Because its set-up cost is smaller than that of the best alternative, the strategy is more likely to be chosen when r is high.

In the case of s, the impact of an increase favours distribution joint ventures at the expense of wholly-owned greenfield distribution facilities, but favours distribution acquisitions and licensing at the expense of both. The net effect on joint-venture distribution strategies therefore depends upon whether the best alternative to joint ventures is greenfield distribution or either acquisitions or licensing.

The implications of these general principles for the strategies of acquisition, franchising and licensing discussed above are summarized in Table 2.3. The table indicates whether an increase in a given variable is likely to increase or decrease the propensity to adopt that strategy in preference to the other two. A question mark indicates that the direction of the effect cannot be known unless relative set-up costs are specified – in this context, the relative cost of building trust after an acquisition, q, and the relative cost of adapting a licensee's production plant, a. If $2q < a$ then an increase in r will favour acquisition and discourage licensing, so that r will have a negative effect on licensing. The effect on acquisition will remain indeterminate, however, because, although it becomes more favoured relative to licensing, it becomes less favoured relative to franchising. The direction of the effect therefore

Table 2.3 *Comparative static analysis of the effects of changes in the values of the explanatory variables on the choice between the three dominant strategies*

Number	Strategy	a	q	s	t_2	t_3	r
1.3	Acquisition	+	−	+	+	+	?
2.1	Franchising	+	+	−	+	−	+
6	Licensing	−	+	+	−	+	?

Notes:
a Adaptation cost of production plant.
q Cost of building trust to access marketing expertise through a newly-acquired distribution facility.
s Value of profit-sharing collusion.
t_2 Additional transaction cost incurred by licensing technology.
t_3 Additional transaction cost incurred in using an external market for the wholesale product.
r Rate of interest.

Table 2.4   Comparative static analysis of the effects of changes in the values of the explanatory variables on the propensity to adopt each possible entry mode

	a	j_1	j_2	j_3	m	q_1	q_2	q_3	r	s	t_1	t_2	t_3	z
1.1	+	+	+	+	−	+	+	+	+	−	+	+	+	+
1.2	−	+	+	+	+	−	−	+	?	+	+	+	+	+
1.3	+	+	+	+	+	+	−	−	?	+	+	+	+	+
1.4	−	+	+	+	−	−	+	−	?	+	+	+	+	+
2.1	+	+	+	+	+	+	+	+	+	−	+	+	−	+
2.2	−	+	+	+	+	−	+	+	?	+	+	+	−	+
3.1	−	+	+	+	−	+	+	+	?	−	−	+	−	+
3.2	−	+	+	+	+	+	−	+	?	+	−	+	−	+
4.1	+	+	+	+	−	+	+	+	+	−	+	+	+	−
4.2	+	+	+	+	+	+	−	−	?	+	+	+	+	−
5	+	+	+	+	+	+	+	+	+	−	+	+	−	−
6	−	+	+	+	+	+	+	+	?	+	+	−	+	+
7	−	−	−	+	+	+	+	+	?	+	+	+	+	+
8	−	−	+	−	+	+	+	+	?	+	+	+	+	+
9	−	+	−	−	+	+	+	+	?	+	−	+	+	+
10	+	+	−	−	+	+	+	+	?	?	+	+	+	−
11.1	+	+	−	−	+	+	+	+	?	?	+	+	+	+
11.2	−	+	−	−	+	−	+	+	?	+	+	+	+	+

Notes:

a   Adaptation cost of production plant.

j_1 Cost of building trust to support technology transfer in a production joint venture.

j_2 Cost of building trust to support access marketing expertise through a distribution joint venture.

j_3 Cost of building trust to support a flow of the wholesale product to or from a joint venture.

m   Cost of acquiring knowledge of the market through wholly-owned distribution.

q_1 Cost of building trust to transfer technology to a newly-acquired production facility.

q_2 Cost of building trust to transfer marketing expertise to a newly-acquired distribution facility.

q_3 Cost of building trust to support a flow of wholesale product to or from a newly-acquired facility.

r   Rate of interest.

s   Value of profit-sharing collusion.

t_1 Additional transaction cost incurred by subcontracting production.

t_2 Additional transaction cost incurred by licensing technology.

t_3 Additional transaction cost incurred in using an external market for the wholesale product.

z   Net additional cost of serving the foreign market by export rather than production in the host market.

depends upon whether licensing or franchising is the best alternative to acquisition. If $2q > a$ then an increase in r will favour licensing and discourage acquisition, so that an increase in r will have a negative effect on acquisition. The effect on licensing will remain indeterminate, however, because, although it becomes more favoured relative to acquisition, it becomes less favoured relative to franchising.

The wider implications of these principles are summarized in Table 2.4. The results reported in the table apply to the market entry problem in its most general form. The additional assumptions used to derive the dominance relations above are now set to one side. A wide range of hypotheses are generated by this table. A comprehensive discussion of them all is beyond the scope of a single chapter. Some of the results are fairly obvious, and appear in an intuitive form in the extant literature. Other results are more surprising. In some cases the element of surprise is a consequence of the specific assumptions that have been made in order to simplify the model. In other cases the element of surprise indicates a hypothesis which is plausible when considered in depth, but not immediately obvious to the intuition.

2.5 DISCUSSION OF RESULTS

Some of the more obvious results are as follows:

1. An increase in z, caused by higher tariffs, transport costs or a loss of economies of scale in domestic production, encourages production abroad. It encourages both licensing and wholly-owned production. This underlines the importance of keeping the distinction between *location* effects and *internalization* effects very clear in any discussion of foreign market entry strategy.
2. An increase in a, reflecting a highly specific type of entrant's technology, discourages acquisition and licensing, and favours greenfield production.
3. An increase in the cost of building trust, q, discourages acquisition and favours either greenfield investment or arm's-length contractual arrangements.
4. A high cost, m, of learning about the foreign market through experience, encourages acquisition, licensing and franchising, and discourages subcontracting or greenfield investment in distribution.
5. A high transaction cost for intermediate output, t_3, encourages the vertical integration of production and distribution. This can be achieved either by the foreign entrant investing in both production and distribution, by the entrant exporting to a wholly-owned distribution facility, or the en-

trant licensing the technology to a vertically integrated domestic firm. It can also be achieved by forming a vertically integrated IJV.

6. A high transaction cost for arm's-length technology transfer, t_1, favours foreign direct investment over arm's-length arrangements, like subcontracting.

7. In general, subcontracting is not a very attractive mode of foreign market entry. This is because it does not give access to the domestic rival's marketing expertise. It also leaves the domestic rival in a strong competitive position, since the contractual commitment to the entrant is of a short-term nature, and the rival's distribution facility is not committed at all. The reason why subcontracting is so often used is because of another motive for entering a foreign country, and that is for access to local resources – notably cheap labour for offshore processing. This motive, though important, is excluded from the present chapter. This shows how important it is to distinguish different strategic motivations when discussing institutional arrangements in international business.

Three interesting and less obvious results are as follows:

1. The existence of large monopoly rents, associated with a high cost of competition, s, favours strategies which give the entrant long-term control over either the domestic rival's production facilities, or their distribution facilities. It favours acquisition over greenfield investment in either production or distribution. It also favours long-term arrangements like licensing over short-term arrangements like subcontracting and franchising.

2. Joint ventures in distribution are a useful mode of market entry when high costs of learning by experience, m, discourage greenfield distribution, high costs of building trust, q_1, discourage the acquisition of distribution facilities, high costs in the arm's-length intermediate output market, t_3, discourage franchising, and high costs of arm's-length technology transfer, t_2, discourage licensing. However, joint ventures in production do not make much sense as a means of market entry, unless the production joint venture is part of an integrated joint venture that handles distribution as well.

3. In general, the analysis confirms that market structure is a crucial factor in the choice between greenfield investment and acquisition. Entry through greenfield investment increases local capacity and intensifies competition, whereas entry through acquisition does not. This explains why governments so often compete to attract inward greenfield investment while taking a restrictive attitude to acquisitions at the same time.

2.6 CONCLUSION AND IMPLICATIONS FOR FUTURE RESEARCH

The model is very flexible, in the sense that it is easy to modify the assumptions to address other issues. It can be extended to include two host-country rivals, or two entrants vying with each other to enter the same market. This requires extending the analysis from duopoly to three-firm oligopoly. Introducing a third player not only increases the scope for competition, but introduces new opportunities for co-operation too. The model can be rendered more dynamic by allowing entrants to determine the timing of entry – a particularly important consideration where growing markets, such as China or Eastern Europe, are concerned.

The host government plays a very passive role in the present model. Strategic interactions between the host government and the entrant can be introduced. The host government may offer tax incentives in return for commitments on local value added or 'job creation' which affect the choice of entry mode. Bargaining may take place over subsidies. Political risk may discourage FDI and encourage the use of arm's-length contracts instead. The possibilities for the firm to minimize global tax liabilities through transfer pricing can also be taken into account.

The model can be extended to take account of foreign investment in services as well as manufacturing. It already takes an important step in the direction of analysing service industries by introducing marketing and distribution activities in addition to production. By modifying the assumptions about the physical relationship between production and distribution in various ways, the model can be applied to a wide range of service industries.

There are many smaller ways in which the model can be modified as well. The analysis of duopolistic rivalry can be refined using models of Bertrand and Cournot competition (Gorg, 1998). The formation of IJVs through greenfield investment can be introduced to supplement the 'buy in' strategy assumed above. Finally, the role of host-country production expertise can be modelled in greater detail by making more explicit the function of adapting foreign technology to local production conditions.

REFERENCES

Agarwal, S. and S.N. Ramaswani (1992) 'Choice of foreign market entry mode: impact of ownership, location and internalisation factors', *Journal of International Business Studies*, **23**, 1–27

Anderson, E.M. and A.T. Coughlan (1987) 'International market entry and expansion via independent or integrated channels of distribution', *Journal of Marketing*, **51**, 71–82

Anderson, E.M. and H. Gatignon (1986) 'Modes of foreign entry: a transaction costs analysis and propositions', *Journal of International Business Studies*, **17**, 1–26

Bakema, H.G., J.H.J. Bell and J.M. Pennings (1996) 'Foreign entry, cultural barriers and learning', *Strategic Management Journal*, **17**, 151–66

Beamish, P.W. (1985) 'The characteristics of joint-ventures in developing and developed countries', *Columbia Journal of World Business*, **20**, 13–20

Beamish, P.W. (1987) 'Joint ventures in less developed countries: partner selection and performance', *Management International Review*, **27**(1), 23–37

Beamish, P.W. and J.C. Banks (1987) 'Equity joint ventures and the theory of the multinational enterprise', *Journal of International Business Studies*, **18**, 1–15

Beamish, P.W. and J.P. Killing (eds) (1997) *Cooperative Strategies* (3 vols), *North American Perspectives, European Perspectives, Asian Pacific Perspectives*, San Francisco: New Lexington Press

Benito, G.R.G. and G. Gripsrud (1992) 'The expansion of foreign direct investments: discrete rational locational choices or a cultural learning process?', *Journal of International Business Studies*, **23**, 461–76

Blodgett, L.L. (1992) 'Factors in the instability of international joint ventures: an event history analysis', *Strategic Management Journal*, **13**, 475–81

Buckley, P.J. (1983) 'New theories of international business: some unresolved issues', in M. Casson (ed.), *The Growth of International Business*, London: Allen & Unwin, 34–50

Buckley, P.J. and M. Casson (1976) *The Future of the Multinational Enterprise*, London: Macmillan

Buckley, P.J. and M. Casson (1981) 'The optimal timing of a foreign direct investment', *Economic Journal*, **92**(361), 75–87

Buckley, P.J. and M. Casson (1988) 'A theory of cooperation in international business', in F.J. Contractor and P. Lorange (eds), *Cooperative Strategies in International Business*, Lexington, MA: Lexington Books

Buckley, P.J. and M. Casson (1996) 'An economic model of international joint ventures', *Journal of International Business Studies*, **27**(5), 849–76

Buckley, P.J. and P.N. Ghauri (eds) (1993) *The Internationalization of the Firm*, London: Dryden Press

Buckley, P.J. and R.D. Pearce (1979) 'Overseas production and exporting by the world's leading enterprises', *Journal of International Business Studies*, **10**(1), 9–20

Casson, M. (1985) 'Multinational monopolies and international cartels', in P.J. Buckley and M. Casson (eds), *The Economic Theory of the Multinational Enterprise*, London: Macmillan

Casson, M. (1991) 'Internalisation theory and beyond', in P.J. Buckley (ed.), *New Horizons in International Business: Research Priorities for the 1990s*, Aldershot: Edward Elgar, 4–27

Casson, M. (1994) 'Internationalization as a learning process: a model of corporate growth and geographical diversification', in V.N. Balasubramanyam and D. Sapsford (eds), *The Economics of International Investment*, Aldershot: Edward Elgar

Caves, R.E. (1971) 'International corporations: the industrial economics of foreign direct investment', *Economica*, **38**, 1–27

Contractor, F.J. (1984), 'Choosing between direct investment and licensing: theoretical considerations and empirical tests', *Journal of International Business Studies*, **15**(3), 167–88

Contractor, F.J. (1990) 'Ownership patterns of US joint-ventures and liberalisation of foreign government regulation in the 1980s: evidence from the Benchmark Surveys', *Journal of International Business Studies*, **21**, 55–73

Contractor, F.J. and P. Lorange (eds) (1988) *Cooperative Strategies in International Business*, Lexington, MA: Lexington Books

Davidson, W.H. (1980) 'The location of foreign direct investment activity: country characteristics and experience effects', *Journal of International Business Studies*, **11**(2), 9–22

Dubin, M. (1975) 'Foreign Acquisitions and the Spread of the Multinational Firm', DBA Thesis, Graduate School of Business Administration, Harvard University

Dunning, J.H. (1980) 'The location of foreign direct investment activity, country characteristics and experience effects', *Journal of International Business Studies*, **11**, 9–22

Flowers, E.B. (1976) 'Oligopolistic reaction in European and Canadian direct investment in the United States', *Journal of International Business Studies*, **7**, 43–55

Franko, L.G. (1971) *Joint Venture Survival in Multinational Corporations*, New York: Praeger

Geringer, J.M. (1991) 'Strategic determinants of partner selection criteria in international joint ventures', *Journal of International Business Studies*, **22**(1), 41–62

Geringer, J.M. and L. Hebert (1991) 'Measuring performance of international joint ventures', *Journal of International Business Studies*, **22**(2), 249–63

Gomes-Casseres, B. (1987) 'Joint venture instability: is it a problem?', *Columbia Journal of World Business*, **22**(2), 97–107

Gomes-Casseres, B. (1991) 'Firm ownership preferences and host government restrictions', *Journal of International Business Studies*, **21**, 1–22

Gorg, H. (1998) 'Analysing foreign market entry: the choice between greenfield investments and acquisitions', Trinity College, Dublin Technical Paper 98/1

Graham, E.M. (1978) 'Transatlantic investment by multinational firms: a rivalristic phenomenon', *Journal of Post-Keynesian Economics*, **1**, 82–99

Graham, E.M. (1992) 'The theory of the firm', in P.J. Buckley (ed.), *New Directions in International Business*, Cheltenham: Edward Elgar

Gulati, R. (1995) 'Does familiarity breed trust? The implications of repeated ties for contractual choices in alliances', *Academy of Management Journal*, **28**(1), 85–112

Hallen, L. and F. Wiedersheim-Paul (1979) 'Psychic distance and buyer-seller interaction', *Organisasjon, Marknad och Samhalle*, **16**(5), 308–24. Reprinted in P.J. Buckley and P.N. Ghauri (eds) (1993), *The Internationalization of the Firm*, London: Dryden Press

Harrigan, K.R. (1988a) 'Joint ventures and competitive strategy', *Strategic Management Journal*, **9**, 141–58

Harrigan, K.R. (1988b) 'Strategic alliances and partner asymmetries', in F.J. Contractor and P. Lorange (eds), *Cooperative Strategies in International Business*, Lexington, MA: Lexington Books

Hennart, J.-F. (1982) *A Theory of Multinational Enterprise*, Ann Arbor: University of Michigan Press

Hennart, J.-F. (1988) 'A transaction costs theory of equity joint ventures', *Strategic Management Journal*, **9**, 361–74

Hennart, J.-F. and Y.-R. Park (1993) 'Greenfield vs acquisition: the strategy of Japanese investors in the United States', *Management Science*, **39**, 1054–70

Hennart, J.-F. and Y.-R. Park (1994) 'Location, governance and strategic determinants of Japanese manufacturing investment in the United States', *Strategic Management Journal*, **15**(6), 419–36

Hill, C.W.L., P. Hwang and C.W. Kim (1990) 'An eclectic theory of the choice of international entry mode', *Strategic Management Journal*, **11**, 117–28

Hirsh, S. (1976) 'An international trade and investment theory of the firm', *Oxford Economic Papers*, **28**, 258–70

Hofstede, G. (1980) *Culture's Consequences: International Differences in Work-related Values*, Beverly Hills, CA: Sage

Horst, T.D. (1972) 'Firm and industry determinants of the decision to investment abroad: an empirical study', *Review of Economics and Statistics*, **54**, 258–66

Hymer, S.H. (1976) 'The International Operations of National Firms: A Study of Direct Foreign Investment', (unpubl. 1960 PhD thesis), Cambridge, MA: MIT Press

Inkpen, A.C. and J. Birkenshaw (1994) 'International joint ventures and performance: an interorganizational perspective', *International Business Review*, **3**(3), 201–17

Johanson, J. and J.-E. Vahlne (1977) 'The internationalization process of the firm – a model of knowledge development and increasing foreign market commitments', *Journal of International Business Studies*, **8**(1), 23–32

Johanson, J. and F. Wiedersheim-Paul (1975) 'The internationalization of the firm – four Swedish cases', *Journal of Management Studies*, **12**, 305–22

Killing, J.P. (1983) *Strategies for Joint Ventures*, New York: Praeger

Kim, W.C. and P. Hwang (1992) 'Global strategy and multinational's entry mode choice', *Journal of International Business Studies*, **23**, 29–53

Kindleberger, C.P. (1969) *American Business Abroad*, New Haven: Yale University Press

Knickerbocker, F.T. (1973) *Oligopolistic Reaction and Multinational Enterprise*, Boston, MA: Harvard University Press

Kogut, B. (1988) 'Joint ventures: theoretical and empirical perspectives', *Strategic Management Journal*, **9**, 319–32

Kogut, B. (1989) 'The stability of joint ventures: reciprocity and competitive rivalry', *Journal of Industrial Economics*, **38**(2), 183–98

Kogut, B. and H. Singh (1987) 'Entering the United States by joint venture: industry structure and competitive rivalry' in F.J. Contractor and P. Lorange (eds) (1988), *Cooperative Strategies in International Business*, Lexington, MA: Lexington Books

Kogut, B. and H. Singh (1988) 'The effect of national culture on the choice of entry mode', *Journal of International Business Studies*, **19**(3), 411–32

Kogut, B. and U. Zander (1992) 'Knowledge of the firm, combinative capabilities and the replication of technology', *Organization Science*, **3**, 383–97

Kogut, B. and U. Zander (1993) 'Knowledge of the firm and the evolutionary theory of the multinational corporation', *Journal of International Business Studies*, **24**, 625–45

Meyer, K.E.E. (1997) 'Determinants of Direct Foreign Investment in Transition Economies in Central and Eastern Europe, PhD thesis', University of London

Nitsch, D., P. Beamish and S. Makino (1996) 'Entry mode and performance of Japanese FDI in Western Europe', *Management International Review*, **36**, 27–43

Penrose, E. (1959) *The Theory of the Growth of the Firm*, Oxford: Basil Blackwell

Prahalad, C.K. and G. Hamel (1990) 'The core competence and the corporation', *Harvard Business Review*, May, 71–91

Root, F.R. (1987) *Entry strategies for International Markets*, Lexington, MA: Lexington Books

Rugman, A.M. (1981) *Inside the Multinationals: The Economics of Internal Markets*, London: Croom Helm

Shane, S. (1994) 'The effect of national culture on the choice between licensing and direct investment', *Strategic Management Journal*, **15**, 627–42

Stopford, J.M. and L.T. Wells, Jr (1972) *Managing the Multinational Enterprise: Organization of the Firm and Ownership of Subsidiaries*, London: Longman

Svensson, R. (1996) *Foreign Activities of Swedish Multinational Corporations*, Uppsala: Department of Economics, Uppsala University, Economic Studies 25

Tirole, J. (1988) *The Theory of Industrial Organization*, Cambridge, MA: MIT Press

Vernon, R. (1966) 'International investment and international trade in the product cycle', *Quarterly Journal of Economics*, **80**, 190–207. Reprinted in P.J. Buckley and P.N. Ghauri (eds) (1993), *The Internationalization of the Firm*, London: Dryden Press

Wilson, B. (1980) 'The propensity of multinational companies to expand through acquisitions', *Journal of International Business Studies*, **12**(2), 59–65

Woodcock, C.P., P. Beamish and S. Makino (1994) 'Ownership-based entry mode strategies and international performance', *Journal of International Business Studies*, **25**, 253–73

Yip, G. (1982) 'Diversification entry: internal development versus acquisition', *Strategic Management Journal*, **3**, 331–45

Young, S., J. Hamill, C. Wheeler and J.R. Davies (1989) *International Market Entry and Development*, Hemel Hempstead: Harvester Wheatsheaf

Yu, C.-M. and K. Ito (1988) 'Oligopolistic reaction and foreign direct investment: the case of the US tyre and textiles industries', *Journal of International Business Studies*, **19**, 449–60

Zejan, M.C. (1990) 'New ventures or acquisitions: the choice of Swedish multinational enterprises', *Journal of Industrial Economics*, **38**, 349–55

3. The boundaries of firms: a global systems perspective

3.1 INTRODUCTION

This chapter analyses the boundaries of the firm from a system-wide perspective. It re-examines some of the issues raised in the previous chapter. New hypotheses are generated by situating the previous analysis within a systems approach. In the previous chapter the unit of analysis was the individual firm. In the present chapter the unit of analysis is the global economy. The analysis predicts not only where the boundaries of any given firm will be drawn, but how many firms there will be, and where their boundaries will interface with one another.

Despite the frequent references to 'globalization' within the IB literature, a coherent account of the economic structure of the global economy is hard to find. When they appeal to formal models, IB scholars tend to cite standard economic theories of international trade: these may be theories of factor substitution, such as the Heckscher–Ohlin–Stolper–Samuelson theory (see for example, Kemp, 1964), or the theories of strategic trade policy based on transport costs and increasing returns to scale (Helpman and Krugman, 1985). It is well known, however, that such theories focus upon industries rather than firms. To take a systems view of the MNE it is necessary to disaggregate the global economy from the industry level to the level of the individual production facilities.

In this chapter the global economy is portrayed as a collection of facilities linked together by a complex web of product and knowledge flows. The facilities that are linked together are of different types. They are differentiated by function – for example, production, marketing or R&D. There are various possible sites at which facilities may be located. Each activity can be concentrated upon a single location, or distributed over all of them. Some sites attract certain types of facilities, and others different ones. Different patterns of location lead to different geographical patterns of product flow and knowledge flow.

A global system needs to be co-ordinated. There are many different types of institutional arrangement that can be used to effect co-ordination – for example, firms, markets, social networks and the state. In the simplest form of internalization theory the focus is on the choice between the firm and the market, and this is the specific choice that is examined here.

A firm may own and control any number of facilities. Where two facilities are controlled by different firms, and there is a linkage between them, the firms involved must negotiate and enforce a contract in order to harmonize their decisions. In this case the linkage is co-ordinated by external market forces. Where two linked facilities are controlled by the same firm, the linkage is co-ordinated internally by managers instead. If the facilities are located in different countries, then internal control creates a multinational enterprise; otherwise a national multi-plant enterprise is created instead.

There are numerous combinations of firm and market by which the global economy can be co-ordinated. At one extreme, a single firm can co-ordinate the entire world – that is it owns all the facilities and internally co-ordinates all the linkages between them. At the other extreme, every facility can be owned by a different firm. In this case external markets effect all the co-ordination between facilities instead. In between these limits are various possibilities, in which different firms control different groups of activities. But how many different firms will there be, and what groups of activities will they control?

This issue has been raised in general terms many times before – for example, by Robertson (1923) and Coase (1937) – but curiously no attempt has ever been made to address it fully in a systematic way. The probable explanation is that most people believe the problem to be much too complex. Analysis almost always focuses upon a single firm, and ignores the interdependencies between different firms which arise from the structure of the system within which the firms are embedded.

There are two main dimensions of the configuration of the global economy: *location* and *ownership*. A full solution of the co-ordination problem requires the simultaneous determination of the location and ownership of facilities. There is a correspondence between the location and ownership of facilities and the pattern of linkages involved. The location of facilities determines the geographical pattern of linkages, whilst the ownership of facilities determines whether each linkage is internal or external to the firm.

The co-ordination problem can be solved either by focusing upon the location and ownership of facilities, and inferring the pattern of linkages, or by focusing upon the pattern of linkages and inferring the location and ownership of facilities. This chapter offers a formal solution based upon the second approach. It shows that the problem is not as complex as it appears. A judicious choice of simplifying assumptions generates a formulation which is fairly transparent in logical terms, and which points to a solution along quite straightforward lines. Within the chosen approach there are further options for solving the problem, which are described in detail in later sections of the chapter.

Before presenting the model, the historical evolution of the systems per-spective is reviewed. This review, in Sections 3.2–3.4, motivates the formal model, which is set up and solved in Sections 3.5–3.10. Applications and extensions are discussed in Sections 3.11 and 3.12, and the conclusions are summarized in Section 3.13.

3.2   HISTORICAL BACKGROUND TO THE SYSTEM-WIDE PERSPECTIVE

Most contemporary accounts of the theory of the firm take the firm itself, rather than the industry, or the economy as a whole, as the basic unit of analysis. Current interest is focused on what goes on inside the firm. This is a reaction against conventional neoclassical theory, which modelled the firm as a 'black box'. There is also considerable emphasis today on firm-specific advantages (or competencies). As a result, the neoclassical concept of a 'representative firm' is rejected because it understates the individuality and character of the typical firm.

However, this reaction against the neoclassical approach can be pushed too far. One important advantage of the neoclassical approach is that it directs attention to the wider economic environment in which the firm operates. Neoclassical industrial organization theory directs attention to the firm's competitors, whilst general equilibrium theory highlights the complementarities and the substitution possibilities that connect firms in different industries.

The need to incorporate a wider perspective on the firm is particularly strong in the light of the continuing 'globalization' of the world economy. This has generated significant changes in the environment of the typical firm. Recent changes in the boundaries of firms are best understood as a rational response to external changes of this kind. Thus a satisfactory theory of the firm needs to encompass the structures of both the firm itself, and the global economic system of which it forms a part.

The system-wide perspective set out in this chapter is not new. It is clearly hinted at by Coase (1937). At the time Coase was writing, controversy raged over the issue of 'planning versus prices'. Socialism was identified with central planning, and capitalism with a market system which decentralized decision-making, using prices. One school of thought on economic systems argued that socialist planners could make use of 'shadow' prices, which would mimic the prices of the market system. Shadow prices would be more accurate than market prices as measures of opportunity costs, because mo-nopolistic distortions could be eliminated, and externalities compensated for. The opposing school of thought argued that central planners would be unable to compute the shadow prices because they would be overwhelmed by the weight of information needed for their calculations (Hayek, 1935). It was also hinted that bureaucrats would distort information under their control for their own ends. The fundamental problems of human deviousness would simply reassert themselves in a different form. The problems would be more difficult to check under central planning, because of the absence of competitive discipline, due to the monopoly power of the state.

Coase's insight was that the choice between planning and prices is not quite so stark as this ideological debate supposed. It is possible to combine the benefits of planning and prices by having planning units embedded in a market system. Indeed, capitalist firms have always performed this planning function. They hire managers to co-ordinate through authority the allocation of resources that would otherwise have been determined through a market system:

> It is easy to see when the State takes over the direction of an industry that, in planning it, it is doing something that was previously done by the price mechanism. What is usually not realised is that any business man in organising the relations between his departments is also doing something which could be organised through the price mechanism. (Coase, 1937, p. 389, fn. 3)

Planning and prices can therefore be combined according to their comparative advantage to co-ordinate different parts of the economic system. Firms institutionalize the planning system, and markets institutionalize the price system. Thus the boundaries of the firm and the market are the interface between the two systems of resource allocation – the points at which their respective advantages are equalized.

Who is to determine where the boundaries should lie? There are two possibilities. Markets can be embedded in a planning system, or planning can be embedded in a market system. These arrangements have very different implications.

If markets are embedded within a planning system, then the planners decide where markets should exist, and set the rules by which they operate. This is the situation that prevails inside decentralized organizations where different divisions trade with each other at transfer prices. Various degrees of decentralization are possible. The internal prices may be fixed by a central planning unit inside the firm, or they can be negotiated directly by the division heads – an arrangement that approximates more closely to the conventional market process.

The other possibility – that planning is embedded in a market system – is the situation assumed by Coase. In the market system, it is private entrepreneurs who determine where the boundaries of firms lie. More specifically, entrepreneurs establish firms by bringing various groups of resources under common ownership and control. To acquire these resources they normally need to borrow funds. These funds will only be forthcoming if investors think that they will be put to proper use. Proper use includes establishing a firm whose boundaries are positioned in a suitable way. If a firm's boundaries are believed to be in the wrong place, then investors will withdraw their funds, or sell out their shares to another firm, which will then take over and put the boundaries in the right place. This process may be implemented through divestment, management buy-in or buy-out, or acquisition.

The process is driven by profit-seeking entrepreneurs. These entrepreneurs are always looking for ways to reconfigure the boundaries of firms in pursuit of greater efficiency. They may divest assets which do not fit with the other assets owned by the firm, and acquire other assets to complement existing ones. Sometimes they form new firms, sometimes they take over existing firms, or merge them. Sometimes they may acquire firms simply for asset-stripping, or to close down loss-making activities.

Each entrepreneur seeks to operate each firm as profitably as he can, which means that, where management is delegated, each manager is 'incentivized' to maximize profit on the owner's behalf. If he fails to do so, then he will lose his job. It might be inferred, therefore, that competitive discipline leads to the maximization of profit as a whole. In other words, the global system is driven to maximize global profit.

However, this conclusion ignores the role of competition in product markets. Competition in the product market serves to eliminate above-average profit. In the short run, competition encourages price-cutting, and in the long run monopolies are undermined by new entrants who imitate or improve the monopolist's technology or product. It is only Marxists who claim that collusion among large firms is so strong that firms are able to maximize profit on a system-wide basis.

It is, however, possible to restate this proposition in a more satisfactory way. In this restatement, there is a crucial qualification – namely that the state of competition is to be taken as fixed. For any given degree of competition in the product markets, competition in the markets for capital and management does indeed create a tendency towards the maximization of system-wide profit. A necessary condition for any firm to maximize profit, conditional on the state of competition in the product market, is that any given level of output is produced at minimum cost. If output is not produced at minimum cost, then there is some cost-reducing change that is bound to increase profit. This implies that within the system as a whole any given set of outputs will be produced at minimum cost. In other words, the global system tends to minimize the global cost of producing any given set of outputs.

A cost-reducing change effected by a firm could involve a change in method of production, but it could equally involve a change in location, or in the boundaries of the firm. It follows that the principle of minimizing system-wide cost governs both the location of production and the boundaries of firms. Given the output mix of the global economy, the location of facilities and the boundaries of firms can be predicted from the principle that system-wide cost is a minimum.

Not only do firms optimize individually, therefore, but the constellation of firms within the economy is optimized too. 'In a competitive system, there is an "optimum" amount of planning!' (Coase, 1937, p. 389, fn. 3). Any failure to minimize the overall cost of the system will create a profit opportunity somewhere in the system which an alert entrepreneur will intervene to correct (Kirzner, 1973).

3.3   FURTHER CONSIDERATIONS

In practice, of course, this entrepreneurial system works far from perfectly, though supporters of the market system argue that, despite its defects, it works better than any alternative system is likely to do. It is worth noting, however, that the market which drives the system-wide minimization of cost is the capital market, together with the market for managers, and not the product markets on which many writers wrongly focus. It is competition for funds, and for managerial ability, that determines which entrepreneurs can realize their business plans and which of them cannot. The capital market allocates funds between different planning units – the firms – each of which establishes boundaries for itself within the product market system. The market for managers allocates managerial ability between different firms according to the firm's demand for management ability, which reflects the complexity of the internal co-ordination problems that the manager must solve.

Some product markets – and in particular, intermediate product markets for components and semi-processed goods – may be wholly internalized within certain firms. Others may be partially internalized, so that firms make components for internal use, but supply the same components to independent firms as well. Product markets are therefore far more 'planned' than many advocates of the market system are willing to recognize. One obvious symptom of this, within the global economy, is the high level of intra-firm international trade.

Equally, however, it is a mistake to suppose that all firms are pure planning units, for as noted earlier, firms may contain market subsystems inside them. Subsystems are particularly common when intermediate products are made in several different manufacturing plants (multiple sourcing) and are used in several different assembly plants (multiple users). Just as firms are found inside the market system, so markets can be found inside firms.

Indeed, it is possible to go further than this. The internal market of a firm normally involves trade between subsidiaries, and each of these subsidiaries can in turn be regarded as an independent firm – indeed, they are usually constituted as such from a legal point of view. Thus inside the firm's internal market other firms are to be found. These firms may be similar to the original firm, though on a smaller scale. Indeed, it is possible to iterate this process further, for inside some subsidiaries there may be local markets too. The economy therefore consists of a nested system of firms and markets. The characteristic of the capitalist system is that the firms are inside the market, rather than the markets inside the firm; by contrast, the characteristic of the socialist system based on shadow prices is that the market is inside the firm, and that the firm is also the state. Both systems are therefore more eclectic than is normally supposed. Both derive flexibility from combining alternative institutional forms, rather than relying on any single one. However, while capitalism relies on private entrepreneurs to decide where the boundaries of firms should be drawn, socialism relies on planners employed by the state. The state may well employ people with entrepreneurial ability to act as planners, but differences of opinion between planners are not resolved by competition for capital, as in the capitalist system, but by reference to the authority exercised by the head of state.

3.4   UPDATING THE SYSTEMS VIEW

The debate over planning and prices was at its height in the 1930s, when high tariffs and a desire for national self-sufficiency inhibited international trade. Foreign direct investment was discouraged by high levels of political risk. The debate was therefore conducted in the context of a closed national economy. Today, however, when trade and capital movements have been liberalized, it is more appropriate to take the global rather than the national economy as the basic unit of analysis. It is also important to recognize the strategic significance of knowledge flows. These did not figure much in the earlier debate. In updating the systems view, therefore, a contemporary formulation must encompass the co-ordination of knowledge flow as well as of ordinary product flow.

The updated model contains the Buckley and Casson (1976) model of the multinational enterprise as a special case. This is no accident. The Buckley and Casson model was based upon a systems view:

> ... the modern business sector carries out many activities apart from the routine production of goods and services: particularly important are marketing, R and D, the training of labour, the building of a management team, the procurement of finance and the management of financial assets, etc. All these business activities are interdependent and are connected by flows of intermediate products. The intermediate products are sometimes ordinary semi-processed materials passed on

from one industry to another, but more often are types of knowledge and expertise, embodied in patents, human capital, etc. Efficient coordination of business activities requires a complete set of markets in the intermediate products. However, markets in certain intermediate products are difficult to organise, and it is our thesis that attempts to improve the organisation of these markets have led to a radical change in business organisation, one aspect of which is the growth of the MNE. (p. 33)

The model presented here articulates the view of the world economy which these authors developed (for subsequent refinements see Casson, 1990, 1992). It was their expectation, at the time they first wrote, that the subsequent development of internalization theory would follow the path set out in the present chapter, but this judgement proved to be wrong. In fact, the concept of internalization was quickly shorn of the generality conferred upon it by Coase. The insights of the systems view were lost, and the concept was applied in a highly specific way.

This was partly due to the influence of Williamson (1975) and Dunning (1977). Williamson concentrated his analysis on the vertical integration of production, and later narrowed the focus still further to the strategic 'hold-up' problem (Klein, Crawford and Alchian, 1978; Williamson, 1985). His analysis was mainly domestic, and focused on the co-ordination of material flow rather than knowledge flow. Dunning's view was wider, in the sense that he took an international perspective, and focused on knowledge flow. But his view was also narrow in a different sense: he initially applied the theory purely to the issue of whether a firm-specific advantage could be licensed or not. He played down the issue of vertical integration of production, until forced to take account of its significance for 'resource-seeking investment' in his later work (for example Dunning, 1983).

The theory of internalization thus became divorced from the systems view of the economy in which it is most naturally embedded. It became relegated to the status of a special theory dealing with specific 'boundary' issues in the context of a single firm. Writers began to emphasize the benefits of internalization at the expense of the costs; consequently, they appeared to some of their critics as mere apologists for vertical integration or for foreign direct investment. The systems view, however, underlines the importance of taking a balanced view of internalization. It is necessary to recognize the costs as well as the benefits of internalization, for it is the costs that account for the benefits of the external market system in which firms are embedded.

3.5   THE MODEL IN OUTLINE

Methodology

Discrete choice models provide a very suitable method of analysing system-wide behaviour, as they do for many other aspects of multinational business strategy. A significant advantage of discrete choice models over their continuous counterparts is that a solution can always be found by enumerating all the possibilities, evaluating each of them in turn, and selecting the best. As the dimensions of the system increase, however, the efficiency of this method of solution decreases rapidly because of 'combinatorial explosion' – the number of different permutations of strategy accelerates dramatically as the dimensions increase (Casson and Wadeson, 1996). This means that it is very important to eliminate those solutions that are always dominated by others. It is also important to examine the remaining solutions in an appropriate order, so that the best solution is encountered early in the process of search.

Economic principles are very important in identifying dominance relations, and in determining an appropriate order of search among the undominated strategies. For this reason, the solution of the problem is discussed below in terms of its economic logic. The mathematical implementation of these principles is fairly straightforward, as the numerical example in Section 3.10 shows.

Basic Structure

Consider an economic system which produces a single consumer good. Three types of activity are involved: R&D ($h = 0$), production ($h = 1$) and marketing and distribution ($h = 2$). There are two locations ($i = 1, 2$). Each activity can take place at one or both locations. The system is portrayed in Figure 3.1. An R&D laboratory is denoted by a triangle, a production plant by a square, and a warehouse and sales office by a diamond.

The facilities are linked to one another either by flows of materials (denoted by thick lines) and/or flows of knowledge (denoted by thin lines). The direction of flow is indicated by an arrow. Three main types of linkage are identified, indexed $m = 0, 1, 2$. The first is a flow of finished product from production to marketing ($m = 0$). The second is a flow of knowledge between R&D and production ($m = 1$), and the third is a flow of knowledge between R&D and marketing ($m = 2$). Product flow is one-way, but knowledge flow is two-way. This is because there is a feedback of knowledge from production and marketing to R&D. There is no flow of knowledge between production and marketing; the transmission of knowledge between production and marketing is entirely intermediated by R&D. This simplification is of little

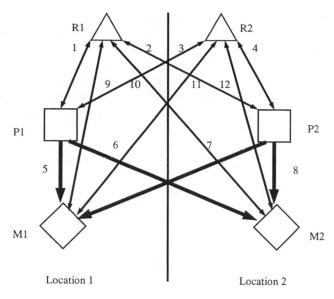

Note: The numbers 1–12 identify the linkages described in the text.

Figure 3.1 Basic configuration of the system

consequence because production and marketing are already linked directly by material flow.

Linkage Costs

The information flows used for co-ordination purposes are not shown in the figure. All linkages are, however, supported by information flow. The cost of maintaining a linkage has two main components: transfer cost and information cost. The transfer cost is the cost of actually moving the resource from one location to another. It has three main components. In the case of material product these are transport costs, tariffs, and the costs of overcoming non-tariff barriers (such as local health and safety regulations). In the case of intangibles such as knowledge, transport costs are replaced by training costs.

Information cost has two main components: communication cost and as-surance cost. Communication costs relate to the costs of agreeing the price and quantity of the resource to be transferred, on the assumption that those involved are honest and competent. Assurance costs are the costs incurred in dealing with misinformation – whether due to incompetence or dishonesty. The term 'transaction cost' is often used to refer to these assurance costs, but it is not employed here because it has become ambiguous: it sometimes refers only to the costs of dealing with dishonesty, while in other cases it includes not only the costs incurred by incompetence, but communication costs also (see Chapter 5).

The three components of transfer cost, together with the two components of information cost, mean that there are five components of linkage cost altogether. These components are listed in the left-hand column of Table 3.1. Each component of linkage cost depends upon a number of factors, five of which are identified in the table.

Table 3.1   Factors influencing the components of linkage cost

	Type of product	Geographical distance	Political difference	Cultural difference	Internalization
Transfer costs					
Transport/Training	X	X			
Tariff	X		X		X
Non-tariff barriers	X		X		
Information costs					
Communication	X	X		X	X
Assurance	X		X	X	X

The nature of the resource to be transferred is clearly an important factor in linkage cost. For example, knowledge transfers often incur higher information costs than material transfers because the quality of the knowledge is not only critical, but also difficult to check. Three of the factors are location-specific. The first is the geographical distance spanned by the linkage. This is clearly an important influence on transport costs. The second relates to political differences, and in particular whether or not the two locations are within the same country. This dimension can also encompass whether the countries are at war or peace, whether they are parties to a treaty, whether they extend most-favoured nation treatment to each other, and whether they are part of a customs union, free trade area, or monetary union. Political differences are also an important influence on assurance costs. The third location-specific factor is cultural difference. Cultural differences are a major influence on communication costs. They sometimes manifest themselves at the sub-national level: thus a metropolis may have a more individualistic and competitive culture than a remote rural area. While cultural differences between countries are often reflected in their political differences, the relationship is not always a simple one. Thus countries are often on bad terms with their neighbours because of territorial disputes, even when their cultures are quite similar, while countries may be on good terms, not because their cultures are similar, but because they have a common political enemy.

The final influence on linkage costs is whether the linkage is internal or external to a firm. This is clearly the most important factor from the standpoint of the model. It impacts mainly on information costs, as noted above. Internalization also affects exposure to tariffs, however, because it facilitates transfer pricing: by undervaluing internal resource transfers, a firm can reduce its liability to *ad valorem* duties. Transfer-pricing economies are particularly significant when the product is unique to the firm, for in this case there is no arm's-length price with which the customs authority can compare the transfer price.

The total cost of a linkage is the sum of the costs of these five components. Since each of the factors listed in the table affects one or more of the components, the total cost depends upon all five factors. It is assumed, for simplicity, that the total cost of a linkage is directly proportional to the quantity of resource transferred.

Figure 3.1 indicates that there are twelve potential linkages in the system, although not all are activated at any one time. The cost of transferring a unit resource along the jth linkage ($j = 1,...,12$) is

$$t_j = t(m_j, d_j, n_j) \tag{3.1}$$

where m_j identifies the type of flow, d_j indicates the distance involved, and n_j represents the internalization decision. All three of these determinants are discrete variables. The variable m_j has already been discussed. When both the source and the destination are at the same location $d_j = 0$, whereas when they are different $d_j = 1$. Distance may be defined in relation to any of the three criteria listed in Table 3.1, or in terms of any combination of them. Unless otherwise stated, it will be assumed that d_j refers to political distance, and therefore indicates whether a linkage is a domestic or international one. Because location-specific factors are accounted for only by the index d_j, distance-related linkage costs are symmetric with regard to the direction of travel: the cost of resource flow from location 1 to the location 2 is the same as it is from 2 to 1.

External linkages are indicated by $n_j = 0$ and internal linkages by $n_j = 1$. The dichotomous nature of this choice excludes intermediate arrangements, such as informal long-term contracts. However, it is not difficult to introduce such possibilities into the model, as explained in Section 3.12.

Of the three determinants of linkages costs, only one has an unambiguous effect. An increase in distance increases linkage costs. For any product, and any degree of internalization, the cost of a distant linkage exceeds that of a local one:

$$t\,(m_j,\,1,\,n_j) > t\,(m_j,\,0,\,n_j) \quad j = 1,\ldots,12 \tag{3.2}$$

Linkage costs for knowledge flows may be either higher or lower than for material flows, and may either increase or decrease with respect to internalization. On the whole, internal knowledge flows are likely to be cheaper than external knowledge ones, particularly where domestic flows are concerned, although this is not specifically assumed by the model.

R&D Costs

Knowledge is a public good. Thus the output of a single R&D laboratory can supply the needs of two production plants just as easily as it can supply the needs of one. It does not follow, however, that only one R&D facility is required. For example, when distance-related knowledge transfer costs are high, each plant may benefit from having its own R&D laboratory. The public good property does imply, though, that each laboratory should operate with only unit capacity, and that no production plant, however large, should be supplied with knowledge by more than one laboratory. These results simplify the model quite considerably, because they mean that R&D output at each location involves just a zero-one choice, and that there will only be two laboratories if there are two plants in operation as well.

There must always be R&D at some location, because without R&D the product cannot be developed and improved. It follows that there are three possible R&D location strategies within the system. Let x_0 denote the R&D strategy: the three possibilities are location at 1 ($x_1 = 0$), location at both 1 and 2 ($x_1 = 1$) and location at 2 ($x_1 = 2$). It is assumed that knowledge is generated using only scientific labour, and that one unit of scientific labour generates one unit of knowledge per period. Let $w_{0i} > 0$ be the wage of scientific labour at location i ($i = 1, 2$). This wage is also the unit cost of knowledge produced by R&D. Thus the system-wide cost of R&D, c_0, is

$$
\begin{aligned}
c_{00} &= w_{01} & \text{if } x_0 = 0 \\
c_{01} &= w_{01} + w_{02} & \text{if } x_0 = 1 \\
c_{02} &= w_{02} & \text{if } x_0 = 2.
\end{aligned} \tag{3.3}
$$

Production Costs

It is assumed that market size is unity at each location. It is also assumed that price at each location is always sufficiently high to make it profitable to serve both markets. Thus system costs are always minimized by setting total capacity to 2. Capacity is available at each location in integer units. Because total capacity never exceeds 2, production strategy can be uniquely described by the amount of capacity at location 2, namely $x_1 = 0, 1, 2$. The correspond-ing capacity at location 1 is $2 - x_1$.

At each location there is a fixed cost of production and a constant unit variable cost of production. Once-for-all set-up costs are ignored; the empha-sis of the model is on a steady state. Fixed costs arise from the exploitation of economies of scale. All fixed costs are recurrent ones incurred in the mainte-nance, repair and replacement of the capital stock. All production and maintenance is labour-intensive, and is undertaken using ordinary local la-bour. Interest costs incurred in funding the capital stock are ignored. It follows that all production costs at the ith location are directly proportional to the local wage for ordinary labour, $w_{1i} > 0$ ($i = 1, 2$). One unit of labour generates one unit of product, whilst $f > 0$ units of labour are required to maintain the capital stock. Thus system-wide production costs, c_1, are

$$
\begin{aligned}
c_{10} &= w_{11} (f + 2) & \text{if } x_1 &= 0 \\
c_{11} &= (w_{11} + w_{12})(f + 1) & \text{if } x_1 &= 1 \\
c_{12} &= w_{12} (f + 2) & \text{if } x_1 &= 2.
\end{aligned}
\tag{3.4}
$$

Marketing

The costs of marketing are fixed and unavoidable, because each market is always supplied with one unit of product. They do not, therefore, impact on cost-minimization, and so can be ignored.

3.6 THE RELATION BETWEEN THE LOCATION OF FACILITIES AND THE GEOGRAPHY OF LINKAGES

This section identifies the set of possible strategies that can be used to co-ordinate the global system. These strategies are not strategies to be pursued by a given firm, but strategies to be pursued by the system as a whole. The strategy pursued by the system determines how many firms there will be in the system, and the strategy that each one of them will pursue. This is because the system minimizes overall system cost, while each firm only minimizes its own cost, given the behaviour of the other firms that the system supports.

Possible system strategies are indexed $k = 1,...,K$. The system optimizes by selecting the value of k that is associated with the lowest overall system cost. System-wide optimization involves the interplay of location and ownership strategies. It has already been noted that location and ownership can be viewed either from the standpoint of linkages, or from that of facilities. As far as location is concerned, the two approaches are very similar, because of the close connection between location of facilities and the geography of linkages. Indeed, under the conditions assumed above, it can be shown that there is a one-to-one correspondence between efficient location strategies for facilities and the geography of the linkages that support them.

It has already been established that R&D location strategy can be uniquely described by the value of x_0, and that production location strategy can be uniquely described by the value of x_1. Since each of these variables can take only one of three values, there are just nine possible location strategies. These nine strategies correspond to the elements inside the 3×3 box in Table 3.2.

Table 3.2   Cost structure

Location of production	$x_0 = 0$	$x_0 = 1$	$x_0 = 2$	Production costs
	1.		2.	
$x_1 = 0$	$t(1, 0, n_1)$		$t(1, 1, n_3)$	c_{10} $+ t(0, 0, n_5)$ $+ t(0, 1, n_6)$
	3.	4.	5.	
$x_1 = 1$	$t(1, 0, n_1)$ $+ t(1, 1, n_2)$	$t(1, 0, n_1)$ $+ t(1, 0, n_4)$	$t(1, 0, n_4)$ $+ t(1, 1, n_3)$	c_{11} $+ t(0, 0, n_5)$ $+ t(0, 0, n_8)$
	6.		7.	
$x_1 = 2$	$t(1, 1, n_2)$		$t(1, 0, n_4)$	c_{12} $+ t(0, 0, n_8)$ $+ t(0, 1, n_7)$
R&D costs *plus* cost of linkage to marketing	c_{00} $+ t(2, 0, n_9)$ $+ t(2, 1, n_{10})$	c_{01} $+ t(2, 0, n_9)$ $+ t(2, 0, n_{12})$	c_{02} $+ t(2, 0, n_{12})$ $+ t(2, 1, n_{11})$	

It was noted earlier that it is never efficient to supply any given production unit with knowledge from more than one R&D facility. This means that two of the nine location strategies, $(x_0 = 1, x_1 = 0)$, $(x_0 = 1, x_1 = 2)$, are always inefficient and can be eliminated. This leaves the seven location strategies, indexed $k = 1,\ldots,7$, indicated by the numbered cells in the table.

Further simplification of the problem can be achieved by noting that three of the seven location strategies are 'mirror images' of one another, created by

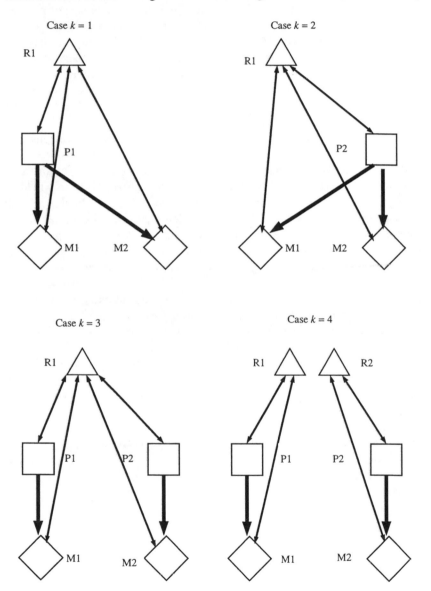

Figure 3.2   Four distinctive linkage structures

interchanging the role of locations 1 and 2. Strategy 7 is the mirror image of strategy 1, obtained by shifting both production and R&D from location 1 to location 2. This symmetry is illustrated by the position of the two elements in the table, where cell 7 is the image of cell 1 reflected in a diagonal running upwards from left to right. Similarly strategy 6 is the mirror image of strategy 2, obtained by interchanging the locations of production and R&D. This is shown by the way that cell 6 is the image of cell 2, reflected in a diagonal running downwards from left to right. Finally, cell 5 is an image of cell 3, reflected in a vertical line through the middle of the box. This indicates that the location of R&D has been altered, while production remains symmetrically located at both. The four distinctive location strategies $k = 1,...,4$ are illustrated schematically in Figure 3.2.

It is easily seen that for three of the four distinctive location strategies, the location of facilities uniquely determines the geographical pattern of linkages that sustains it. The exception is strategy $k = 4$, which can be sustained by two alternative patterns of linkage. Each plant may supply its own local market, or it may supply the other local market instead. In this second instance the product is 'cross-hauled' between plant and market, but in the light of earlier assumptions, such cross-hauling is inefficient. It replaces two domestic linkages with two more expensive international linkages, and is therefore more costly in total. Thus the pattern of linkages is also uniquely determined by location of facilities in this final case.

Given the one-to-one correspondence between linkages and facilities within the location problem, the advantage of working with linkages or facilities is determined by the internalization problem. Since internalization is a property of a linkage, it is natural to work in terms of linkages wherever possible.

It is a very simple matter to determine location strategy conditional upon internalization strategy. Once the internalization of each linkage is specified, the cost of that linkage is known. The total cost C_k, of each of the seven location strategies can then be computed directly by summing the R&D costs (shown in the bottom row of Table 3.2), the production costs (shown in the right-hand column of the table) and the linkage costs shown in the cells within the box. The cost of each strategy is derived by identifying the appropriate cell in the box and then adding to the element in the cell the element at the base of the corresponding column and the element at the end of the corresponding row. Comparing the costs C_k ($k = 1,...,7$), and selecting the lowest, identifies the efficient location strategy k^* and the cost associated with it.

3.7   OPTIMIZING INTERNALIZATION: THE 'TRIANGLE PROBLEM'

In order to complete the solution, it is necessary to apply the principle of minimum cost to determine internalization strategy. If the internalization decision for any given linkage is independent of the internalization decision for any other linkage, then this is a straightforward matter. System-wide costs are minimized by a two-step procedure. The first step is to identify separately the least-cost internalization strategy n_j^* for each of the six types of linkage ($m_j = 0, 1, 2; d_j = 0, 1$). This information is then used to determine the minimum cost $t_j^* = t_j (m_j, d_j, n_j^*)$ for each of the twelve linkages shown in Figure 3.1, conditional upon this internalization decision. The second step is the same as the one described above: to identify the linkages that are activated by each location strategy, then sum the linkage costs, production costs and R&D costs, and thereby identify the least-cost strategy.

There is a difficulty, however. Internalization decisions about individual linkages cannot always be made independently of one another. Some combinations of internalization decisions are incompatible with a coherent set of boundaries between firms. The one-to-one mapping between facilities and linkages which applies in the location dimension is not replicated by a one-to-one mapping between facilities and linkages in the ownership dimension. The problem is that the internalization of any two linkages involving the same facility implies that any linkage between the two facilities it is linked with must be internal too. Some elementary implications of this result were discussed in Casson (1992).

Consider, for example, the triangular pattern of linkages shown in Figure 3.3. This pattern involves linkages between production, marketing and R&D, and is found within each of the four types of location strategies shown in Figure 3.2. An internal linkage is denoted by the letter N and an external linkage by the letter E.

Consider first the the top-left-hand corner of the figure (case 1). Both the linkages emanating from R&D are internalized. This means that the firm that owns the R&D laboratory also owns both the production plant (by virtue of internalizing the linkage from R&D to production) and the marketing facility (by virtue of internalizing the linkage from R&D to marketing). Thus all three facilities are owned by the same firm. It follows that the third linkage, from production to marketing, must be internal as well. Thus where Ns appear along two sides of the triangle, there must be an N along the third side of the triangle too.

The same result does not apply where external markets are concerned, however. If two markets are external then the third does *not* have to be external too. Thus if both the linkages from R&D are external, the linkage

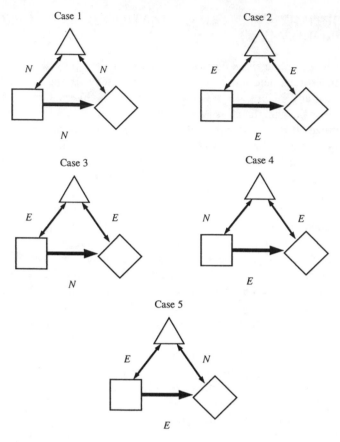

Note: All configurations of the form *N–N–N*, *N–N–E* and *E–E–E* are permitted. No configuration of the form *N–N–E* is permitted.

Figure 3.3   Feasible triangular relationships

between production and marketing can be either internal or external. The case of a third external linkage is illustrated in the top-right-hand corner (case 2). Each of the three activities is independently owned, so the link between any pair of activities is an external one. The case of an internal linkage is illustrated by case 3. Production and marketing are integrated within a single firm, but R&D is independently owned; thus the owner of the R&D laboratory deals at arm's length with both the production and marketing activities owned by this integrated firm. Other instances of two external linkages combined with a single internal linkage are illustrated by cases 4 and 5.

The triangle problem is a special case of a more general problem. The general problem involves any number $n > 2$ facilities. If facility A_1 is linked to facility A_2, A_2 is linked to A_3 and so on, until the last facility, A_n, is linked back to A_1, then internalization of all but one of the links implies that the last remaining link must be internalized as well. In the model discussed in this chapter, however, the problem occurs only for $n = 3$ – in other words, it is always a 'triangle' problem.

The triangle problem is not a mere mathematical curiosity. It has important economic implications. It means that a linkage may be internalized purely as a consequence of a desire to internalize other linkages to which the facilities concerned belong. Specifically, case 1 shows that a vertical linkage between production and marketing may be internalized purely because both of the facilities concerned need to be linked internally to R&D. This illustrates a special case of a more general phenomenon: that linkages involving ordinary product flow may be internalized purely because knowledge-based linkages are also involved. When the gains from internalizing knowledge-based linkages are greater than the gains from internalizing ordinary product flow, product flows may be internalized even when, in the absence of knowledge-based linkages, they would be external instead. Thus attempts to explain the vertical integration of product flow purely in terms of factors impinging on product flow may be misguided, because these factors alone would imply externalization of the product linkage instead. Failing to take a systems view means that when knowledge-based flows are omitted, the real factors driving internalization may be overlooked, and spurious factors governing the internalization of product flow may be emphasized instead.

3.8 SOLUTIONS TO THE TRIANGLE PROBLEM

When there is just a single triangle within a system of linkages, the problem can be dealt with quite easily. A solution can always be found either by turning one of the two internal linkages into an external one, or by turning the solitary external linkage into an internal one. All of these solutions involve changing just one of the linkages. It is never efficient to change two of the linkages, because changing two will be more costly than changing just one. Indeed, changing two linkages can sometimes be quite counterproductive since, if an internal linkage is externalized at the same time that an external linkage is internalized, then the problem is simply recreated in a different form. Since changing any one of the three linkages will solve the problem, it follows that making the cheapest of the changes is the most efficient strategy.

Where two or more triangles are involved, matters are more complicated. However, if the several triangles are independent, in the sense that they have no linkages in common, then each triangle problem can be solved separately using the method described above. Where a linkage is common to two or more triangles, a more sophisticated approach is required, as explained in detail below.

The triangle problem arises in each of the seven location strategies discussed above. Two triangles are involved in each case. This is because there are two separate markets, and each market supports a triangle of its own. For $k = 3$, 4 and 5, the two triangles are independent, and the situation can be resolved by two separate applications of the principles described above. The simplest case is case 4, in the bottom-right-hand corner of Figure 3.2. In this case the two triangles involve completely separate sets of facilities. The first, $R1–P1–M1$, is based entirely at location 1 whilst the other, $R2–P2–M2$, is based entirely at location 2. Case 3, in the bottom-left-hand corner of the same figure, is a little more complicated, because the two triangles involve the same R&D facility. This is not an important difference, however, because it is common linkages, and not common facilities, that are the source of the triangle problem. While the two triangles $R1–P1–M1$ and $R1–P2–M2$ have a facility in common, they have no linkage in common, and each triangle problem can be resolved independently of the other.

For strategies $k = 1$, 2, 6 and 7, however, the two triangles are linked. In each case the common link is between production and R&D. The problem is illustrated by cases 1 and 2 at the top of Figure 3.2. In case 1 the triangles $R1–P1–M1$ and $R1–P1–M2$ have the common linkage $R1–P1$, and in case 2 the two triangles $R1–P2–M1$ and $R1–P2–M2$ have the common linkage $R1–P2$. Apart from the location of the production facility, however, the two cases are the same. Thus while they differ in location strategy, the internalization issues that they raise are the same. It is therefore sufficient to focus on the solution for case 1: the solution for case 2 follows by substituting $P2$ for $P1$ into the solution for case 1.

When triangles are interdependent, the incremental method of solution described above loses much of its power. The solution to a problem in one of the triangles can 'spill over' to create a problem in the other triangle, because it may require the internalization of the common linkage to be changed. It is better to adopt an alternative solution method instead.

The alternative approach involves enumerating all the possible boundary structures associated with the location strategy concerned. Although this approach seems complicated, it is usually quite manageable. This is because double triangles usually occur only when the number of active linkages is small. This means that the number of possible boundary structures is small as well. This makes it easy to explore the various possibilities in a systematic way.

Suppose to begin with that the common linkage is internalized, so that $R1$ and $P1$ belong to the same firm. The only question then is whether $M1$ and

*M*2 will belong to the same firm as well. This involves two independent decisions. It is necessary either to internalize both $R1-M1$ and $P1-M1$, or to internalize neither one. Similarly, it is necessary either to internalize both $R1-M2$ and $P1-M2$, or to internalize neither one. Comparing the costs of these alternatives determines the optimal internalization strategy conditional on the internalization of $R1-P1$.

Now suppose that $R1-P1$ is externalized instead. Once again, there are two independent choices, concerning the ownership of *M*1 and *M*2 respectively. But now there are three options in each case. *M*1 can be integrated with *R*1 by internalizing $R1-M1$ and externalizing $P1-M1$, it can be integrated with *P*1 by internalizing $P1-M1$ and externalizing $R1-M1$, or it can be made independent of both by externalizing both $R1-M1$ and $P1-M1$. Similar options apply in respect of *M*2. Choosing the cheapest of the three options in each case gives the optimal internalization strategy conditional upon the externalization of $R1-P1$. It only remains to compare the total costs of the least-cost strategies conditional on the internalization and on the externalization of the common linkage, and the triangle problem is solved.

3.9   THE SCOPE FOR SIMPLIFICATION

The complications connected with the triangle problem raise the question of whether a simpler approach can be devised. Two approaches will be discussed. Both attempt to avoid the triangle problem, but neither is entirely successful.

The first approach is to dismiss the triangle problem as a spurious one, on the grounds that a firm always has the option of mimicking a market when operating a linkage, even when it owns both the activities concerned. Suppose, for example, that a firm based entirely at location 1 wishes to internalize the linkages $R1-P1$ and $R1-M1$, but would like to externalize the linkage $P1-M1$. The triangle problem says that the firm cannot do this, because its internalization of the first two linkages means that it is the owner of both *P*1 and *M*1, and so the linkage between them must be internal as well. The counter-argument is that the $P1-M1$ linkage can be operated as though it were external by creating an appropriate internal market within the firm. Thus while the first two linkages – both knowledge-based, incidentally – may be co-ordinated centrally, the third linkage – involving product flow from factory to warehouse – can be co-ordinated by negotiations between production and marketing divisions instead.

This argument hinges on the view that an 'internal market' is identical to an external market linkage. There are two objections to this view, however. The first is that it is unrealistic to suppose that a market within a firm functions in exactly the same way as a market between two firms, because the firm has far more control over an 'internal' market than it does over a normal external one. Internal markets can certainly be introduced into the model, as is explained in Section 3.12 below, but they are most appropriately considered as a special type of internalization, and not as equivalent to a normal external market.

The second objection is that, if firms can run markets internally just as well as external markets can run themselves, then there is no need for external markets at all, because firms can reproduce the most efficient aspects of the external market for themselves. The theory would predict that all markets would be internalized, and that some of the internal markets would then be set up to mimic external ones. The prediction that all markets are internalized emerges as a trivial consequence of the extreme assumption being made.

The second approach is to suppress some of the linkages in the model in order to prevent triangles from forming. The knowledge-based linkages are the obvious candidates for suppression, since without the product linkages the customers would never receive deliveries at all. Given that technology transfer is such an important phenomenon, and a well-established component of modern theories of the firm, it seems appropriate to preserve the R&D–production linkages and to suppress the R&D–marketing linkages instead. This second approach is discussed as a special case of the numerical example presented below.

3.10   A NUMERICAL EXAMPLE

Specification

The method of solution may be illustrated using a numerical example. Suppose that the global economy consists of a single industry with modest technological sophistication, in which production affords little scope for economies of scale. Feedback of information from marketing to R&D is crucial in meeting consumer tastes, while information flow from R&D to marketing is crucial in explaining to consumers the best way in which to use the product.

The structure of facility costs is indicated in Table 3.3 and the structure of linkage costs in Table 3.4. With constant returns to scale, there are no fixed costs of production, $f = 0$. Location 1 has a comparative advantage in R&D, and location 2 a comparative advantage in production. This is reflected in the wage rates for ordinary workers and for scientific workers reported in Table 3.3. Wages for scientific workers are lower in country 1, and wages for ordinary workers are lower in country 2.

Product flow from production to marketing is best externalized. This is reflected in the top two lines of Table 3.4, corresponding to the linkage type

Table 3.3   Example of facilities costs

Type of activity		Location	
		$i = 1$	$i = 2$
R&D	$h = 0$	$w_{01} = 4$	$w_{02} = 6$
Production	$h = 1$	$w_{11} = 4$	$w_{12} = 3.5$

Table 3.4   Example of linkage costs

Type of resource flow		Domestic/ international	Internalization	
			$n = 0$	$n = 1$
Product	$m = 0$	$d = 0$	1*	2
		$d = 1$	4*	5
Technology	$m = 1$	$d = 0$	4	1*
		$d = 1$	3*	5
Marketing knowledge	$m = 2$	$d = 0$	3	1*
		$d = 1$	4	2*

$m = 0$. For both domestic ($d = 0$) and international ($d = 1$) linkages, the cost is lower in an external market ($n = 0$) than in an internal one ($n = 1$). Whether internal or external, the international linkage is more expensive than the domestic one, as required by inequality (3.2).

The case for internalization is stronger where knowledge-based flows are concerned. Domestic technology transfer benefits from internalization, but international technology transfer does not. If the technology were more sophisticated, internalization of international technology transfer would be beneficial as well. These properties are reflected in the two middle lines of Table 3.4, corresponding to linkage type $m = 1$. The strategic significance of marketing means that internalization of both domestic and international linkages between marketing and R&D is worthwhile, as indicated in the two bottom lines of the table, corresponding to $m = 2$.

Solution of a Simplified Problem

Consider to begin with a simplified version of the model which avoids the triangle problem by suppressing the linkages between marketing and R&D. The first step in the solution is to choose the degree of internalization for each type of linkage. Because there is no triangle problem, each linkage can be considered independently of the others. The results are indicated by the asterisks in the two right-hand columns of Table 3.4. Each asterisk identifies the minimum cost of the linkage concerned. The column in which the asterisk appears indicates whether the linkage is an internal or external one.

In the second step, these minimum values are substituted into Table 3.2, giving the results shown in Table 3.5. The system-wide cost of each of the seven location strategies is then computed, by adding to the value in each numbered cell the values of the corresponding cells in the bottom row and the

Table 3.5　Overall cost structure of the simplified example

Location of production	Location of R&D			Production costs
	$x_0 = 0$	$x_0 = 1$	$x_0 = 2$	
$x_1 = 0$	1. 1		2. 3	$8 + 5 = 13$
$x_1 = 1$	3. $1 + 3 = 4$	4. $1 + 1 = 2$	5. $1 + 3 = 4$	$7.5 + 2 = 9.5$
$x_1 = 2$	6. 3		7. 1	$7 + 5 = 12$
R&D costs *plus* cost of linkage to marketing	4	10	6	

Table 3.6　Costs of alternative location strategies

Location strategy k	Minimum cost C_k
1	$1 + 13 + 4 = 18$
2	$3 + 13 + 6 = 22$
3	$4 + 9.5 + 4 = 17.5*$
4	$2 + 9.5 + 10 = 21.5$
5	$4 + 9.5 + 6 = 19.5$
6	$3 + 12 + 4 = 19$
7	$1 + 12 + 6 = 19$

right-hand column. The minimum cost location strategy, $k = 3$, is identified by finding the smallest element in Table 3.6, $C_3 = 17.5$.

Properties of the Simplified Solution

The optimal combination of location and ownership strategies is shown in Figure 3.4. It can be seen that R&D is concentrated in country 1, which has a comparative advantage in scientific labour. Production is replicated in both countries. The decision not to concentrate production in country 1 reflects the absence of economies of scale. It also reflects the high costs of exports from country 1 compared to the cost of international technology transfer to country 2, and the fact that country 2 has a comparative advantage in production.

Internalization strategy calls for four separate firms to be involved in the global system. The boundaries between the firms are shown by the lines *AE*, *BE*, *CE* and *DE*. Firm 1, which owns the facilities shown in black, is a high-technology domestic producer. It licenses its technology to a foreign firm, firm 2, which owns the production facility shaded in dark grey. Both firms maintain arm's-length relations with their distributors – firms 3 and 4 (indicated by lighter shading). These arm's-length relationships reflect the economies of externalization in product flow. The resulting pattern of owner-ship reflects the type of economic organization favoured by those who

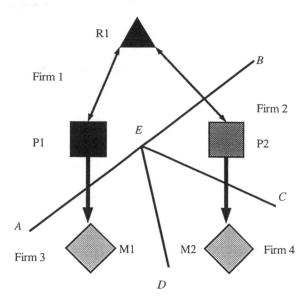

Figure 3.4   Optimal locational and ownership strategies for the simplified example

emphasize the contribution of entrepreneurial small firms to the overall performance of the global economy. As noted earlier, it is competition in the market for capital that maintains this small firm structure, and discourages mergers between the firms involved.

Solution of the Full Model

Now consider the solution of the full model. Because of the triangle problem, a different approach is required. In principle, it is necessary to evaluate alternative internalization strategies for each possible location strategy. In practice, however, some location strategies can be ruled out from the start.

The introduction of flows of marketing knowledge does not affect the location-dependent components of linkage cost. This is because the location of marketing facilities is already fixed. Furthermore, moving the R&D facility from one country to another will not affect location-dependent linkage costs because the marketing linkages comprise one domestic linkage and one international one, independent of R&D location. Thus the costs of these linkages are independent of the direction of knowledge flow. Introducing an additional R&D facility will merely increase both the facility costs and the linkages costs, and so can be ruled out. In terms of Table 3.5, the effects are confined to the bottom row. The additional costs incurred by the R&D strategies $x_0 = 0$, 1, 2 as a result of the additional knowledge flows are respectively 3, 2 and 3.

Location strategy is only affected by the existence of a triangle problem when the relocation of facilities helps to resolve the problem by substituting alternative linkages whose degree of internalization is easier to change. The savings in ownership-dependent linkage costs that arise from substituting a different geography of linkages are likely to be quite small, however. This suggests that the search for a solution to the full problem should begin with the location strategy that minimizes costs when the triangle problem is ignored. In the light of the previous remarks, this is the location strategy $k = 3$ that solved the simplified problem.

Examination of Table 3.4 shows that, when considered independently, each marketing linkage needs to be internalized. The gains from internalization are equal to 2 for both the domestic and international linkages. Given the internalization strategy shown in Figure 3.4, the triangle problem arises only in respect of domestic linkages in country 1. It does not arise in country 2 because the externalization of both the linkages to production, $R1–P2$, $M2–P2$, is fully compatible with the internalization of the linkage $R1–M2$. It simply means that production is subcontracted in country 2: the firm that owns the R&D facility employs an independent producer to make the product, and then buys it back to market it under its own control.

The triangle problem arises in country 1 because the internalization of both $R1–P1$ and $R1–M1$ is incompatible with the externalization of $P1–M1$. There are three simple options which are worth investigating first. Externalizing $R1–P1$ will increase costs by 3. Externalizing $R1–M1$ will increase costs by 2. Internalizing $P1–M1$ will increase costs by 1. Hence internalization of $P1–M1$ is the appropriate response within the limits of location strategy 3.

However, with the costs of location strategy 3 increased to 18.5 (or 21.5 gross of the costs of the marketing links), its cost now exceeds that of strategy 1. It is therefore necessary to determine whether or not strategy 1 encounters a triangle problem. If it does not, then strategy 1 is the optimal location strategy. If it does, then strategy 3 remains the optimal strategy provided that the additional cost of resolving the triangle problem for strategy 1 is not less than 0.5. It is readily established that strategy 1 encounters exactly the same problem as strategy 3 regarding domestic linkages in country 1. Once the triangle problem is resolved, therefore, the costs of strategy 1 rise to 19 (or 22 gross of the costs of the marketing links). Hence, the optimal location strategy continues to be strategy 3, but the ownership strategy is now different from before.

The full solution is illustrated in Figure 3.5. The internalization of marketing knowledge flows generates a multinational enterprise – namely firm 1, identified by its ownership of the facilities in black. The firm's domestic operations are fully integrated, but it subcontracts foreign production to an independent firm – firm 2, whose production facility is shown in grey. The

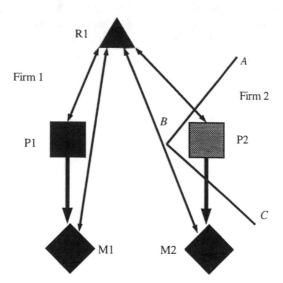

Figure 3.5   *Optimal locational and ownership strategies for the full example*

boundary between the firms is indicated by the line *ABC*. Thanks to greater internalization, the new equilibrium involves fewer firms. The transition to Figure 3.5 is effected by a merger of the firms 1, 3 and 4 in Figure 3.4; only firm 2 remaining unaffected by the change.

The solution illustrates nicely the point made earlier about the internalization of certain linkages being driven by factors connected with other linkages. In this example the internalization of the flow of knowledge between marketing and R&D is so important that it leads to internalization between production and marketing in country 1. In the absence of this knowledge flow, the link between production and marketing would be external instead.

The example also illustrates the importance of international business effects. The interaction of geography and ownership is reflected in the way that knowledge flows between R&D and production are best internalized when they are domestic, but best externalized when they are international. When combined with the economic logic of the knowledge flow between marketing and R&D, this leads to the subcontracting of production in country 2 even though production is internalized in country 1. This reflects the 'foreignness' of country 2 when viewed from the perspective of the R&D laboratory located (for reasons of comparative advantage) in country 1.

Finally, the model also demonstrates the difference between optimizing the behaviour of a single firm, such as firm 1, and optimizing the structure of the entire population of firms within the global system. The step from the single-firm problem to the full-system problem shows how the emergence of new linkages can significantly alter the number of firms in the system, either by concentrating ownership through merger or acquisition, or dispersing ownership through divestment.

3.11 APPLICATIONS

Economic models are usually applied using the method of comparative statics. Hypotheses are derived by changing the values of exogenous variables, and calculating the direction and magnitude of the impact on endogenous variables. In the present model the key exogenous variables are the costs of R&D, c_0, the costs of production, c_1, and – above all – the linkage costs, t_j ($j = 1,...,12$).

It is not only the absolute levels of these costs that are important, but also the relative costs. The relative costs of R&D and production in each country determine the underlying pattern of comparative advantage, which is a major influence on location strategy. The relative costs of different types of linkage influence both location and ownership strategies. In deriving predictions that link ownership strategy with location strategy, therefore, changes in linkage costs are particularly significant.

The most obvious application of the model is to analyse the process of globalization. The key driver of globalization is the decline of linkage costs. As costs decline, so a larger number of linkages can be sustained. This means that the global system is becoming much more complex.

Some of the factors driving down linkage costs apply at both the domestic and international level. This means that the globalization of economic activity is to some extent paralleled by increasing complexity at the domestic level. Thus computer systems using sophisticated inventory management programmes can support 'just-in-time' lean production systems involving large numbers of different component manufacturing facilities. This growth in domestic complexity is reflected in the way that global systems are increasingly seen as connecting urban or regional 'clusters' or 'agglomerations' in which local activities are tightly connected.

The focus of globalization is, however, upon changes that specifically affect international linkages. These include advances in international liner shipping due to containerization, the increasing use of jet aircraft for business travel, and advances in electronic mail, and in satellite communications generally. A paramount influence, however, has been political change. These include trade liberalization, through GATT, UNCTAD and the WTO, and the development and enlargement of regional trading blocs such as the EC, ASEAN, NAFTA, MERCOSUR and the like. The impact of these changes is to reduce international linkage costs relative to domestic linkage costs.

Thus there are two distinct but related changes that can be examined using the model. The first is a general reduction in all linkage costs, and the second an additional reduction in international linkage costs compared to domestic linkage costs. The first increases the complexity of the system in general, and the second increases the complexity of international linkages relative to domestic ones. The model in this chapter has been designed specifically with the second purpose in mind. The modelling of the system at each location is far too basic to accommodate shifts in the degree of complexity at the domestic level. The modelling of the overall system is, however, well adapted to capturing the increasing use of international linkages as economic integration advances. This is particularly true when the model is extended in the directions suggested below.

Application of the model in this way generalizes many of the well-known results of IB theory which pertain to the behaviour of a single firm to a system that comprises any number of firms instead. It also reveals new connections between location and ownership strategies which stem specifically from system effects. In the context of globalization, for example, it shows that the emergence of new linkages is likely to be associated with new patterns of ownership which may involve substantial changes in the overall concentration of global power.

3.12   EXTENSIONS

The model set out in this chapter is sufficiently simple that it can be extended
in a number of ways. The most important of these is to enlarge the range of
institutional arrangements available for the co-ordination of linkages. A natural extension is to allow for two types of internal and two types of external
linkage.

As already noted, internal linkages can be effected either by centralized
planning systems, or by transfer prices that attempt to mimic the market.
Internal transfer pricing differs from an external market in two respects. First,
the process of negotiation is controlled by the firm, rather than regulated by
social convention, and compliance with contracts is enforced through the
internal authority structure of the firm rather than through an external legal
system. Second, different internal prices can be used for different purposes;
thus one set of transfer prices can be used to allocate resources, while another
is used to minimize overall tax and tariff liabilities, whereas in an ordinary
market only one set of prices can prevail.

Similarly, it is well known that external markets can be personal as well as
impersonal. A common feature of personal markets is 'goodwill': firms purchase from each other on a regular basis instead of shopping around for the
best short-term deal on price. There is an informal long-term contract that
underlies the sequence of formal short-term contracts that they make. This
arrangement is often dubbed 'network-type', although the terminology is
misleading since the arrangement is not a property of the system as a whole,
but of an individual linkage within it. Just as the internal market gives a
'market-like' quality to internal arrangements, so these network relations give
a 'firm-like' quality to external ones.

Additional arrangements are easily accommodated in the model by extending the range of values taken by the decision variable n_j from 2 to 4. Let
internal planning be denoted $n = 0$, an internal market $n = 1$, a network
relation by $n = 2$ and an impersonal external market by $n = 3$. As before,
when linkages are independent, the arrangement used for the jth linkage can
be determined simply by minimizing $t(h_j, d_j, n_j)$ with respect to n_j, giving n_j^*
and the associated cost t_j^*. When the linkages are interdependent, problems
arise only with respect to internalization and externalization, and not with
respect to the form that the internalization or externalization takes. There is
no reason why a firm cannot co-ordinate one linkage internally using prices
and another using central planning, or why a firm cannot deal with one
independent firm on a network basis and another on an impersonal basis. It is
true, of course, that it may be somewhat cheaper for a firm to adopt a single
internal arrangement, and a single external arrangement. The additional cost
of hybrid arrangements would certainly be something that could be allowed

for in a more sophisticated model. It seems inadvisable, however, to introduce such a complication at this stage.

It may be asked how firms can agree upon the form of external linkage to be used. If one firm prefers a network relation and the other prefers an impersonal relation, whose view will prevail? Will the firm that wants an impersonal relationship be able to refuse the advances of the other firm? From the point of view of the present model, the answer is very simple: the firms agree upon whichever arrangement minimizes the overall costs of running the system. It is assumed that the firm that favours the arrangement that maximizes overall performance will be able to compensate the other firm out of the greater profits that are obtained.

The model can be enriched from a locational perspective too. An obvious refinement is to relax the symmetry of linkage costs. There are several reasons for doing this. First, while tariffs between trading partners are often harmonized, this is not invariably the case. Differences in tariff rates imply asymmetry in linkage costs for products. A second consideration concerns transport costs. 'Back haulage' of products in otherwise empty ships or vehicles may be much cheaper than haulage at normal rates in the other direction. This is particularly true of shipping, which would otherwise have to carry ballast for reasons of stability.

Asymmetries can apply to knowledge transfers too. Suppose, for example, that the two locations are Japan and the US. If more Japanese scientists speak English than US scientists speak Japanese, then technology may be easier to transfer from the US to Japan than from Japan to the US. The same effect would be produced if cultural factors stimulate Japanese scientists to be more receptive than US scientists to knowledge generated in foreign R&D facilities. This scenario implies that knowledge-based linkage costs are higher for flows from Japan to the US than they are from the US to Japan. Within the context of the model, this encourages the location of R&D in the US and the location of production in Japan.

The introduction of asymmetric linkage costs complicates the specification of the model slightly, but does not affect the method of solution in any substantial way. Its only effect is to increase the number of different types of linkage which must be considered when optimizing internalization.

Another extension involves increasing the number of locations. Unlike the previous changes, this complicates considerably the analysis of location. For example, if the number of locations is increased from 2 to 3, the number of potential location strategies increases from 9 to 70. However, the principle that no production plant should have dual-sourcing of knowledge restricts the number of efficient locations strategies to 52. This extension is extremely useful in analysing the role of customs unions in international trade, as discussed in the previous section. By identifying each location with a separate country, the impact on third countries of alliances between two countries can readily be examined. The analysis of trade creation and trade diversion can be coupled with an analysis of knowledge-creation and knowledge-diversion, and with changes in multinational activity induced by internalization effects.

The introduction of an additional location can also be effected while preserving the structure of a two-country model, by introducing a second location within an existing country. For example, a distinction could be drawn between a metropolis and its hinterland, or between a coastal region and an inland one. The impact of international trade on regional growth could be analysed in terms of location effects, while at the same time taking account of 'branch plant' effects caused by the internalization of linkages between the metropolitan or mercantile 'core' and its more remote 'periphery'.

The final options for extension concern the introduction of new types of facility. One possibility is to distinguish between upstream and downstream production in order to provide a fuller analysis of vertical integration. This option was highlighted in Buckley and Casson (1976, pp. 45–9) and was developed empirically in Casson *et al.* (1983). The vertical integration of production can be examined in both a domestic and international context. In a domestic context, the role of industrial districts, or 'clusters' (Porter, 1990) can be investigated. In an international context, off-shore production based on cheap labour and export-processing zones can be analysed, and also raw materials-seeking investments.

Another possibility is to distinguish between different types of R&D, such as basic R&D and adaptive R&D (Pearce and Papanastassiou, 1996). The location of adaptive R&D, and the potential for attracting basic R&D, are important industrial policy issues for many newly-industrializing countries, and for some transitional economies too.

In addition to new types of activity in existing industries, it is also possible to introduce new industries. This involves specifying additional final products, and introducing new marketing facilities to go with them. This extends the model in the direction of inter-industry linkage models, which are already established in the economics literature (Leontief, 1958). These models have been applied in a locational context by Isard (1972) and other regional scientists. However, the mainstream analysis of inter-industry linkages has never been properly integrated with internalization theory, as its focus of analysis has remained on the industry rather than the firm. Research at the interface of inter-industry economics and internalization theory should yield substantial dividends in the future.

3.13 CONCLUSIONS

This chapter has picked up the threads of a research agenda which has been allowed to lapse. It has, indeed, lapsed twice. When Coase first set out the agenda, most of his contemporaries failed to recognize the significance of what he had done. His institutional approach to modelling the economic system was eclipsed by advances in the mathematical modelling of the neoclassical general equilibrium system. Forty years later, the 'globalization' of the Coasian perspective by Buckley and Casson was perceived by some of their contemporaries as a specific technical contribution to the analysis of licensing, or of raw-materials-seeking investment, and not as a general approach to analysing the global economy as a whole. As a result, 'internalization theory' was conventionally stated in terms of decisions taken by a single firm, whose existence was assumed to be given, rather than in terms of interdependent decisions taken within an efficiency-driven system, in which the existence of firms was not assumed, but where instead the rationale of the firm had to be proved in relation to the benefits of using the market.

The obvious explanation for this double lapse is that scholars shied away from the complexities that they supposed would exist in implementing the full system-wide view. This chapter has shown that these anxieties are misplaced. Discrete choice modelling provides a viable approach to solving the problem of efficient system-wide organization. There are certainly complications – notably, the triangle problem – but they are not insuperable ones.

It has been shown that the model developed in this chapter can be extended in several different directions. The model presented here was selected as the simplest possible one in which interesting system effects could be investigated. It is other, more complex models, that afford the greatest promise for practical application – in particular, three-location models that allow for network effects.

It is often observed that research which answers one question only leads to the emergence of another. 'Asking the right questions' is the key to successful research, but the right question cannot be asked until at least part of the problem has been understood. By answering the question 'How can a systems view of location and ownership strategies be formally articulated?' this chapter suggests another question as a sequel. The question is 'How do entrepreneurs within the international business system actually arrive at an efficient structure? Do they, in some sense, mimic the algorithms used to compute the efficient solution in the model described above, or do they use a completely different approach instead?' This issue concerns not only the way in which entrepreneurs formulate their plans, but also the way in which capital markets allocate resources between rival plans put forward by competing entrepreneurs. This issue is addressed in a companion book (Casson, 2000, Ch. 3).

REFERENCES

Buckley, P.J. and M. Casson (1976) *The Future of the Multinational Enterprise*, 2nd edn 1991, London: Macmillan

Buckley, P.J. and M.C. Casson (1998) 'Analysing foreign market entry strategies: extending the internalisation approach', *Journal of International Business Studies*, **29**(3), 539–61

Casson, M. *et al.* (1983) *Multinationals and World Trade: Vertical Integration and the Division of Labour in World Industries*, London: Allen & Unwin

Casson, M. (1990) *Enterprise and Competitiveness: A Systems View of International Business*, Oxford: Clarendon Press

Casson, M. (1992) 'Internalisation theory and beyond', in P.J. Buckley (ed.), *New Directions in International Business*, Aldershot: Edward Elgar, reprinted in M. Casson (1995), *The Organization of International Business*, Aldershot: Edward Elgar, 22–46

Casson, M.C. (2000) *Enterprise and Leadership: Studies on Firms, Markets and Networks*, Cheltenham: Edward Elgar

Casson, M. and N. Wadeson (1996) 'Information strategy and the organisation of the firm', *International Journal of the Economics of Business*, **3**(3), 307–30

Coase, R.H. (1937) 'The nature of the firm', *Economica* (New Series), **4**, 386–405

Dunning, J.H. (1977) 'Trade, location of economic activity and the multinational enterprise: a search for an eclectic approach', in B. Ohlin, P.O. Hesselborn and P.M. Wijkman (eds), *The International Allocation of Economic Activity*, London: Macmillan

Dunning, J.H. (1983) 'Changes in the structure of international production: the last 100 years', in M.C. Casson (ed.), *The Growth of International Business*, London: George Allen and Unwin, 84–139

Hayek, F. von A. (1935) 'The present state of the debate', in F.A. von Hayek (ed.), *Collectivist Economic Planning*, London: George Routledge & Sons, 201–43

Hayek, F. von A. (1937) 'Economics and knowledge', *Economica* (New Series), **4**, 33–54

Helpman, E.M. and P.R. Krugman (1985) *Market Structure and Foreign Trade: Increasing Returns, Imperfect Competition and the International Economy*, Cambridge, MA: MIT Press

Isard, W. (1956) *Location and Space Economy*, Cambridge, MA: MIT Press

Isard, W. (1972) *General Theory: Social, Political, Economic and Regional*, Cambridge, MA: MIT Press

Kemp, M.C. (1964) *Pure Theory of International Trade*, Englewood Cliffs, NJ: Prentice-Hall

Kirzner, I.M. (1973) *Competition and Entrepreneurship*, Chicago: University of Chicago Press

Klein, B.A., R.G. Crawford and A.A. Alchian (1978) 'Vertical integration, appropriable rents and the competitive contracting process', *Journal of Law and Economics*, **21**, 297–326

Leontief, W. (1953) *Studies in the Structure of the American Economy*, New York: Oxford University Press

Leontief, W.W. (1958) *Studies in the Structure of the American Economy*, Oxford: Oxford University Press

Pearce, R.D. and M. Papanastassiou (1996) 'R&D networks and innovation: decentralised product development in multinational enterprises', *R&D Management*, **26**(4), 315–33

Porter, M.E. (1990) *The Competitive Advantage of Nations*, New York: Free Press

Robertson, D.H. (1923) *The Control of Industry*, London: James Nisbet

Williamson, O.E. (1975) *Markets and Hierarchies: Analysis and Anti-trust Applications*, New York: Free Press

Williamson, O.E. (1985) *The Economic Institutions of Capitalism*, New York: Free Press

4. Bounded rationality, meta-rationality and the theory of international business

with Nigel Wadeson

4.1 INTRODUCTION

The concept of bounded rationality is often applied to international business behaviour (see for example, Kogut and Zander, 1993). It is a key element in Williamson's (1975) version of transaction cost theory, and underpins Hedlund's (1993) arguments in favour of the 'heterarchy' – otherwise known as the 'network firm'. There is, however, no consensus over what exactly 'bounded rationality' signifies. The term itself is a curious one. It indicates what it is not – namely full or substantive rationality – but not exactly what it is. There are a number of different views. As a result, a casual reference to bounded rationality is ambiguous, since it is not clear to which particular interpretation of bounded rationality it refers.

The object of this chapter is to clarify the concept of bounded rationality by reinterpreting it in terms of information costs. This introduces much-needed rigour and precision into the analysis of the organization of multinational firms. Many of the effects imputed to bounded rationality can be explained more simply in terms of a rational response to information costs.

According to Simon (1947, 1982, 1992), bounded rationality involves the use of satisficing routines. The concept of satisficing indicates, first, that decision-making involves a search for solutions, and, second, that the search is likely to terminate before the ideal solution has been found. The chosen solution is merely satisfactory – it is not necessarily the fully optimal one. The concept of routine indicates that satisficing problem-solvers tend to follow the same search procedure time after time. The behavioural perspective favoured by Simon suggests that these routines are programmed into people. They are not the product of individual choice. The routines may be either innate – being biologically programmed – or socially acquired – for example, by a programmed propensity to imitate other people's behaviour.

While Simon argues that bounded rationality is necessary to explain administrative behaviour within a firm, Williamson (1975) emphasizes that bounded rationality has implications for the nature of the firm itself. In

Williamson's theory, bounded rationality has one major job to do. It explains why complex contingent contracts cannot be written, and why labour must be hired to work under the management of a firm. The same idea can be used to explain the integration of successive stages of production too.

Prior to Williamson, Cyert and March (1963) developed a behavioural theory of the firm in which they specified algorithms that managers could use to set prices, output and inventory levels. These specifications were essentially *ad hoc*, however. They were not so much an *explanation* of what managers did, as a *description* of what they did in a typical firm. The theoretical content was restricted to abstracting from minor details of the administrative process.

The behavioural approach, in its simplest form, suggests that managers cannot modify their patterns of behaviour when circumstances change, yet there is plenty of evidence to suggest that such modifications do occur. These modifications are not arbitrary – the direction of change is dictated by the need for efficient adaptation. A successful firm selects whichever routine is most efficient under the prevailing circumstances. Indeed, Baumol and Quandt (1964) demonstrated that successful routines can be reinterpreted as rational rules once the appropriate managerial costs of decision-making are taken into account. This is a point to which we return below.

Nelson and Winter (1982) revitalized the behavioural approach by allowing for greater flexibility in organizational behaviour. They also widened the scope of the theory to incorporate rivalry between firms. However, the degree of flexibility permitted to the firm within their theory is still relatively small. Moreover, key elements of the theory remain *ad hoc*. Nelson and Winter argue that much of the intangible knowledge base of the firm is comprised of routines. These routines are tacit: they are not sufficiently codifiable to be bought or sold through licensing agreements. Managers are so thoroughly bounded in their rationality that they can only memorize these routines through carrying them out. They habitually repeat a routine just as long as it performs reasonably well. The routine with which a firm commences is arbitrary. Managers learn from their mistakes, but only in a myopic way: the unexpected failure of a routine stimulates a search for another routine that is as good as the original routine used to be. This search is modelled as a behavioural satisficing process. The incremental effects of learning gradually adjust a firm towards an optimum, without it ever actually getting there.

Firms that learn most effectively tend to increase in size at the expense of others, since following each shock to the industry they tend to increase their market share. One consequence of this is that the industry as a whole tends to converge upon a rational pattern of routine behaviour. Despite the emphasis on bounded rationality in individual firms, therefore, the evolutionary process that selects in favour of the most rational firms means that rationality reasserts itself at the industry level in any case. This shows that even in a theory that is meant to be critical of orthodoxy rationality, the tendency to rational behaviour proves to be quite robust, because it is underpinned by evolutionary selection mechanisms.

The modelling of evolutionary selection mechanisms is potentially very complex (see for example Moss and Rae, 1992). For this reason, evolutionary models are usually solved by simulation. The properties exhibited by these simulations are often difficult to understand at an intuitive level. Their short-run dynamics, while usually more interesting than their long-run ones, can prove particularly difficult to interpret. The long-run dynamics are usually easier to interpret because they often involve convergence on a rational outcome, as explained above. It is only where there are multiple equilibria, or no equilibria at all, that such convergence tends not to occur. It is thus by appeal to the properties of the model's equilibria that the long-run dynamics are most readily understood. These equilibrium properties in turn reflect the obstacles to achieving full rationality within the system. Thus the successful interpretation of simulation results often depends upon an appeal to the rationality principle in any case.

4.2   BOUNDED RATIONALITY – AN EMPTY BOX?

Bounded rationality is appealing because it seems to explain in a single stroke all the quirks of behaviour that we observe in other people. But this explanation is an illusion. Bounded rationality is certainly *consistent* with such behaviour, but only because it is consistent with just about any type of behaviour at all. Unless it is coupled with other assumptions, it actually predicts nothing, since it rules out nothing.

The fact that bounded rationality rules nothing out is underlined by the fact that it is not usually taken to imply that all behaviour is irrational. If bounded rationality were indeed construed in this way, then it would at least predict that nothing explicable in rational terms would ever occur. But writers on bounded rationality usually leave open the possibility that behaviour may sometimes be rational too. They know that the predictions of total irrationality are false. As a consequence of this, many modern writers invoke bounded rationality without recourse to either behaviourism or artificial intelligence. The main consequence is to make the use of substantive rationality within the theory optional. Thus a scholar who invokes bounded rationality for one purpose may invoke substantive rationality for some other purpose. For example, Williamson (1985) explains the authority relation created by the contract of employment in terms of bounded rationality, but then analyses managerial choice between alternative contractual arrangements as a substantively rational one.

While the benefits of postulating bounded rationality are largely illusory, the costs of postulating bounded rationality are very real. These costs stem principally from the problem of ambiguity noted at the outset. Different writers invoke different *ad hoc* behavioural rules, and the same writer may even invoke different rules at different stages of the same argument. Thus bounded rationality hardly ever means quite the same thing in one context as it does in another.

Ambiguities of this kind do not make for good theorizing. A good theory is easy to understand. There is a logical transparency to the way it works. This logical transparency is needed because, just as the bounded rationality postulate suggests, people have difficulty understanding theoretical constructs and putting them to proper use. From this perspective, logical transparency is necessary in theories constructed for use by boundedly rational people, because it makes the theories easy to understand. The assumption of rational action provides just the kind of logical transparency that is required in a good theory. It is necessary to assume that people behave *as if* they were rational, simply because we know that we would otherwise have difficulty in understanding their behaviour. A rigorous theorist needs to assume rationality because students of the theory cannot cope with the complexity that an alternative approach would involve. The paradox of rationality is that rationality often has to be assumed, precisely because we know that it isn't true. More precisely, rationality has to be assumed in the agents in the model because it isn't true of those who study the model. If the rationality postulate is rejected, then some other equally simple postulate must be put in its place. So far, a satisfactory alternative has not been found.

Logical transparency is also important in revealing inconsistencies and contradictions in the construction of a theory. Scholars of any persuasion are unfortunately prone to logical error in the construction of their theories because, being boundedly rational, they share in human fallibility. The fallible individuals who invoke the rationality postulate are easily found out when they make a mistake, because the symptoms of the problem are so clear, and this obliges them to correct the fault. However, those who refuse to invoke the rationality principle, or any equivalent postulate, may escape detection because of lack of clarity in what they write. Bad theorists dislike the rationality postulate, because they know that if they used it they would be quickly found out. They take refuge in postulating bounded rationality instead.

There is certainly a lot of bad theory to be found in international business. Contemporary organizational theories of international business are particularly prone to logical flaws because of their heavy dependence on the bounded rationality postulate. Modern writers exploit the freedom to switch between rationality and irrationality in order to construct theories that have no internal logical consistency at all. An example drawn from the literature on globalization will illustrate the point. Following Bartlett and Ghoshal (1987) there has been an increasing flow of visionary papers purporting to demonstrate the benefits of flexible organizational structures in meeting global competition (Hedlund and Ridderstrale, 1992). There is no sign of this flow abating (see for example, Hamel and Prahalad, 1996). But none of the writers who set out these ideas invoke an explicit assumption, such as rational action, which would guarantee the internal logical consistency of their analysis. Instead they use the concept of bounded rationality to disguise the fact that their underlying assumptions about human behaviour are changing as their argument develops. No coherent view of human behaviour emerges from their work, because the discipline imposed by the rationality postulate is missing in each case.

The problem of maintaining intellectual standards in international business theory is particularly regrettable when the foundations for a more rigorous approach have already been laid. Egelhoff (1991) has shown how multinational organizations can be analysed coherently from an information-processing perspective. This more rigorous approach is set out at length in Chapter 5 below. It is based on the principle that rational organization minimizes overall information cost. According to this principle, the essence of organization is a division of labour in information processing, with senior managers synthesizing information channelled to them from junior ones. This arrangement allows the junior managers – functional specialists and managers with local knowledge – to specialize in collecting information from the specific sources that they know best. It permits the senior managers, who have more general knowledge, and wider vision, to specialize in synthesizing information from these diverse sources in order to take decisions. These decisions are then communicated back to junior managers for implementation. Issuing instructions from headquarters is a parsimonious way of sharing a synthesis of information within the organization (Casson, 1994). This approach is perfectly consistent with arguing that hierarchy should take a flexible form. Indeed, it is a direct implication of the theory that the form that a hierarchy takes must adapt to the changing pattern of volatility in the environment (Casson, 1995, Ch. 4). This is, nonetheless, far removed from suggesting that hierarchies themselves should be replaced by some totally different form.

4.3   RATIONALITY – WHAT EXACTLY DOES IT MEAN?

Distinguishing the rational from the irrational is not, in fact, as simple as it may seem at first sight. To define properly what is meant by bounded rationality it is first necessary to know precisely what rationality means. Different definitions of rationality have different implications for the concept of bounded rationality (Elster, 1986; Hargreaves Heap, 1989).

In economic theory the most useful interpretation of rationality is an instrumental one (Blaug, 1980). Rationality is a feature of the choice of the means by which a given end is to be achieved. It is not a property of the end itself. A successful business executive who makes a large anonymous donation to charity is not behaving irrationally, even though a selfish and materialistic person might perceive it this way. It is not irrational to be altruistic. The executive may be fully aware that their disposable income will be reduced by this action. The most likely explanation is that the executive has a conscience which is eased by the donation; a rational altruist will increase the magnitude of the donation to the point where the marginal emotional benefit from a further increase in the amount donated is just equal to the material sacrifice involved.

When ends are given, it is not possible to say that one end is more rational than another. The only sense in which ends are rational is that preferences must be transitive – consistency requires that if strategy A is preferred to strategy B, and B is preferred to C, then A is preferred to C.

It may, however, be possible to persuade people that some ends are more *reasonable* than others. Thus a Kantian philosopher may persuade a young vandal that damaging public property is unreasonable because, if everyone did the same, then it would be self-defeating. There would be no undamaged property left to vandalize, while the cumulative effect of the damage would make everyone worse off. This argument does not show that vandalism is irrational, since the vandal may be someone who derives so much satisfaction from it that it pays them to run greater risks than other people in order to carry it out. It is more of an attempt to influence preferences, so that the vandal associates guilt with acts of vandalism, and therefore finds that such acts no longer make him feel better.

This manner of treating ends can, if handled wrongly, trivialize the principle of rational action, since it can be used to 'rationalize' any action in terms of unusual ends. Restrictions need to be imposed on ends if instrumental rationality is to have predictive implications. An obvious restriction is that 'more is always better' as far as ordinary goods are concerned. Tastes may be constrained to be convex, implying that people prefer variety to monotony in the range of goods that they consume. The idea that ends are fixed is also important. It is this assumption that is used in economics to predict that decision-makers will substitute against means that have become relatively scarce. If ends are allowed to change, then their laws of change must be fully specified, so that the effects of these changes can be accounted for before the effects of changes in means are considered as well.

Different views of instrumental rationality also prevail. A very narrow view of rationality is that a rational decision is based on full information. This is a very strict criterion which is hardly ever satisfied in practice. For this reason, it is the definition favoured by those who wish to argue that bounded rationality is ubiquitous. In terms of constructing an alternative model of human behaviour, however, this approach does not get us very far.

A broader and more helpful view of rationality is that it involves making the best possible use of available information. On this view the decision-maker acts under uncertainty, but responds to it in a particular way. Missing information is replaced by subjective beliefs. These beliefs are expressed as probabilistic statements. This approach is fairly common in modern neoclassical microeconomic theory (Lippman and McCall, 1979). It is nevertheless controversial. There are those who claim, on the basis of experimental evidence, that people cannot think logically about probabilities. Against this, it is argued that such evidence is generated by placing people in contrived and unfamiliar situations, and that in situations with which they are familiar people behave as though their logic were sound.

A refinement of this broader view allows people to decide how much information they will collect before they make their decision (Marschak and Radner, 1972). Decision-making then becomes a two-stage process. In the first stage the decision-maker decides what information to collect, and in the second stage they decide how to act on the basis of what they have found out. The logic of the process requires the rational decision-maker to consider at the outset how they would behave in each case according to what they have found out. Each possible item of information needs to be considered, and its implications for the ensuing decision worked out (Casson and Wadeson, 1996). If the information would make no difference to the decision, whatever it turned out to be, then there is no point in collecting it. To know which particular discovery would make a difference, the decision-maker must know at the start what his decision would be in the absence of any information. This decision reflects his subjective probabilities. Having decided what the consequences of various items of information would be if he had them, the decision-maker then decides which items are worth collecting and which are not.

While this refinement may seem a little complicated, it has one very significant implication. This implication alone indicates that the approach is very useful. It shows that a rational decision-maker will normally gather information as a sequential process. Indeed, provided there are no physical economies in observing several things at once, it is impossible to improve upon a sequential information-gathering approach with a simultaneous one. The optimal procedure is always to gather one particular item of information first, and then to gather a second item depending upon what the first one turns out to be. The first item may well be decisive, in the sense that further investigation is unnecessary because it is already obvious what decision to take. If the first decision is not decisive, then the second may well be, and so on. In a typical case, the decision-maker goes on to collect several items of information, but not all of them. He stops before collecting all of them, because the cost of collecting and processing the next item of information is less than the benefit it is expected to confer. The benefit conferred by reducing the risk of a mistaken decision is more than outweighed by the cost of the additional information. The implications of this result are examined in detail in later sections of this chapter.

4.4   META-RATIONALITY

The remainder of this chapter is concerned with developing the implications of rational behaviour in situations where information is costly to process. It is assumed that a rational agent takes full account of the information costs they face. This is known as *meta-rational* behaviour. The key feature of meta-rational behaviour is that the decision-maker takes account of information costs in deciding how he will take his decision. The simplest example of meta-rational behaviour is a decision-maker who is uncertain about a single parameter in the environment, and who decides whether to observe the value of this parameter before taking the decision. A more sophisticated example of meta-rational behaviour is a decision-maker who faces several uncertainties, and decides to investigate them in turn, in a specific order, using a rule which prescribes how to proceed at each step according to what the information discovered at the previous steps turns out to be. The key point about meta-rationality is that this rule is an optimal one, and not just arbitrary. It is optimal because it provides the best possible trade-off between information cost and the risk of making a mistaken decision.

Meta-rationality also applies to decisions jointly taken by the members of a group. The obvious reason for joint decision-making is that it allows people to specialize in different aspects of decision-making according to their personal comparative advantage. Economic decisions are typically taken in a complex environment where a variety of factors need to be investigated. Information on these different factors is likely to be dispersed. The dispersion may be geographical; for example, different sources of information may be located in different countries. Information also may be dispersed by product, so that specialists in different markets have to be consulted. Finally, information may be dispersed by functional area; it is quite common, for example, for a synthesis of production information and sales information to be used to plan next period's output of a product.

The division of labour is not the only reason for using joint decisions. Joint decision-making can reduce the incidence of errors by allowing people to act as checks and balances against each other when some of the information collected may be wrong (Sah and Stiglitz, 1986). It can also improve the implementation of a decision. People who have participated in a decision are more likely to feel a share of the responsibility for it, and so work harder to make it a success. Greater efficiency in the implementation of collective decisions is one of the advantages of the democratic political process, and also of adopting a consultative style of corporate management.

In a centralized group a single individual – the leader – will normally take responsibility for deciding upon the division of labour in decision-making. The leader will choose a set of individual procedures that harmonize with each other, and determine which person should have responsibility for implementing each procedure. The group therefore operates as an organization. Its structure is geared to the implementation of a particular set of administrative routines. Meta-rationality implies that the structure is optimized by the leader, and that the routines constitute an efficient response to the costs and benefits of information.

In a decentralized group the division of labour will normally be set by negotiation. This can complicate the analysis quite considerably. Fortunately, decentralization is often a partial process. Instead of everyone negotiating for themselves, everyone belongs to one of a small number of subsidiary organizations. These organizations, together with their interorganizational links, constitute the organization of the group. The leader of each subsidiary organization negotiates on behalf of its members. Thus in an example discussed below, all the individuals belong to one of two firms. One firm buys a product from the other. The leaders of the two firms negotiate over who investigates what, and who takes responsibility for communicating which type of information to the other. Each leader decides upon the internal routines that are appropriate to carry out the investigations that his firm has to make.

An obvious objection to meta-rationality is that a decision-maker who selects a procedure, or set of procedures, has to know what the costs of information are. If he does not know the costs, then he cannot do his calculations. He could find out what the costs are by investigation, but then the question would arise as to whether this investigation was itself worth carrying out. The decision-maker would then embark upon an infinite regress, in which every decision would require the cost of information to be known, and where, in order to decide whether this cost was worth discovering, the cost of finding out this cost would need to be discovered as well.

Although this problem may seem insuperable, it is not in fact as serious as it first appears. To begin with, the theory does not require that the cost of information should actually be known, but only that subjective probabilities of the cost should be available. If the decision-maker is risk-neutral, then the missing value of information cost can simply be replaced in the calculations by its expected value. In this case the solution of the problem is no more complicated with uncertainty than it is without it. If the decision-maker is risk-averse, however, then additional calculations will need to be carried out.

4.5 PROCEDURES AND ROUTINES

Meta-rationality is particularly useful in explaining the origins of procedures and routines. It has already been emphasized that optimal information strategies are sequential. This means that they have an obvious procedural quality to them. In general, they specify that a certain type of information should be collected first, and that further action should be taken, depending on what this information turns out to be.

Many of the situations faced by a typical decision-maker are similar to one another, in the sense that the value of the resources committed, the risks attributable to ignorance, and the cost of gathering information, are roughly the same in each case. This is certainly the case within the typical firm, which confronts the same set of markets in each successive period. Under these conditions, an optimal procedure for one decision is an optimal procedure for every similar decision too. Thus the same procedure will be applied in each successive case. This procedure identifies the transitory factors in the recurrent situations, and indicates how to respond to the various sets of transitory events that may occur. The optimal procedure forms the basis of a procedural routine.

The significance of this result is most clearly seen when there are set-up costs in devising the optimal procedure. One important cause of set-up costs is that there are certain persistent factors in the environment which dictate what particular form the response to transitory factors should take. These persistent factors are costly to investigate. Once they have been investigated, the chosen procedure can be repeated successfully as long as these factors remain unchanged. The fixed cost of collecting this information on the persistent factors can therefore be spread over all subsequent applications of the procedure.

Suppose, for example, that in every period the demand for a product undergoes a transitory change caused by changes in fashion. The procedure dictates how output should respond to this change. It dictates, for example, that the state of fashion should be observed, and output adjusted in some prescribed way. The way that output is adjusted depends upon a persistent factor in the situation. Suppose that following a transitory shock, demand tends to revert towards some long-run norm. The level of this norm is a persistent factor which governs the rational response to a transitory shock. Suppose furthermore that this norm is governed by the availability of substitutes for the product, and that the number of substitutes is not known at the outset. The set-up cost of the rule therefore includes the cost of investigating the number of substitutes. Once this investigation has been made, the information so obtained is encoded in the procedure that is to be applied on all subsequent occasions. Thus the cost of devising the strategy is spread over numerous decisions.

Meta-rationality, therefore, predicts that where a decision-maker faces a succession of similar and uncertain situations, behaviour will be governed by the routine application of a particular procedure. This shows that the use of procedures does not have to be explained as a consequence of programmed behaviour, nor as a consequence of some all-pervading, bounded rationality. It is a direct consequence of meta-rational behaviour in a particular type of environment. In this environment intermittent disturbances create temporary problems within a basically stable system. From this perspective, the firm is a functionally specialized organization dedicated to the formulation and implementation of a particular type of decision process based upon procedural routines.

4.6 MEMORY

Repeated application of a procedure requires that the procedure be memorized. If memory costs are high, then it may be cheaper to investigate the persistent factors all over again each period, rather than to remember the procedure. In general, the decision-maker faces a trade-off between memorizing a procedure, and 'reinventing' it each time it is required (Casson, 1995, Ch. 6).

Memory costs generally depend upon the complexity of the procedure. Complexity in turn depends on a number of factors: in particular, on the number of different combinations of circumstances that can be identified by the information collected, and the number of different strategies that are conditional on this information. The ease with which the conditions can be formalized is important too. If the procedure is complex and difficult to formalize then memory costs are high, remembering the procedure is discouraged, and repeated improvisation of the procedure is preferred instead.

To reinvent a procedure, the persistent factors in the environment must be observed again. Memorizing a procedure involves observing the persistent factors only once. Use of memory, therefore, spreads the costs of observing the persistent factors over repeated uses of the procedure in a way which improvisation does not. The less frequently the procedure is required, the more difficult it is to spread the memory costs. A procedure is more likely to be memorized the more frequently it is used. The higher the cost of observing these persistent factors, the greater the advantage of memorizing the procedure in order to spread the cost.

Much recent research on organizational behaviour is preoccupied with the idea that procedures are memorized inside people's heads, rather than recorded in a written form. It is said that all the managers within an organization rely upon essentially the same procedures. Managers socialize with each other in order to reinforce their memories of these procedures. This is linked with the view that problems of any given type are liable to occur almost anywhere within an organization: procedures are not specific to particular functional or geographical areas, but are common to all the areas in which the firm is involved. Those who regularly use a given procedure should, therefore, share their knowledge with those who only need to use it on an intermittent basis. These procedures are said to constitute the organizational culture of the firm, and they are claimed to be crucial to the firm's success. When the persistent factors in the firm's environment change, these procedures need to change as well, but they may be deeply embedded in managerial psychology, and legitimated by the past successes that are widely imputed to them. Under these conditions, the prime requirement for effective leadership of the firm is 'change management' – to legitimate changes in the key routines without damaging the social cohesion of the management team.

While there is a good deal of insight in this view, there is a danger that, when exclusive emphasis is placed on the social aspects of management, some of the impersonal aspects are overlooked. In many technologically progressive industries scientific competence in the application of formal procedures in functionally specialized areas remains crucial to the firm's success. For example, the ability to decide intelligently how much information is required to resolve a technical issue in product development governs the speed with which the firm can innovate in order to 'stay ahead' of the competition. Similarly, in mature industries facing intense price competition, the control of cost through highly formal accounting procedures is crucial to competitive success. Scientific and accounting procedures of this kind are usually implemented by technical experts who do not need to socialize extensively with other managers in order to do their job. Moreover, the procedures they employ can be formalized sufficiently for subordinates to be given a rule book to allow them to play their part in carrying the procedures out. Organizational memory is localized in functional areas, and not distributed evenly throughout the firm. Moreover, a good deal of it is not locked away inside people's heads, but is recorded in writing to facilitate dissemination within the relevant functional group.

The same point may be made about the localization of organizational memory within multinational firms. While local memories may be socially embedded in the managerial teams of individual national subsidiaries, the case for teams from different subsidiaries to share their memories is often weak. The more specific the marketing and production requirements in each country, the less is to be gained by sharing organizational memories on a company-wide basis.

4.7   INTERNAL COMMUNICATION

Communication costs are of two main kinds. There are geographical costs of transmitting information over distance, and there are costs of interpersonal transfer of information. The geographical costs reflect such factors as higher telephone charges for long-distance calls, and higher postal charges for international mail. The costs of interpersonal communication include the costs of encoding messages in a manner that is intelligible and unambiguous to the people to whom they are addressed.

Recent literature on international business emphasizes the tacit nature of much of the information communicated within the firm, and argues that such communication is possible only because of the shared values and beliefs created by the corporate culture. This is equivalent to the proposition that costs of communication are much lower within firms than they are between them.

However, this proposition sits uneasily with the growing evidence for strong interorganizational links between independent firms (Ebers, 1997). A closer examination of the issue suggests that many firms rely upon professional cultures to mediate relationships between managers. Thus a high-technology manufacturing firm may rely upon the culture of the engineering profession, a financial conglomerate may rely upon the culture of the accounting profession, and so on. It makes economic sense for firms to 'free-ride' wherever possible on other institutions which build up understanding and trust between the managers they employ. This strategy also affords the flexibility to build interorganizational links with other firms that employ people from the same professional group.

The problem with the conventional approach to tacit information is twofold: first, it assumes that tacitness, and not transactions cost, is the dominant factor dictating the boundaries of the firm. Second, it plays down the influence of tacitness on the internal organization of the firm. While tacitness is of limited significance for the boundaries of the firm, it is of considerable significance for organizational structure and management style. By mistakenly emphasizing the former effect, the latter effect has been overlooked.

The high communication costs associated with tacit information tend to impair the managerial division of labour within the firm. The more tacit the information, the more difficulty managers have understanding one another. If people cannot understand what other people say, then there is little point in basing their decisions on what other people try to tell them. If a chief executive cannot understand what his subordinates tell him, then he will manage in a highly autocratic style. The only information that he will use in arriving at a decision is information that he has collected himself. This may be adequate if the firm depends upon just a few key sources of information – for example, a small number of business publications to which the chief executive subscribes. It may also be adequate if the sources of volatility in the firm's environment are very few, so that it is easy for one person to monitor them all (see Lawrence and Lorsch, 1967, p. 117). However, if information sources are dispersed, and there are many different kinds of volatility to contend with, an autocratic management style is likely to result in seriously mistaken decisions.

An autocratic style normally implies a highly centralized organizational structure, but this is not invariably so. It is possible for a firm to operate as a federation of autocrats, who bargain with each other on behalf of the groups each controls. Each senior manager collects his own information locally and acts upon it without consulting his subordinates. He bargains with other senior managers on an individual basis if he needs resources from them. Communication is confined to giving orders within each group, and quoting prices to other groups. This model is most appropriate where activities are loosely coupled – for example, where the firm is exploiting different local brands in different national markets. In this case the strategies pursued in one national market have few knock-on effects so far as other markets are concerned. It is, however, inappropriate where the firm's activities in different locations are tightly coupled – for example, where production in different countries involves different stages of a vertically integrated process, or where different national sales subsidiaries are responsible for maintaining the reputation of the same global brand.

Explicit information affords lower communication costs and therefore permits a more consultative management style. The consequent pooling of information from diverse sources generally results in a better decision. It may help to sustain higher levels of innovation too. Much of the information contributed by a manager to a consultation process involves updating other managers on how circumstances have changed in his own particular field. Through the consultation process, therefore, managers as a group come to appreciate the full extent of the changes they confront, and to appreciate the collective need to respond. By contrast, an autocratic style of management tends to suppress information on change, and therefore allows outdated strategies to be sustained. Low communication costs not only improve the static efficiency of the firm, therefore; they also boost dynamic efficiency by encouraging consultation which promotes regular change. This is one reason why an evolving business environment, in which persistent factors change from time to time, tends to favour a consultative management style. The faster the pace of evolution, the greater the need for consultation, and the greater the incentive for the firm to invest in lowering communication costs.

This result links back to the discussion of corporate culture earlier on. It shows that the advantages of reducing communication costs are particularly great in situations of rapid change. Insofar as a homogenizing corporate culture reduces communication costs, it increases managers' appreciation of the scope of change, and builds consensus on the need for innovation. Volatile environments therefore favour investing in corporate culture in order to reduce communication costs, as an instrument for promoting innovation.

4.8   EXTERNAL COMMUNICATION

External communication costs are a neglected topic in the modern theory of the firm. This is most surprising, given the great importance attached to the marketing function in modern consumer societies. It is also surprising in the light of the growth of inter-firm linkages relationships noted above.

External communication costs are fundamental to marketing strategy. It is by communication with customers that the nature of the product is explained to them. More important, it is by listening to its customers that the firm discovers the kinds of improvement in the product that its customers would most like to see. Effective marketing therefore requires a two-way flow of information, in which customers are not confined to receiving advertising messages from the firm, but also get an opportunity to express their preferences for different products. These preferences relate not merely to existing products – which customers can easily signal through their purchasing decisions – but to products which do not yet exist.

The idea that firms need to engage in dialogue with their customers is an attractive one. There is a problem, however. If customers were to share all their information with the firms, then they would almost certainly express preferences for certain types of product which it is quite impossible to produce. This is because customers can visualize what their ideal product is like, but lack the technical knowledge to assess whether it is feasible or not. Likewise, if firms were to share all their knowledge of the production possibilities with their customers, they would almost certainly describe many kinds of product which are irrelevant to customers' needs.

What is required is a system by which customers and producers can select information that is relevant for each other (Casson and Wadeson, 1998). This selection needs to be informed by a message previously received from the other party. The object of this message is not to convey a lot of information in itself, but rather to indicate what kind of information it is desired to receive. In other words, the opening message may simply be a question. The answer sought to this question is not a comprehensive one. It is one that is just sufficient to determine the follow-up question that needs to be asked. After a number of questions and answers, the really crucial information begins to be exchanged. This is information which has been selected, by the preceding conversation, from all the information that might conceivably have been communicated, for its pertinence to the problem. It may, for example, relate to which variant of the product a customer would choose from two highly desirable variants, both of which are feasible for the firm to produce.

By structuring questions and answers in different ways, the exchange of the really crucial information is arrived at in varying numbers of steps. The most efficient dialogue is the one that achieves an exchange of pertinent and decisive information in the minimum number of steps. The exchange of this pertinent and decisive information is what brings the communication process to a close, since it establishes which among a small number of highly desirable and technically feasible variants is closest to what the customer really wants.

Of course, the most efficient form of dialogue depends upon what the optimal variant of the product really is. Since this is not known in advance, the dialogue is chosen using subjective probabilities of what the best solution may turn out to be. In terms of the meta-rational approach, the producer and the customer agree to maximize the joint benefit from their conversation. They agree on the subjective probabilities to be used in the calculation of the optimal conversation. They then optimize the structure of the conversation, and proceed to share their information in the agreed way.

There are a number of different dimensions of a conversation that need to be optimized. One is the subject to which the questions are addressed. The producer and the customer must agree on which aspects of the product design are to be considered. The sequencing of the conversation needs to be decided too – should the customer ask the first question, or should the producer initiate the process? Should the conversation be terminated if it does not seem to be getting far, in terms of matching product design to customer needs, and if so how quickly should it be abandoned?

If a producer is trying to improve a mass-produced branded product, then he will naturally consult a very large number of customers before he makes any change. These customers will be chosen as a representative sample of the wider population of customers with whom he deals. The conversation will normally be implemented through market research. This implies that the protocol governing the conversation will be a fairly rigid one. The producer will take the initiative in approaching the customer, and only after the customer has answered a few questions will the producer begin to divulge information of his own, such as what kinds of new variants he considers that it may be feasible to produce. The customer may be offered prototypes of these products to examine, and in some cases may even be able to try them out. The results of the market research are then fed back into the product development programme. When the prototypes have been modified the process may iterate again.

The opposite extreme to mass production is where each unit of output is customized to a particular buyer's requirements. This is often the case with intermediate products, and in particular with capital equipment. A producer of durable capital goods may liaise individually with each customer over the design of the good. This resembles the kind of one-to-one conversation which is common in normal social intercourse. The customer may begin by indicating, in general terms, the kind of performance requirements he has in mind. The producer then sketches out a couple of designs, and the customer indicates which is the most preferred. He may also indicate that either will do, and that the cheapest is preferred, or that neither will do, and that a new set of designs should be submitted instead. Compared to the previous process, the dialogue is more likely to begin with the customer, rather than with the producer. The customer's requirements are likely to be stricter, with less scope for substitution between different product characteristics than in the other case. The process is also more likely to terminate with no feasible solution to the customer's problem being found.

The meta-rational approach to external communication, therefore, predicts that the protocols governing the inter-firm marketing of intermediate products will differ significantly from those that apply to the marketing of consumer products. Although this result is already familiar from the industrial marketing literature, the meta-rational approach affords a rigorous explanation of the result in terms of efficient communication. It also provides a means of extending the analysis to deal with differences in the marketing of various types of intermediate product, and also of various types of consumer product.

It is important to emphasize that, although these dialogues take place across the boundaries of the firm, the question of how the dialogue is constructed is logically distinct from the more familiar issue of where the boundaries of the firm are drawn. Although distinct, the issues are related, as might be expected. The greater the degree of distrust, the stronger the connection. Each party incurs costs in terms of the time tied up in the process of conversation. At each stage of the conversation, one party may learn more useful things from the other than the other learns from them. At various points where the process may be terminated without success, one party may have sunk far greater costs in the conversation than the other. When each party is suspicious of the other, each party will wish to minimize their own contribution to the conversation. They will try to persuade the other party to divulge information which is useful to them for other purposes, while minimizing the amount of such information they divulge themselves. The producer will be reluctant to go to the expense of constructing prototypes in case the customer should reject them on quite trivial grounds. A devious customer may claim that a prototype is unsuitable for his purposes when it really is quite suitable, in the hope of acquiring the prototype for a heavily discounted price. In general, when each firm reduces its commitment to the communication process, misunderstandings are likely to become more frequent, and the efficiency of the outcome is reduced. When the gains from collaboration between the firms are high, but the level of trust is very low, it may therefore be advantageous for the firms to integrate. By pooling the financial interests of the firms, neither any longer stands to gain from economizing on communication cost at the expense of the other. Communication becomes much richer, and it is much more likely that an appropriate product will be supplied for a reasonable cost. It is, therefore, because of distrust, and the need to control its consequences, that the location of the boundaries of the firm and the pattern of communication across these boundaries are linked.

4.9   RATIONAL LEARNING

Meta-rationality also provides a means of tackling the difficult issue of what is meant by 'rational learning'. Learning is a key theme of the recent literature on organizational change (see for example, Nohria and Ghoshal, 1994). Learning is clearly connected with bounded rationality in the sense that bounded rationality defines the initial conditions in which learning takes place. A fully informed individual would have nothing to learn. Once again, however, there is a tendency in the recent literature to discuss the issue in a superficial way. The meta-rational approach provides greater analytical rigour. As a result, it becomes possible to derive a connected set of hypotheses concerning when and where learning will occur, and how it will actually take place.

Rational learning may be said to involve the updating of subjective probabilities in the light of new information. Bayes' Rule provides the logical framework in which this is done. The decision-maker begins at the outset with a set of alternative hypotheses, but is unsure which of them is true. These hypotheses typically relate to the unknown value of a key parameter, such as the rate of growth of the market, or the price elasticity of demand.

The implementation of Bayes' Rule is not a simple matter, though (Kirman and Salmon, 1995). Non-linearities make it computationally complex. It is much easier to update probabilities using simple procedures that approximate to the non-linear relations implied by Bayes' Rule. The use of these alternatives may be rational when the costs of calculation are particularly high. A rational individual can compare alternative learning strategies, and select the one that is most suitable for their purposes.

A common objection to arguments of this type is that the kind of uncertainty that learning has to contend with is too radical to permit the apparatus of rational choice to be used. Subjective probabilities cannot be formed, it is said, and the underlying model into which they are supposed to be inserted is not known either. People may know that they are uncertain, but not what they are uncertain about.

A person confronted with radical uncertainty of this kind can still pursue a strategy of trial and error, however. It is still possible to 'play around' with something and to remember which experiment produced the best result so far. The crucial questions in experiments of this kind are twofold. The first is to decide in what order to try out the various possibilities. The second is to decide when to stop experimenting and to stick with the best strategy discovered up to that time.

The interesting thing is that these are essentially the same problems that were discussed earlier, but in a different guise. Both sets of issues concern the optimization of a search strategy. The difference between them lies in the nature of the information collected, and the use to which it is put. In the first case the information concerns some aspect of the firm's environment, and it is inserted into the model of the firm's environment that the decision-maker is using to guide his decision. In the second case the information relates to the performance achieved by a trial action of a given type. This is not inserted into a model of the firm's environment because such a model does not exist in this case. It is put into a model of the learning process instead. This model estimates, in the light of past experience, how much further improvement may be possible in the light of further experiment. Information on the latest trial informs the judgement on whether further improvement is likely if another trial were to be made.

It could, of course, be asserted that, because of the radical nature of the uncertainty, it is impossible to apply any model of the learning process in this way. The alternative view is that the order in which the experiments are undertaken is arbitrary, and so is the time at which the experiments stop. However, this negative view ignores the possibility that a decision-maker, confronted over time with a succession of radically uncertain situations, can experiment with different experimental procedures. If these radically uncertain situations have certain elements in common, then the adequacy of the solution obtained by a given learning procedure in any given case can be taken as an indicator of the probable efficiency of the procedure in other cases. Given a sufficient number of radically uncertain situations with which to experiment, therefore, the decision-maker will tend to converge, by pragmatic adjustment, upon an efficient learning procedure. This efficient learning procedure is the one that trades off correctly the expected gain from fewer mistaken decisions in the future against the expected cost of experimental failure today.

The analysis of learning by experiment indicates that the accumulation of experience is the key to successful decision-making. Those who have encountered similar cases of radical uncertainty before can form a better judgement about what learning procedure works best than can those who have not. Even those with no experience of their own, however, can attempt to free-ride on the experiences of others, copying what they do. Even if other people's learning procedures cannot be observed directly, the speed of learning achieved by the most successful people acts as a bench-mark against which a person's own performance may be judged. The discrepancy between current performance and bench-mark performance indicates the scope for improvement in learning procedures that could be achieved by further experiments.

It follows that, even under conditions of radical uncertainty, useful predictions about behaviour can be derived from the rationality postulate. Rational action is a principle whose scope is not confined to well-specified situations. The application is certainly easier when situations are well-specified, but the principle is not so fragile that it disintegrates when confronted with loosely specified problems instead.

4.10   SUMMARY AND CONCLUSIONS

The essence of meta-rationality is that the decision-maker calculates in advance of any decision how they will respond to various components of information cost. Five main components of information have been identified, and three have been discussed in detail. From a meta-rational perspective, the most straightforward type of information cost is observation cost. Meta-rational analysis of observation cost illustrates very simply the costs and benefits of dispelling uncertainty in decision-making. Memory costs are a little more difficult. To analyse memory costs it is necessary to adopt a dynamic, or intertemporal, perspective. Memory allows the set-up costs of gathering information on persistent factors to be spread over all subsequent decisions where information on these factors is required. The meta-rational perspective on memory explains why routine procedures are memorized in order to deal with repetitive situations in which the same persistent factors apply.

Communication costs add a further dimension to the analysis. Unlike observation and memory costs, it is impossible to analyse communication costs fully without allowing for the fact that more than one person is normally involved. Communication costs are incurred both within and between organizations. The easiest communication costs to analyse are those within an organization. In this context, an employer seeks to optimize the internal division of labour in information-handling by structuring information flow between his employees. This optimization process is easiest to see in the planning of routine procedures. It is the optimization of the implementation of routines that governs the organizational structure and management style of the firm.

Communication between organizations is most readily handled by assuming that the organizations seek to maximize their joint rewards. Again, it is most useful to situate the analysis in terms of the planning of routines, or protocols, which structure communication between the organizations on a regular basis. Meta-rational structuring of communication between two organizations is exemplified by the arrangements used for collaborative design between an assembler and a subcontractor.

Meta-rational theory places many of the insights of conventional organization theory on a more rigorous footing. An important consequence of this greater rigour, however, is that it highlights the contingent nature of many of the conclusions which have previously been advanced in an unqualified way. In other respects, meta-rational theory undermines some of the claims to be found in the recent literature. It shows, for example, that the hierarchical form of organization has many inherent advantages. It suggests that the key issue in organizational design for international business is not so much whether hierarchy is appropriate, as what form of hierarchy works best under what conditions. Firms in a stable and sheltered environment may operate most effectively under a fairly autocratic style of management, but the greater the number and diversity of shocks, and the greater the need for innovation, the more appropriate a consultative management style becomes. Meta-rational theory has the power to predict exactly what form such consultation will take. It can predict the decision procedures used within the firm, and the way in which different parts of each procedure are allocated to different people. As such, it goes into much further detail than the more visionary discussion of organization characteristic of recent international business literature.

REFERENCES

Bartlett, C.A. and S. Ghoshal (1987) 'Managing across borders: new strategic requirements', *Sloan Management Review*, Summer, 6–17

Baumol, W.J. and R.E. Quandt (1964) 'Rules of thumb and optimally imperfect decisions', *American Economic Review*, **54**(1), 23–46

Blaug, M. (1980) *The Methodology of Economics: or How Economists Explain*, Cambridge: Cambridge University Press

Casson, M.C. (1994) 'Why are firms hierarchical?', *International Journal of the Economics of Business*, **1**(1), 43–81

Casson, M.C. (1995) *The Organization of International Business*, Aldershot: Edward Elgar

Casson, M.C. and N. Wadeson (1996) 'Information strategies and the theory of the firm', *International Journal of the Economics of Business*, **3**(3), 307–30

Casson, M.C. and N. Wadeson (1998) 'Communication costs and the boundaries of the firm', *International Journal of the Economics of Business*, **5**(1), 5–27

Coase, R.H. (1937) 'The nature of the firm', *Economica* (new series), **4**, 386–405

Commons, J.R. (1934) *The Legal Foundations of Capitalism*, New York: Macmillan

Cyert, R.M. and J.G. March (1963) A *Behavioural Theory of the Firm*, Englewood Cliffs, NJ: Prentice-Hall

Ebers, M. (ed.) (1997) *The Formation of Inter-organizational Networks*, Oxford: Clarendon Press

Egelhoff, W.G. (1991) 'Information-processing theory and the multinational enterprise', *Journal of International Business Studies*, **22**(3), 341–68

Elster, J. (ed.) (1986) *Rational Choice*, Oxford: Blackwell

Hamel, G. and C.K. Prahalad (1996) 'Competing in the new economy: managing out of bounds', *Strategic Management Journal*, **14**(1), 23–46

Hargreaves Heap, S. (1989) *Rationality in Economics*, Oxford: Blackwell

Hedlund, G. (1993) 'Assumptions of hierarchy and heterarchy: an application to the multinational corporation', in S. Ghoshal and E. Westney (eds), *Organization Theory and the Multinational Corporation*, London: Macmillan, 211–36

Hedlund, G. and J. Ridderstrale (1992) 'Towards the N-form corporation: exploitation and creation in the MNC', paper presented at the Conference on Perspectives on International Business: Theory, Research and Institutional Arrangements, University of South Carolina, Columbia, SC

Kirman, A.P. and M. Salmon (eds) (1995) *Learning and Rationality in Economics*, Oxford: Blackwell

Kogut, B. and U. Zander (1993) 'Knowledge of the firm and the evolutionary theory of the multinational corporation', *Journal of International Business Studies*, **24**(4), 625–45

Lawrence, P.R. and J.W. Lorsch (1967) *Organization and Environment: Managing Differentiation and Integration*, Cambridge, MA: Division of Research, Graduate School of Business, Harvard University

Lippman, S.A. and J.J. McCall (eds) (1979) *Studies in the Economics of Search*, Amsterdam: North-Holland

Marschak, J. and R. Radner (1972) *The Economic Theory of Teams*, New Haven, CT: Yale University Press

Moss, S. and J. Rae (1992) *Artificial Intelligence and Economic Analysis: Prospects and Problems*, Aldershot: Edward Elgar

Nelson, R. and S.G. Winter (1982) *An Evolutionary Theory of Economic Change*, Cambridge, MA: Harvard University Press

Nohria, N. and S. Ghoshal (1994) 'Differentiated fit and shared values: alternatives for managing headquarters-subsidiary relations', *Strategic Management Journal*, **15**(6), 491–502

Sah, R.K. and J.E. Stiglitz (1986) 'The architecture of economic systems: hierarchies and polyarchies', *American Economic Review*, **76**(4), 716–27

Simon, H.A. (1947) *Administrative Behaviour*, New York: Macmillan

Simon, H.A. (1982) *Models of Bounded Rationality*, Cambridge, MA: MIT Press

Simon, H.A. (1992) *Economics, Bounded Rationality and the Cognitive Revolution* (with M. Egidi, R. Marris and R. Viale), Aldershot: Edward Elgar

Williamson, O.E. (1975) *Markets and Hierarchies: Analysis and Anti-trust Implications*, New York: Free Press

Williamson, O.E. (1985) *The Economic Institutions of Capitalism*, New York: Free Press

5. The organization of the multinational enterprise: an information cost approach

5.1 INTRODUCTION

The object of this chapter is to summarize in a non-technical way some of the insights into the theory of the multinational enterprise (MNE) that can be derived from the theory of information costs. Information costs are not the same thing as transaction costs. While most transaction costs are information costs, the converse does not apply. Information cost is a more general concept than transaction cost. Consequently, there are many information costs that are not transaction costs, as that term is commonly understood. For example, information costs incurred in appraising investments, planning experiments and searching for new production locations are not transaction costs, but nevertheless attempts to minimize these costs have a significant effect on the organization of the firm.

The intellectual pedigree of the theory is different too. As explained in Chapter 4, information cost analysis derives from decision theory, and in particular from the theory of co-operative decision-making known as the theory of teams (Marschak and Radner, 1972). This theory provides useful techniques for formalizing some of the earlier insights of Hayek (1937) and Richardson (1960) into the nature of the co-ordination problem in economics. The process of co-ordination benefits from a division of labour in which functionally-specialized organizations emerge. The MNE is one important organization of this kind. It co-ordinates on a global basis the decisions of households which supply labour (and of other factors of production) for the production of a given product with the decisions of households which consume that product.

Such co-ordination makes intensive use of information. Different kinds of information need to be collected from different sources. The various items of information must then be synthesized to make decisions. Different functional areas of the firm specialize in collecting and processing different types of information. Information can be thought of as an abstract commodity (Stigler, 1961), flowing along the channels of communication defined by the organizational structure of the firm. The economic logic of information dictates the form that this structure takes. It also dictates that the production and use of information is governed by procedures. It identifies optimal procedures, and determines the factors on which they depend. It thereby predicts how these procedures will change in response to changes in the business environment.

Information gathered by the firm can be used not only to track the changes in the environment, but also to learn more about the laws of change themselves. Under these circumstances, the evolution of the firm is governed both by the firm's response to exogenous change, and also by endogenous changes in the firm's understanding of its environment as a whole.

Explaining organization in these terms is much more satisfactory than appealing solely to the theory of transaction costs. Transaction cost analysis – as reflected in internalization theory, for example – is concerned first and foremost with explaining the boundaries of the firm. It explains the boundaries of the firm extremely well, as other chapters in this book clearly demonstrate. What lies inside the boundaries of the firm is not explained so well, however, because this is not the focus of the theory.

Internal organization needs to be explained in terms of what the firm sets out to do. Firms set out to hire factors of production, which they combine to generate goods and services which they aim to sell. To sell their goods they need to make contact with their customers, and win their confidence. This marketing activity makes intensive use of information. Similarly, the procurement of factors of production requires intensive flows of information, in assessing the skills of workers, and in keeping shareholders informed of how their funds are being used. To understand the organization of the firm, it is necessary to appreciate the importance of linking the information flowing through the product market with the information flowing through the factors markets. Marketing activities need to be integrated with procurement activities so that the overall performance of the firm is optimized. The efficient integration of these activities through the structuring of information flow is the principal factor dictating the internal organization of the firm (see, for example, Egelhoff, 1988).

The chapter is organized as follows. Sections 5.2–5.5 examine the relationship between information costs and transaction costs. It is argued that too much emphasis has been placed on opportunism in analysing transaction costs. As a result, opportunism is often introduced into the analysis of issues where it is of little or no practical significance. This applies, in particular, to explanations of the organizational structure of the firm. Sections 5.6–5.9 systematically develop the theory of information costs, beginning with some elementary yet fundamental points. They explain the concept of decisiveness and use it to show why decision-making is a sequential, procedure-driven process of the kind that is assumed, but never proved, in alternative theories of organization (see Ch. 4). Sections 5.10–5.17 extend the theory to encompass a series of interdependent decisions in which many different executives participate. An important distinction is drawn between transitory and persistent information. It is shown that the properties of transitory information govern organizational routine, while the properties of persistent information govern how these routines evolve over time. Different types of information have different sources, and the way these sources are distributed over space affects the decentralization of the firm. The path-dependent nature of efficient decision-making is elucidated, and its application to the internationalization process of the firm is explored. The conclusions are summarized in Section 5.18.

5.2   INFORMATION COSTS AND TRANSACTION COSTS

The idea that information costs are somehow distinct from transaction costs may appear strange to some readers. The need to emphasize this distinction arises partly because of an ambiguity in the way the term 'transaction cost' has become used in the literature. It may seem natural to construe as a 'transaction cost' any cost that is incurred in setting up a transaction. Thus the cost of specifying the product to be bought and sold would be a transaction cost, as would the cost of exchanging the names and addresses of buyers and sellers, where this was necessary in order for the product to be delivered safely, and for the payment to be made securely in return. This very general concept of transaction cost – as a cost relating in some way to a transaction of any sort – is the concept used by North (1991). It is also the concept employed in everyday discourse.

However, according to Williamson (1985), opportunism is a key element in transaction costs. Williamson often gives the impression that in the absence of opportunism, transaction costs would invariably be lower, and possibly even zero. This is a fundamentally different view of transaction cost from that held by North, but the difference is not always recognized by other writers who draw upon their work, and who often switch back and forth between the two different notions of transactions cost without realizing the confusion that this causes.

The problem is a serious one, since some of the costs connected with transactions are incurred quite independently of whether or not opportunism is present. Thus opportunism does not necessarily arise in connection with either of the cases discussed above: the specification of a product, or the exchange of information about addresses. It does not necessarily pay a buyer to mislead a seller about the type of product he desires: the result of lying might be that he was offered a totally unsuitable product. Dishonesty would make his approach to the seller a complete waste of his own time. Similarly, it does not normally pay a seller to say that an acceptable means of payment, such as a credit card, is actually unacceptable, because he is liable to lose a sale as a result of this. As far as exchange of addresses is concerned, it would be a foolish buyer who gave the wrong address if it meant that the seller delivered the product to the wrong person as a result. The costs of specifying products, and exchanging addresses, are certainly information costs, because in both cases resources of time, and possibly money, are tied up in communication. However, they are not necessarily transactions costs, in Williamson's sense, because opportunism is not always involved. Opportunism may sometimes be involved (for example, concealing the true address when using a stolen credit card to purchase a good that the customer intends to carry away), but these cases are often the exception rather than the rule.

Even if the narrow focus on opportunism is rejected, as several critics of Williamson have urged (see, for example, Kay, 1993), there would remain important information costs that were still not transaction costs in the usual sense of the word. For example, the cost of market research is not really a transaction cost, because it is not linked to any particular transaction. Insofar as it is linked to transactions, it is linked to all transactions in the product which is developed in response to the findings of the research. If the concept of transaction cost were broadened to include all costs of this type, however, then many other kinds of cost, such as the overhead costs of the firm's entire headquarters, would have to be included too. The most obvious way of addressing the terminological problem is simply to recognize that there are many information costs that are clearly not transactions costs.

It is important, however, not to go from one extreme to the other, and to deny any connection at all between information and transaction costs. While not all information costs are transactions costs, many transactions costs are information costs. In particular, many of the transactions costs that stem directly from opportunism are information costs as well as transactions costs. This is because information is often collected as a means of mitigating the threat of opportunism. Opportunism in a transaction implies that some of the information supplied by the other party may be false. It may be a false claim – for example, 'I can't afford to pay any more', or 'A cheque is in the post' – or a false promise, 'I'll give you the best quality I've got, and deliver it tomorrow'. When an item of information is liable to be false, a common response is to collect another item of information. This may be intended simply as a check. More likely, however, it is hoped that a transactor subject to sanctions, who knows that his information is liable to be checked, will prefer to tell the truth. It is the threat of being checked, rather than the check itself, which is important in this case. It is also possible to check out the transactor himself. The aim is to find out what incentive the transactor is under. Reputation is relevant here: a transactor who already has a reputation for honesty has more to lose if he is caught telling a lie. The important point is that, whatever form the information takes, the transaction cost incurred in checking one item of information is spent on another item of information. Thus many transaction costs attributable to opportunism are information costs as well.

Not all the costs that stem from opportunism are information costs, however. For example, the costs involved in coercing defaulters to make payment, or in persuading suppliers to replace defective items, may also involve expenditure of physical resources. Thus while many transactions costs are information costs, some are not.

The relationship between information costs and transaction costs is summarized in Figure 5.1. On the left-hand side of the figure are two concentric circles, and on the right-hand side is an ellipse that intersects them both. The outer circle represents all transaction costs – in the everyday sense of all costs that are normally associated with individual transactions. The inner circle represents all those transaction costs that are attributable to opportunism. The annulus – the ring formed by the circumferences of the two circles – represents all those transaction costs which are not due to opportunism – such as the costs of specifying the product and exchanging addresses, as discussed above.

The intersection between the circles and the ellipse identifies three components of information cost. Type I information costs correspond to the intersection of the inner circle and the ellipse. They are the information-cost

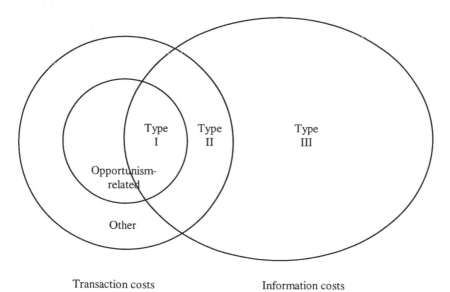

Transaction costs   Information costs

Figure 5.1   Relationship between information costs and transaction costs

components of opportunism-related transaction costs, such as the costs of checking up on the incentives under which a trading partner operates. Type II information costs are associated with the intersection of the annulus with the ellipse. They are the information costs that relate to transactions, broadly defined, but are independent of opportunism. These are exemplified by the costs of specifying the product and exchanging addresses. Type III information costs correspond to the remaining area of the ellipse. They are costs that are independent of any specific transaction. They can only be attributed to large sets of transactions. In the limit, they are costs attributable to all the transactions in which the firm is involved – in other words, they are basically overhead costs of remaining in business, such as the costs of monitoring the market environment for new competitive threats to the firm.

5.3   MARKETING AND PROCUREMENT: THEIR INFLUENCE ON ORGANIZATIONAL STRUCTURE

The focus of internalization theory is upon Type I information costs. The focus of this chapter, by contrast, is on Type II and Type III information costs. Type II and Type III information costs are particularly important in the marketing of finished products, and in the procurement of factors of production. To appreciate the significance of these costs for the organization of the firm, it is important to recognize that the issues which arise in marketing output and in procuring factors of production are rather different from those which are the focus of attention in internalization theory. This is because internalization is relevant to intermediate products flowing between one part of the production sector and another, while final product marketing and factor procurement involve flows of resources between firms and households. Marketing and procurement activities bring firms into direct contact with households, but intermediate product markets do not.

This difference is significant because, when markets need to be organized, it is normally firms that take responsibility for this. Firms play an important role in reducing information costs in product markets. Households do not participate in organizing transactions on the same scale as do firms. Firms are usually much larger economic units, and they tend to specialize in selling one particular type of product. The typical household consumes a wide variety of different products, each on a small scale, while a firm typically sells just one or two types of product on a much larger scale. All of this means that a typical firm handles a given product on a far more regular basis than does a typical household.

Because they specialize in handling a particular type of product, firms are in a good position to invest in specialized facilities. They are also in a good position to develop special methods for reducing information costs. Thus firms operate retail premises for the convenience of customers, where the product is displayed, and where advice and after-sales service can be obtained. This assists consumers in evaluating the product specification in terms of quality and price. Firms also advertise their products, and locate their retail premises in convenient centres – such as large cities – where consumers can have confidence that prices are set at competitive levels. Firms also set the rules of the game by which consumers can negotiate over price. For low-value items the price is usually set on a non-negotiable, take-it-or-leave-it basis, while on high value items discounts may be negotiated within certain limits, especially when demand is slack or where a larger-than-usual order is concerned.

The result is that firms bear the brunt of the information-processing activities through which the product market works. They recover their information-processing costs by setting a margin between their costs of production and their retail price. The more efficient the procedures that the firm employs in marketing, the lower the information costs it incurs in supplying a given standard of service to its customers, and the more profitable the firm is likely to be.

Firms also bear many of the information-processing costs incurred in the procurement of factors of production. The concentration of costs upon the firm instead of the household is somewhat less in the case of factor markets, however. Firms are not so narrowly specialized where inputs rather than outputs are concerned. Thus a firm may employ many different types of worker, each with different skills, while producing a relatively narrow range of products. A firm may sell to thousands of different customers, but employ only tens or hundreds of workers. Thus workers share with firms the costs of transacting in the labour market to a greater extent than consumers share with firms the costs of transacting in final product markets. Workers have to make more effort when searching out a suitable job than they do when searching out a source of supply for a consumer product. Nevertheless, most firms still find it worth their while to take the initiative in advertising vacancies and quoting rates of pay, while many firms also devise routine procedures for recruiting and training staff. Similar considerations apply to the procurement of other factor inputs such as land and capital. Firms generally take the initiative in approaching factor owners in order to secure their supplies of factor inputs. They also invest in procedures for the smooth and speedy processing of information relating to the inputs they procure, but only to a limited degree.

The organization of the firm is, therefore, driven from one side by the information-processing demands of marketing, and from the other by the information-processing demands of procurement. Marketing and procurement decisions are linked. A firm's demand for factor inputs derives from the demand for its product. Conversely, constraints on the availability of factor inputs constrain the firm's supply of the product. The organizational structure of the firm is, therefore, dictated by the need to integrate the two sorts of information processing.

At this point, however, the reader may notice that an important activity has been left out of the picture – namely the production of the product. While this is a striking omission, it is not so serious as it may at first seem. One advantage of the information-cost approach to the firm is that it puts the organization of production in its place. In some instances this is a relatively subordinate place.

To understand why this is so, it is important to recognize that conventional theories of the firm tend to be biased towards overstating the economic significance of production as far as the organization of the firm is concerned. The information-cost approach is a useful corrective to this bias. The typical firm is usually assumed to be a manufacturing one. It has become a convention in the theory of the firm to focus upon its productive activities – that is on the physical transformation of labour and other factor inputs into finished product. This approach is highly dubious in the modern 'information age'. Indeed, it was never a very good assumption to begin with. There have always been firms that have supplied services rather than goods. More significantly, there have been many firms, like brokers and banks, which have handled goods and payments without transforming them in a physical sense. Historically, many of the most prosperous firms have been those owned and operated by merchants and middlemen, who have, at most, stored and transported the goods in which they have traded – that is they have transformed them in time, through storage, and transformed them in space, through transport, but have not physically transformed them through production.

Nevertheless, it is important when developing a balanced view of the firm, to give the organization of production due attention. The need for efficiency in the production process creates additional demands on information processing. The flow of goods needs to be monitored continually to avoid shortages, or the build-up of excessive stocks, caused by the interaction of leads and lags within the production process. Machinery too needs to be monitored through programmes of preventative maintenance, and labour needs to be supervised to control for human error. These information demands must be added to the other demands stemming from the marketing and procurement activities described above.

Of all these sources of demand, it is normally marketing ones that are the most intense. This is why marketing strategy is usually rated so highly as the key to the success of a firm. Much of the information required in marketing falls into the Type II category described above. It involves making contact with customers, advertising the product specification, and informing customers of which retailers stock the goods and where their premises can be found. None of this information is exposed to serious risk of opportunism. As explained above, lying would normally be self-defeating in activities of this kind. The key to success is to process information efficiently, and not to invest at great expense in checking that every item of information supplied by other people is true.

5.4   THE CO-ORDINATION OF INTERMEDIATE PRODUCT FLOW

Given the importance of minimizing Type II information costs, it might be asked whether other types of information cost really enter the picture at all as far as the behaviour of the firm is concerned. The answer, of course, is that they do, but in a much more limited way than is normally assumed.

Type I costs connected with opportunism are very important where intermediate product flows are concerned. Intermediate products are generated naturally within a multi-stage production process. According to internalization theory, an intermediate product generated at a given stage of production can either be sold on to an independent firm through an arm's-length transaction, or passed on internally to another part of the same firm. The main difference between the first arrangement, based on an external market, and the second arrangement, based on an internal market, lies in the incentive to cheat on the transaction. This is where Type I information costs come into their own.

Type I transaction costs are not the only type of transaction cost that is relevant in this case, however. Type II information costs are relevant as well. This is because the internalization of an intermediate product market provides a wider range of options for organizing information flow between the adjacent stages of production. An integrated firm that has internalized an intermediate product market can implement a fully centralized procedure to co-ordinate the flow of product between adjacent stages, whereas two independent firms linked by an external market cannot use a centralized procedure of this type. The integrated firm does not have to implement a centralized procedure if it does not want to, however; it also has the option of using a decentralized procedure if it wishes. For example, it could instruct the manager of the upstream plant and the manager of the downstream plant to negotiate internal transfer prices as a means of co-ordinating their production decisions. One advantage of internalization, therefore, is that it provides an option, but not an obligation, to use a centralized control procedure to co-ordinate upstream and downstream production if desired. The degree of centralization impacts on the level of Type II costs incurred by the firm. Thus it is not only Type I costs, but also Type II costs, that impinge on the internalization of intermediate product markets.

The failure to distinguish properly between Type I and Type II information costs has led to further confusion on this particular topic. Some writers have assumed that centralized co-ordination is the only form, or at least the most natural form, of internal co-ordination for an intermediate product market. Thus Williamson (1975) uses the term 'hierarchy' as if it were interchangeable with 'internal market', suggesting that firms will opt for centralization whenever internalization makes it feasible. Hennart (1986) goes even further, and appears to suggest that a market is not really internalized unless it takes a hierarchical form. Although Williamson and Hennart discuss internal decentralization in the context of multi-product firms (the 'M-form' firm, for example), they do not appear to fully recognize its significance where the co-ordination of multi-stage production for a single product is concerned.

Buckley and Casson (1976), by contrast, leave open the question of whether internal co-ordination is centralized or not. They regard a decentralized internal market, co-ordinated by transfer prices, as the most natural analogue of the external market, although they recognize that the hierarchical alternative is viable too. This position is clarified further in Casson (1982), where it is suggested that the degree of centralization of the internal market is governed by the logic of the resource allocation problem that needs to be solved.

The main reason why it makes sense to focus on Type I costs when discussing the internalization of intermediate product markets is that one of the most important intermediate products within the firm is knowledge. The classic argument in the internalization theory of the MNE is that in the absence of adequate patent protection, the best way to protect property rights in technology is to exploit a technology within the firm. This is because the use of internal markets helps to protect proprietary knowledge through secrecy. Yet, even here, Type I information costs are not the whole of the story. Type III information costs are potentially important too. Technological breakthroughs effected by corporate R&D depend upon inputs of general scientific knowledge. An innovative firm needs to be effective in procuring the latest results of academic research. The use of this knowledge cannot easily be imputed to any single transaction with which the firm is involved, however. The same point applies to general knowledge about long-run market trends which have implications for the investment policies of the firm. The main problem for the firm is in gaining access to the people who possess information of this kind, rather than being misled by them once the firm has found out who they are. The firm is therefore faced with the problem of addressing Type III information costs in an efficient way.

Taking all these points together, it is clear that the theory of the firm has suffered from a number of distortions in recent years. The traditional emphasis on production has led scholars to see the organization of production as the major organizational challenge facing the firm, when in fact the major challenge is typically the organization of marketing, and the integration of marketing with other activities, including, not only production, but also factor procurement and R&D. Second, there has been confusion over the nature of transaction costs, which has in turn obscured the crucial difference between transaction costs and information costs. There has been a failure to recognize that the relative importance of Type I information costs and Type II information costs differs between final product markets and intermediate product markets. Type II information costs are the dominant factor in final product markets, while Type I information costs tend to be more important in intermediate product markets, especially where knowledge is concerned. Even in intermediate product markets, however, Type I costs may not be as dominant as some writers have suggested they are. Finally, there has been confusion over whether or not internal intermediate product markets are always centrally co-ordinated.

5.5   THE MARKET-MAKING MULTINATIONAL

The present chapter aims to correct for these problems in the literature by highlighting the importance of information costs of Types II and III. In doing so, it is convenient to focus on a particular type of firm that has received extensive discussion elsewhere – namely the market-making firm (Casson, 1997, 2000). In the present context, the focus is on the market-making multinational (MMM).

The essence of an MMM is that it establishes international trading links which would not otherwise exist. It exploits its entrepreneurial skills and its international reputation to co-ordinate factor suppliers and final consumers in different countries who would not otherwise be linked with each other. It identifies changes in international demand and supply conditions which create opportunities to organize new markets in certain types of product.

The purest form of MMM simply buys and resells the same product. It may also transform it, but whether this is necessary depends largely on the nature of the product. For example, a tea supplier has little to do apart from blending and packaging the product before delivery to the customer, while a chocolate supplier needs to heat and mould his product in addition. Whether the MMM chooses to produce the product itself, or to subcontract its production to other people, is an internalization issue driven by the need to assure the quality and the continuity of supply. While the MMM may well engage in conventional production, market-making is its key activity. This seems realistic: it is probably no exaggeration to say that most MNEs which engage in production are strategically driven, not by the technology they use, or by the co-ordination of their intermediate product flow, but by their ability to make a market for their product.

The concept of the MMM captures Schumpeter's (1934) view that innovation is not merely technological but also encompasses creating new products, developing new export markets, and tapping new sources of supply (see also Ch. 8). It gives more analytical depth to the idea of marketing skill as a component of the ownership and competitive advantages mentioned by Dunning (1977) and Porter (1980). It is also consistent with recent empirical work which suggests that market-making leads large-scale technology generation in the internationalization process of the firm (Mitchell *et al.*, 1996).

It is interesting to note that market-making innovators often receive a much worse press than technological innovators, even though historically their contributions to economic well-being have been just as great. Even today, market-makers are often described as social parasites (de Monthoux, 1993). The same cultures that despise the market-maker often praise innovative scientists and engineers as heroes. Technological innovation, it would seem, is valued for its symbolic demonstration of human control of nature. The market-maker, by contrast, is more a symbol of uncontrollable volatility, as prices rise and fall in response to unforeseen shortages and surpluses of the product.

Numerous examples of MMMs can be found in multinational service industries, such as catering and hotels, banking and insurance, and retailing. Many examples can be found in manufacturing industries too. A particularly good example is provided by the personal computer (PC) industry of the mid-1990s. Some of the most successful PC suppliers buy in almost all their key components, and do little more than assemble and warehouse the product. In a few cases they merely badge an almost fully-assembled product and configure it for its destination market by adding pre-loaded software and operating manuals in the appropriate language. An important competitive advantage for the well-established firms lies in the brand, which assures the customers of component quality and after-sales service. But the relative ease of entry shows that brands alone are not enough. Effective management of the distribution channel is the really crucial factor.

Distribution of PCs is an information-intensive activity. Tele-sales departments handle large volumes of credit-card sales, which are converted promptly into requisitions for particular specifications of product. Inventories have to be kept low, not only because of high interest charges but also because of the continual risk of technological obsolescence. The PC supplier is a good example of the so-called 'hollow firm' or 'flagship firm' described, for example, by Rugman and D'Cruz (1996). Insofar as it develops good relations with a few loyal supplier firms, it may also be described as a 'network firm' (Chesnais, 1988). The key point is that it is only production that has been 'hollowed out' from these firms. Taking a production-centred view of the firm, there is a paradox here, but from a market-making point of view there is no paradox at all. These firms are simply an unusually pure form of the market-making firm. The fact that even in a very high-technology industry they outsource all their major technological requirements indicates that technology is not the key to their success. Even the firms that do carry out R&D tend to specialize in areas unconnected with the PC market. Their success resides in the fact that they recognize the logistical imperatives of mass distribution and possess organizational procedures that are well adapted to the information-processing needs of the distribution channel. The PC industry therefore makes an appropriate case study with which to illustrate the analysis below.

5.6   PRINCIPLES OF INFORMATION ECONOMICS

Decisions by definition, involve a choice between alternatives. A rational decision requires information on the costs and benefits associated with these alternatives. The emphasis in this chapter is on discrete choice between a finite number of alternatives. Discrete choice models are a powerful means of simplifying problems and overcoming otherwise intractable analytical ones. The simplest possible discrete choice is whether or not to proceed with a given project. It is simple because, not only is it a pairwise choice, but also one of the pair is the null strategy of doing nothing at all. The net return from the null project is known to be zero at the outset. The decision therefore only requires information on the costs and benefits of a single project. For example, a PC supplier needs information about two key factors – potential demand and the cost of memory chips – when deciding whether or not to launch a model with a new specification.

Most decisions are taken under uncertainty. Uncertainty exists because information is scarce. If information were not scarce, then it would be possible to collect and assimilate sufficient information to dispel all uncertainty about each decision. Although the existence of uncertainty is taken for granted, in most situations the information required is in principle available. It is just that it is only available at prohibitive cost. For example, if the PC supplier could costlessly interview all potential purchasers of a new model and record their preferences then he would know exactly what specification would best meet their requirements.

The degree of scarcity of any commodity is measured by its cost. In this respect information is like any other commodity. The scarcity of information is measured by information cost. Several components of information cost can be distinguished. These include:

- *observation costs* incurred in direct measurements of the firm's environment;
- *communication costs* of transmitting information between one location and another and between one person and another;
- *memory costs* of holding information in store for use on a future occasion;
- *deposit and retrieval costs* of putting information into store and getting it out again; and
- *calculation costs* associated with processing information using logical or mathematical operations in order to arrive at decisions, and in order to make it easier to store and to share.

For example, a PC supplier incurs observation costs in noting the prices charged by its competitors, and how these change over time as new models are introduced and established models obsolesce. A PC supplier incurs communication costs in receiving customers' orders and passing these orders on to the factories in which the PCs are built. The PC supplier incurs memory costs in storing details of the customers it has supplied on a database that can be used by help-line advisors and by engineers undertaking warranty repair work. A PC supplier incurs deposit and retrieval costs in entering records of deliveries into the database and in accessing the database when providing after-sales service. A PC supplier incurs calculation costs when the information stored in the database is aggregated and used to generate forecasts of demand as a guide to future investment decisions.

When information is costly, it is only worth collecting if there is some compensating benefit. A rational decision-maker invests in information only if the expected benefit exceeds the cost. The benefit of information is that it dispels uncertainty; this benefit is measured in terms of the increase it achieves in the expected value of the outcome. The expected value of the outcome is calculated using subjective probabilities that the decision-maker attaches to the various aspects of the situation. To calculate the value of information, the decision-maker needs to know what he would do with it if he had it, and must compare the way he would act with the information with the way he would act without it. For example, if the information would not change the decision then it is irrelevant and of no value at all. Normally the value of the information will be positive, because actions chosen in the light of the information will be correct while those taken without it may be wrong. Under these conditions taking a decision is a two-stage process. In the first stage the decision-maker asks what he would do with the information if he had it, and in the second he decides whether, in the light of this, he wants it or not. This contrasts sharply with the situation that prevails in the absence of information costs, where the decision-maker simply collects all the information he needs at the outset, reducing the decision effectively to just a single step.

For example, it may be quite rational for a PC supplier planning to launch a new model not to carry out market research before investing in production if he believes that the market research will be very expensive. It is better for him to take a calculated gamble that the model will be a success than to spend a large amount of money avoiding a possible failure.

Consider the special case where just a single item of information is required for a decision. To calculate the expected value of acting with the information the decision-maker must assess the correct response to each possible situation, and then weight the outcomes associated with these responses using the subjective probabilities described above. Summing the values of the probability-weighted outcomes gives the required expected value. This value must then be compared with the expected value of acting in ignorance of the situation. For each possible action in turn, the expected value of the outcomes is evaluated on the assumption that the true situation is not known. Each of these calculations is similar to the one made before. The highest expected value identifies the optimal course of action when in ignorance of the situation.

It can be shown that the value of information, as measured by the difference between these two expected values, tends to be greater, the more equal the probabilities attached to different situations, and the more unequal the outcomes associated with different actions in any given situation. Conversely, the difference between the two expected values is smallest when the probabilities attached to the different situations are very different, but the outcomes associated with each course of action in any given situation are very much the same.

The differences between the subjective probabilities measure the decision-maker's confidence that a particular situation, or subset of situations, is likely to prevail. The differences in the values of the outcomes generated by different strategies in the same situation measure the costs of error. It follows that information is most valuable to a decision-maker when he lacks confidence that he knows the true situation, and where the cost of error is high. Conversely, the value of information is low when the decision-maker is confident that he knows the true situation and when cost of error is low. The more confident the decision-maker, and the lower the cost of error, the less he feels that he needs additional information, and the more likely he is to take a calculated risk instead. The less confident the decision-maker, and the higher the cost of error, the more he feels that he must acquire the information in order to avoid a mistake.

For example, a PC supplier is more likely to carry out market research when he is very unsure about the potential size of the market, and where the non-recoverable costs sunk in the launch of a new model are large. Conversely, if the supplier is confident that he already knows the size of the market, then he may decide not to bother with the market research. If he believes that the market is large, and the set-up costs of the launch are small, then he will invest right away, while if he believes that the market is small, and the set-up costs are large, then he will reject the idea instead. In other words, the self-confident optimist invests and the self-confident pessimist does not. It is the supplier that is unsure who investigates before he invests because he needs the information that the market research will provide.

5.7 SYNTHESIS

The typical decision requires a synthesis of several different items of information. It has already been noted that the evaluation of a project requires information both about its revenues and its costs. The choice between two projects requires information about the benefits and costs of both projects; in other words, it requires four items of information in all. The principle of synthesis demonstrates that there are positive externalities between different items of information. By itself, a single item of information may have no significance for any decision, but when combined with others it may play an important role.

For example, a PC supplier trying to decide between two alternative models to fill a given niche requires information about the revenues and costs of each model before he can decide which one to invest in. He therefore requires four items of information in all. None of these items may be commercially sensitive in themselves but, when combined to identify a profitable project, they become very sensitive indeed.

When more than one item of information is required, the decision-maker no longer faces a binary choice of whether to collect a single item of information, but a more graduated choice of exactly how much information to collect. At one extreme lies the null strategy of collecting no information, at the other extreme the comprehensive strategy of collecting all the information. Between these two extremes lies a wide range of possibilities.

If n items of information are required for a correct decision then in practice any number $m \leq n$ different items can be collected. Moreover any m items can be made up in $n!/m! (n - m)!$ different ways. This means that there are 2^n possible subsets of information in all. Thus while for $n = 1$ there are just two possibilities, as noted above – namely to collect the single item or not – for $n = 2$ there are 4 possibilities, for $n = 3$ there are 8 possibilities, and so on. The complexity of the decision problem increases exponentially as the amount of information required increases.

The art of modelling situations of this kind is to discover general principles which can be used to systematically construct solutions to problems, however complex they may be. They can also be used to develop intuition about the general properties of the solution. These principles can be derived from familiar economic logic, and corroborated by formal mathematical proof. Three important principles are:

- The more information that is collected, the higher the expected value of the outcome tends to be. This principle generalizes the previous result that a single item of information normally increases the expected value of the outcome.
- There is a trade-off between the expected value of the outcome and the cost of information incurred. This generalizes the previous result that a costly item of information will not be collected unless a compensating benefit can be obtained.
- As the amount of information collected increases, diminishing marginal returns to the collection of information will eventually set in. This principle applies only when several items of information are required. It applies because a rational decision-maker will collect the most valuable items of information first, and the less valuable items later on.

Under these conditions a rational decision-maker optimizes the trade-off between information cost and the quality of decision by collecting information up to the margin where the expected benefit of the next item of information is just outweighed by its cost (Casson, 1995b, Ch. 4). In a few cases a rational decision-maker may opt for one of the extreme strategies described above, but in many cases he will choose an intermediate strategy, collecting some of the information but not all of it.

Consider, for example, the trade-off between sales revenue and marketing cost. A PC supplier can in principle carry out market research on all the design features of a new model that influence demand. The more features he investigates, the more computers he can expect to sell. This is because more of the features will be finely tuned to customer needs. But targeting customers in this way eventually encounters diminishing marginal returns. With a small market research budget, only the most important characteristics of the model will be finely tuned, but as the budget increases, so less important characteristics will become finely tuned as well. These later design changes make a smaller contribution to the growth of demand. Eventually the design changes will become so trivial that the contribution to revenue of a further increase in the marketing budget will be just offset by the additional expense involved. At this point the marketing budget has been optimized by equating marginal revenue (net of production cost) to marginal marketing cost.

5.8   DECISIVENESS: WHY SEQUENTIAL PROCEDURES HAVE OPTION VALUE

When a synthesis of information is required, a subset of information can sometimes turn out to be decisive. Although it may seem at the outset that all of the information is always required, it may turn out that, if only some of the information is collected, then it will become perfectly clear what ought to be done because, whatever the rest of the information turns out to be, it cannot possibly affect the decision. This will only happen if the facts revealed by the subset are of a certain kind. If it always happened this way, then the subset would invariably be sufficient for the decision and the rest of the information would be strictly irrelevant.

Decisiveness emerges because of the logic of rational choice between discrete alternatives. An optimal choice is characterized by a set of inequalities which are necessary and sufficient for a maximum. If each variable appearing in these inequalities is believed to have a finite range, then when some of the variables take extreme values, other variables may have no effect on the inequality relations. Their range of variation is too small to outweigh the differences generated by the extreme values of the other variables. Since they cannot reverse the inequalities, they cannot affect the decision, hence there is no point in collecting information on them.

To take advantage of this decisive property, it is necessary to avoid committing to the collection of all the information at the outset. This rules out the simultaneous collection of all the information. When information is collected simultaneously, it is impossible to use the results of the investigation of a subset to inform the decision as to whether the rest of the information should be collected as well. The initial commitment must be to collect only a subset of the information. The smallest subset of this kind is a single item. A thorough-going implementation of this principle therefore requires that information should be collected one item at a time – in other words, it supports a sequential information-gathering strategy (Radner, 1996).

The logic of decisiveness implies that information on the most variable items be collected first. The wider the variation of one item relative to the others, the more likely it is to establish an inequality so great that the others are unable to reverse it. If all the items required for synthesis are ranked in descending order of their range of variation, then there will be a tendency for investigation to stop at the point of greatest discontinuity, where the decline in range between adjacent items is steepest.

Decisiveness is most significant for decision-making when it is viewed in probabilistic terms. In practice there are few situations in which it can be said that some subsequent observation on a variable will always lie within some range where it cannot affect the decision, but there are many situations in which it can be said that it will probably do so. Although there is a chance that, if the information were gathered, then the decision would be altered, the chance is so remote that it is a risk worth taking. It therefore pays to act as though decisiveness were guaranteed, even though in fact it is no more than a strong probability.

The simplest case involves collecting just two items of information. Instead of collecting both items together, one of the items is selected to be collected first. Normally this is the one with the greatest variation. The results of this investigation are then used to decide whether it is necessary to collect the second item as well.

For example, a PC supplier contemplating the launch of a new model may consider that if the demand looks extremely buoyant then he should proceed with the investment whatever the cost of components turns out to be. This is because he believes that the potential variation in the intensity of demand is very wide, while the potential variation in costs is relatively small. He therefore investigates demand conditions first, with the aid of market research, and only investigates cost conditions if the demand turns out to be fairly small. This is because it is only when demand is fairly small that adverse cost conditions could make the investment uneconomic.

One way of expressing this result is to say that a sequential investigation strategy confers option value. The option value arises from the costs that are saved from avoiding the collection of unnecessary information. This option value extends the range of externalities between different items of information, since it shows that one item of information can determine whether or not another item of information is a necessary component of a synthesis.

An important feature of sequential investigation strategies is that different strategies confer different option values. The strategy that confers the greatest option value is the rational choice. This means that it is possible, using this approach, not only to explain why information-gathering is sequential, but to predict which particular sequence will be chosen. The most important factor conferring option value on a sequential strategy is the speed with which it terminates. The earlier the procedure is expected to stop, the fewer items of information, on average, have to be collected, and therefore the lower the information costs incurred in achieving a given expected value for the outcome. Other factors matter too, of course, but in most cases they are of a second order of importance. Thus a strategy that defers collecting the more expensive items of information until the cheaper ones have been collected will also tend to have a high option value, provided of course that there is a reasonable chance that the cheaper items will reveal that the collection of some of the more expensive ones is unnecessary.

For example, a PC supplier planning to invest in a new model has a choice of two sequential strategies with option value. The first begins by investigating the state of demand for the model, and then proceeds to investigate the state of costs only if a certain level of demand prevails (a relatively low level in the case discussed above). The second reverses this order, and begins by investigating the state of costs first. Only if costs are at a certain level does it investigate demand as well. For instance, if costs are low then the investment may proceed immediately, while if costs are high then investment will proceed only if investigation of demand reveals it to be high. If demand is believed to be highly variable then the first strategy will normally be followed, whereas if cost conditions are thought to be highly variable, then the second will be adopted instead. This implicitly assumes, however, that the costs of investigating demand and the costs of investigating cost conditions are roughly equal. If one of the costs, say the cost of market research, was actually much higher than the other then the option strategy that made the cheaper investigation first would normally be preferred – in this case, the strategy of investigating cost conditions first. Only if demand was enormously more variable than costs would demand conditions be investigated first.

The same principle applies when more than two items of information are involved. As the scope of the synthesis increases, the analysis of the option values becomes more complex, however. An additional principle must be invoked to guide the solution process. This is the principle of backward recursion. The solution process begins by considering all the cases in which only one item of information remains to be collected. It is irrelevant in which sequence the rest of the information was collected. The cases that need to be considered differ only in what the remaining item happens to be. This means that if n items need to be collected, then there will be n different cases in which one item is missing. Recall that, in order to assess whether a further item of information needs to be collected, the question of how this information will be used must be addressed. When this further item of information is the final item of information, the exercise is straightforward since, if this item is collected, then the decision-maker is fully informed about the situation and is therefore able to take the right decision. The solutions can be found for each of these cases using the method described above.

The next step backwards involves considering those cases in which not just one but two items of information still remain to be found. There are $n(n-1)$ different cases of this kind, each of which must be investigated separately. In every case there is now a choice, not only of whether to collect additional information, but of which of the two items to collect first. After one step forward through this remaining part of the sequence, however, the decision-maker finds himself in one of the situations already analysed, where only one item of information remains to be found. The solutions obtained in the first step back can therefore be fed into the solution two steps back, obviating the need for these calculations to be repeated from scratch. Each situation resembles the case discussed above where the decision-maker had to choose between two option strategies which sequenced the collection of information in different ways. For each of the $n(n-1)$ cases the values of the two option strategies must be compared with each other, and with the strategy of collecting no further information at all. This determines the best way of carrying forward the search for information, conditional on the information that is available two steps away from the end of the process.

Considering in turn the case where three items of information still remain to be collected, and then four, and so on, it can be seen that for any finite set of information needing to be synthesized the recursion will eventually bring the problem back to the first stage. By this stage there is just one problem to be solved, because the starting point of total ignorance about the set of information to be gathered is unique. On the other hand, the number of possible ways in which the investigation can evolve from this point onwards is the largest of all, but apart from the initial move, these possibilities have all been explored before in earlier steps of the recursive process. The final step of the solution procedure therefore follows exactly the same format as the others. Because it builds on all the other steps, it solves the problem in its entirety. Its solution determines the full sequence in which information is collected.

Consider, for example, a multinational PC manufacturer deciding whether to source a given component, such as a memory chip, from one overseas location or another. The manufacturer knows at the outset that one location uses labour-intensive methods and the other capital-intensive methods which afford economies of scale. The relative cost of components depends on three factors, each of which can be independently observed: the cost of labour in the first location, the cost of labour in the second location, and the scale of output, as determined by the level of demand. The manufacturer is aware that, if the cost of labour in the first location is low relative to the second, then the first location should be chosen, but if it is high then the second location should be chosen instead, provided that both labour costs in the second location are moderate and demand is high. The PC manufacturer believes initially that labour costs in the second location are likely to be high. Given this belief, the optimal investigation strategy is to observe labour conditions in the first location first. If they are low then production will be committed to the first location right away, and only if they are high will further information be sought. In the latter case demand will be investigated next. If demand turns out to be high, then the second location will be chosen, while if it turns out to be low then labour costs in the second location may be investigated as well to test whether the initial belief is really correct. The firm therefore follows a fairly elaborate procedure of international consultation before arriving at a final decision. Exactly who is consulted depends on how the process evolves in the light of the reports on conditions received at each stage.

5.9   EXPLOITING CORRELATION TO IMPROVE DECISION PROCEDURES

A complication in this analysis stems from the question of correlation between the different factors that impinge on the decision situation. Suppose to begin with that each item of information that impinges on the decision relates to a separate factor in the situation, and that each factor varies independently of the others. Independence means that the probability of any given factor being in any given state is independent of what states the other factors are in. If this independence is recognized by the decision-maker, then he has no need to revise the probability he associates with a given factor being in a given state in the light of what he may have learnt from previous investigations about the states that the other factors are in. In other words, while the decision-maker learns more about the situation as a whole as his investigation proceeds, he never learns more about any given factor than he learns from directly observing that factor himself.

   This situation changes when the factors in the decision situation are correlated with each other. When there is correlation, an observation on any one factor indirectly provides information on others. A rational decision-maker must respond to this situation by conditioning the probability that a given factor is in a given state on the states of all the other factors that he has observed. As he learns more about these other factors, so the subjective probabilities he attaches to the remaining factors will change. In the context of the calculations described above, this means that the probabilities used to assess whether a further item of information should be collected are dependent on the other items already collected. What is more, the decision-maker must anticipate how these subjective probabilities will change according to what information he is planning to collect. Although this complication is a nuisance from an analytical point of view, it can be a powerful aid to efficient decision-making. This is because the strategic exploitation of these correlations can allow the measurement of one factor to obviate the need to make observations of other factors which are highly correlated with it. In other words, correlations generate external economies in observation. An important consequence is that it is generally advantageous to observe factors which are highly correlated with other factors at an early stage of the investigation, because the information so gathered may avoid the need to make other observations later on.

Consider for example a PC supplier planning a model for a global market. Each national market is potentially different from the others. Specific local factors can be discovered only from local investigation. There is, however, one national market which is fairly typical of all, in the sense that demand at this location is highly correlated with demand at other locations. To avoid investigating demand at all locations, the supplier may decide to investigate demand in the typical location and gross the figure up.

5.10 THE ECONOMICS OF MEMORY

The sequential nature of optimal decision-making reflects the externalities that exist between different items of information. Externalities have so far only been considered in the context of a single decision, however. When the same decision-maker is involved in several decisions, additional kinds of externality come into play. An item of information used to make one decision can also be used to make others. This reflects the 'public good' property of information. Every item of information is a public good in the sense that it is not used up when it is exploited. The economic significance of this property of information hinges on the similarity of different decision situations. This similarity arises from the presence of a common factor. Once information has been gathered on this factor, it can be reused in other situations where this factor is at work. In this context it is useful to distinguish between general information, pertaining to a factor that simultaneously affects several situations, and specific information, pertaining to a factor that affects only one.

Because decisions are usually made sequentially, the reuse of information also requires that the factor to which it relates is persistent, in the sense that it tends to remain in the same state. If the factor is transient, and frequently changes state, then information about it will quickly obsolesce. This makes it difficult to reuse the information in subsequent decisions; to guarantee accuracy, the factor must be re-examined every time a new decision is made. It is therefore useful to distinguish not only between general and specific information, but also between persistent and transitory information. Considered as an abstract commodity, therefore, persistent information is a durable good.

The reuse of persistent information raises the question of memory. In principle information needs to be memorized in every sequential operation, including the synthesis of information within a single decision. Few decisions take so long, however, that there is a danger of forgetting what was collected at the outset before the decision is finally made. Where several different decisions are involved, however, there may be a significant lag between one decision and the next. Memory becomes a non-trivial issue in this case, because information must be stored throughout the period that elapses between the decisions.

The cost of memory depends on the kind of technology that is used to supplement the human mind. The existence of memory costs indicates that information is still costly to use even if it has been acquired before. For any given memory bank, including the human mind, memory capacity is finite. Once the store is full, further information can be accommodated only by forgetting something – that is, by deleting it from the store. This situation can be formalized by treating the marginal cost of storage as variable. As the store fills up, so the marginal cost increases until at full capacity the cost becomes infinite. It is important, however, to distinguish between the short-run and the long-run economics of storage. In the long run it may be possible to design and build larger stores – certainly in the case of computers, if not in the case of people – and to replicate stores of given size under constant returns to scale.

Filing and retrieval cost will also tend to vary with the amount of information that is stored. When a larger amount of information is stored, more effort has to go into finding the appropriate file location, and more sorting is required to retrieve it later.

The demand for memory varies according to the kind of information involved. General persistent information is most suitable for memorizing because it applies to a wide range of decisions for a long time to come. Scientific knowledge is a good example of this. Specific persistent information is also useful to memorize, provided the specific situation remains relevant to the decision-maker. The addresses of regular customers is a case in point. Transitory information is generally unsuitable for memorizing, although a record of transitory information that is continually updated may well prove useful in analysing the dynamics of change. Creating an archive of transitory information is one way of improving predictive power. For example, a record of sales over a five-year period may indicate a seasonal pattern and an underlying trend.

Consider for example a PC supplier planning his price and output levels on a regular monthly basis. The overall balance of supply and demand each month depends upon general transient factors. General transient factors affecting demand include not only obvious factors such as macroeconomic fluctuations in supply and demand, but also more subtle factors such as changes in the kind of software that customers wish to run. General transient

Table 5.1   Factors governing market-making in the PC industry

	Transient		Persistent	
	Demand	Supply	Demand	Supply
Specific	Individual's need for new or replacement PC	Wage rates at each component plant	Delivery cost to individual customers' addresses	Transport costs for each component plant
General	Software releases affecting PC memory requirements	Raw material costs affecting all component suppliers	'Lifestyle' determinants of PC demand	General state of computer science

factors affecting supply include the prices of raw materials like silicon and gallium which are used to make components. In targeting individual customers, specific transient factors come into play, such as whether the customer needs to replace their PC. Where individual consignments from particular suppliers are concerned, specific transient factors like the producer's local labour costs are important. Examples of transient factors are given on the left-hand side of Table 5.1.

Provided that the persistent factors remain unchanged, management can be confident that the same procedure for collecting information on the transient factors can be followed each period. The firm therefore remembers the procedure from one period to the next. The nature of the procedure – which observations are made first, for example – depends on the persistent factors in the situation. Persistent factors affecting the PC supplier are shown on the right-hand side of Table 5.1. At any one time the PC supplier memorizes the values of the persistent factors and the optimal procedure associated with them. The transient factors are not memorized, except for use in a research archive devoted to improving forecast accuracy.

5.11   TRADITION VERSUS REINVENTION

It might be asked why a rational decision-maker ever contemplates a sequence of decisions in the first place. Surely the rational decision-maker looks forward to the end of time (in the case of a firm) or the end of his life (in the case of an individual) and attempts to solve for a single fully integrated plan? Such a decision-maker will sequence his future decisions on the basis of when and where he plans to collect various items of information. He will not collect all the items at the outset because he will recognize that it is normally better to defer the collection of items about future states until those states have actually occurred.

A single integrated plan of this kind can be extremely difficult to derive, because the optimization problem is so complex. There are many different possibilities to examine. Fortunately, though, complex problems can sometimes be decomposed into sub-problems, each of which is much simpler to solve. The distinction between the different kinds of information made above provides a key to how this can be done. Given that persistent factors tend to be stable while transient factors do not, each future period can be thought of as bringing new values of the transient factors and repeating the values of the persistent ones. If the objective is to maximize performance on a period-by-period basis, then the solution to the problem is simply to identify the best procedure for dealing with the transient factors and repeat it on a regular basis.

The best procedure depends on what the values of the persistent factors happen to be. If the persistent factors never change, then they can be investigated at the outset and never examined again. But this condition is rarely fulfilled in practice. Persistent factors do change, and this raises a number of related issues.

The first is the frequency with which persistent factors should be monitored. Uncertainty about a factor cannot be eliminated altogether except by observing it every period, but this is uneconomic. At the other extreme the factor can be ignored altogether, on the assumption that it still has the same value as when it was last observed, and the risk of the error accepted. The cost of the error reflects the consequences of applying an inappropriate decision procedure to transitory information. This cost increases as the frequency with which the factor is observed is reduced. A rational decision-maker will trade off the cost of the observation against the cost of error by choosing the appropriate frequency of observation.

The second issue is whether the decision-maker should memorize the optimal procedures associated with every possible persistent state. Every time a persistent factor is seen to change, the decision-maker needs to switch procedures. This raises the question of whether the new procedure should be retrieved from memory or worked out from scratch. Memorizing every procedure that could possibly be required will incur significant costs. On the other hand, never memorizing any procedure means that a new procedure has to be improvised every time new conditions occur.

There are, in fact, two approaches to memorizing procedures rather than just one. The first is to memorize the procedure from the outset, and the second to memorize it only from the time when it is first used. Memorizing from the outset guarantees that the procedure must be derived only once, but runs the risk that what is memorized may never need to be used at all. Memorizing from the first occasion it is used requires the procedure to be improvised once at most. However, if improvisation must be effected under greater pressure of time, then this may prove more costly than deriving the procedure at the outset instead.

The decision-maker therefore faces a trade-off between the cost of improvising the procedure on the one hand, and the cost of memorizing it on the other. As the procedure becomes more complex, both costs become higher, and the importance of the trade-off increases. The key to the trade-off is the frequency with which a decision situation is likely to recur. This is determined by the ergodicity of the persistent factor. If the factor has only a small number of possible states, and transitions between any pair of states are easy to make, then the probability of recurrence of any state is reasonably high. The factor is then said to be highly ergodic. The actual time frame involved depends on how frequently the persistent factor changes. Although this frequency is by definition low where a persistent factor is concerned, there is still scope for variation. A higher frequency of change leads on average to a shorter wait for a recurrence to occur. High frequency therefore combines with high ergodicity to encourage the decision-maker to memorize procedures that are not in current use. Conversely, low frequency combined with low ergodicity encourages improvisation instead.

This result can be refined in a number of ways. In practice most market-making firms face several persistent factors rather than just one as assumed above. Different factors will be monitored with different frequencies according to the probability that they change. Because the number of possible configurations proliferates as the number of factors increases, the probability that any situation recurs diminishes, so memorizing the response becomes less worthwhile. The more factors involved in the situation, therefore, the greater the propensity to improvise.

A further refinement is to distinguish the states of the environment that recur regularly from those that do not. A sophisticated decision-maker will memorize the procedures relating to the most commonly occurring states, and improvise a response to the rest. This means that the organization has a selective memory. Its traditions address the most commonly recurring situations, but leave the decision-maker to improvise in other cases.

These results have important implications for evolutionary theories of the firm (Nelson and Winter, 1982; Cantwell, 1995). Evolutionary theories invoke a principle of memorizing by doing, which implies that a firm will forget a procedure as soon as it stops using it because otherwise the memory costs would be too great. The emphasis on evolution supports this strategy too, for one of the characteristics of an evolutionary trajectory is that past situations almost never recur. It is interesting to note, therefore, that according to this view the firm would actually operate with no conventional memory at all, in the sense of remembering the way things were before. The firm has no traditions on which to draw when circumstances similar to the past are recreated. In business environments where situations do tend to recur, this lack of relevant tradition could prove a serious competitive disadvantage to the firm.

An example of a firm that may have little need for tradition is the PC supplier described above. The PC industry is notable for the fact that even persistent factors are relatively volatile; thus quite small changes in the technology of integrated circuit design can have dramatic effects on operating performance. Remembering how the industry was run today is unlikely to be of much help in addressing problems ten years hence, because past situations are most unlikely to recur.

By contrast, firms in the oil industry face recurrent periods of political instability which can disrupt supplies. Although every case differs in detail from the previous ones, the procedures used in previous crises retain their relevance. Experience of these procedures is thus a significant advantage. This is reflected in the greater role of tradition in the corporate cultures of major oil firms, and the persistence of lifetime career structures in many of them. The value of these traditions may also explain the lower frequency of competitive entry into the oil industry as compared to the PC industry.

5.12   SYMPTOMS AND THE CONTROL OF OBSERVATIONAL ERROR

Observations are not necessarily accurate. What is usually observed is a symptom of a situation, rather than the true situation itself. Provided the risk of error can be estimated, however, allowance for it can be made in the choice of procedure. For example, if a factor in a situation is particularly difficult to observe directly, and several symptoms are available, then they can be combined to provide an overall assessment of the situation. The most useful symptoms are those closely correlated with the true situation, but whose causes of error are independent of each other. The first quality makes even a single observation useful, while the second means that pooling observations quickly reduces the remaining error.

Procedures can allow for error in various ways. If the symptom conflicts quite sharply with the decision-maker's prior beliefs, then he may rationally require a second symptom to corroborate the first before he alters his proposed course of action, whereas if the symptom confirms his beliefs then he may require no corroboration at all. If a mistaken change in strategy could have serious consequences, then he will rationally require more corroboration than if the damage would be slight. This is why a rational organization will provide for unusual results to be checked before a decision is made, based on them.

The difficulties caused by relying on symptoms are more acute in some cases than in others. The greatest difficulties tend to arise when there are many different symptoms of the same thing, but none of them is very reliable. In this case the challenge is to sequence the collection of symptoms in an appropriate way. Should several symptoms be collected on a given factor first, or is one symptom enough? Should one factor be examined in depth before a second factor is considered, or should all factors be examined superficially at the outset? Should investigation of different symptoms proceed simultaneously in order to save time, even though the savings from the exercise of options will be lost as a result?

The use of symptoms to recognize a market opportunity is the basis for the foundation of a market-making firm. The opportunity is associated with a specific configuration of persistent factors which other people have failed to recognize (Casson, 1982). Searching out such opportunities resembles prospecting for treasure, in the sense that the aim is to cover as wide a field of investigation as possible, looking in likely places, but avoiding places which others consider likely too. Since discoveries of new markets occur infrequently, improvisation rather than tradition is usually the basis for the foundation of an innovative firm.

Over time the persistent factors can change, and the subsequent consolidation and growth of the firm depends crucially on periodically updating information on these factors. Diagnostic skills are needed to respond effectively to symptoms of a change, such as an unexpected rise in costs, or a decline in demand as mentioned above. Diagnostic skills are rather different from the prospecting skills required to found a firm. Once a change is recognized, the procedures must be altered. This can cause a problem for a firm whose employees are committed to a particular procedure. Leadership skills may be required to change the culture of the firm. Skills in diagnosis and in cultural change are thus an important source of competitive advantage to the mature market-making firm. They are rather different to the skills required to found the firm, which may explain why many firms replace top management when they reach a certain size.

Consider, for example, a European marketing manager of a US PC supplier who is facing falling sales. At first he suspects a general decline in European demand. He therefore begins by assessing whether his firm's market share has changed or not. It is discovered that market share has fallen, and so alternative explanations, such as poor promotion of the product, have to be considered instead. As the explanations sought become more subtle so the expertise required for diagnosis grows. The problem remains unsolved, and is referred up to global headquarters, who bring wider experience to bear upon the issue. They in turn decide to call in consultants. Finally the consultants discover from a sample survey that customers perceive a problem with product reliability which has not been properly revealed because of the lack of an extended warranty scheme. The problem comes from the way the customers handle the machine. The technological solution is to modify the keyboard design. The organizational solution is to create a database to record incidents reported under the warranty scheme. By interrogating the database, emergent problems revealed by warranty work can be tackled before the reputation of the product is badly damaged.

5.13   INFORMATION AS A BY-PRODUCT

It was demonstrated earlier that decision-making is a two-stage process. The first stage acquires information, and the second determines the action. In practice, however, the distinction is not quite as sharp as this, because the second stage may generate information too. This information emerges as a by-product of the action. The information can then be memorized and used in a subsequent decision. This shows that successive decisions are interdependent. It raises the possibility that decisions could be sequenced in order to maximize the positive externalities derived from the by-product, information.

Actions generate information either from their outcome or from the process of implementation. Implementation sometimes generates information simply because it takes the decision-maker to a specific location where a certain type of information is freely available. The more important case is where the outcome of the action is the source of information. This is because the outcome acts as a symptom of the underlying situation – in other words, it indicates the state of a persistent factor which has not been observed at the outset.

The systematic exploitation of this kind of situation requires pragmatic experimentation. Experimentation is involved because what is learnt about the situation depends, in general, on the action that is performed. Certain actions are more informative than others because they reveal more about the state of the persistent factor. In the short run, therefore, they tend to be risky actions, since if the state is unfavourable the outcome may be very poor. The advantage of the risky action is that it reveals information which is useful in later decisions. Experimentation is thus favoured by decision-makers who take a long-run perspective on a problem.

An alternative to gathering information by experiment is to gather it by observation at the outset instead. This dramatically reduces the risk of an unfortunate outcome. It is in this sense that the experimental approach is also pragmatic – it involves a 'try and see' approach to gathering information, in contrast to the more analytical approach of gathering it before anything else is done.

The strategic implications of the by-product principle depend upon how the information obtained is eventually used. There are two main possibilities. The first is that the information relates directly to the situation in which the decision was taken, and so is fed back into the next decision of the same kind. If the information pertains to a transient factor, then it simply keeps the regular decision-making going in an economical way. If, on the other hand, the information pertains to a persistent factor, then it provides greater depth of understanding of the situation and helps to fine-tune the decision procedure. Repeated feedback of information of this kind can endow the decision-maker with impressive specialist expertise.

For example, the response of customers to a new PC model may provide information about customer preferences which was not revealed by initial market research. If these preferences are stable, then the information can be fed into the design of the model's successor. This suggests that a design strategy which systematically captures information from the launch of the previous model to feed into the design of the current one will enhance long-run profitability.

The other possibility is that the information relates to a situation elsewhere in which the decision-maker is not involved. The exploitation of such information may lead the decision-maker to diversify his activities. For instance, a firm that regularly receives feedback on a factor that impinges on other markets may benefit from entering those markets as well. The firm may cease to specialize in an individual market, and come to specialize instead in a set of markets governed by a common factor on which it gathers information.

Consider a PC manufacturer who needs to update his knowledge of how his major customers use their computing hardware. His enquiries generate information relating to the other components of a PC system too – monitors, printers, scanners, and so on. The manufacturer responds to this by developing a separate retail division which handles a full range of hardware compatible with the PC. While the retail division feeds off information gathered by the manufacturing division, the manufacturing division reciprocates by using information gathered by the retail division to improve the design of its models. The ultimate scope of the firm is therefore governed by its commitment to gathering information on the way its customers use their PC systems.

Certain types of experiment are more conducive to corporate diversification than others. A firm committed to basic research is more likely to generate information relevant to other industries than one committed more to applied research. The more basic the research, therefore, the greater the inducement to diversification. Technological externalities are not the only cause of diversification, however. Firms committed to applied research also encounter information externalities, but they are more likely to relate to customer preferences. Thus a firm with a small number of key industrial customers may specialize in mastering the technology of the user industry and eventually enter into partnership with its customers to exploit spin-off innovations. Again, a consumer product firm whose sales are concentrated on a particular socioeconomic group may generate information about this group which pertains to other products they wish to buy. This may induce it to diversify into other consumer product industries. All of these examples show how some of the major insights of evolutionary theories of the firm can be deduced using the simple calculus of information costs.

5.14   PATH DEPENDENCE

The implementation of a sequential strategy exhibits path dependence of a distinctive kind. The path dependence arises from the way that the sequential strategy conditions the next step in the investigation process on what has been learnt in the previous ones. Whether a given item of information is collected depends upon whether certain other items of information were collected first. In a given situation, a strategy beginning with one item may lead to a particular item being collected later, whereas a strategy beginning with a different item may not. If this particular item is actually crucial, then the outcome of the decision hinges on the item of information with which the procedure begins. This choice sets the investigation off along a distinctive path which, by ignoring crucial information, can lead to the wrong decision.

The important point to note, however, is that, within a framework of rational choice, this wrong decision represents a risk worth taking. The chosen procedure is selected only because the probability of the situation which makes the missing item crucial is very small indeed. The chosen procedure is favoured because it avoids the greater risks to which the alternative procedures are prone. If the risk associated with the missing item were really as great as supposed, then another procedure would indeed be used – for example, a safety-first procedure that collected every conceivable piece of relevant information. The moral is that path-dependence in decision-making is a desirable feature because it is a consequence of the way that a rational decision-maker controls for risk at acceptable information cost. It is certainly not a reflection of irrationality and, on average, does not lead to an inefficient outcome. Indeed, the reason why path-dependence is an important feature of decision-making is that it contributes to efficiency in a significant way.

The path-dependent nature of sequential procedures becomes particularly evident when each step in the procedure generates information as a by-product of resources committed as a result of the previous information obtained. This is illustrated by the way that a firm learns by experience when it invests abroad. In the Scandinavian model of the internationalization process of the firm, the firm invests in a sequence of foreign markets, one at a time (Johanson and Vahlne, 1977). Entry into each market generates information about that market as a by-product of the investment. If certain markets are believed to be similar to one another in certain respects, then information gleaned from one market can be used to inform decisions about whether to enter other markets. By entering markets in an appropriate sequence, the firm can maximize its opportunities for learning. By entering first those markets that are believed to be most similar to other markets, it maximizes the option value of the sequential strategy (Casson, 1995a).

The sequence that is chosen will reflect the initial beliefs of the firm about the characteristics of the markets concerned. Different sets of beliefs will lead to different sequential strategies. Thus different firms with different beliefs will enter different markets first. As a result, they will learn different things. These differences in what they have learnt may well reinforce the initial differences in beliefs. If so, then they will enter different markets at the next stage too, and this will in turn reinforce the differences between them in what they know.

If they continue investing, then eventually their beliefs will tend to converge because, as the entry process continues, they will tend to have entered the same markets (albeit at different stages) and so their market knowledge will tend to become the same. Thus once experiences become sufficiently broad, investment behaviour becomes similar. On the other hand, their early experiences, combined with their initial beliefs, may discourage them from further investment beyond a certain point. In this case their early beliefs may never be corrected, and initial discrepancies will remain. There will be considerable diversity among such firms in the countries in which they have invested, reflecting both the initial differences in their beliefs and the way that these differences have been compounded by the diversity of early experiences.

In general, therefore, inexperienced investors will tend to follow very different paths of expansion, while experienced investors will tend to behave in a similar way. Many investors may never become sufficiently experienced, because their early experiences discourage them from further investment. The path-dependent nature of foreign investment is therefore most significant among firms which have internationalized to only a limited extent.

Consider a recently established PC supplier in the US who has developed a new model with the specific needs of domestic customers in mind. It is unsure how far the model has global appeal. It is aware that the global market is partitioned into different cultural areas. A model that lacks appeal in any given area is most unlikely to have appeal in a more distant cultural area. Within each cultural area there is one market that is relatively small; here model launches require little investment, the reputational consequences of failure are negligible, and so mistakes can be made at little cost. Under these conditions internationalization will consist of a sequence of market-entry investments, in which the results of the first investment are used to decide whether to carry out the second, and so on. The rational sequence reflects the information spillovers determined by the subjective correlations between demand conditions in the various cultural areas.

The PC supplier is unsure about the cultural obstacles to entering each market. In fact, Europe is the nearest cultural area, then Latin America, then South East Asia, and so on. Other things being equal, the firm will invest in markets in ascending order of perceived 'cultural distance'. If its beliefs are correct, then it will invest first in supplying a small European market and, if this is successful, will proceed to supply the rest of Europe, while investing in a small Latin American market too. If this second investment is a success, then it will supply the rest of the Latin American market and invest in a small South East Asian market, and so on. Other things may not be equal, of course. A fuller analysis shows that the sequence will also be affected by the expected profitability of the market, and by country-specific competitive threats such as the danger of pre-emption by a global rival or the threat of imitation by local firms. Even so, the basic pattern of investing in the markets in ascending order of cultural distance will remain.

Path-dependence arises because a different sequence of market entry may well lead to a different set of markets finally being served. If the PC supplier believed wrongly that South-East Asia offered the lowest cultural distance, then he would investigate South-East Asia first. If he found that the cultural distance was too great, then he might decide that it was not worth investing in Europe at all. He would therefore never correct his mistaken belief about Europe. In general, the supplier will achieve the greatest commercial success with the most appropriate initial beliefs, that is the one whose subjective probabilities correspond most closely to the true situation. It is only when beliefs are inappropriate that path-dependence in investment is likely to cause really serious problems.

5.15   DIVISION OF LABOUR AND COMMUNICATION

No account of organizational structure is complete without an analysis of how the classic principle of the division of labour applies to the processing of information. Information is an abstract commodity, and it benefits from a division of labour in the same way that any other commodity does. While the preceding analysis has discussed the case of multiple decisions, based on multiple sources of information, the involvement of more than one individual has only been implicit. In one sense the previous discussion merely lays the foundations on which the theory of the division of labour can build. It is the division of labour which explains why different people co-operate in taking a decision, and why they relate to one another in a particular way (Buckley and Carter, 1996; Carter, 1995).

The need for synthesis in decision-making indicates one obvious advantage of a division of labour in information. Because synthesis is usually more difficult than observation, or at any rate calls for rather different skills, it is advantageous to have different people performing these two tasks. Specialization improves efficiency in both activities.

If a synthesis involves a large number of items of information, then several collectors may supply a single synthesizer. The number of items it is economic to collect will tend to reflect, among other things, the importance of getting the decision right. This suggests that in key decisions the synthesizer is likely to be supported by several people supplying him with information.

This tendency is reinforced by the localization of sources of information. When sources are dispersed, it may be impossible for one person to cover them all. For each source local people on the spot have a comparative advantage in supplying the information. This applies in both the spatial and functional dimensions. It explains why, even when only a few items of information need to be synthesized, they may still be supplied by different people.

The by-product principle becomes relevant at this point. It links the division of labour in the provision of information to the division of labour in the implementation of decisions. Where implementation generates information relevant to the next decision of a similar kind, those who specialize in implementation have a natural advantage in being the source of information too. This leads to a very simple structure of organization in which information feeds back from the same people who carry out instructions. The structure is also amenable to simple, if crude, methods of accountability based on the synthesizer supervising subordinates who both carry out his orders and feed him with information. The synthesizer sits at the apex of a hierarchy in which subordinates gather information to feed up to him, and receive orders in return. In carrying out these orders, they obtain as a by-product the information they need to feed up for the next decision. The synthesizer consults his subordinates according to a sequential procedure in which he obtains information on the most volatile aspects of the environment first. These are aspects about which he is most uncertain and whose variation has the greatest impact on the short-run profits of the firm. Under this arrangement the synthesizer clearly has more power than his subordinates, but there are inequalities of power between the subordinates too. This is because those who are consulted first may supply decisive information which terminates the consultation process before others have been consulted. Subordinates who handle the more volatile transient factors enjoy more power than others, because they always have an opportunity to give their views, while others do not (Casson, 1994).

Consider again the PC supplier discussed in the second example of Section 5.8, who each month follows a procedure of synthesizing transient information on supply and demand. He now implements a division of labour by allocating responsibility for marketing to one manager and responsibility for procurement to another. The marketing manager obtains information on demand as a by-product of selling last month's production. Similarly, the procurement manager obtains information on supply as a result of taking delivery of last month's components. The PC supplier combines this transient information to formulate explicit instructions which the managers carry out. The cycle then repeats itself.

When demand is more volatile than supply, then the marketing manager is likely to be consulted first. The procurement manager is consulted later only if the marketing manager's report is not decisive. This gives the marketing manager more power and creates a marketing-led firm. Conversely, if supply is more volatile than demand then the procurement manager is likely to be consulted first. This confers greater power on the procurement manager and creates a procurement-led firm.

Synthesis is not the only special skill that promotes a hierarchical type of organization. Diagnosis of certain types of symptom also requires special skills. Some diagnostic skills are very scarce indeed. Some are intuitive, and are inherited rather than acquired, but most are the product of lengthy training. Most organizations therefore involve a hierarchy of expertise. At the bottom of the hierarchy is the ordinary manager, who fulfils the role of the local general practitioner so far as diagnosis is concerned. At head office is a team of functional specialists to whom particular kinds of problem are referred. At the top of the hierarchy is the generalist who handles problems that have never been encountered by anyone else in the organization before. He is supported by the specialists and intervenes when they cannot agree. Because the senior people diagnose problems rather than take decisions, relationships between adjacent levels in the hierarchy are based more on professional respect than on authority. The placement of personnel within the hierarchy is based first and foremost on perceived competence, underpinned by experience, qualifications and track record. The greater the complexity of diagnostic problems, the more necessary it is for the organization to adopt a meritocratic form of this kind.

Consider a PC supplier who has established a help-line for important corporate customers with operational problems. The routine management of this line is the responsibility of the product support division. Some problems are too difficult for the support staff to resolve. They are referred to the specialists in the design team, who work closely with top management in developing new models. Because they designed the product, the design team normally understand the problems better. If the design team cannot solve a problem, then the matter is referred to the chief executive, who decides how the customer is to be handled – whether the firm will continue to accept responsibility for the problem, whether it will offer a rebate, or perhaps accelerate the development of another model which will overcome the problem.

5.16   COMMUNICATION COSTS AND DECENTRALIZATION

Communication costs are a major impediment to the division of labour in information processing. Communication costs are of two main kinds. The first kind is incurred in encoding and decoding messages, and the second in transmitting them.

Difficulties in encoding and decoding messages reflect both the inherent tacitness of the information and the cultural differences between those who send and receive messages. In the context of this chapter tacitness is simply one of several causes of high communication cost. It is mainly a characteristic of the content of the message: the nature of the subject to which it refers and the degree of confidence that it seeks to convey. For example, it is notoriously difficult for people to encode their own feelings in explicit grammatical sentences.

Cultural differences mean that a message may be encoded and decoded using different basic assumptions. Ambiguous encoding and inappropriate decoding can lead not only to factual misunderstanding, but also to unintended offence. In the short run a rational response to cultural differences is to restrict communication to a few important issues which can be articulated explicitly. The long-run response is to promote informal social contact, unrelated to immediate decisions, so that attitudes can be better understood and possibly aligned more closely. This investment will be repaid by future savings in communication costs.

The second kind of communication cost is concerned with the transmission of the message once it has been encoded. This cost is a function of the medium – fax, phone, electronic mail, face-to-face and so on – which is chosen in the light of the need for speed, clarity, confidentiality, and so on. It is also a function of the distance involved, though this is of limited importance today.

Communication costs encourage decision-makers to be very selective about whom they consult. In many organizations communication costs exceed observation costs because the by-product principle makes observation almost free. The relatively high cost of long-distance communication – especially face-to-face communication – reinforces this result in MNEs. This suggests that a major factor governing organizational structure is a simple trade-off between the advantages of functional specialization in effecting a broad-based synthesis of information and the costs of communication which this involves.

This trade-off has important implications for the degree of decentralization within a firm. If certain kinds of information are almost always decisive, then there is little need for regular consultation. Those who have access to the decisive information may as well take responsibility for the decision themselves. If a firm faces a single major source of volatility each period, for example, then the person who monitors this source may as well control the firm. This leads to an autocratic style of management. Top management takes decisions without consulting other people, and other managers are relegated to a passive role.

This pattern of volatility is characteristic of local markets rather than global ones. Global markets generally have multiple sources of volatility generated by shocks arising in different parts of the world. This puts a premium on a broad-based synthesis of information. The only justification for autocratic management under these conditions is that costs of communication are so high that consultation is impossible. Under these circumstances the decision-maker simply formulates his plans using an aggregated global view and accepts that local errors will be made.

If, on the other hand, communication costs are very low then there is no obstacle to synthesizing all the information required before a decision is taken. This leads to a highly consultative style of management. Low communication costs generally reflect cultural homogeneity, lack of urgency and an absence of tacit information. They may also support a flat collegial structure with wide participation in decision-making, though this is possible only if there is widespread capacity for synthesis among members of the management team.

In practice few organizations correspond to either of these idealized types. This is because communication costs are not uniformly high or low. There is often a difference between the costs of communicating information obtained centrally by head office and the costs of communicating information obtained locally around the periphery. When the costs of communicating information differ according to the source, it is advantageous for the synthesizer to provide the more costly information for himself, since this makes the greatest contribution to controlling communication costs. Thus if local information is relatively explicit, and so easy to communicate, then it is advantageous to effect a synthesis centrally. The tacit information is supplied directly by top management. They combine their tacit information with the explicit information they receive from local managers and encode their decision in explicit instructions. This renders all communication explicit and so reduces communication costs.

In the opposite case, local information is tacit and central information is explicit. It then becomes advantageous to decentralize decision-making to the local level. The problem is to harmonize local decisions with each other. For a start, the head office must publish the information it has gathered, so that all local managers have access to it. Second, each local manager must be prescribed an appropriate decision rule. This rule tells him how to synthesize his own information with the information received from head office. The rules are designed by head office so that, when they are implemented under any given set of conditions, the local decisions are compatible with each other. Sometimes compatibility is achieved by imposing uniform procedures through standardized conventions, but in many cases compatibility depends on each locality employing its own distinctive rule. Using this principle, global strategy and local responsiveness can be reconciled under conditions of tacit local information (Bartlett and Ghoshal, 1990).

Table 5.2   Influence of communication costs on organizational structure

Communication costs of central factors	Communication costs of peripheral factors	
	Low	High
Low	Full consultation	Decentralization
High	Consultative hierarchy	Autocratic hierarchy

The various organizational structures are summarized in Table 5.2. This table does not exhaust all the possibilities by any means. For example, it is possible to draw a further distinction between the strategic and tactical uses of information, and evaluate strategies of partial decentralization within which head office sets a strategic framework in which local tactical decisions can be taken. This is appropriate when both the centre and the periphery are sources of both explicit and tacit information. The centre combines its own tacit information with reports of explicit information it receives from the periphery, and encodes these in a strategic plan formulated at a highly aggregated level. This plan is then published, and its contents are synthesized with local tacit information to formulate local tactics. The formulation employs procedures designed to harmonize the local plans. This process of harmonization may be strengthened by requiring local plans to be vetted at head office before they are finally implemented.

Consider for example a PC supplier launching a regular sequence of new models. The technological possibilities constitute tacit information held by the design team at headquarters. The capabilities of a given design, once a prototype is available, constitute explicit information, since an operating manual can be drafted and other people allowed to try out the prototype for themselves. The design team can therefore communicate with local management by supplying them with a prototype which they can use. Customer requirements constitute tacit information held by local managers in each country. Local managers also hold explicit information, such as sales of existing models, which is easily passed up to head office.

Given these constraints, the PC head office will centralize design but decentralize marketing in the following way. The design team incorporates its tacit technical information in a number of alternative prototypes for the new model. Local managers then compare the performance of the prototypes, taking account of their customers' working practices, and perhaps even allowing loyal customers to use the machines themselves. Information on customer response is fed back to the design team in the explicit form of a ranking of the different prototypes, and requests for particular features to be added to the preferred design. Finally, head office aggregates this explicit information and selects one prototype for development.

5.17   NEW INFORMATION TECHNOLOGY

No discussion of information costs would be complete without some reference to the role of new information technology (IT). The biggest impact on the organization of the MNE has come from reductions in communication and memory costs. Until recently, reductions in processing costs were relevant mainly to scientific computing. Indeed, even now their relevance to business stems mainly from faster filing and retrieval of records rather than from faster calculations. The reduction in communication and memory costs has stimulated investment in relational databases which store large amounts of highly specific information and are widely accessible to members of the organization (Casson and Wadeson, 1996). The storage of information on individual households, hotel rooms, airline flights, and so on, has had a major impact on market-making firms in the service sector – for example, the development of computerized reservation systems for travel and tourism, and the widespread use of computerized bank account and credit ratings in the financial sector.

An important feature of new IT is that it favours explicit over tacit information. It therefore encourages the conversion of qualitative information to a quantitative form. It favours the sharing of this quantitative information, because its cost of communication is so low. Information on past transactions can be stored as an archive for future research. The marketing department of the firm can use this archive to target mail-shots, to prioritize customers making telephone enquiries, to optimize the location of retail outlets, and so on. Entrepreneurial employees can use the database for researching new products. This stimulates the diversification of the firm along particular lines. By exploiting the database as a public good within the firm, the firm is driven into making markets in the areas which it covers.

Computers can implement sophisticated decision procedures driven by expert systems. These procedures may be too difficult for ordinary managers to learn. Even if they could learn them, they would probably be too slow in executing them. Where time is of the essence (as in financial speculation, for example), expert systems have much to recommend them. Implementation of an expert system shifts power from ordinary managers to those who design the system. Where the designers rely on tacit information, they will be centrally located so that the chief executive can consult them face-to-face. Ordinary managers therefore experience a shift of power. They surrender power to the systems analysts, who configure the computer system, but are able to share access to a vast amount of data along with everyone else in the organization. The extent of the 'empowerment' effected by this access depends on how entrepreneurial and computer-literate the individual manager is.

How far the systems analysts are forced to share their power depends on whether other sources of tacit information are also important. For example, tacit information on the credit standing of a major borrower is very important to a bank. While the application of tacit information to the design of expert systems will be centralized, an efficient bank will continue to give discretion to local managers to put their tacit information on borrowers to proper use. This illustrates the general point that, while computerization favours centralization of systems expertise, decentralization remains important when there is tacit information within the organization that cannot be included in the computerized calculations.

5.18   CONCLUSION

This chapter began by distinguishing three different types of information cost. It was argued that in explaining the behaviour of the firm too much emphasis has previously been placed on Type I costs – that is opportunism-related transaction costs. Type I costs are relevant mainly to explaining the boundaries of the firm. They are much less useful in explaining how the firm is organized – in other words, how the various activities within its boundaries are co-ordinated. Type II costs and Type III information costs are much more relevant for this purpose. These are the costs of handling information which is believed to be honest. The information may not be entirely accurate because of measurement error, and errors may be aggravated by the incompetence of those who are responsible for making observations. Nevertheless, the quality of the information will not be improved significantly by altering incentives, because those involved have no particular reason to lie.

The organizational structure of the firm is determined by the need to co-ordinate the firm's activities at minimum information cost. This means that the total cost of collecting, communicating, storing and processing Type II and Type III information must be kept to a minimum. The main activities that need co-ordinating are marketing, procurement, production and R&D. The relative importance of these activities varies according to the nature of the firm's environment. The more volatile the factors impinging on a particular activity, the greater the importance of collecting and processing information about the factors impinging on that activity. Where there is an internal division of labour in information processing, the managers responsible for processing the information in the areas of greatest volatility acquire considerable power.

The discussion has focused on MMMs, for which the principal source of volatility is in marketing, and to a lesser extent in procurement. Volatility in production has been discussed only to a limited extent. The chapter has set out a number of general principles related to the efficient processing of information, and illustrated them with reference to a multinational PC supplier. It has been shown that optimal decision-making procedures are sequential, with information on the most volatile factors normally being collected first. Only if this information is not decisive is information on other factors collected as well. This priority in consultation is the basis of the power possessed by those who collect information on the principal sources of volatility.

The entire internationalization strategy of the firm can be thought of as one big decision which could, in principle, be taken at the outset. The sequential principle implies that information on foreign markets should be collected in a number of separate steps, however. Furthermore, the by-product principle implies that much of this information can be fed into the decision process after initial foreign investments have been made. As a result, the entire decision process becomes stretched out in time. The initial commitment is merely to enter markets in a sequence which is contingent on the outcomes of previous investments. This makes the firm's expansion path-dependent, but it is not path-dependent in an irrational sense, because the path-dependence is, in fact, a crucial feature of a rational strategy.

These and other results are all deduced from a simple economic theory of information costs in which decision-makers trade off the costs of information against the expected costs of mistaken decisions. While this theory of information costs is certainly not the only way of analysing organizational behaviour, the results reported above show that it is a highly productive one where IB studies are concerned.

REFERENCES

Bartlett, C. and S. Ghoshal (1990) *Managing across Borders: The Transnational Solution*, London: Routledge

Buckley, P.J. and M.J. Carter (1996) 'The economics of business process design: motivation, information and coordination within the firm', *International Journal of the Economics of Business*, **3**(1), 5–24

Buckley, P.J. and M.C. Casson (1976) *The Future of the Multinational Enterprise*, London: Macmillan

Cantwell, J.A. (1995) 'Multinational corporations and innovatory activities: towards a new evolutionary approach', in J. Molero (ed.), *Technological Innovation, Multinational Corporations and New International Competitiveness*, Chur: Harwood Academic Publishers, 21–57

Carter, M.J. (1995) 'Information and the division of labour: implications for the firm's choice of organization', *Economic Journal*, **105**, 385–97

Casson, M.C. (1982) *The Entrepreneur: An Economic Theory*, Oxford: Martin Robertson, reprinted, Aldershot: Gregg Revivals, 1991

Casson, M.C. (1994) 'Why are firms hierarchical?', *International Journal of the Economics of Business*, **1**, 47–76

Casson, M.C. (1995a) 'Internationalisation of the firm as a learning process: a model of geographical and industrial diversification', *Revue d'Economie Industrielle*, special issue, 109–34, rev. version in Casson (1995b), Ch. 5

Casson, M.C. (1995b) *The Organization of International Business*, Aldershot: Edward Elgar

Casson, M.C. (1996) 'Comparative organisation of large and small firms', *Small Business Economics*, **8**, 1–17, rev. version in Casson (1995b), Ch. 6

Casson, M.C. (1997) *Information and Organisation: A New Perspective on the Theory of the Firm*, Oxford: Clarendon Press

Casson, M.C. (2000) *Enterprise and Leadership: Studies on Firms, Markets and Networks*, Cheltenham: Edward Elgar

Casson, M.C. and N. Wadeson (1996) 'Information strategies and the theory of the firm', *University of Reading Discussion Papers in Economics*, No.334, forthcoming in *International Journal of the Economics of Business*

Chesnais, F. (1988) 'Technical cooperation agreements between firms', *STI Review*, **4**, Paris: OECD, 51–119

Coase, R.H. (1937) 'The nature of the firm', *Economica* (New Series), **4**, 386–405

de Monthoux, P.G. (1993) *The Moral Philosophy of Management: From Quesnay to Keynes*, Armonk, New York: M.E. Sharpe

Dunning, J.H. (1977) 'Trade, location of economic activity and the multinational enterprise: the search for an eclectic approach', in B. Ohlin, P.O. Hesselborn and P.M. Wijkman (eds), *The International Allocation of Economic Activity*, London: Macmillan, 395–418

Dunning, J.H. (1981) *International Production and the Multinational Enterprise*, London: Allen & Unwin

Egelhoff, W. (1988) *Organizing the Multinational Enterprise*, Cambridge, MA: Ballinger

Hayek, F.A. von (1937) 'Economics and knowledge', *Economica* (New Series), **4**, 33–54, repr. in F.A. von Hayek, *Individualism and Economic Order*, London: Routledge and Kegan Paul, 1959, 33–56

Hennart, J.-F. (1986) 'What is internalization?', *Weltwirtschaftliches Archiv*, **122**, 791–804

Johanson, J. and J.-E. Vahlne (1977) 'The internationalisation process of the firm – a model of knowledge development and increasing foreign market commitments', *Journal of International Business Studies*, **8**(1), 23–32

Kay, N.M. (1993) 'Markets, false hierarchies and the role of asset specificity', in Christopher Pitelis (ed.), *Transaction Costs, Markets and Hierarchies*, Oxford: Blackwell, 242–61

Marschak, J. and R. Radner (1972) *The Economic Theory of Teams*, New Haven, CT: Yale University Press

Mitchell, W., R. Morck, J. Miles Shaver and B. Yeung (1996) 'Causality between international expansion and investment in intangibles, with implications for financial performance and firm survival', *mimeo*

Nelson, R.R. and S.G. Winter (1982) *An Evolutionary Theory of Economic Change*, Cambridge, MA: Belknap Press of Harvard University Press

North, D.C. (1991) 'Institutions, transaction costs and the rise of merchant empires', in James D. Tracy (ed.), *The Political Economy of Merchant Empires*, Cambridge: Cambridge University Press, 22–40

Porter, M.E. (1980) *Competitive Advantage*, New York: Free Press

Radner, R. (1996) 'Bounded rationality, indeterminacy and the theory of the firm', *Economic Journal*, **106**, 1360–73

Richardson, G.B. (1960) *Information and Investment*, Oxford: Oxford University Press

Rugman, A.M. and J.R. D'Cruz (1996) 'Strategies of multinational enterprises and governments: the theory of the flagship firm', in G. Boyd and A.M. Rugman (eds), *Euro-Pacific Investment and Trade: Strategies and Structural Interdependencies*, Aldershot: Edward Elgar

Schumpeter, J.A. (1934) *The Theory of Economic Development* (trans. R. Opie), Cambridge, MA: Harvard University Press

Stigler, G.J. (1961) 'The economics of information', *Journal of Political Economy*, **69**, 213–25

Williamson, O.E. (1975) *Markets and Hierarchies: Analysis and Anti-Trust Implications*, New York: Free Press

Williamson, O.E. (1985) *The Economic Institutions of Capitalism*, New York: Free Press

6. International joint ventures

with Peter J. Buckley

6.1 INTRODUCTION

In a global environment, participation in an international joint venture (IJV) is an important strategic option (Beamish and Banks, 1987). Explicit assumptions are particularly crucial when studying IJVs. No IJV, however configured, performs perfectly, and so to understand why an IJV is chosen it is necessary to understand the shortcomings of the alternatives. Moreover, IJVs are configured in many different ways, and different configurations are associated with different kinds of behaviour (Tallman, 1992).

When the firm's objective is profit-maximization, the choice of any strategy, such as an IJV, is driven by the structure of revenues and costs. This structure is determined by the firm's environment. By identifying the key characteristics of this environment, the firm's behaviour can be modelled in a very parsimonious way. The predictions of the model emerge jointly from the profit-maximization hypothesis and the restrictions imposed by the modeller on the structure of revenues and costs. Predictive failure of the model is addressed by re-examining these restrictions and not by discarding the maximization principle which is at the core of the theory (Buckley and Casson, 1988).

The variables entering into the theory do not have to be of a strictly economic nature. The criterion for inclusion is that they can be analysed from a rational action point of view. The modelling of IJVs illustrates this very well. A wide range of factors impact upon IJVs (Geringer and Hebert, 1989): not just traditional economic factors, such as market size, but technological, legal, cultural and psychological factors too. Variables of all these kinds appear in the model developed below.

Economic models permit judgements about efficiency to be made. While IJVs may be commended on social and political grounds, they could be criticized as being inefficient for, say, large firms that are leaders in their industries. An economic model can address this issue head-on. Since no firm, however large, can be completely self-sufficient, it is readily shown that participation in IJVs is definitely efficient, provided that the conditions are right. The main objective of this chapter is to set out these conditions in full. It is because these conditions are now more widely satisfied than they were in the past that IJVs have become such an important aspect of international business.

6.2   THE TYPOLOGY OF IJVS

The role of IJVs in the global economy has already been discussed in Chapter 1. This discussion emphasized that IJVs can take many different forms. The strategic significance of IJVs for a firm entering a foreign market was discussed in Chapter 2. The importance of modelling IJVs in a formal way was emphasized at this stage. Formal modelling puts the advantages and disadvantages of IJVs, relative to other modes of market entry, into a clearer light.

Because so many different forms of IJVs are possible, and because they have so many different roles, it is important to fix ideas before pursuing the analysis of IJVs in further depth. This chapter focuses on the case of an equity-based joint venture between two private firms. The firms each hold 50 per cent of the equity in the IJV. The rationale of the IJV, it is assumed, is to combine complementary resources. These resources comprise firm-specific knowledge, and the combination is effected by each firm sharing its knowledge with the other. Firms do not normally share all their knowledge through an IJV, but only a subset of it, and this is reflected in the model below.

The assumptions made about the revenues and costs associated with an IJV are rather different from those made in the earlier chapters. Because the analysis focuses on a special type of IJV, it is appropriate to specify revenues and costs with greater care. The assumptions are therefore more subtle than those that were made before. The assumptions become even more sophisticated in Chapter 7.

The knowledge provided by a firm may relate to technology, or to market conditions, or both. The geographical scope with which technology is exploited is normally wider than that of marketing expertise, which tends to be of a more localized nature. This has important implications for the structure of an IJV, and for the degree of symmetry between the partner firms (Harrigan, 1988). It means that the combination of two technologies through R&D collaboration is normally geared from the outset to global market exploitation. The partner firms are in a symmetric situation in the sense that both of the assets that they contribute to the IJV are of global application.

By contrast, the combination of a new technology with marketing expertise usually involves market access of a more local nature. There is an asymmetry between the globally-oriented asset contributed by the high-technology firm and the locally-oriented asset contributed by its partner. In the course of globalizing the exploitation of its technology, the high-technology firm may make a series of market-access alliances with firms in different localities. This gives the high-technology firm more experience of joint ventures and may also allow it to play off one partner against another later on.

A final possibility is that each of the firms contributes marketing expertise in a different locality. This restores the symmetry of the first case, but does not restore the global dimension unless the partners' skills, when combined, span the whole of the global marketplace. The principal motive for such collaboration is the co-ordination of prices in different geographical segments of the world market. Such collusion is potentially significant when the product is easily traded, and there are barriers to entry or over-capacity in the industry (for example, the steel industry).

These possibilities are summarized in the first two rows and columns of Table 6.1, and are illustrated schematically in Figure 6.1. The two firms are indexed 1 and 2, with firm 1 based in country A and firm 2 in country B. The figure employs the conventions introduced in Buckley and Casson (1988), refined in Casson (1995) and extended in Casson (1997). Two physical activities are identified – production, represented by a square, and distribution, represented by a diamond. Physical activities are linked by product flow, which is indicated by a thick black line; the direction of flow is shown by an arrow. Two knowledge-based activities are distinguished – R&D, indicated by a triangle, and marketing, indicated by a circle. R&D generates techno-

Table 6.1 Typology of IJVs according to the kind of knowledge shared

	Firm 2		
Firm 1	Technology	Marketing expertise	Both
Technology	1. R&D collaboration	2. Market access by firm 1 to country B	7. R&D collaboration with access to market B (Firm 2 'buys back')
Marketing expertise	3. Market access by firm 2 to country A	4. Collusion in markets of A and B	9. Firm 2 supplies technology for use in both markets (Firm 2 'buys back')
Both	6. R&D collaboration with access to market A (Firm 1 'buys back')	8. Firm 1 supplies technology for use in both markets (Firm 1 'buys back')	5. R&D collaboration with access to both markets (Both firms 'buy back')

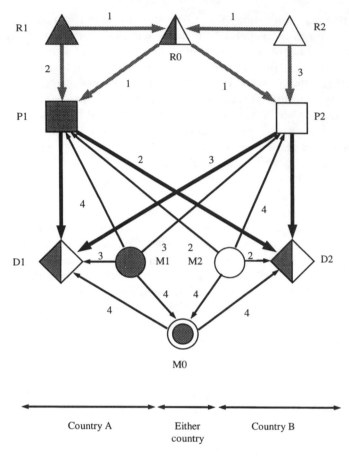

*Figure 6.1   Schematic illustration of four IJV configurations generated by
the sharing of technology and marketing expertise contributed
by two firms*

logical know-how which is exploited in production. Marketing is also a
source of know-how, but in the context of this model, it is mainly a co-
ordinating activity. Marketing acts as an information hub, co-ordinating
distribution with production, and distribution in one country with distribution
in another. Thus, in the figure technological know-how flows from R&D to
production, while co-ordinating information flows from marketing to both
production and distribution. Flows of technological know-how are represented by a thick grey line, while flows of co-ordinating information are
represented by a thin black line. In practice, of course, R&D and marketing
are linked by flows of information as well, but these flows are not directly

relevant to the analysis in this chapter and in the interests of simplicity they are omitted from the figure.

Ownership of an activity by firm 1 is indicated by shading in grey, while ownership by firm 2 is indicated by an unshaded area. Jointly-owned facilities are partly shaded and partly not. The IJV facilities are the laboratory R0 and the marketing headquarters M0. These can be based in either A or B, or in a third country C, as circumstances warrant.

Table 6.1 identifies nine types of IJV configuration altogether. Four of them, shown in the top-left-hand block of the table, combine one type of knowledge from each firm, while the other five involve at least one of the firms contributing both types of knowledge. The four simple types are distinguished by the numerical labelling of the linkages in Figure 6.1. Pure research collaboration (type 1) is represented by the links from the partners' own laboratories R1 and R2 to the IJV laboratory R0, and the flow of new technology to the partners' production plants P1 and P2. Market access by firm 1 to country B (type 2) is represented by the flow of exports from the production plant P1 to the IJV distribution facility D2. Technology from laboratory R1 is embodied in the product, and marketing expertise from M2 is used to co-ordinate the export flow. Conversely, market access by firm 2 to country A (type 3) is represented by the flow of exports from the plant P2 to the distribution facility D1. This combines technology from the laboratory R2 with marketing expertise from M1. Finally, collusion in the distribution of the products (type 4) is represented by the synthesis of marketing expertise from M1 and M2 effected by the jointly-owned facility M0, which co-ordinates the jointly-owned distribution facilities D1 and D2.

The simplest case to analyse, and the one which has therefore attracted most attention from economists, is pure R&D collaboration (type 1) (Veugelers and Kesteloot, 1994). The practical difficulty with this case is that when the results of R&D are shared, competition between products exploiting the same technology can dissipate partners' rents. This encourages collusion in the marketing of the final product, and such collusion is likely to be most effective if the partners share their marketing expertise as well. This combination of R&D collaboration (type 1) and shared marketing expertise (type 4) generates a type 5 IJV. Because of its practical significance, this case forms the main focus of this chapter. Other cases are possible too, however. Studying the third row and third column of Table 6.1 reveals cases where both firms contribute technology but only one contributes marketing expertise (types 6 and 7). Such cases can arise where a new technology controlled by one firm has to be adapted to local production conditions and local customer requirements in an idiosyncratic market controlled by another firm. Alternatively, both firms may contribute marketing expertise but only one of them may contribute technology (types 8 and 9). This can occur where a new technology generates a new product that requires a distinctive approach to retailing, which is familiar to the innovating firm, but where a knowledge of the local customer base is possessed only by the partner firm.

So far nothing has been said about joint ownership of production. This issue is highly relevant to globalization. It is well known that many new products are nowadays developed with global markets in mind. The lower the transport costs and tariffs, the greater the opportunity for exploiting economies of scale in production. If the existing plants of the partner firms exhibit economies of scope – for example, they have flexible equipment with unused capacity – then it may be possible to achieve economies of scale without investing in a production facility dedicated to the new product. However, even if such plants exist, they may not be in an ideal location, given the specific input requirements of the product and the geographical distribution of its demand. If a new dedicated facility is indeed required, then it is natural that it should be jointly owned, particularly in a type 5 IJV where each firm is contributing both technology and marketing expertise. In fact, globalization affords a particular stimulus to joint ventures of type 5: the development of a product with global appeal usually requires a synthesis of technical expertise, while the realization of sales potential requires a synthesis of marketing expertise as well. The greater the fixed costs of R&D, and the economies of scale in production, the more important the marketing synthesis in achieving the critical level of global sales becomes.

A joint-owned production facility P0 is illustrated in Figure 6.2. While the wholly-owned facilities P1 and P2 continue to be used for other products, the product developed and marketed by the IJV is now produced in P0. It is assumed that production is based in a country which has ready access for its exports (through free trade and low transport costs) to the major centres of global demand. To preserve the symmetry of the configuration, this location is assumed to be a third country C.

The figure is used to illustrate the types 5–9 which appear in the third row and third column of Table 6.1. The only symmetric type is number 5, in which both firms combine their technologies in the research laboratory R0 and co-ordinate their distribution using the marketing headquarters M0. A useful feature of this configuration is that each of the firms 'buys back' some of the output to which it has contributed a technological input. This gives each firm a strong incentive to ensure that its input is of high quality. It also gives it a strong incentive to ensure that the production facility P0 is operated in an efficient way. Buy-back from a joint facility occurs with types 6–9 as well (as Table 6.1 makes clear), but the incentives are not so strong, because only one of the firms is involved.

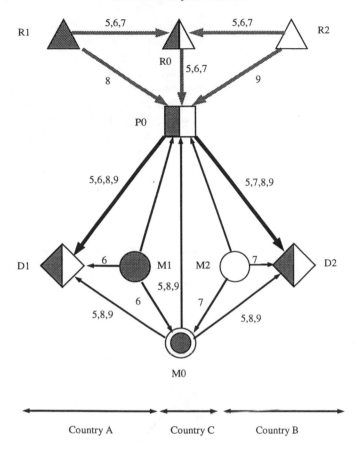

R1   5,6,7   R0   5,6,7   R2

8   5,6,7   9

P0

5,6,8,9   5,7,8,9

D1   6   M1   M2   7   D2

5,8,9

6   7

5,8,9   5,8,9

M0

Country A   Country C   Country B

Figure 6.2   *Schematic illustration of IJV configurations 5–9 based on a single shared production facility*

6.3   THE STRATEGY SET

Not only are there many different configurations of IJV, but there are many contractual alternatives to each particular configuration. It is impossible to discuss IJV strategy rigorously unless both the particular IJV configuration and the alternatives to it are clearly specified. The alternatives considered here are those suggested by internalization theory (Buckley and Casson, 1976): namely, a merger and a licensing agreement. All three of these strategic options involve combining both the technology and the marketing expertise of the two firms, but they combine them in different ways.

All three options require the consent of both firms. If no consent is achieved then no collaboration occurs (this is the null option, strategy 0). To simplify the analysis it is assumed that firm 1 takes the initiative in promoting inter-firm collaboration and that firm 2 plays an entirely passive role. The consequences of relaxing this assumption are considered later. It is firm 1 which evaluates the profits from the merger, IJV and licensing strategies and compares them with each other. Firm 2 agrees to any proposed arrangement provided that the terms of the arrangement leave it no worse off than before (that is than under the null strategy). Under these conditions the private gains to firm 1 coincide with the overall gains from each strategy, and in economic terms firm 1's decision is Pareto-efficient even though to an outsider the distribution of rewards may seem unfair.

The IJV option is presented in Figure 6.3; this corresponds to the type 5 linkages indicated in the previous figure.

A merger could in principle be effected either by firm 1 acquiring firm 2, or by firm 2 acquiring firm 1, or by a third firm acquiring them both. It is

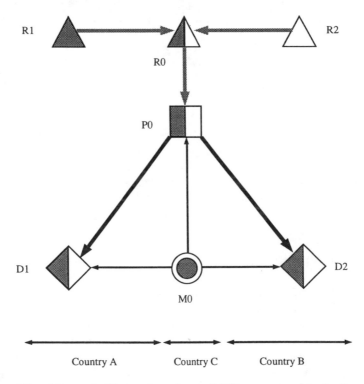

Figure 6.3   Schematic illustration of type 5 IJV as assumed in the formal model

assumed that because firm 1 takes the initiative, it is firm 1 that acquires firm 2. Note, however, that even though firm 1 may be better at spotting opportunities, firm 2 may be better at managing a large organization, and it might, in fact, be more profitable for firm 1 to arrange a reverse takeover instead. Likewise with licensing: it is possible for firm 1 to license in firm 2's technology (and the associated marketing expertise) or for firm 1 to license its own technology out to firm 2. It is assumed that firm 1 licenses in firm 2's technology, so that it retains its full independence, as in the case of acquisition. If, however, firm 1's technology was much easier to value than firm 2's, then it might be easier for it to license out its own technology instead. This is another complication which will not be considered here.

It is assumed that firm 1 extracts its rewards from collaboration through the terms on which its deals with firm 2 are made, and not through the proportion of equity which it holds. If the equity stake were the sole consideration, then acquisition of firm 2 would always be more profitable than a joint venture, which in turn would be more profitable than licensing, which is clearly

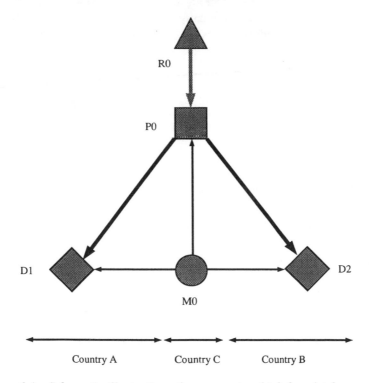

*Figure 6.4   Schematic illustration of a merger in which firm 1 takes over
firm 2 and rationalizes R&D, as assumed in the formal model*

absurd. In the context of an acquisition it is the price at which firm 2's equity is valued which is crucial; in the case of an IJV it is the management fees that the IJV must pay to firm 1, while in the case of licensing it is the royalty rate offered to firm 2.

The configuration of the merger is illustrated in Figure 6.4. The shading throughout indicates that firm 1 has acquired all the facilities previously owned by firm 2. R&D has been rationalized: the laboratories R1 and R2 have been eliminated and all research concentrated on R0. Such rationalization is not an inevitable consequence of merger, but it is undoubtedly one of the advantages of merger that it is easier to do. Marketing has also been rationalized; as with the IJV, the local marketing activities M1 and M2 have been eliminated in favour of global marketing through M0.

The same conventions are used in Figure 6.5 to illustrate the licensing option. Licensing does not afford the same opportunities for rationalization as mergers and IJVs. Under licensing, firm 2's laboratory R2 supplies technology direct to its 'opposite number' R1, which combines it with its own technology and transfers the resulting package internally to plant P1. The resulting product is supplied internally to D1, and externally to D2, both flows being co-ordinated by M1 using information supplied to it under the

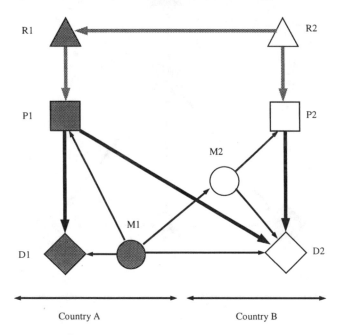

Figure 6.5   Schematic illustration of a licensing arrangement as assumed in the formal model

licensing agreement by M2. This particular configuration of licensing has been chosen because it affords the most direct comparison with the configurations assumed for the other options discussed above.

6.4 INTERNALIZATION FACTORS IN STRATEGIC CHOICE

An important advantage of the IJV is that it allows both the partner firms to acquire some of the benefits of internalizing knowledge flow without incurring the full set-up costs of a merger. By contrast, licensing affords no benefits of internalization, but it avoids the more modest set-up costs of an IJV.

There are many internalization factors which potentially impact on IJVs (Buckley and Casson, 1988). Some of the most important ones are listed on the left-hand side of Table 6.2, together with their notation, which is used in Section 6.6 below. The column entries indicate the impact of each factor on the costs of each strategy.

Table 6.2 Key determinants of the costs of alternative strategies

Determinant	Notation	Strategy		
		Licensing	IJV	Merger
Obstacles to licensing				
Economies of scale	z	+	0	−
Lack of patent rights	p	+	0	0
Uncertainty about technological competence	t	+	0	0
Obstacles to IJVs				
Cultural distance leading to misunderstanding and distrust	d	0	+	+
Obstacles to merger				
Protection of firm's independence	n	0	0	+
Scope economies in technology unrelated to other technologies of acquiring firm	s	0	0	+

Note: A positive sign indicates that costs increase while a zero sign indicates that costs are unaffected.

It has already been noted that licensing offers limited opportunities for rationalization compared to a merger, with an IJV occupying an intermediate position between the two. The greater the economies of scale, generally the higher the gains from rationalization. The first line of the table therefore indicates that economies of scale increase the costs of licensing, while reducing the costs of a merger.

The best-known internalization factor is the general security of property rights and, in particular, the existence of patent rights on technology. It is far easier to sell access to a technology at arm's length when it is patented than when it is not. Thus patent coverage encourages licensing at the expense of both mergers and IJVs.

A more subtle point concerns the uncertainty that firms experience about their own degree of technological competence. A key feature of a joint venture contract, in contrast to a licensing agreement, is that it does not specify in detail exactly what technological expertise each partner will contribute to the venture. While neither partner normally commits themselves to supplying all they know, they do not attempt to restrict what they supply as explicitly under an IJV as they would under a licensing agreement. Each firm generally agrees to contribute, within reason, whatever is necessary to achieve the agreed objective, such as the solution to a technical problem or the development of a new product. This arrangement provides mutual insurance to the partners under conditions where they are unsure, not only about their partner's technological competence, but about their own as well. If each partner firm knew exactly what it was capable of, and understood fully the requirements of the project, then it would be able to specify exactly what it required from its partner. At the same time, it would be perfectly clear about what it was able to supply itself. Licensing would therefore involve no risk that either firm would lack the competence to fulfil its specific commitments. The more uncertain the partners are about their competence relative to the technical goal, however, the greater are the risks of specifying exactly what is required from their partner to complement their own skill, and conversely the greater the risks of accepting an obligation to supply specific skills themselves.

This is evidently related to the tacitness of the knowledge involved (Polanyi, 1966). Although tacitness is normally discussed in terms of the costs of communicating knowledge to other people, a related, and indeed more fundamental issue, is whether people can actually communicate what they know to themselves. In other words, do managers truly understand where their competencies really lie before they get to put them into practice? It would seem that the concept of uncertainty about own-competence is a useful way of conceptualizing this difficult issue.

The lack of specificity in the joint venture agreement, therefore, provides each firm with the flexibility to modify what it requires of its partner in the light of what it discovers about its own expertise. The same flexibility of response can be achieved by merger, as the third line of Table 6.2 makes clear. The greater the firm's uncertainty about its own technological competence, therefore, the stronger the preference for a merger or an IJV is likely to be.

It is possible to construct a number of variations on this theme – for example, where the partners discover one another's shortcomings rather than discovering their own – but the basic principle remains the same. The lack of specificity in the IJV arrangement affords a degree of mutual insurance through flexible response that is missing in an ordinary licensing agreement.

Mutual insurance only works, however, if the other partner can be trusted to make the appropriate response (Casson, 1991; Ring and Van der Ven, 1994). Insuring people against their own incompetence creates a 'moral hazard' problem. They may plead incompetence merely to demand support from the other party, while claiming to be unable to deliver support themselves. Licensing requires less trust than an IJV, because the contract, being more explicit in detail, is easier to enforce in law. This advantage of licensing depends, however, on the effectiveness of international law, which in turn depends upon the sanctions available, the rules of evidence, access to an impartial judiciary, and so on.

While IJVs are less dependent on the law for their success, they are more dependent on culture. From an economic perspective, culture may be defined as shared values and beliefs. Cultural homogeneity, acting through shared beliefs, reduces transactions costs by avoiding misunderstandings, while shared values – notably integrity and loyalty – underpin the willingness to share knowledge which is crucial to an IJV. Prudence requires that knowledge is shared only with those who can be trusted to reciprocate, which favours partnership with members of the same cultural group. This is reflected in the fourth line of Table 6.2, where cultural distance is identified as an obstacle to an IJV. Cultural distance may also be an obstacle to merger – although, contrary to popular opinion, the obstacle may not be so great as in the case of an IJV. This is because a merger permits hierarchical monitoring to be substituted for socially-mediated trust, and in the long run allows corporate leadership to engineer a high-trust culture internal to the firm itself.

The last two factors in the table are classified as obstacles to merger. There is the well-known problem that some 'national champions' are protected from foreign takeover by their governments, while others are family firms whose shareholders value independence more than they value their profit stream. Such constraints can raise the cost of merger to a prohibitive level. Competition policy and anti-trust policy can also protect firms from takeover, and in some cases anti-trust policy may inhibit IJVs as well.

Then there is the nature of the acquired technology. If the acquired technology has many applications besides the particular application for which it is required, then the acquiring firm may need to diversify into these applications, or to license such applications out to other firms. In either case it may be more advantageous for the acquiring firm to leave the original owner to do this, rather than to attempt this in addition to all the other things it has to do. The more unrelated the acquired technology is to the other technologies (if any) possessed by the acquiring firm, the greater the disadvantages of acquisition.

6.5   THE DYNAMICS OF INNOVATION IN A GLOBAL ECONOMY

The choice of strategy can be analysed either as a one-off decision made afresh every time an opportunity for collaboration arises, or in terms of a commitment to handling a succession of opportunities of a given type using the same strategy. When technological innovation is spasmodic, then the first approach is the most appropriate, but in industries where innovation is a regular occurrence the second has more to recommend it. It is the second approach that is followed here.

Suppose that each firm is committed to combining one of its technologies with those of another firm, but that the firm it partners with keeps changing as new innovations continually occur. This is because innovative ability is dispersed across a number of potential partners in the industry, and indeed some major innovations may originate with entirely new entrants. When subsequent innovation renders an existing partner's technology obsolete, a change of partner is required. At any one time the firm has only one partner, but the identity of the partner changes with a frequency that reflects the rate of innovation in the industry.

Switching partners incurs considerable costs where merger is concerned, because of the expense of the legal reconstruction of the firms and their subsequent rationalization (as indicated in Figure 6.4). While commitment to merger affords significant internalization benefits, its costs are large as well. Thus rapid innovation which leads to frequent partner switching considerably increases the average recurrent cost of the merger strategy. The formation of an IJV also incurs significant set-up costs, though not so large as those of a merger. Correspondingly, the internalization gains are lower too. At the opposite extreme to a merger is the licensing option, which involves low set-up costs but offers no internalization economies at all. Licensing is therefore much cheaper than merger, and somewhat cheaper than an IJV, when technological change is rapid.

The costs of switching to a new partner are normally incurred at the outset of an arrangement, while the benefits are deferred: they are distributed continuously over time. There is, therefore, an element of interest cost in switching, and this must be allowed for when calculating the costs and benefits of alternative strategies.

Unlike the costs, the benefits of internalization are continuing ones. Moreover, they normally vary directly with the size of the market in a way that set-up costs do not. The greater the value of the market for the product that the partner firms produce, the greater the gains from internalization. One reason for this is that internalization enhances the proportion of the rents from the marketing of the product that the firms can appropriate for themselves.

6.6   A FORMAL MODEL OF IJV SELECTION

There is a subtle inter-play between the different factors mentioned above which requires a formal model for its elucidation. Let the three strategies be indexed in ascending order of internalization: $k = 1$ for licensing, $k = 2$ for an IJV and $k = 3$ for a merger. In addition, there is a null strategy ($k = 0$) which involves no collaboration between firms. The strategy is chosen by firm 1 to maximize its overall profit, π.

Profit has three components: the basic gains from collaboration, which are independent of the chosen strategy but vary with the size of the market; the benefits of internalization, which vary according to the strategy and according to market size; and the costs of internalization, which are independent of market size but vary according to the chosen strategy, the frequency of partner change and a number of other factors described below.

Let π_k be the profit per period generated by the consistent pursuit of strategy k through a succession of collaborations with innovative partner firms. Let c_k be the set-up costs incurred by strategy k when switching to a new partner firm. All of the costs identified in Table 6.2 may be construed as costs of this kind. Reading down the right-hand columns of the table shows that the set-up cost of a licensing arrangement, c_1, is an increasing function of economies of scale, z, missing patent rights, p, and uncertainty about the firm's technological competence, t. The set-up cost of an IJV, c_2, is an increasing function of cultural distance, d, while the set-up cost of a merger, c_3, is a decreasing function of economies of scale, z, and an increasing function of cultural distance, d, the degree of protection of the independence of the partner firm, n, and the scope economies of the technology, s:

$$c_1 = c_1 \, (p, \, t, \, z) \qquad (6.1.1)$$
$$c_2 = c_2 \, (d) \qquad (6.1.2)$$
$$c_3 = c_3 \, (d, \, n, \, s, \, z) \qquad (6.1.3)$$

Let $f \leq 1$ be the frequency with which a change of partner occurs. This frequency may be interpreted as the probability that a change will occur in any given period. The value of f reflects the pace of innovation in the global economy. Let $r \geq 0$ be the rate of interest in the international capital market. When interest charges associated with repaying the set-up costs are allowed for by summing the relevant geometric series, the average recurrent expense equivalent to a unit set-up cost turns out to be

$$v = (f + r) / (1 + r) \tag{6.2}$$

provided that r is suitably small. It is readily established that v is an increasing function of the frequency, f, and the rate of interest, r,

$$\partial v/\partial f = 1/(1 + r) > 0 \tag{6.3.1}$$
$$\partial v/\partial r = (1 - f) / (1 + r)^2 > 0 \tag{6.3.2}$$

Let b_k be the benefit from internalization accruing when strategy k is applied to a market of unit size. It is assumed that the total benefit is directly proportional to the market size, x. As indicated above, the internalization benefit of merger exceeds that of an IJV, which in turn exceeds that of licensing – which is, of course, zero; thus

$$b_3 > b_2 > b_1 = 0 \tag{6.4}$$

Since profit is by definition the excess of benefit over cost,

$$\pi_0 = 0 \tag{6.5}$$
$$\pi_k = (a + b_k) x - c_k v \quad (k = 1, 2, 3)$$

where $a > 0$ is the basic gain from collaboration per unit market size. The chosen strategy, k, satisfies the inequality constraint

$$\pi_k \geq \pi_i \quad (i \neq k) \tag{6.6}$$

The choice of k is unique when the inequality (6.6) is strictly satisfied.

All of the factors shown in equation (6.5) affect the choice of k, as do the factors which in turn determine them; thus

$$k = (a, b_2, b_3, d, p, n, s, t, f, r, x, z) \tag{6.7}$$

Not all of these factors impact on IJV strategy all of the time. They only affect the choice when it is marginal, and there are three different margins that are involved. The marginal choice between an IJV and licensing depends on all of these factors except b_3, n and s, which are specific to a merger, and a, which is common to both. The marginal choice between an IJV and a merger depends on all of these factors except p and t, which are specific to licensing, and a, which is again common to both. The marginal choice between an IJV and the null strategy depends on a, b_2, d, f, r and x. In principle, all of these margins can be relevant, though only one of them will be relevant at any time.

6.7 THE INTERACTION OF MARKET SIZE AND VOLATILITY

Discrete-choice models of this kind have many applications in international business. Indeed, Buckley and Casson (1981) use a variant of the present model to analyse entry through FDI to a foreign market. Their model excludes IJVs, but includes exporting as an alternative to foreign direct investment and licensing. Exporting is already included in the present model, as a component of all three strategies, and does not need to be treated separately as in the previous model. The previous model also excludes volatility; it takes only a short-run view of technological change compared to the present chapter. The formal similarities can be seen by examining the influence of market size on strategic choice, as illustrated in Figure 6.6.

The figure measures profit vertically and market size horizontally. The zero-profit axis is $A_0 A_0'$, corresponding to the null strategy; the bottom axis is used purely to clarify the labelling of the figure. The variation of profitability with market size under licensing is indicated by the line $A_1 A_1'$; since licensing affords low set-up costs, but no internalization benefits, the intercept is only slightly below that of $A_0 A_0'$, while the slope (measured by a) is fairly modest. The situation under an IJV is indicated by $A_2 A_2'$; the intercept is lower, because the set-up costs are higher, but the slope (measured by $a + b_2$) is steeper because internalization benefits are available. Finally the schedule $A_3 A_3'$ shows the situation under merger; the intercept is very low because the set-up costs are very high, but the slope (measured by $a + b_3$) is the steepest of all because the full benefit of internalization is being obtained.

The envelope $A_0 B_0 B_1 B_2 A_3'$, indicated by the heavy line, indicates the maximum profit generated at each market size. The strategy that generates this profit is determined by which of the schedules forms the envelope at the appropriate point. The corresponding strategy can be read off along the horizontal axis, as indicated in the figure. The figure has been drawn so that all of the strategies have a role to play – no one strategy is dominated by the others. Under these conditions there is a steady progression, as market size

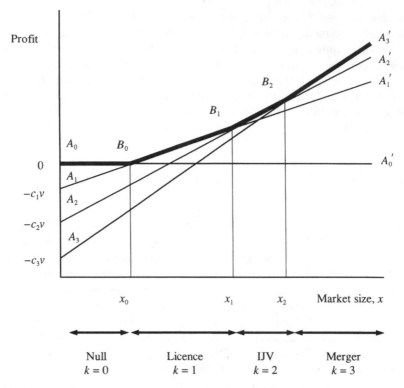

Figure 6.6   Influence of market size on strategic choice

increases, from no collaboration, to licensing, to an IJV and finally to a merger. This is because, as the size of the market grows, the set-up costs of internalization, which are fixed costs independent of market size, can be spread more thinly and greater investment in internalization becomes worthwhile. This is a very partial picture of the situation, however. While it is the size of the market that governs the benefits of internalization, it is the factor v that governs costs. The factor v may be termed the volatility factor; it reflects the impact of both the pace of technological progress and the cost of capital.

A complementary view to Figure 6.6 is presented in Figure 6.7, which shows how the profitability of the different strategies varies with volatility for a given market size. The profits of licensing, IJV and merger are indicated by the respective schedules D_1D_1', D_2D_2' and D_3D_3'. The envelope of maximum profit is $D_3E_1E_2E_3D_0'$. It can be seen that as volatility increases so internalization becomes less attractive. There is first a switch from merger to IJV, then from IJV to licensing, and finally collaboration is abandoned altogether.

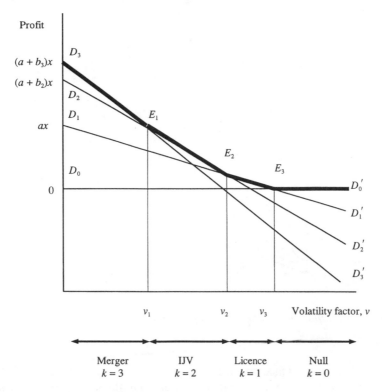

Figure 6.7   Influence of the volatility factor on strategic choice

This diagram provides a simple explanation of joint venture instability. Compared to a merger, the advantage of an IJV stems from the ability to switch partners as technology evolves. It is intrinsic to an IJV that the arrangement is not as long-lasting as a merger would be. Indeed, if an IJV turned out to be very long lasting, it would suggest that management had made a strategic error, and that a merger would have been better instead. For example, a merger would have allowed for a more thorough rationalization of activities than an IJV. The fact that many IJVs lead on to merger confirms this view, as it shows that such strategic errors can be corrected later. It also confirms the recent view that short-lived IJVs are not necessarily a failure. Indeed, it goes further than this, and shows that a firm that participates in a succession of short-lived IJVs, far from being a poor performer, may be sticking consistently to a successful strategy that affords flexibility under conditions of rapid technological change.

It seems natural to combine these two partial analyses by studying the interaction between volatility and the size of the market. An exercise of this kind is illustrated in Figure 6.8. Market size is plotted horizontally and

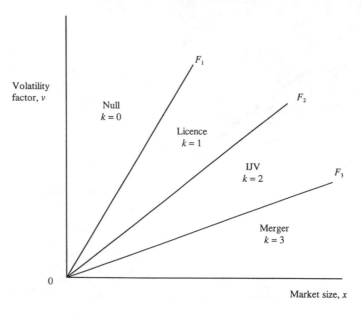

Figure 6.8   Combined impact of market size and volatility on strategic choice

volatility vertically. Once again it is assumed that no strategy is completely dominated by the others. Applying this condition to the inequalities (6.6), and invoking (6.4), shows that

$$k = \begin{array}{ll} 0 & \text{if } \ v > a/c_1 \\ 1 & \text{if } \ b_2(c_2 - c_1) < v \leq a/c_1 \\ 2 & \text{if } \ (b_3 - b_2)/(c_3 - c_1) < v \leq b_2/(c_2 - c_1) \\ 3 & \text{if } \ v > b_2/(c_2 - c_1) \end{array} \qquad (6.8)$$

These conditions indicate how the boundaries OF_1, OF_2 and OF_3 between the regimes shown in the figure vary in response to the costs and benefits of internalization.

There are four regimes in the figure, each corresponding to one of the strategies. If the market size is very small and volatility very high, then the null strategy is chosen. As the market size increases and/or volatility falls, licensing is preferred instead. The IJV is preferred when either market size and volatility are both low – that is the market, though small, is subject to little innovation – or both high – that is there is a large market with considerable innovation. Finally, merger is selected when the market is very large but volatility is very low.

Table 6.3   Impact of market size and volatility on strategic choice

Market size	Degree of volatility	
	Low	High
High	Merger	IJV
Low	IJV	Licensing

The major implications of these results are summarized in Table 6.3. IJVs are favoured in the symmetric situations where market size and volatility are either both low or both high. Licensing is favoured in the asymmetric situation where the market is small but volatile, and merger in the opposite situation where the market is large but stable.

Given the dependence of volatility on both the pace of technological change and the rate of interest, the results can also be summarized by saying that IJVs are favoured under the following conditions:

1. limited innovation, low rate of interest and small market;
2. moderate innovation, moderate rate of interest and moderate size of market; and
3. rapid innovation, high rate of interest and large market.

It is suggested below that it is scenario 3 that is most relevant to the increase of IJV activity in the 1980s. Scenario 2 is also interesting, however, because it shows that IJVs can also occur under conditions of 'moderation in all things'. Other variants of this moderation theme can be generated by allowing one factor to increase while there is a compensating decrease in another factor; for example, size of market.

The impact of the other factors can be analysed by examining their effects on each of the four regimes. Figure 6.9 illustrates how the impacts described in Table 6.2 are reflected in the directions in which the various boundaries rotate in response to changes in cultural distance, d, the degree of protection of the independence of the partner firm, n, the extent to which patent rights are missing, p, the scope economies of the technology, s, and uncertainty about technological competence, t. It can be seen that in addition to the results reported above, IJVs are favoured by a high degree of protection of the independence of the partner firm, n, missing patent rights, p, the scope economies of the technology, s, and by uncertainty about technological competence, t. The effect of cultural distance, d, is ambiguous, for while it may encourage IJVs at the expense of mergers, it also encourages licensing in-

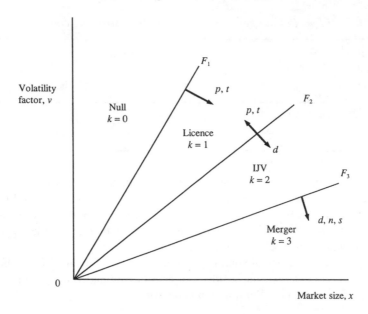

Figure 6.9   Impact of cultural heterogeneity, economies of scope and technological uncertainty on strategic choice

stead of IJVs. Similarly, the effect of economies of scale in production is ambiguous, because while economies of scale encourage IJVs instead of licensing, they discourage IJVs when the alternative is merger. IJVs are definitely encouraged by economies of scope in technology, s, because such economies are difficult to exploit through a merger. Finally, IJVs are favoured by uncertainty about technological competence, t, because this makes licensing a relatively inflexible arrangement.

6.8   APPLICATION OF THE MODEL: IJVS IN THE GLOBAL ECONOMY

The model can be used to explain the increasing use of IJVs in international business during the 1980s and 1990s (Dunning 1993, 250–55) in terms of

1. reductions in trade barriers and improvements in freight transportation, which have 'globalized' markets and so increased effective market size;
2. the rapid increase in national income, particularly in the Asia-Pacific region, which has also increased market size, particularly for consumer durables;

3. accelerated technological innovation which has increased volatility;
4. the emergence of new technologies, combining ideas from different scientific traditions, which has increased firms' uncertainties about their own technological competencies;
5. new technologies such as information technology, biotechnology and genetic engineering which seem to exhibit greater economies of scope than the dominant engineering technologies of the 1960s.

In terms of Figure 6.10, factors 1–3 represent a shift from area Z_0 – moderate market size and low volatility – in the 1960s, to Z_1 – large market size and high volatility – in the 1980s and 1990s. Factor 4 corresponds to the anti-clockwise rotation of the boundary OF_2 to OF_2', while factor 5 corresponds to the clockwise rotation of the boundary OF_3 to OF_3'. As a result some collaborations which would have been effected by merger are now effected by IJVs. Moreover, some collaborations which would have been effected by IJVs and might now be effected by licensing because of greater volatility are still effected by IJVs because technological uncertainty has increased as well.

IJVs have not had matters entirely their own way, however. Barriers to merger caused by the existence of 'national champions' have tended to diminish, allowing more foreign acquisitions to take place in high-technology

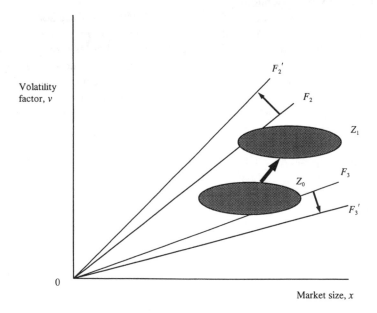

Figure 6.10   Comparative analysis of the international business environment in the 1960s and 1990s

industries. The speculative boom in the 1980s reduced the effective cost of capital to large firms and so also reduced the interest burden of financing mergers and acquisitions. Moreover, expanding market size and a degree of 'technological protectionism' in the European Union has produced a combination of large market size and more moderate volatility which is conducive to mergers between 'protected' firms. Indeed, such mergers have sometimes been favoured by the industrial policy-makers on the grounds that they will help to create not national but 'European' champions.

6.9   EXTENSIONS OF THE MODEL

The scope of every economic model is restricted by the nature of the assumptions that the modeller is required to make, and the present case is no exception. Because it is such a simple model, however, it is a straightforward matter to extend it. Greater relevance can be obtained at little cost in terms of analytical complexity.

It is not difficult, for example, to augment the set of strategies. One possibility worth considering is that the firm could 'go it alone' and attempt to replicate its partner's expertise for itself. Another is that the firm could license out its own technology rather than license in its rival's technology. Economies of scope and technological uncertainties introduce some complications here, however. Suppose that both firms have other technologies besides the ones that they plan to combine in the IJV. If the other technologies of firm 2 have greater complementarity (or 'synergy') with the technology offered by firm 1 than have the technologies of firm 1 with the technology offered by firm 2, it is then appropriate for firm 1 to license out to firm 2 instead of the other way round. This ensures that the complementarities between the different technologies within the firms' portfolios are used to greatest effect.

Firm 2 will be willing to license in the technology, however, only if it is sure that the technology will match its own competence. If firm 2 is more uncertain of its own competence than firm 1, then it may be reluctant to license in, so that firm 2 may still finish up licensing out as a response to this difficulty. It is only when firm 2 is reasonably certain of its competence that it will be willing to act on the basis that the greatest complementarities lie between its own technologies and the technology on offer from firm 1.

This leads to a further point concerning the passive role that has been imputed to firm 2 up till now. The possibility that firm 2 will license firm 1's technology suggests a more active role for firm 2. In particular, it suggests that firm 2 may attempt to bargain with firm 1 over the distribution of the rewards from collaboration. It will no longer be the case, therefore, that all the gains from collaboration accrue to firm 1. If the two firms have similar information about the total gains to be generated by the different strategies, then they may as well dispense with negotiations and agree right away upon the strategy that maximizes their total gain. They can then divide this gain between themselves in some equitable way – such as a 50:50 split.

When the gains are always divided in some fixed proportion, then the choice of strategy will be the same as when only one of the firms takes an active role. This is because the ordering of the strategies by the active firm in any given situation is unchanged when the profits of all the strategies are reduced by the same fixed proportion. Unfortunately, however, this condition is not always satisfied in practice.

It is also possible to augment the list of exogenous variables both by addressing wholly new issues, such as the impact of tax incentives, and by refining the treatment of existing ones. Consider, for example, the impact of the pace of technological change on switching costs. When established firms are good at 'learning by doing' (Nelson and Winter, 1982), future technological improvements are likely to accrue to existing partners. It is mainly when established partners are poor at learning by doing that improvements are more likely to originate with entrants to the industry. The capability of established firms to maintain their leadership is, in turn, likely to be stronger when technological change is incremental, within an existing paradigm, rather than radical, involving the emergence of a new paradigm. This suggests that it is not just the overall pace of technological change that needs to be incorporated into the model, but that the pace of incremental change and the pace of radical change need to be distinguished, and their impacts separately assessed. Rapid incremental change may be perfectly compatible with the merger strategy, because the enduring value of the other firm's competence is reasonably assured; but rapid radical change is likely to subvert the merger strategy and favour the IJV, or licensing, instead.

6.10   GENERALIZATION OF THE RESULTS

The application of the model has focused on the growth of innovation-driven and rationalization-driven IJVs of the kind which predominate in high-technology industries. The emergence of such IJVs has been associated with the downsizing and delayering of some large multinationals. These firms have been restructured in a more entrepreneurial and flexible form as a network of alliances. At the same time, however, a more traditional kind of IJV, concerned with market access, has continued to flourish. Such IJVs are favoured by Japanese firms seeking to consolidate their share in the European market. How far do the results derived above apply to these type 2 and type 3 IJVs, and indeed to other types of IJV as well?

The short answer is that many of the results remain unchanged, but some do not. Factors such as missing patent rights, government protection against foreign acquisition, and cultural distance continue to affect IJV decisions in the same way as before. This reflects the generality of the internalization theory from which they derive. The rate of interest and market size are basic economic variables which remain important too. Other factors, though, are more specific to the type 5 IJV.

Where other types of IJV are concerned, the interplay of technological expertise and marketing expertise takes a slightly different form. For example, where market access is concerned, the speed of learning becomes more important than the pace of technological change. The faster the high-technology firm can acquire the local expertise of the market-oriented firm, and the slower the market-oriented firm is to acquire technology, the more beneficial is the IJV as a transitional method of market entry to the high-technology firm. Uncertainty about the quality of marketing expertise becomes more important too.

6.11   CONCLUSIONS

The development of an economic model is often stimulated by the desire to explain certain 'stylized facts'. In the present case the stylized fact has been the increasing number of IJVs in high-technology global industries. Economic models offer a simple yet rigorous explanation of facts which other disciplines sometimes explain in more complicated and more heuristic terms. If economic models did no more than rationalize what everyone already knows, however, then their value would be rather limited. Fortunately, the way that economic models are constructed means that they do not merely explain the facts they were designed to explain, but provide new predictions as well. It is their ability to draw attention to phenomena that have not been noticed, and to integrate the explanation of these phenomena with the explanations of already known phenomena, that is the true measure of their success.

The model developed in this chapter explains the formation of IJVs in terms of nine distinct but related factors. These factors are listed on the left-hand side of Table 6.4. They govern the margins of strategic interaction between IJVs and licensing on the one hand, and IJVs and mergers on the other. The impact of each factor on each of these strategies is indicated by the entries in the table.

The model shows that the impact of any given factor can only be understood by controlling for all the other factors in the analysis. It is also necessary to control for the *levels* of some of the factors; in particular, the impacts of market size, the pace of innovation, and the rate of interest reverse direction as their level increases.

Table 6.4   Impact of key explanatory factor on strategic choice

Explanatory factor	Notation	Strategy		
		Licensing	IJV	Merger
Market size	x	−	X	+
Pace of technological change	f	+	X	−
Rate of interest	r	+	X	−
Cultural distance	d	+	?	?
Protection of independence	n	+	+	−
Missing patent rights	p	−	+	+
Economies of scope	s	+	−	−
Technological uncertainty	t	−	+	+
Economies of scale	z	−	?	+

Note: X indicates positive at a low value and negative at a high value.

The gist of the results can be summarized by saying that IJVs represent a strategy of moderation. Just as the equity participation in an IJV is intermediate between that in a licensing agreement and that in a full-scale merger, so the IJV emerges as intermediate in strategic terms as well. This may help to explain why the empirical evidence on IJVs is so difficult to interpret in terms of models which seek to relate IJV activities to extreme values of particular factors, such as the sunk costs of R&D.

The results summarized in Table 6.4 generate detailed predictions about how IJV formation will vary within industries, between industries, across countries, and over time. Factors such as technological uncertainty are firm-specific, and can therefore explain why firms in the same industry adopt different strategies. The pace of technological change is industry-specific, and can explain differences in the frequency with which IJVs are encountered in various industries. Cultural distance is specific to pairwise combinations of countries, and can therefore account for differences in the international distribution of IJVs within an industry. With globally-integrated capital markets, the rate of interest tends to be uniform across industries and countries, and is therefore mainly a time-specific factor.

The other factors mentioned also vary with time of course, although some (such as the pace of technological innovation) may vary more than others (such as cultural differences). Despite the apparently restrictive nature of the assumption of profit-maximization applied to a representative pair of firms, therefore, a wide variety of relevant results can be obtained.

REFERENCES

Beamish, P.W. and J.C. Banks (1987) 'Equity joint ventures and the theory of the multinational enterprise', *Journal of International Business Studies*, **19**(2), 1–16

Buckley, P.J. (1988) 'The limits of explanation: testing the internalisation theory of the multinational enterprise', *Journal of International Business Studies*, **19**, 181–93

Buckley, P.J. and M.C. Casson (1976) *The Future of the Multinational Enterprise*, London: Macmillan

Buckley, P.J. and M.C. Casson (1981) 'The optimal timing of a foreign direct investment', *Economic Journal*, **91**, 75–87

Buckley, P.J. and M.C. Casson (1988) 'A theory of cooperation in international business', in F.J. Contractor and P. Lorange (eds), *Cooperative Strategies in International Business*, Lexington, MA: Lexington Books, 31–53

Casson, M.C. (1991) *The Economics of Business Culture: Game Theory, Transaction Costs and Economic Performance*, Oxford: Clarendon Press

Casson, M.C. (1995) *The Organisation of International Business*, Aldershot: Edward Elgar

Casson, M.C. (1997) *Information and Organisation: A New Perspective on the Theory of the Firm*, Oxford: Clarendon Press

Dunning, J.H. (1993) *Multinational Enterprises and the Global Economy*, Wokingham, Berks: Addison-Wesley

Geringer, J.M. and L. Hebert (1989) 'Control and performance of international joint ventures', *Journal of International Business Studies*, **20**(2), 235–54

Harrigan, K. (1988) 'Strategic alliances and partner asymmetries', in F.J. Contractor and P. Lorange (eds), *Cooperative Strategies in International Business*, Lexington, MA: Lexington Books, 205–26

Nelson, R.R. and S.G. Winter (1982) *An Evolutionary Theory of Economic Change*, Cambridge, MA: Belknap Press of Harvard University Press

Polanyi, M. (1966) *The Tacit Dimension*, New York: Anchor Day

Ring, P. Smith and A.H. Van der Ven (1994) 'Developmental processes of cooperative interorganisational relationships', *Academy of Management Review*, **19**, 90–118

Tallman, S.B. (1992) 'A strategic management perspective on host country structure of multinational enterprise', *Journal of Management*, **18**, 455–71

Veugelers, R. and K. Kesteloot (1994) 'On the design of stable joint ventures', *European Economic Review*, **38**, 1799–815

7. Real options in international business

with Mohamed Azzim Gulamhussen

7.1 INTRODUCTION

The study of real options is a relatively new field (Campa, 1994; Dixit and Pindyck, 1994). It has important implications for the analysis of business behaviour. It can explain many of the characteristics of real-world decisions which until recently were believed by many people to defy analysis. It can explain the 'wait and see' approach to investment, which often seems to indicate procrastination and indecisiveness. In fact, 'wait and see' can be an entirely rational risk management strategy. Similarly, it is observed that many managers make only a token commitment of resources at the start of a project. The project has to 'jump' a succession of hurdles in order to expand to its full size. This apparently over-cautious 'bureaucratic' approach can also be understood as a rational risk management strategy.

Not all the behaviour explained by real options is seemingly irrational, however. Real options can also explain sophisticated aspects of behaviour (Schmitzler, 1991). Real options can be used to analyse the pursuit of flexibility in modern international business strategy, as described in Chapter 1 (Kogut and Zander, 1993).

Because the field of real options research is so new, some important conceptual issues need to be clarified. The term 'real option' is not always used in the same way by different writers. It is necessary to clear up some potential confusions when introducing the topic.

Real options are non-trivial. Their logic is quite complex. They typically involve situations spanning several time periods, where items of information relevant to decisions are released only one period at a time. Real options involve complicated strategic aspects of decision-making which cannot be analysed merely in terms of 'frameworks', 'paradigms' or heuristics (see Chapter 10). It is crucial to set out the assumptions of the analysis in a totally explicit manner. Formal modelling is indispensable. It is an area of business strategy where the standard techniques of economic analysis come into their own.

Options are ubiquitous. Real option theory provides a straightforward and realistic means of 'dynamizing' existing static theories. For every static phenomenon, there is some corresponding options perspective. There is, there-fore, no area of international business, or of economics as a whole, to which real option theory cannot be applied, but in many cases, the values of options are likely to be small. It is therefore necessary to investigate many different cases in order to identify those in which the values of real options are likely to be large.

7.2   PRINCIPLES OF REAL OPTION THEORY

There are four key aspects of option theory. They are:

- intertemporal optimization;
- uncertainty;
- deferred information; and
- irreversibility.

It is useful to consider each of them in turn.

Option theory is a special case of the optimization of the allocation of resources over time. The principles of rational intertemporal decision-making have already been applied by economists in many different contexts: for example, household-saving behaviour, cost–benefit analysis for public projects, and net present value techniques for private investment appraisal (Hirshleifer and Riley, 1992; Marschak and Radner, 1972). Intertemporal optimization has been used to model the investment expenditures of firms over time, by assuming that shareholder wealth is maximized subject to a production func-tion constraint and a given set of product and factor prices (Jorgenson, 1963, 1967).

The simplest versions of these models all assume perfect certainty. Uncer-tainty is key to option theory, however. Interviews with business managers invariably suggest that uncertainty is a crucial issue in investment decision-making (a classic study is Shackle, 1970). It is sometimes argued that the effects of uncertainty can never be properly modelled, because uncertainty affects the way that a problem is formulated in the first place. Notwithstand-ing this, a large body of theory has already been developed which models uncertainty in a formal way. This theory is invaluable in formulating a rigor-ous theory of options. The standard approach to uncertainty in economic modelling is to identify a set of mutually exclusive and collectively exhaus-tive states of the world, and to postulate that the decision-maker can attach a subjective probability to each of them. A common objection to this approach is that the set of all possible states is either infinite, or at least so large as to make this exercise impractical. However, another way of looking at the issue is to suppose that the decision-maker simply takes the set of all possible states of the world and partitions it into various subsets by classifying these states in various ways. A simple partition may distinguish just two states of the world, one of which is 'good' as far as investment is concerned, and the other of which is 'bad'. A refinement of this is to distinguish states which mainly affect demand from states which mainly affect supply, and to distinguish good and bad conditions separately for demand and supply. This approach does not commit the decision-maker to identifying every conceivable state of the world, but simply to exercise judgement in classifying these unspecified states in a realistic way. Provided the chosen distinctions exist in reality to some degree, a model of this kind may have considerable predictive power. This approach to handling uncertainty, based on mentally 'pigeonholing' situations into simple categories, is widely used in practice, and is immune to some of the criticisms of modelling noted above. It is this approach that is used in the real option models presented below.

Prior to the development of formal models of decision-making under uncertainty, it was widely believed that the introduction of uncertainty into economic models would radically alter predicted patterns of behaviour. This turned out to be false. For example, even under uncertainty, rational agents continue to substitute against the more expensive factor inputs, and in favour of products whose prices have risen relative to others. The most powerful effects of uncertainty only emerge when decision-makers act in the belief that *present uncertainty will be resolved in the future*. Certain things will be known in the future that cannot be known today. This confers an advantage on the postponement of decisions, since future decisions will be better informed, and so incur lower risks of a mistake. A formal way of expressing this important property is to say that the decision-maker's information set is time-dependent. As time passes, the information set gets richer as new information is added. Although certain parts of the information set may shrink if memory is poor, the old information that is lost is likely to be less relevant to the future than the new information which is being added (though not invariably so).

When an investment decision is postponed, the investment is effectively deferred. This has costs as well as benefits, of course. While a decision, when taken later, may involve fewer mistakes, given the circumstances at the later time, it could have been a mistake to delay the commitment of resources in the first place. For example, the cost of inputs, such as plant and equipment, may have risen in the meantime, or a competitor may have pre-empted the market opportunity. In general, there is a trade-off between deferring an investment to await additional information, and committing resources right away to deter pre-emption by others. A key strength of real option theory is that it addresses this trade-off head-on. It generates substantive hypotheses regarding the timing of investments. While the theory of investment under certainty, described at the outset, has proved relatively weak at explaining empirical evidence, and the general theory of uncertainty has effected little improvement, real option theory offers the prospect of a significant advance in explanation, although it is still too soon to say whether all of this potential will be realized or not.

It was asserted above that postponing an investment decision is equivalent to deferring the investment. In fact, matters are not quite as simple as this. If every investment could be costlessly reversed, then a commitment to invest today could be made without prejudice to a review of the investment decision planned for tomorrow. If tomorrow's decision was that, with hindsight, today's decision was wrong, then it would simply be reversed. In fact, the 'commitment' of resources made at the outset would have been illusory, in the sense that all the resources could be recovered simply by reversing the decision at a later date. The reason why today's decision is linked to tomorrow's decision is that in fact the investment is not reversible.

It is important to emphasize that in option theory irreversibility is an economic phenomenon rather than a technical one. These two aspects of irreversibility are easily confused. It is sometimes suggested, for example, that investments in real assets are irreversible while purchases of financial assets are not. While this may often be true in a technical sense, it is not true in an economic one. Although, technically speaking, a purchase of a financial asset can be reversed by selling it again, the asset cannot necessarily be sold for the same price that it was bought for. In economic terms, the transaction is not fully reversible unless the asset can be sold for the same price for which it was bought – for example, through a 'money back' guarantee.

Conversely, a real investment that is technically irreversible may carry little risk of capital loss if it is highly versatile. Although an asset may be fixed in position, and have no second-hand value, there may be plenty of alternative uses to which it can be put. Although it cannot be sold, it is highly unlikely that the owner would wish to sell it, because if one use turns out badly then another use is likely to do just as well. Thus the owner of the asset may feel very secure about getting their money back by one means or another – more secure, indeed, than the owner of a financial asset with a highly volatile price.

The concept of irreversibility is often expressed in terms of sunk costs. These are the costs of an investment which cannot be recovered once the investment has been made. Thus if an asset is bought for P_1, but can only be sold second-hand for $P_2 < P_1$, then the sunk cost of the purchase is $P_1 - P_2$. The point just made above applies to sunk costs as well: it is important to remember that sunk cost is an economic property of the situation in which the decision-maker is placed, and not a physical characteristic of the asset. Sunk cost is measured relative to the best alternative use of the asset at the future date. Thus the measure of sunk cost derived above is valid only when selling off the asset is the best alternative to keeping it in its original use.

Because sunk cost is defined with respect to alternative uses, the concept is more subjective than is often supposed. This subjectivity is not unique to sunk cost – it applies to all costs which are measured as opportunity costs (Wiseman, 1989). Statements of real option theory which treat sunk costs as objective will cause confusion whenever an asset has several alternative uses in a future period.

7.3 RELATIONSHIP BETWEEN REAL OPTIONS AND FINANCIAL OPTIONS

Almost everyone has heard about financial options – in particular 'put' and 'call' options based upon stock market prices (for a review see Dempster and Pliska, 1997). These options involve a contract between two parties. This contract creates a right to buy or sell an asset at a future time at a pre-specified price – either a fixed price, or one specified by some agreed rule. This right can be traded: it can be bought and sold, just like the underlying asset to which it relates. The main object of option theory, as developed in finance, is to price such options correctly.

There is a good deal of confusion about the relationship between real options and financial options. There are two opposing views that can be found in the popular literature, and both of them are wrong. The first is that real options and financial options are basically the same thing – that real options relate to real assets, and financial options relate to financial assets, but that the underlying principles are the same. The second view is that real options and financial options are fundamentally different: real options are about the timing of irreversible investment decisions, while financial option theory is about the valuation of 'derivative' contractual instruments. Those who take the second view believe that those who take the first view are misled by the use of the same term 'option' to describe two different phenomena. In fact, the first view is closer to the truth than the second, in the sense that financial options are simply a special case of real options, and the same principles – as described in Section 7.2 – apply to both. The mistake of the first view is to suppose that the difference lies simply in whether the asset is real or monetary. The nature of the asset is important, but the key issue is whether the asset is tradable or not, rather than whether it takes a real or monetary form. In practice, almost all monetary assets are tradable, but the converse does not apply: not all real assets are non-tradable. Because some real assets are tradable, tradability is a separate issue from whether the asset is a real or monetary one.

The nature of the option is important too. Some options are contractual, while others reflect the physical properties of the asset. For example, some options are exercised by buying and selling an asset, whereas others are exercised by retaining ownership of the asset and reallocating it to an alternative use. The importance of distinguishing between contractual and non-contractual options is reflected in the second view described above. Where this view goes wrong is to suppose that different principles apply to the valuation of contractual options and non-contractual options. In fact they do not. The principles are the same. This is fortunate, because it means that there is, in fact, just one body of option theory, and not two. Financial option theory is just a special case of a more general theory of options which is based on the principles set out in Section 7.2 above. Real option theory is the body of theory that has applied these general principles to non-contractual options on non-tradable assets, and neglected their applications to financial options. The applications of real option theory given below clearly demonstrate that the principles commonly ascribed to real option theory apply to financial options as well.

These remarks are elaborated in Table 7.1. The table classifies different types of options using two main dimensions. The first dimension, indicated by the columns, specifies whether the asset is tradable or not. A tradable asset is an asset which can always be bought and sold. When there are no transac-

Table 7.1   Classification of options by type of option and type of asset, with examples

Type of option	Type of asset		
	Tradable		Non-tradable
	Monetary	Real	Real
Contractual			
Formal	Bond or currency option	Commodity option Equity option	Option to purchase land or building Option to acquire a non-quoted firm
Informal			'First refusal' option to acquire a firm in which a minority stake is held
Non-contractual	Holding money as a source of liquidity		Option to up-size, down-size or re-locate a factory: see also Table 7.2

tion costs or other 'market imperfections', the purchase price of a tradable asset is equal to its selling price. This is a crucial property used in standard option-pricing models in the theory of finance. The columns also identify a secondary distinction between real and monetary assets, but as indicated above, this is of no real significance. It is of no significance because, as emphasized above, it is the economic value of the asset that matters in option theory, and the physical form that the asset takes is of no consequence unless it also affects some other more relevant aspect of the problem.

The second dimension, indicated by the rows, specifies whether or not the option takes a contractual form. This distinction is not important for the mathematical structure of the models, but it is important in understanding how an option model is applied. The distinction shows that option theory can be used to value the flexibility provided both by contractual arrangements and by the physical properties of an asset. A minor distinction is between contractual arrangements of a formal and an informal kind. While formal arrangements are the more conspicuous, informal arrangements may be of greater consequence where long-term corporate strategies are concerned – for example, informal options agreed with partner firms to acquire or divest joint venture companies.

The options of greatest relevance to IB theory appear in the bottom-right-hand corner of the table. They are real options rather than financial ones. They include options to vary the size, location, timing and utilization of an investment project once the initial phase of it is complete. These are non-contractual options, which are highly relevant to *location* issues in IB. Another important set of options discussed above are contractual options to acquire or divest assets owned wholly or partly by other firms. These contractual options are highly relevant to *ownership* issues in IB. Between them, these two issues – ownership and location – dominate the modern economic theory of IB. It follows that real options have a key role in generating a dynamic version of IB theory.

7.4 TECHNIQUES OF ANALYSIS

The modern theory of option pricing is a highly technical branch of the theory of finance. It is based on highly specific assumptions which are necessary in order for these techniques to be applied. For example, the famous Black–Scholes pricing formula assumes Brownian motion in the movement of the price of the underlying financial asset, and 'risk neutrality' – a rather misleading term which in option theory connotes a particular feature of the arbitrage process. These highly specific assumptions obscure some of the more general – and, indeed, more powerful – insights that emerge when the value of real options – in particular, non-contractual real options – are considered instead.

Much of the technical difficulty in contemporary financial option theory stems from the commitment to continuous time models. Continuous time is a reasonable approximation to reality in stock markets and currency markets where trading is virtually instantaneous, but it is a poor approximation to the circumstances under which non-contractual decisions relating to the deployment of real assets are made. Here, discrete time models, based on dividing up time into a finite number of periods, are generally more realistic. Since discrete time models are much simpler to solve than continuous ones, there is much to be gained from studying options from the outset in terms of discrete time. This is the approach adopted in this chapter.

The discrete time models used in this chapter involve rational, intertemporal decision-making under uncertainty. All the models can be solved by explicit analytical methods, although for certain types of model approximations are useful. The general method of solution is a recursive technique. This technique solves for the rational choices in the final period, conditional on the choices made in the previous periods, and then uses these results to determine the optimal choices in the preceding period. This method is repeated until the initial period is reached. Initial decisions are optimized on the assumption that, in the light of these decisions, the most appropriate choices in subsequent periods will then be made. This determines a comprehensive contingent plan of action covering every period.

Most of the models are presented in numerical rather than algebraic form. This is the most convenient way of expounding models like the present ones, which involve choices between discrete strategies over discrete periods of time. It is straightforward to re-formulate the models in algebraic form and interested readers may like to do this for themselves. The only difficulty is that the derivation of solutions is relatively tedious, and the algebraic inequalities that characterize the optimum strategy are cumbersome to write down (see, for example, Chapter 2). Because the present chapter has a mainly expository role, numerical examples are preferable because they are much quicker to present and are more readily understood.

To illustrate the discrete time approach, consider the following numerical example, which places a standard financial option problem in a discrete time framework. Because the example involves a tradable financial asset, it possesses the special feature that the purchase price of the asset is always equal to its selling price. The decision-maker has to decide whether to purchase a contractual option which will allow him to buy the asset in the future at a pre-specified price, if he wishes to.

Consider a single indivisible asset whose future value may be either 20 or 10, depending on whether conditions are good ($s = 1$) or bad ($s = 0$). Conditions are good with probability p. The asset can be purchased today ($t = 0$) for 15 units, or purchase can be deferred until tomorrow ($t = 1$), when tomorrow's price will be known. A call option can be purchased today for 2 units, which gives the right to purchase the asset tomorrow for 15 units – that is for the same price as today. The objective of the risk-neutral decision-maker is to maximize the expected profit *v*. Because of the short period of time elapsing between today and tomorrow, discounting is ignored.

There is an element of irreversibility in today's purchase because a purchaser cannot guarantee to sell the asset tomorrow for the price at which he bought it. Such a guarantee can only be acquired through the separate purchase of a 'put' option, which allows him to sell the asset at a pre-specified price, such as the price at which he bought it. To keep the model simple, the put option is ignored.

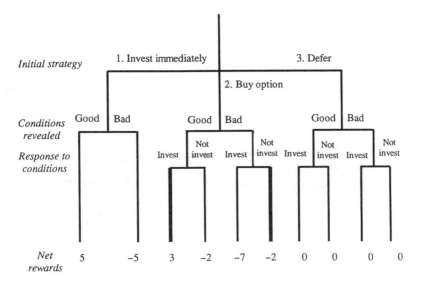

Figure 7.1   Decision tree for appraisal of option purchase

The problem is represented using a decision tree in Figure 7.1. Starting from the top of the figure, the decision-maker has three initial alternatives:

1.   To purchase the asset immediately.
2.   To purchase the call option instead.
3.   To defer a decision on purchasing until later.

Once conditions have been revealed, the decision-maker faces further decisions. If he has purchased the option, then he must decide whether or not to exercise it. The net rewards, derived from the data given above, are indicated by the numbers along the bottom of the figure. If conditions are good, then it will pay to exercise the option, whereas if conditions are bad then it pays not to exercise it. The optimal choices are indicated by the thicker branches in the figure. If the decision-maker has deferred a decision, then he can decide whether to purchase the asset the following day. However, the special conditions assumed in this problem mean that this decision is of no consequence. Since the purchase price is always equal to the value of the asset, the decision-maker is indifferent to purchase, whatever conditions prevail. It is assumed for simplicity that in these circumstances the decision-maker will choose not to make a purchase.

It follows from this discussion that three strategies can be valued as follows. Let v_i be the expected value of the ith strategy; then

$$v_1 = (20p + 10(1 - p)) - 15 = -5 + 10p \qquad (7.1.1)$$
$$v_2 = ((20 - 15)p + 0 (1 - p)) - 2 = -2 + 5p \qquad (7.1.2)$$
$$v_3 = 0 \qquad (7.1.3)$$

The first term in equation (7.1.1) is the expected revenue from an initial investment when it is sold in the following period, while the second term is today's purchase price. The first term in equation (7.1.2) is the value of the option when exercised, weighted by the probability that conditions are good. The second term is its value (zero) when conditions are bad, and the third term is its purchase price.

Selecting the highest value of v for any given value of p gives the solution:

$$i = \begin{array}{ll} 1 & if \quad p \geq 0.6 \\ 2 & if \quad 0.4 \leq p < 0.6 \\ 3 & if \quad p < 0.4 \end{array} \qquad (7.2)$$

Thus, as the probability of good conditions increases from zero to one, the decision-maker switches from no purchase to option purchase, to immediate purchase, illustrating his growing confidence that conditions will be good. The inequalities specified here assume that, when two strategies are of equal value, the strategy with the lower number is always chosen; this convention is used throughout the chapter.

The solution is illustrated graphically in Figure 7.2. The vertical axis measures the expected profit and the horizontal axis measures the probability of good conditions. The schedule V_1V_1' indicates the expected value of the initial purchase strategy. The relatively low intercept and steep slope shows that this is the riskiest strategy. The investor is exposed to a serious risk of capital loss if conditions turn out to be bad. The schedule V_2V_2' indicates the value of the option strategy. Holding an option eliminates the risk of capital loss, while offering the prospect of a capital gain by preserving the right to

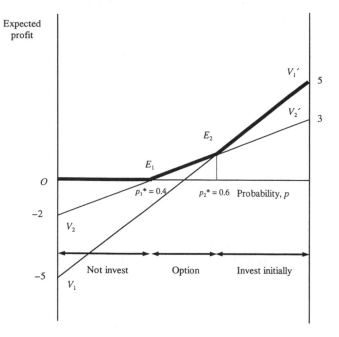

Figure 7.2   Graphical solution of the financial option problem

purchase the asset at a pre-specified price equal to the initial price. The option therefore provides a speculative opportunity while controlling the risk involved. The horizontal axis represents the null value of the third strategy.

To maximize expected profit it is necessary to identify the upper envelope of the three schedules. This is the schedule $OE_1E_2V_1'$, which has kinks at the points E_1, E_2, where some pair of strategies has equal value. For any given value of p, the optimal strategy is the one that forms the portion of the envelope at the relevant point along the horizontal axis. The kinks E_1, E_2, correspond to the two critical values of probability $p_1^* = 0.4$, $p_2^* = 0.6$, where switches of strategy take place. At the first switch point, the no purchase strategy and the option strategy are of equal value, while at the second switch point the option strategy and the immediate purchase strategy are of equal value.

The same diagrammatic technique can also be used to measure the value of an option. Suppose that the decision-maker does not know that an option can be purchased for 2 units. A decision rule is required to determine when to purchase an option. Let a be the unknown value of the option. Equation (7.1.2) then becomes

$$v_2 = -a + 5p \qquad (7.3)$$

and the decision rule is to purchase the option if

$$v_2 > \max[v_1, v_3]$$

that is if

$$a < \max[-5 + 10p, 0] + 5p \qquad (7.4)$$

The determination of the value of the option for $p = 0.5$ is shown in Figure 7.3. This involves a two-stage procedure. In the first stage the maximum expected value obtainable from the two alternative strategies is determined by constructing the envelope OE_3V_1' from the higher of V_1V_1' (representing strategy 1) and the horizontal axis (representing strategy 3). In the second stage, a line OV_1' is drawn connecting the two ends of the envelope at O and V_1'. The vertical distance between OV_1' and OE_3V_1' is a measure of the value of the option. A line WW is drawn parallel to OV_1'

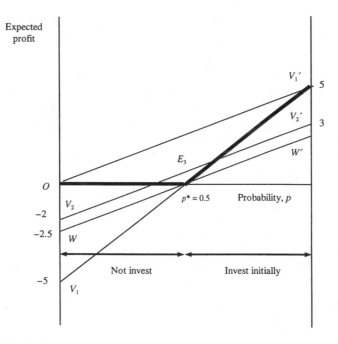

Figure 7.3   Valuation of a financial option

through E_3. The distance in the figure can be measured by comparing the intercepts O and W on the left-hand vertical axis. The value of the option is 2.5. Since its purchase price is only 2, the option should be acquired when p = 0.5. This agrees with the result obtained in Figure 7.2, which showed that the option should be purchased whenever p was in the range between 0.4 and 0.6.

7.5 THE TIMING OF A REAL INVESTMENT: A SIMPLE ROLE FOR CONTRACTUAL OPTIONS IN INTERNATIONAL BUSINESS

Consider a firm contemplating entry into a foreign market. The firm has identified an investment opportunity which it alone can exploit. Exploitation of the opportunity begins in period 2, but the investment expenditure can be incurred in either period 1 or period 2; the problem is to determine which is best. It is convenient to assume that the second period, beginning tomorrow, is very much longer than the first. Because the period is much longer, it is difficult to justify ignoring issues relating to the discount rate. However, to keep the model simple it is convenient to take the rate of discount as fixed and specify the entire problem in terms of discounted values. Discounting is introduced explicitly in Sections 7.10 and 7.11.

The opportunity generates a known flow of income with a present value of 20 units. To appropriate this income stream, the firm needs to acquire a site for the erection of a factory. Conditions in the local market for industrial property are very uncertain, however (as they are in many transitional economies). At the moment, a site is available at a price of 15 units, but in the following period a similar site could become available for either 10 or 20 units, depending upon whether supply conditions in the property market are good or bad. Conditions are good (the price is 10 units) with probability p.

Once the site has been bought, the factory must be erected immediately, and once this has occurred, the site has no alternative use, and no resale value. The owner of the site is willing to fix the price for a sale tomorrow at 17 units, provided that a non-refundable deposit of 2 units is paid. The reservation on the site can be cancelled tomorrow if desired. Cancelling the reservation would allow the firm to make a spot purchase at a price of 10 units if conditions were good.

This example has been chosen to illustrate the close connection between real options and financial options, as described in Section 7.3. The situation closely resembles the financial option problem discussed above. The principal change is that the asset in which the firm invests is no longer tradable. The future value of the asset depends not upon what it can be *sold* for, but only upon what it can be *used* for. The purchase is technically irreversible, but economically it incurs little risk because the owner is certain that the asset is worth 20 units from the outset. The only risk is that the owner may pay more for the asset than is really necessary.

Because the asset is not tradable, a wedge can be driven between its purchase price and its value to the firm. This is reflected in the fact that, whether it is purchased for 10, 15 or 20 units, it is still worth 20 units to the firm. By contrast, in Section 7.4 the asset was always worth what it was purchased for at the time.

There are three dominant strategies, each of which corresponds to one of the strategies in example 1:

1. invest at the outset;
2. place a deposit (the call option) and exercise it if the spot price is high; cancel the order and purchase spot if the price is low; and
3. defer the decision, and invest only if the price is low.

The expected profits generated by these strategies are

$$v_1 = 20 - 15 = 5 \tag{7.5.1}$$
$$v_2 = 20 - 2 - 10p - 15(1-p) = 3 + 5p \tag{7.5.2}$$
$$v_3 = (20 - 10)p = 10p \tag{7.5.3}$$

The first equation shows that initial purchase carries no risk, since both the value of the asset (20 units) and the purchase price (15 units) are known at the outset. The second equation shows that the option will not be exercised if conditions are good – a cost of 10 units is incurred with probability p – but will be exercised if conditions are bad – a cost of 15 units is incurred with probability $1-p$. The third equation shows the profit to be made by deferring the decision when conditions turn out to be good.

Expected profit is maximized by setting

$$i = \begin{array}{ll} 1 & if \quad p \le 0.4 \\ 2 & if \quad 0.4 < p \le 0.6 \\ 3 & if \quad p > 0.6 \end{array} \tag{7.6}$$

The solution is illustrated in Figure 7.4. The conventions are the same as for Figure 7.1. The expected value of the three strategies are represented respectively by the schedules V_1V_1', V_2V_2' and OV_3'. The maximum attainable value of profit for a given value of p is indicated by the height of the envelope $V_1E_1E_2V_3'$. The figure shows that when the future purchase price of the asset is expected to be very high (p is low), the investment will be made at the

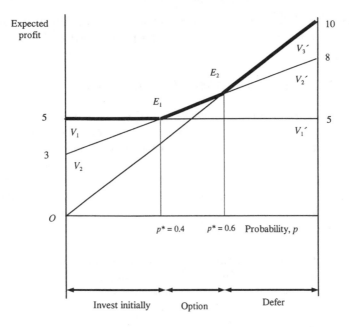

Figure 7.4 *Option to purchase a real asset with an uncertain future price but known value in use*

outset (strategy 1 is chosen), while if it is expected to be very low (p is high), the investment will be deferred (strategy 3 is chosen). A deposit will be placed on the asset (strategy 2) if the firm believes that a high or low price will occur with a probability in the mid-range of values between 0.4 and 0.6. Indeed, it is readily established, using the method described in the previous section, that the option is most valuable when the uncertainty is greatest, that is when $p = 0.5$.

The similarity between this example and the previous one is illustrated by the appearance of the same critical probability values, $p_1^* = 0.4$, $p_2^* = 0.6$. Indeed, a comparison of Figure 7.4 with Figure 7.2 shows that the two figures are almost identical except for the fact that all the schedules have been pushed upwards by 5 units. This explains why the critical values are the same. The only substantial difference arises from the fact that the role of the strategy 1 in the previous example has now been taken over by strategy 3, and vice versa. The role of strategy 2 – the option strategy – remains exactly the same. The interchange of the roles of strategies 1 and 3 is explained by the fact that in the previous example risk was eliminated by not purchasing the asset, while in the present one it is eliminated by purchasing the asset at the outset. Although the new model relates to a real asset rather than a financial one, it is still driven by the same kind of speculative forces as before.

7.6   UNCERTAIN DEMAND CONDITIONS

The previous section discussed a contractual option governing the purchase of a real asset. This is only one of several types of option relating to real assets, and it is certainly not the most important one as far as IB is concerned. When real options were introduced in Chapter 1, the emphasis was on their role in coping with uncertainty about *demand* for the asset's services – and specifically with uncertainty about the foreign demand for the product from which the demand for these services is derived. The previous example, by contrast, focused on uncertainty about the *supply* of the asset instead.

Table 7.2   Classification of non-tradable real options by source of uncertainty and type of asset, with examples

| | Source of uncertainty | | |
Type of option	Cost of supply	Intensity of demand	Either supply or demand, or both
Contractual	Option to purchase land or building		IJV
Non-contractual	Build flexibility into sources of input supply	Build flexibility into range of demands that can be satisfied	Build in potential to up-size, down-size or relocate plant at low cost

Both demand and supply are potential sources of uncertainty, and the relationship between them is illustrated in Table 7.2. The columns of the table distinguish three sources of uncertainty: supply, demand, and a combination of the two. The rows of the table distinguish two types of option: contractual and non-contractual. The most important type of contractual option is the IJV, which is useful in coping with uncertainty in both demand and supply. Non-contractual options involve issues such as the size, timing, location and versatility of investments. Both contractual and non-contractual options can take numerous forms – indeed, there are far too many to do justice to them all in a single chapter.

The remaining sections of this chapter concentrate on a few important cases, beginning with some simple cases relating to non-contractual options that reduce the risks relating to uncertainty in demand. By switching attention from uncertainty about supply to uncertainty about demand some classic examples of real option models are obtained.

Demand uncertainty is an important factor in foreign market entry decisions. Entry is often deferred, even when it would be profitable to go ahead immediately, because it would be even more profitable to wait until later. The strategy of deferring foreign market entry was discussed by Buckley and Casson (1981), but only under conditions of certainty. Under these conditions, the main motive for deferring entry is to await further growth in the market. Once uncertainty is introduced, another motive for waiting is also introduced – namely, to dispel uncertainty about whether the market is likely to grow or not. Entry is postponed until some crucial information relating to the prospective size of the market has become available. This is the gist of the example that follows.

Consider an initial investment in a foreign market. This could be an investment in marketing and distribution facilities, or it could involve investment in production facilities as well. As before, there are two periods, with the second period being very long. Investment today generates a revenue of 2 units today, and one of 20 units tomorrow if conditions are good and 10 units if they are bad. Demand conditions are good with probability p. If the asset is not purchased until tomorrow then only tomorrow's revenues are obtained. The purchase price of the asset is 15 units in both periods. The advantage of purchasing tomorrow is that the purchase decision can be made when the state of demand is known. An asset purchased today cannot be sold off again tomorrow: the entire purchase price is a sunk cost.

By deferring the entry decision, the firm can guarantee that it will not make a loss. When the decision is deferred, the optimal strategy is to enter if and only if demand conditions are good. This generates an expected profit of $5p$. It follows that deferred investment with conditional entry dominates a strategy of not investing at all.

As a result of this, there are only two strategies worth distinguishing:

1. invest at the outset; and
2. defer the investment decision, and invest tomorrow only if demand conditions are good.

The expected profits generated by these strategies are

$$v_1 = 10(1 - p) + 20p + 2 - 15 = -3 + 10p \qquad (7.7.1)$$
$$v_2 = (20 - 15)p = 5p \qquad (7.7.2)$$

The first two terms in equation (7.7.1) express expected revenue in period 2: namely, 10 units when demand conditions are bad, and 20 units when they are good. The third term captures the revenue generated in period 1, while the final term is the outlay on the investment. The derivation of equation (7.7.2) has already been explained. There is no revenue stream and no outlay when demand conditions are bad, because the firm does not invest in this case. There is no revenue from period 1 either, because investment does not take place until period 2.

Expected profit is maximized by setting

$$i = \begin{array}{ll} 1 & if \quad p \geq 0.6 \\ 2 & if \quad p < 0.6 \end{array} \qquad (7.7)$$

The solution is illustrated in Figure 7.5. The expected profit generated by immediate investment is indicated by the height of the schedule V_1V_1', while the expected profit generated by deferral is indicated by the height of the schedule OV_2'. The maximum attainable profit is indicated by the envelope OEV_1', which has a kink at E. The point E identifies the critical probability p^* = 0.6 at which the firm switches from deferral to immediate entry. Thus for low values of p, where the firm is pessimistic about demand conditions, entry is deferred, while for high values of p, where the firm is optimistic about

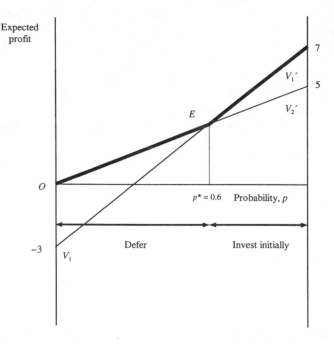

Figure 7.5   Decision to defer investment when future demand is uncertain

demand conditions, entry is immediate because the firm is so confident that conditions will be good.

7.7   SCALE AND REVERSIBILITY OF INVESTMENTS

In the previous example the only strategy conferring option value was deferment. In practice, however, real option value is often generated by choosing an alternative, more flexible, form of investment. This section examines a variant of this strategy which is particularly relevant to foreign market entry (for a similar application to corporate growth see Kulatilaka and Perotti, 1998).

Suppose that there is an alternative to the irreversible investment described in the previous section, in the form of a smaller investment which is partially reversible. This small investment can be upgraded to a full investment in the following period if desired. It involves an initial outlay of 10 units, 7 of which can be recovered if the investment is abandoned in the following period. The cost of an upgrade is assumed to be 6 units. The small investment yields the same revenue as the large investment in the initial period – namely 2 units. This is because the market is initially small, and can be served just as adequately from a small investment as from a large one. However, the small investment is much less effective in the second period. Because of its small scale it can generate an income of only 5 units whatever the size of the market.

The obvious way to exploit the small investment is to use it for initial entry and then either scale it up, if demand is strong, or liquidate it if demand is weak. The alternative to scaling up is to liquidate the investment in the second period and put the proceeds towards a purchase of the larger asset. This is uneconomic, however, because the cost is $15 - 7 = 8$ units, as against 6 units for the upgrade. The alternative to liquidation is to keep the asset in use, but this is uneconomic because the income from use is 5 units, whereas the proceeds from liquidation are 7 units.

It follows that there is only one further strategy that is worth considering in addition to the strategies already considered above.

3.   Invest on a small scale with a view to scaling up if demand is buoyant and liquidating if demand is weak.

The expected value of the new strategy is

$$v_3 = -10 + 2 + (20 - 6)p + 7(1 - p) = -1 + 7p \qquad (7.9)$$

The first term in (7.9) is the initial outlay, and the second is the revenue from period 1; the third term is the expected profit from an upgrade when demand conditions are good, and the final term is the expected proceeds from liquidation when conditions are bad.

The new solution is

$$i = \begin{array}{ll} 1 & if \quad p \geq 0.67 \\ 2 & if \quad p \leq 0.5 \\ 3 & if \quad 0.5 < p < 0.67 \end{array} \qquad (7.10)$$

The solution is illustrated in Figure 7.6. The value of the new strategy 3 is indicated by the height of the schedule V_3V_3'. This intersects OV_2' at E_1 and V_1V_1' at E_2, determining the critical probabilities $p_1^* = 0.5$, $p_2^* = 0.67$ between which the small-scale investment is preferred. This is a good example of the way that small flexible investments are preferred when future demand conditions are highly uncertain.

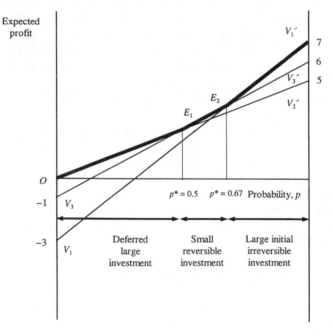

Figure 7.6   Advantages of a small-scale reversible initial investment when future demand is uncertain

7.8 INVESTMENT IN INFORMATION-GATHERING AS A REAL OPTION

While the previous example clearly demonstrated the advantages of small reversible investments, the value of the option that was generated was not sufficiently large to make the strategy dominant. It was efficient only when there was a high degree of uncertainty. Given the prevalence of such investments in real-world market entry situations, this suggests that something important may have been omitted from the model.

The obvious omission is a factor that has been extensively discussed in the earlier chapters of this book – namely, investment in the collection of information. So far it has been assumed that information about the state of demand is automatically revealed in the second period whether the firm has invested in the first period or not. Under these conditions, deferred investment is very attractive when market prospects are poor, because investing at the outset confers no information advantage. On the other hand, the problem with making an irreversible investment at the outset is that it is too late to do anything useful with the information once it has been obtained.

Suppose now that information on demand conditions can only be obtained in the second period if an investment has been made in the first period. While the values of both of the initial entry strategies remain unchanged, the value of the deferred entry strategy is dramatically reduced. Because it now confers no information advantage, the value of the deferred investment strategy falls to

$$v_2 = 10(1 - p) + 20p - 15 = -5 + 10p \qquad (7.11)$$

It is now totally dominated by the initial full-scale investment strategy, because the only remaining difference between them is that the initial investment generates 2 units of profit from period 1, whereas the deferred investment does not.

The deferred investment strategy previously dominated the null strategy of no investment in either period, but as deferment is now less profitable, this is no longer the case. It is therefore necessary to reintroduce the null strategy explicitly into the strategy set. It is convenient to introduce it as a replacement for the deferred investment strategy. The new strategies that need to be evaluated are therefore

1. invest on a large scale at the outset;
2. do not invest at all;
3. invest on a small scale at the outset with a view to scaling up if demand is buoyant and liquidating if demand is weak.

The new solution is

$$i = \begin{array}{ll} 1 & \text{if} \quad p \geq 0.67 \\ 2 & \text{if} \quad p \leq 0.14 \\ 3 & \text{if} \quad 0.14 < p < 0.67 \end{array} \qquad (7.12)$$

The modified solution is illustrated in Figure 7.7. The schedules V_1V_1', V_3V_3' remain in their previous positions (see Figure 7.6). The value of strategy 2, which is now the null strategy, is represented by the horizontal axis. V_3V_3' intersects the horizontal axis at E_1, corresponding to a critical probability p_1^* = 0.14. It intersects V_1V_1' at the same point, E_2, as before, corresponding to the critical probability $p_2^* = 0.67$. The range of probability values for which the small reversible strategy is chosen has therefore more than tripled as compared with the previous case.

This modified example shows very clearly why a small-scale reversible investment is so often chosen as an initial entry strategy. It can act as a 'listening post', helping the investor to collect information on the future prospects of the market. Using another metaphor, it can be described as a 'toe

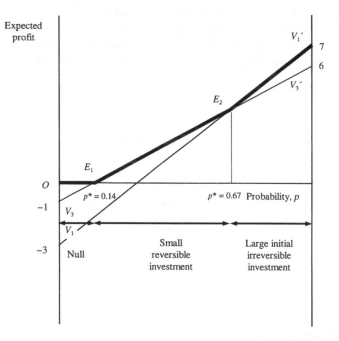

Figure 7.7   Role of a small-scale reversible investment for collecting information on demand conditions in a market

in the water': it is an exercise in collecting important information which affords the option of a quick withdrawal if necessary. This metaphor is also consistent with the picture of FDI as a process of increasing commitment to the foreign market, as described in the Scandinavian model of the internationalization of the firm (Johanson and Vahlne, 1977).

7.9 INTERNATIONAL JOINT VENTURES AS REAL OPTIONS

International joint ventures are primarily contractual real options. Although an IJV's physical assets may embody a certain degree of flexibility, the distinctive feature of an IJV from an option perspective is the flexibility afforded by the joint ownership arrangement. There are many different types of IJV, as noted in Chapter 6. This section presents an example which has been chosen to illustrate the option perspective on IJVs in the simplest possible way.

The basic idea is that a partner in an IJV possesses both a 'call option' to buy out the other partner, and a 'put' option to sell out to the other partner, depending upon how the IJV performs in the future (Kogut and Zander, 1993; Chi and McGuire, 1996). The question arises, however, as to why the other partner would be willing to trade on especially favourable terms. One reason is that transaction costs are lower between the partners than they are between ordinary firms, because the partners have got to know and trust each other. They share the gains from this trust by trading equity with each other on mutually favourable terms. This means that the partners possess options to trade on these terms instead of on the terms that would prevail if there were no previous connection between them.

Another explanation is that one of the partners is better informed than the other. Their reputation for being better informed gives them an advantage in negotiations over equity purchase. As the IJV evolves, the more sophisticated partner makes offers to the less sophisticated partner which the latter is willing to accept. In this way information rents accrue to the partner who is better at valuing the joint venture – that is is better at forecasting the IJV's future stream of profits. This mechanism for appropriating information rents will only work, however, if the other partner receives no rival offers from third parties. One reason why they may not receive such offers is that other firms are not so well informed about the prospects for the IJV, because they lack the 'inside knowledge' that is shared by the partner firms. They therefore lack the confidence to make rival offers. The other partner may not possess sufficiently tangible evidence to go out and solicit such offers to test the offers received from the more sophisticated firm. It is this case of asymmetric information which is the basis of the example that follows.

Consider two firms which can go into partnership by sharing ownership of equity on a 50:50 basis. One firm provides finance and the other the human capital, such as the ideas. The issue is analysed from the standpoint of the financial investor, which is the more sophisticated firm. This investor, it is assumed, has identified a small, high-technology, start-up venture which requires capital in order to fund further R&D. The owner of the start-up will sell 50 per cent of his equity for 5 units, or sell out completely for 10 units. These sales must be effected at the outset (period 1), before the outcome of the R&D is known.

In the future (period 2) the outcome of the R&D is revealed to the owners of the firm. The financier knows that if the research is successful then the project will be worth 20 units, whereas if it is unsuccessful, then it will be worthless. The partner, however, is not as good at valuing projects, and believes that if the outcome is successful then it will be worth only 12 units, while if it is unsuccessful, it will still be worth 7 units. These beliefs are reflected in negotiations between the firms, in which the sophisticated firm extracts maximum rents from the unsophisticated one. The unsophisticated partner is willing to sell his 50 per cent stake for $12 - 5 = 7$ units if the outcome is good, and to buy the financial investor's stake for $7 - 5 = 2$ units if the outcome is bad. The outcome does not become public knowledge, so these offers will not be affected by rival bids. The partners come to an informal understanding on these terms when they enter the IJV. Because of the trust between them, they both honour these terms in the following period, even though their initial contributions have been 'sunk' by the start of the second period.

The financial investor has three main alternatives:

1.   Acquire the firm immediately.
2.   Enter a joint venture immediately and review the situation in the next period.
3.   Avoid the project altogether.

If he participates in the IJV then it always pays him to exercise the call option if the outcome is good, because the unsophisticated partner undervalues the project. Thus instead of earning 50 per cent of 20 units, namely 10 units, the investor can pay out an additional 7 units to obtain an additional 10 units, that is the entire 20 units, for himself. Similarly, it always pays him to exercise the put option when the outcome is bad. This is because the unsophisticated partner overvalues the project, since he is willing to pay 2 units to buy more of a project that is actually worthless. Thus the sophisticated partner will not continue with the IJV in its initial form, but will either take over the IJV, or divest his share of it, depending on the outcome of the R&D.

Let the probability of a successful outcome perceived at the outset by the sophisticated investor be p. Then the expected profits of the three strategies are

$$v_1 = -10 + 20p \tag{7.13.1}$$
$$v_2 = -5 + (20 - 7)p + 2(1 - p) = -3 + 11p \tag{7.13.2}$$
$$v_3 = 0 \tag{7.13.3}$$

The first term in equation (7.13.1) is the purchase price for an outright acquisition, and the second term is the profit from the entire project when its outcome is good. The first term in equation (7.13.2) is the cost of buying a stake in the IJV. The second term is the expected profit generated by exercising the call option, and the third is the expected profit generated by exercising the put option.

The solution is

$$i = \begin{array}{ccl} 1 & if & p \geq 0.78 \\ 2 & if & 0.27 \leq p < 0.78 \\ 3 & if & p < 0.27 \end{array} \tag{7.14}$$

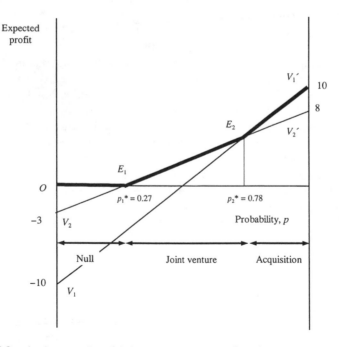

Figure 7.8   An international joint venture as a real option

The solution is illustrated in Figure 7.8. As before the expected profit associated with the ith strategy ($i = 1, 2$) is indicated by the height of the schedule V_iV_i', with the horizontal axis indicating the expected profit of the null strategy (strategy 3). The envelope $OE_1E_2V_1'$ indicates the maximum attainable profit. The IJV is the preferred strategy between the critical values $p_1^* = 0.27$, $p_2^* = 0.78$, which correspond to the switch points E_1, E_2. The figure reveals the IJV as a classic option strategy – namely one that is pursued when the investor is highly uncertain about the outcome of a project.

7.10   INVESTMENT IN AN INTERNATIONAL HUB

All of the previous examples have analysed option strategies within a two-period framework. To keep the models simple, discounting over time has been subsumed by simply taking the interest rate to be fixed, and implicitly discounting income flows at this rate of interest when valuing the asset under different sets of conditions. Not all real options can be analysed in this way, however. This section presents a more complicated problem, in which the exercise of options is a repeated process. It is shown that under certain conditions the solution of such a problem can nevertheless be reduced to the solution of an equivalent problem defined over just two periods of time. The example discussed in this section is a very simple one. A more complex example is discussed in the following section.

This example concerns the real option potential of an international production and distribution hub. Consider a firm that is confronted with a fixed level of global demand, $z > 0$. Demand commences in period 2 and continues in perpetuity at the same level. However, the geographical distribution of this demand is uncertain. There are two possible locations at which demand could be based. In any given period, demand is either all at one location, or all at the other. Demand is distributed at random: in each period the probability of demand being concentrated in one particular location is 0.5, independently of where demand was located in previous periods. Customers at each location demand a specific variant of the product; thus the variety of product acceptable at one location is unacceptable at the other. Both variants of the product sell for a unit price.

The firm can choose between two types of equipment for the production and distribution of the asset. One is a rigid type of equipment, which can only produce one variety of product, and the other is versatile equipment, which can be switched from producing one variety of product to another (see van Mieghem, 1998). Rigid equipment can only service demand at one location, whereas the versatile equipment can service demand at either location. Both types of equipment never wear out. Specific equipment costs $x > 0$ units, while versatile equipment costs y units. Versatile equipment is more expensive than specialized equipment, but is less than double the cost: $x < y < 2x$. Investment in equipment is financed by borrowing at the rate of interest $r > 0$. Each time the versatile equipment is re-tooled to produce a different variety of product, an adjustment cost $a > 0$ per unit output is incurred.

Equipment can be located at one of three places: the two market locations and an intermediate hub. Site costs are the same at each location. If product is exported from one market to another then it passes through the hub, where it has to be trans-shipped. Unit transport costs between each market and the hub are $t > 0$, and the unit cost of trans-shipment at the hub is $s > 0$. It is assumed that total costs are sufficiently low that the null strategy of no production in any location is always dominated by some other strategy.

The problem involves a simultaneous choice of two interrelated factors: the type of equipment, and its location. It is readily established, however, that certain combinations of location and type of equipment are dominated by others. It never pays to use versatile equipment to supply just a single market, because the capital cost is greater. It never pays to locate a specific type of equipment at the hub, because it is cheaper to supply the relevant market locally. It never pays to export from one market to another because, for any given type of equipment, it is always cheaper to export to both markets from the hub.

It follows that whenever specific equipment is used, two items of equipment will be bought, and one will be located in each market. This equipment will be utilized on average only half the time, since for the other half of the time global demand will be concentrated in the other market instead. If versatile equipment is bought, then a single item will be bought, and it will be installed at the hub. It will be utilized continuously.

It follows that there are two main strategies that need to be considered:

1. Invest in rigid equipment in each location and use each piece of equipment only to supply the domestic market.
2. Invest in versatile equipment at the hub and export to both locations.

When versatile equipment is used at the hub, the probability that it needs to be switched in any period is 0.5, because in any two successive periods demand will be in the same location with probability 0.5, and in different locations with probability 0.5. It is assumed that the location of demand in period 2 is not known at the time that the equipment is set up in period 1, so that adjustment costs are liable to be incurred as soon as production commences in period 2.

The expected profits associated with these respective strategies are

$$v_1 = -2x + (z/r) \qquad (7.15.1)$$
$$v_2 = -y - (a/2r) - (t/r) + (z/r) \qquad (7.15.2)$$

The first term in equation (7.15.1) is the cost of purchasing two items of rigid equipment, while the second is the present value of the revenue stream generated by selling z units of product in perpetuity at a unit price. The first term in equation (7.15.2) is the cost of purchasing a single versatile piece of equipment. The second term is the expected present value of the cost of switching the versatile equipment from one variety to another, given that the probability of switching is 0.5. The third term is the cost of transporting product each period from the hub to the relevant export market, whichever market it happens to be. The final term is the present value of the export sales.

For future reference, it is useful to note that expected profits can also be expressed in terms of flows. The net flow of profit each period under strategy 1 is equal to the value of sales, z, less the interest charges on the rigid equipment, $2xr$. Similarly, the net flow of profit under strategy 2 is equal to the value of sales, z, less expected adjustment costs, $a/2$, less transport costs, t, less the interest charges on the versatile equipment, yr. Stating profit as a flow of income is equivalent to multiplying equations (7.15) through by r:

$$v_1' = v_1 r = -2xr + z \qquad (7.16.1)$$
$$v_2' = v_2 r = -yr - (a/2) - t + z \qquad (7.16.2)$$

Subtracting equation (7.16.1) from equation (7.16.2) shows that strategy 2 (the hub) is preferred if

$$(a/2 + t) < (2x - y)r \qquad (7.17)$$

This condition asserts that the sum of expected adjustment cost and transport cost must be less than saving in capital costs effected by purchasing just the single versatile asset.

The condition (7.17) is illustrated in Figure 7.9. The parameter values for which the hub strategy is chosen are indicated by the shaded area in the figure. The figure shows that the hub strategy is most likely to be preferred when adjustment costs are low, transport costs are low, the price premium on flexible equipment is low, and the interest rate is high.

This model demonstrates that hub strategies work best when two aspects of flexibility reinforce each other. The first aspect is the versatility of the equipment – that is how easily it can be switched from producing one variety of product to another – and the second is the ease with which different export markets can be accessed from the same location.

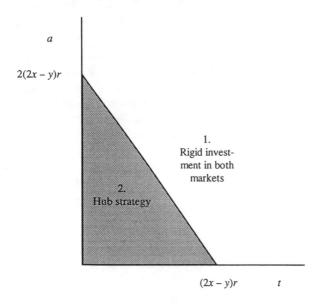

Figure 7.9   A hub strategy as a real option

7.11   PRODUCTION FLEXIBILITY WITHIN THE MULTINATIONAL ENTERPRISE

The preceding models have shown how real option theory can add a new dimension to the analysis of some traditional business issues, such as foreign market entry, and also to some newer issues, such as the pursuit of flexibility through IJVs and production hubs. There is, however, a distinctive body of literature, which has not yet been discussed, which argues that the multinational enterprise affords an intrinsic source of flexibility in its own right (see for example DeMeza and van der Ploeg, 1987; Capel, 1992; Kogut and Kulatilaka, 1994; Mello, Parsons and Triantis, 1995; Rangan, 1997). This flexibility is attributed to the multinational's organizational form: it is asserted that MNEs can use their internal markets to switch production between locations more effectively than non-multinational firms.

While this literature raises an interesting issue, it is by no means evident that its assumptions are sound and its conclusions correct. While an MNE may be well placed to switch production between locations at which it already operates, it may be poorly positioned to switch production to locations where it has never operated before. In the modern global economy many firms seek flexibility through international subcontracting arrangements rather than through FDI, because such arrangements facilitate the relocation of production to newly industrializing countries and transitional economies where they have never operated before.

Nevertheless, the models of multinational flexibility are interesting for the issues that they raise, and they also provide a natural extension of some of the models presented above. It is therefore useful to conclude the sequence of models presented in this chapter with a model of this kind. The model presented here is only loosely based on previous models of this type, because previous models did not use the discrete time–discrete choice approach followed in this book.

The essence of the present model is that there are costs of switching production between locations, and that these costs are lower when the switching is done by an MNE. The nature of the switching is not quite the same as in the previous section, however. The adjustment costs are incurred when a given source of demand is met from a different source of supply. In contrast to the previous model, where uncertainty related to the distribution of demand, uncertainty in the present case relates to the relative costs of alternative sources of supply. The model predicts that volatility in relative costs of production at different locations favours the multinational organization of production.

The model is more complicated than the previous ones, and will be presented in some detail. Algebraic solutions will be derived, similar to those in the previous section. Consider a firm that has a choice of two locations from which to source a given market. This market could be either a global or a local one, but to fix ideas it is useful to regard it as a global one. Production takes place under constant returns to scale. Cost conditions at each location vary independently of each other. At each location the unit cost is b_1 when local conditions are good and $b_2 > b_1$ when local conditions are bad. In the interest of simplicity, the costs imputed to each location are inclusive of distribution costs (that is the costs of transporting the product to the market).

Conditions at each location are revealed at the beginning of each period, in time for production to be allocated in response to cost differentials. The volatility of cost conditions is measured by the transition probability, p; this is the probability that if conditions are good today, then they will be bad tomorrow. Transitions are symmetric: thus p is also the probability that if conditions are bad today then they will be good tomorrow.

The firm controls the distribution of the product to consumers, and it has a choice of whether or not to integrate backwards into production. At each location the firm can either own the production facilities, or subcontract production to an independent firm. Integration reduces the costs of switching production between locations. If the firm owns the production facilities at both locations, then it can internalize the switching of production between the plants. Internalization allows the switching decision to be taken centrally, and co-ordinated administratively from headquarters (although the internal market does not have to work in this particular way). Otherwise the firm must rely on external market co-ordination. With external markets, cost conditions are revealed by subcontractors' price quotations, and production is shifted by re-assigning contracts between producers.

Switching costs are a special type of adjustment cost. For simplicity, it is assumed that adjustment, like production, operates under constant returns to scale. The costs of switching production from one location to another are a_1 with internalization and $a_2 > a_1$ with external markets. The cost differential reflects the problem of bluffing in negotiations, and the legal cost of enforcement, which are encountered under the external strategy (see Chapter 2).

Internalization is not necessarily the best choice, however, because there are costs involved. Internal markets require an organization to be set up. This organization is created by merging the independent producers into the firm. The set-up cost incurred by the merger is $m > 0$. This cost is incurred in the first period, when the merger decision is taken, with production commencing in the second period. The cost of the merger is financed by perpetual borrowing at a fixed interest rate, r. The set-up cost of the organization is the only set-up cost to appear in the model. To keep the model as simple as possible, it is assumed that the production process itself has no capital requirements.

The market served by the firm is of fixed size, z, and price is fixed at unity. This price is sufficiently high, and costs sufficiently low, that production at one location or the other is always profitable.

There are basically two decisions that the firm has to make: whether to switch production between locations as conditions change, and whether to internalize production or not. It never pays to internalize and then not switch production, because under the assumed conditions the only benefit derived from internalization is the reduction of adjustment costs. Thus of the four possible permutations, three strategies dominate:

1. Internalize through merger, and switch production whenever circumstances require.
2. Externalize production, and switch location whenever circumstances require.
3. Externalize production but never switch location.

Because of constant unit costs of production and adjustment, production is always shifted completely from one location to the other: if it pays to shift one unit, then it pays to switch them all. Similar reasoning establishes that, if it pays to switch on one occasion when a cost differential can be exploited, then it pays to switch on every such occasion. Conversely, if it does not pay to switch on one occasion, then it never pays to switch at all.

At the time the strategic decision on multinationality is made, it is assumed, the firm does not know the cost conditions that will prevail in any period. All it knows is that cost conditions at any given location are equally likely to be good or bad, that is that the probability of good conditions at the outset is 0.5 in each location. This belief is consistent with a steady state of the transition process described above: given the symmetry of the transitions, each location is equally likely to experience good or bad conditions at any arbitrarily chosen time.

Since production is always profitable, price is independent of cost, and market size is fixed, the revenues of the firm are independent of its costs. Revenue is a lump sum, and so the maximization of expected profit is equivalent to the minimization of expected cost. The minimization of expected cost occurs over an infinite time horizon but within this time horizon every period from the second period onwards is the same as every other one. Thus minimizing cost in a representative period also minimizes cost over an infinite horizon. Moreover, because the market size is fixed, minimizing total cost is equivalent to minimizing unit cost. It is therefore sufficient to minimize the expected unit cost in a representative period.

In a representative period, picked at random, costs conditions at each location are equally likely to be good or bad. With a switching strategy, it is possible to guarantee that production will take place at the lowest possible cost. Given that cost conditions at each location are independent of each other, a unit cost of b_1 can be achieved with probability 0.75; minimum attainable unit cost is b_2 only when conditions at both locations are bad, which occurs with probability 0.25. Without a switching strategy, however, the probability of incurring a unit cost b_1 falls to 0.5, and conversely the probability of incurring a unit cost b_2 increases to 0.5. Thus the overall expected unit saving from switching in a representative period is $0.25(b_2 - b_1)$.

It is now necessary to calculate the probability, q, that a switch will be necessary. This probability is not the same as the volatility factor, p, introduced earlier, though it depends upon it. When a switching strategy is pursued, production has to be relocated only when the existing location is high-cost and the alternative location is low-cost, because in all other cases the existing location affords the lowest attainable cost. Moreover, under a switching strategy the existing location must have afforded the lowest attainable cost in the previous period.

- If both locations previously had low costs, then a switch is required only if conditions at the existing location change (with probability p) while conditions at the other location do not (with probability $1 - p$). Thus if both locations are low-cost then a switch is required with probability $p(1 - p)$.

- If both locations previously had high costs, then a switch is required only if conditions at the other location change while conditions at the existing location do not; since both locations face identical volatility, a switch is required with probability $p(1 - p)$ once again.
- If the initial location was previously low-cost and the other location was high-cost then a switch is required only if their roles are reversed: this requires two changes, and the probability of this joint event is p^2.

There are only three possibilities to consider, because the fourth possibility is incompatible with the pursuit of a switching strategy. Each of these possibilities is equally likely at an arbitrarily chosen time, so each is weighted by a probability of $1/3$. The probability of a switch is calculated by summing the weighted probabilities derived above:

$$q = (2p(1 - p) + p^2)/3 = p(2 - p)/3 \qquad (7.18)$$

The maximum attainable value of q is $1/3$, which corresponds to a situation where conditions alternate every period at each location, $p = 1$.

The only qualification concerns the initial period. It is assumed that cost conditions in the initial period become known after the strategic decision has been made, but before the allocation of production for that period takes place. Thus there is no need for adjustment in the initial period, because the firm can choose an appropriate location at the outset. The stream of adjustment costs therefore commences a period later than the stream of production costs, and so needs to be discounted to allow for this.

The expected unit costs of the three dominant strategies are

$$c_1 = ((3b_1 + b_2)/4) + (a_1q/(1 + r)) + (mr/z) \qquad (7.19.1)$$
$$c_2 = ((3b_1 + b_2)/4) + (a_2q/(1 + r)) \qquad (7.19.2)$$
$$c_3 = (b_1 + b_2)/2 \qquad (7.19.3)$$

The first term on the right-hand side of each these expressions is the relevant expected unit production cost, the second term (where it appears) is the expected unit adjustment cost, while the third term in equation (7.19.1) is the unit cost of financing a merger. The solution is

$$i = \begin{array}{ll} 1 & if \quad (a_1q/(1 + r)) + mr/z < a_2q/(1 + r); \\ & \quad (a_1q/(1 + r)) + mr/z < (b_2 - b_1)/4 \\ 2 & if \quad (a_1q/(1 + r)) + mr/z > a_2q/(1 + r); \\ & \quad (b_2 - b_1)/4 > a_2q(1 + r); \\ 3 & if \quad (b_2 - b_1)/4 < (a_1q/(1 + r)) + mr/z; \\ & \quad (b_2 - b_1)/4 < a_2q/(1 + r) \end{array} \qquad (7.20)$$

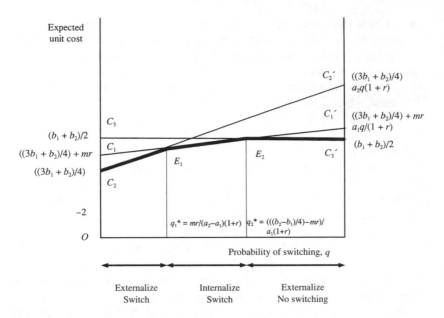

Figure 7.10 Optimization of production sourcing strategies with randomly varying production costs

A typical solution is illustrated in Figure 7.10. The figure has been chosen to illustrate all the possible strategies. Expected unit cost is plotted vertically and the frequency of switching is plotted horizontally. The cost of the ith strategy is indicated by the height of the schedule C_iC_i'. For low frequencies of switching the externalization switching strategy (strategy 2) is always best. A necessary condition for the internalization switching strategy (strategy 1) to be efficient is that the unit cost of financing the merger is less than the expected saving in unit production costs effected by switching, $mr/z < (b_2 - b_1)/4$. Provided a_1 is sufficiently small compared to a_2, the internalization switching strategy will be efficient for some range of frequencies, indicated in the figure by the interval to the right of the critical value q_1^*. The internal switching strategy will become more expensive as the frequency of switching increases, and unless the cost of internal switching is very low, a critical frequency q_2^* will be reached at which it pays to stop switching altogether. The relevant range of frequencies lies to the right of q_2^* in the figure.

The overall conclusion is that the 'multinational solution' based on internalized switching is most likely to be chosen when the cost of internal switching is low, the cost of merger is low, the market size is high, and the rate of interest is low. The most important result, however, is that a moderate frequency of switching favours the multinational strategy – it needs to be sufficiently high to encourage internalization, but not so high that the cost of implementing a switching strategy becomes prohibitive. Using equation (7.18), and inverting the relationship between p and q, shows that a moderate frequency of switching corresponds to a moderate degree of volatility in the cost environment.

7.12 WIDER IMPLICATIONS: THE RELATIONSHIP BETWEEN VOLATILITY, INFORMATION GATHERING AND FLEXIBILITY

With one exception, all the preceding models have assumed that key information cannot be obtained prior to a certain time. In the case of the investment decisions discussed in Sections 7.5–7.7, crucial information about the demand for the asset's services, or its future supply conditions, could not be obtained until the second period. This was the rationale for either deferring the decision, or making a small commitment rather than a large one. In the case of production switching, discussed in Sections 7.10 and 7.11, information about the future distribution of demand, or the future pattern of relative costs, could not be obtained until the date at which the switch had to be made.

These assumptions ignore the possibility that the decision-maker can forecast the relevant events. There are often current symptoms of a future event which can be used to infer whether it will occur, and what form it will take. Such symptoms may be observable at a certain cost. The question then arises whether the expenditure for gathering the information is worthwhile (see Chapter 4). Expenditure on the information resembles an option. Instead of reducing risk by deferring commitment, it reduces risk by raising the chances of making a correct decision when committing resources right away. This was the theme of the model discussed in Section 7.8.

In fact, there may be a spectrum of such information-gathering options. Forecasts based on symptoms are rarely fully accurate. The accuracy of the forecast depends upon how far ahead the forecast has to be made. There are thus two ways of improving a forecast: to defer the forecasting exercise until nearer the date of the forecast event, and to collect more current data with which to forecast ahead. This trade-off exists for every period before the event. The optimal risk-management strategy therefore trades off both information cost against forecast accuracy at any given date, and one date against another in respect of when the forecast is made.

The fact that information is costly to obtain prior to the event to which it relates indicates that information is time-specific to some degree. The cost of collecting information early has a parallel in the spatial dimension – namely, the cost of collecting information at a distance from where the event occurs.

This reflects the location-specificity of information. The time- and location-specificity of information explain why it is so important to be 'at the right time and the right place' as far as the appraisal of investments is concerned.

This point can be extended even further. Information on certain subjects accrues naturally to specialists working in particular fields. One reason is that the information is often generated as a by-product of the implementation of investment projects. The implementation of one project may generate information that is relevant to the appraisal of subsequent projects of the same type. This means that one investment project may actually possess an option value for subsequent projects, because it reduces the risk of mistakes in their appraisal.

It is not only subsequent projects that may benefit from information by-products, however. When a firm has a portfolio of projects underway, information gathered from one project may be used to refine decisions made regarding other projects coming on stream at the same time. Information externalities may well benefit projects operating simultaneously, as well as projects operating sequentially.

Information by-products cannot be effectively utilized, however, if there is no flexibility to respond to the information obtained. To exploit information from one project on another project that is already underway, the second project must be flexible. It must be designed with real options in mind. The greater the potential information externalities, the greater is the advantage of designing real options to go into projects from the outset. This relates to both contractual options like IJVs and non-contractual options such as those afforded by flexible equipment. Cheap information, obtained as a by-product, therefore encourages the systematic pursuit of flexibility. The converse also applies: if one activity is potentially very flexible, then it may be useful to initiate complementary activities which generate information that will help to exploit this potential in the most effective way.

These two-way linkages indicate that the connection between information-gathering and the flexibility of investments is not just an issue that relates to a single investment project, considered in isolation from others, but is an issue that applies to the entire portfolio of activities with which an investor may be involved. A sophisticated investor will optimize the link between information-generation and project flexibility by taking account of all the information externalities that link the projects in his portfolio.

This link between information-gathering and project flexibility has significant implications for the globalizing firm (and also for firms that are already globalized). It shows that the entry strategies pursued in different markets are all linked to one another. The most successful globalizing firms will be those that use the information gathered in each market to exploit the opportunities for flexible responses in all the other markets in which they participate.

7.13 CONCLUSION

This chapter has set out to demonstrate some of the modelling techniques that can be used to implement the research agenda put forward in this book. Real options are only one aspect of the full agenda, but they are a very important element nevertheless. They provide a way of rationalizing many practical aspects of business behaviour which until recently defied analysis: the seeming irrationality of procrastination and delay in committing resources to new foreign markets, and the cautious incremental approach to investment that is so often pursued once the market is entered.

The application of real options to IB issues has been discouraged by confusions over the relation between real options and financial ones. This chapter has sought to clear up some of this confusion by demonstrating that a single set of four key principles underlies both branches of options theory. The principal difference between the two branches of theory lies in the fact that one deals mainly with tradable assets and the other deals mainly with non-tradable ones.

Options reduce risk by providing the flexibility to respond to new information when it becomes available. The key to a successful exploitation of real options is to foresee the kind of information that is likely to become available, and plan the options to exploit this information from an early stage. Flexibility can take many forms: IJVs provide flexibility through contractual options, whereas small reversible investments in versatile assets provide flexibility in a non-contractual form. These forms of flexibility can be combined – for example, by holding a portfolio of IJVs, each of which operates versatile assets, and utilizes information by-products from other IJVs, as well as supplying its own information by-products to them.

This chapter has introduced and synthesized ideas rather than presented an exhaustive treatise on its subject. Much work remains to be done in producing algebraic versions of the numerical models presented above, and in simulating the algebraic models to determine the sensitivity of various option strategies to the parameters which govern them. This chapter has focused on applications to manufacturing, but real options also apply to marketing and R&D (see for example Huchzermeier and Loch, 1997). New models can be generated by modifying the assumptions of the models presented above. The new models can be made more realistic than the ones presented here – for example, by introducing oligopolistic rivalry (Lambrecht and Perraudin, 1996) – but they are also likely to be more complicated too.

Insights from these models can be used to construct 'dynamic' versions of existing static theories. The real option perspective can be applied to standard IB theories, including classic theories such as the product cycle model and its variants (Vernon, 1966, 1974, 1979). The real option perspective can provide a formal analysis of the leads and lags in the internationalization process which is missing from many orthodox accounts of the subject.

REFERENCES

Buckley, P.J. and M.C. Casson (1981) 'Optimal timing of a foreign direct investment', *Economic Journal*, **91**, 75–87

Campa, J.M. (1994) 'Multinational investment under uncertainty in the chemical processing industries', *Journal of International Business Studies*, **25**(3), 557–78

Capel, J. (1992) 'How to service a foreign market under uncertainty: a real option approach', *European Journal of Political Economy*, **8**, 455–75

Chi, T. and D.J. McGuire (1996) 'Collaborative ventures and value of learning: integrating the transaction cost and strategic option perspectives on the choice of market entry modes', *Journal of International Business Studies*, **27**(2), 285–307

DeMeza, D. and F. van der Ploeg (1987) 'Production flexibility as a motive for multinationality', *Journal of Industrial Economics*, **35**(3), 343–51

Dempster, M.A.H. and S.R. Pliska (eds) (1997) *Mathematics of Derivative Securities*, Cambridge: Cambridge University Press

Dixit, A. and R.S. Pindyck (1994) *Investments under Uncertainty*, Princeton, NJ: Princeton University Press

Hirshleifer, J. and J.G. Riley (1992) *The Analytics of Uncertainty and Information*, Cambridge: Cambridge University Press

Huchzermeier, A. and C.H. Loch (1997) 'Evaluating R&D projects as real options: why more variability is not always better', Fontainebleau: INSEAD Working Paper 97/105/TM

Johanson, J. and J.-E. Vahlne (1977) 'The internationalization process of the firm – a model of knowledge development and increasing foreign market commitments', *Journal of International Business Studies*, **8**(1), 23–32

Jorgenson, D.W. (1963) 'Capital theory and investment behaviour', *American Economic Review*, **53**, 247–59

Jorgenson, D.W. (1967) 'Investment behaviour and the production function', *Bell Journal of Economics and Management Science*, **3**, 220–51

Kogut, B. and N. Kulatilaka (1994) 'Operating flexibility, global manufacturing and the option value of a multinational network', *Management Science*, **40**(1), 123–39

Kogut, B. and U. Zander (1993) 'Knowledge of the firm and the evolutionary theory of the multinational corporation', *Journal of International Business Studies*, **24**(4), 625–45

Kulatilaka, N. and E.C. Perotti (1998) 'Strategic growth options', *Management Science*, **44**(8), 1021–31

Lambrecht, B. and W. Perraudin (1996) 'Real options and preemption', Discussion Paper, Department of Economics, Birkbeck College, University of London

Marschak, J. and R. Radner (1972) *Economic Theory of Teams*, New Haven, CN: Yale University Press

Mello, A.S., J.E. Parsons and A.J. Triantis (1995) 'An integrated model of multinational flexibility and hedging policies', *Journal of International Economics*, **39**, 27–51

Rangan, S. (1997) 'Do multinationals shift production in response to exchange rate changes? Do their responses vary by nationality? Evidence from 1977–1993', Fontainebleau: INSEAD Working Paper 97/84/SM

Rivoli, P. and E. Salorio (1996) 'Foreign direct investment under uncertainty', *Journal of International Business Studies*, **27**(2), 335–54

Schmitzler, A. (1991) *Flexibility and Adjustment to Information in Sequential Decision Problems: A Systematic Approach*, Berlin: Springer-Verlag, Lecture Notes in Economics and Mathematical Systems 371

Shackle, G.L.S. (1970) *Expectation, Enterprise and Profit*, Cambridge: Cambridge University Press

van Mieghem (1998) 'Investment strategies for flexible resources', *Management Science*, **44**(8), 1071–7

Vernon, R. (1966) 'International investment and international trade in the product cycle', *Quarterly Journal of Economics*, **80**, 190–207

Vernon, R. (1974) 'The location of economic activity', in J.H. Dunning (ed.), *Economic Analysis and the Multinational Enterprise*, London: Allen & Unwin, 89–114

Vernon, R. (1979) 'The product cycle hypothesis in a new international environment', *Oxford Bulletin of Economics and Statistics*, **41**, 255–67

Wiseman, J. (1989) *Cost, Choice and Political Economy*, Aldershot: Edward Elgar

8. Entrepreneurship and the international business system: developing the perspective of Schumpeter and the Austrian school

8.1 INTRODUCTION

The Annual Conference of the Academy of International Business for 1998 was held in Vienna. The conference provided a useful opportunity to examine the contribution to IB studies of two major schools of economic thought which have their intellectual roots in Vienna – the Schumpeterian school and the Austrian school. As the capital of the Austro-Hungarian empire and a hub of East–West European diplomacy and trade, turn-of-the-century Vienna was a major cultural centre, which attracted many gifted intellectuals (including many recently emancipated Jews). It is not altogether surprising, therefore, that Vienna incubated not merely one but two important schools of economic thought.

Although founded at the end of the nineteenth century, these schools retain considerable intellectual vitality at the beginning of the twenty-first century. The schools are today regarded as 'heterodox' because they reject some of the more restrictive assumptions of the orthodox neoclassical approach to economics. However, as emphasized in Chapters 4 and 5, some of the more restrictive assumptions of the neoclassical approach are quite unnecessary, and indeed are very unhelpful when analysing institutional issues. By relaxing some of the less important and more restrictive neoclassical assumptions, propositions similar to those advanced by the Schumpeterian and Austrian schools begin to emerge within the neoclassical approach. This suggests that Schumpeterian and Austrian approaches are fundamentally more orthodox than they often appear.

They are also more similar to one another than they sometimes appear. Proponents of a heterodox view often stress the differences, not only between their own views and orthodoxy, but between their own views and alternative heterodoxies too. Austrians are often identified with a 'right-wing', pro-market policy stance, and Schumpeterians with a 'left-wing' interventionist one. Yet in one important respect the two approaches are very similar. They share an emphasis on the role of entrepreneurship in the market process. It is, in fact, hardly surprising that the two schools have important factors in common, given that their roots both lie in Vienna, and that Schumpeter himself studied under the early leaders of the Austrian school.

The chapter is structured into three main parts. Sections 8.2–8.5 summarize the main ideas put forward by the two schools, emphasizing those ideas that have the greatest importance for IB. The strengths and weaknesses of the two approaches are evaluated. A comparison of the two approaches suggests that their strengths and weaknesses are much the same. Their principal strength lies in their common emphasis on entrepreneurship. Unlike much contemporary literature on entrepreneurship, which focuses on individual small-firm start-ups, Schumpeter and the Austrians embed their theories of entrepreneurship within a coherent systems view of the economy. Unlike most neoclassical writers, however, they do not take the structure of the economic system as fixed and immutable. Under entrepreneurial stimulus, the structure of the system is permitted to evolve over time. The two schools of thought therefore offer the basis for a *flexible systems* view of the economy, with the flexibility being provided by the entrepreneur. The principal weakness of both theories lies in a rather idiosyncratic view of individual psychology which hinders rather than helps their analysis of entrepreneurial motivation. In fact, many of the aspects of entrepreneurial behaviour that they attribute to idiosyncratic psychology can be readily explained as a consequence of rational action involving the pursuit of non-pecuniary goals subject to information costs, as explained in previous chapters of this book. The other major limitation of the theories is that they apply the flexible systems approach primarily to the national economy. It is, however, a fairly small step, in analytical terms, to extend the flexible systems view from the national to the global economy. This extension provides the basis for a *flexible global systems* view of the economy which is extremely useful for the analysis of IB issues.

Sections 8.6–8.8 show how the flexible global systems view can be used to analyse the evolution of IB operations within the international economy. The schematic approach employed in previous chapters is extended to analyse long-term changes in patterns of foreign trade, foreign investment and international technology transfer. This emphasis on the dynamics of long-term change reflects Schumpeter's historical interest in the rise of capitalism. The basic idea is that entrepreneurial activity leads to continual advances in the international division of labour, which restructure the international economy over time. Small regions become integrated into larger regions as trade, investment and technology flows intensify. Regions integrate into nations, and nations integrate into a global economy. Throughout this process, the web of international trade flows, investment flows and knowledge flows becomes ever more complex. In this way the modern global business system is represented as the outcome of entrepreneurial activity throughout the past millennium.

Sections 8.9 and 8.10 consider potential extensions of the analysis, and discuss the implications of the flexible global systems view for future IB research.

8.2 FROM A NATIONAL TO A GLOBAL PERSPECTIVE

Until recently neither the Austrian school nor the Schumpeterian school paid much attention to IB issues. Their units of analysis were fixed firmly at the national level. Ever since Menger (1871) and Bohm-Bawerk (1884), Austrian writers have taken a national perspective because of their overriding concern to constrain the influence of the nation-state. This stance was a reaction to the Marxist research agenda, which supported the socialization of industry through expropriation. The intellectual influence of Marxism peaked around the turn of the century, and this stimulated the Austrian economists to rebut its economic arguments by exposing its fallacies. Furthermore, it was customary during the later years of the Austro-Hungarian Empire for leading academics, such as the members of the Austrian school, to become involved in government and public administration, and this further sharpened their focus on national rather than global issues.

The Austrian economists claimed that Marxist government was unworkable. They insisted that only the free market system can support efficient economic co-ordination, because only the free market provides price information of the quality needed if choices are to be made in an efficient way. In Austrian theory the entrepreneur has a crucial ideological role as a personification of the market process. The proper role of the state is limited to providing a framework of law that safeguards private property. Private property provides the security that people require if they are to calculate carefully where their best interests lie. The prospect of increasing one's personal holdings of private property also provides the incentives required to stimulate entrepreneurial activity. The state should not intervene directly in the allocation of resources because this will distort incentives – only the market is capable of assigning the ownership of resources in an intelligent way.

Schumpeterians have neglected IB issues for a rather different reason – namely, that they have been distracted by other issues. One of these issues is whether future progress in technology and social organization requires a shift from capitalism to socialism, and an allied centralization of economic power (Schumpeter, 1942). This is clearly related to the Austrian issue concerning the proper limits of the state, and to the Marxist agenda as well. Schumpeterians have tended to line up on one side of the policy divide, however, favouring state intervention to promote industrialization, and the Austrians on the other. Schumpeterians support selective R&D subsidies, indicative planning, and government-funded strategic investments, while modern Austrians favour 'getting the incentives right' (that is defining appropriate property rights) and leaving the market to do the rest.

Another important Schumpeterian issue concerns the cyclical instability of industrial capitalism. Building on the statistical work of the Russian economist Kondratieff, Schumpeter claimed that 'long waves' of between fifty and sixty years duration could be detected in major industrial economies. Kondratieff's evidence referred to prices, but Schumpeter claimed that long waves also occurred in quantities, such as employment and output. He supported this claim with a wealth of historical evidence, documented in his book on *Business Cycles* (1939). This book adopts a comparative international perspective, and charts the shift of technological leadership in the West from the United Kingdom to France, Germany and the United States over two centuries (see also Landes, 1969). However, Schumpeter did not develop his comparative international perspective into a fully-fledged theory of the transmission of cycles from one country to another within an integrated global economy.

According to Schumpeter, long waves occur because technological innovations are clustered in time (see also Mensch, 1979; van Duijn, 1983). Modern followers of Schumpeter have also examined the clustering of innovations in space. Clustering of innovations in space is clearly very relevant to IB issues. The emergence of new locations for innovation clusters may well be a key factor in explaining the shift of technological leadership from one country to another. Clustering at the regional level has been examined by Audretsch (1995). Clustering in different countries has been discussed by Pavitt (1989), while Krugman (1991) has considered its implications for international trade.

Unlike the Schumpeterians, IB scholars have tended to focus on the diffusion of innovations, taking the location of innovations as given (Vernon, 1966). It is claimed that the advantages of diffusing technology within the firm explain why multinational enterprises are so common in innovative industries (Buckley and Casson, 1976). The social cost of communicating an innovation within a firm may be lower too (Teece, 1977).

It is clearly desirable to integrate the IB and the Schumpeterian approach. An integrated view would link the localization of innovation to its subsequent international diffusion through foreign direct investment (FDI). It would make it possible to explain the international pattern of FDI flows between source and host countries in terms of nation-specific comparative advantages in innovation. The link between innovation and diffusion in an international business context has recently been explored by Cantwell (1989, 1995) and Kogut and Zander (1993), and more work is clearly required on the subject.

8.3   THE SCHUMPETERIAN AND AUSTRIAN PERSPECTIVES

Despite the differences of emphasis noted above, Schumpeterians and Austrians have many concepts and ideas in common. One of the most important shared concepts is a well-articulated 'systems view' of the economy. One of the apparent paradoxes of the history of economic thought is Schumpeter's great admiration for Walrasian general equilibrium theory (Schumpeter, 1953) – a theory which gives a distinctive mathematical expression to the structure of the economic system. Walrasian theory is usually perceived as a paradigm of neoclassical theory, because of its emphasis on rational action and equilibrium, and Schumpeter's admiration of Walras is particularly worrying for those modern Schumpeterians who like to emphasize the heterodox nature of Schumpeterian theory. Part of the explanation for the paradox may lie in Schumpeter's elitism, which respected Walras's genius, and in particular his mathematical abilities. However, the most likely explanation is that Schumpeter admired the elegant way in which the Walrasian model formally encapsulates the interdependence found within the economy (Heertje, 1981). A similar emphasis on interdependence is found in Marx's work, which Schumpeter also admired, but here the independence arises from the interplay of social classes. However, where Walras perceives the harmony of equilibrium, Marx perceives the conflict of class warfare. Schumpeter uses the Walrasian model of the interdependence of the economic system in the opening chapters of his seminal work on entrepreneurship (Schumpeter, 1934), and he exploits the system view of the economy throughout the rest of the book.

While Austrians too appreciate the harmony and interdependence of the Walrasian system, they object to the way that the abstract notion of the Walrasian auctioneer displaces the real-world entrepreneur. They also complain that the number of markets in a Walrasian model is fixed. The number of markets is not determined exogenously by the number of different commodities that can be produced, they rightly assert, but endogenously by the initiatives of numerous entrepreneurs. The system is therefore less static and rigid, and more dynamic and flexible, than Walras makes out.

Both Austrians and Schumpeterians also agree on the importance of capital accumulation (another Marxist theme!). The Austrians emphasize that capital consists of intermediate products. The productivity of capital derives from the use of more 'roundabout' methods of production. Both fixed and working capital are included in this analysis. Fixed capital represents a diversion of resources from the production of consumer goods to the production of durable capital goods such as buildings and machinery. This diversion is warranted on the grounds that the capital enhances the productivity of labour, so that over the lifetime of the asset the total amount of consumption goods produced by a given amount of labour will be higher than before. Working capital arises from the fact that production takes time. When a single complicated process is resolved into a set of much smaller processes, economies of specialization are achieved. But the total time required to complete the production of any one item increases as a result. While each worker is kept fully occupied on his speciality, the circulation of work in progress may be delayed by materials being stored while they are passed on from one stage of production to another. The division of labour therefore tends to increase the capital intensity of production, not only because it promotes the mechanization of the simplest stages of production, but because it increases the volume of work in progress too.

8.4 LIMITATIONS OF THE SCHUMPETERIAN AND AUSTRIAN PERSPECTIVES

Another connection between Austrians and Schumpeterians is that both approaches have become imbued with distinctive psychological postulates which are incompatible with a literal interpretation of the neoclassical notion of 'rational economic man'. It would be nice to be able to claim that this common deviation from orthodoxy is due to a 'Viennese connection' – such as the influence of Freud or Jung – but there is no direct evidence to support this. The psychological connection means, however, that both schools of thought have become 'outsiders' where modern economic orthodoxy is concerned.

Schumpeter believed in the distinctive psychology of the entrepreneur. He is motivated by the

> dream and will to found a private kingdom ... what may be achieved by industrial or commercial success is still the nearest approach to medieval lordship possible to modern man ... Then there is the will to conquer; the impulse to fight, to prove oneself superior to others, to succeed for the sake, not of the fruits of success, but of success itself ... Finally there is the joy of creating, of getting things done, or simply of exercising one's energy and ingenuity ... Our type seeks out difficulties, changes in order to change, delights in ventures. This group of motives is the most distinctly anti-hedonist of the three. (Schumpeter, 1934, pp. 93–4)

This quotation indicates the distinctive sociological strand of thinking which Schumpeter introduced into his economic theory in order to do justice to the history of innovation.

Modern Austrian economists have taken a far darker view of human motivation. In his later work, Hayek (1994) abandoned utility theory for a view of human nature in which greed and envy are biologically programmed into human habits and routines. Kirzner (1997) suggests that the opportunities to profit from arbitrage have a magnetic attraction for many human beings. Markets are efficient, he suggests, because people are drawn to them by a compelling prospect of capital gain which dominates any rational calculation of where profits are most likely to be found.

Such 'psychologism' is an unnecessary embellishment of the systems view of the economy referred to above. Insofar as the psychology affords a valid insight into human motivation, the insight can be summarized either as a constraint on the form that an individual's utility function takes, or a statement about the level of information costs they face (Buckley and Casson, 1993). Essentially, Schumpeter argues that individuals value status as well as money, while Kirzner argues that money obtained through the use of private information is valued more highly than money gained through hard work. Schumpeter believes that some individuals (the entrepreneurs) have very much lower information costs than the average person, while the later Hayek believes that information costs are generally so high that few people perceive any real choices at all.

8.5   COMPLEMENTARITY OF THE PERSPECTIVES

Once the psychologism is rejected, the relevance of these theories to IB can be more clearly perceived. The Schumpeterian and Austrian approaches complement each other nicely. Schumpeter offers a model of an evolving economic system driven by intermittent waves of investment stimulated by major innovations. He distinguishes five main types of innovation: process innovation; product innovation; the discovery of a new export market; the discovery of a new source of raw materials; and the creation of a new type of institution (cartels and trusts are what he seems to have had in mind). His own emphasis lay on the first two – namely, the major technologically-driven innovations, such as railways, electricity generation and chemical manufacturing, which have become the main focus of his followers. However, in interpreting the historical record, Schumpeter also recognized the importance of innovations in trade (the third and fourth type of innovation). This establishes a link to the Austrians, who emphasize even more strongly than Schumpeter the importance of innovations in marketing. The Schumpeterian emphasis on technology and the Austrian emphasis on marketing together provide a nicely balanced view of the sources of growth in the international economy.

The two approaches are also complementary with respect to the size of firm. Schumpeter visualizes the entrepreneur as a heroic individual who creates a major business organization to exploit his innovation in a systematic way. The Austrians, on the other hand, emphasize the collective importance of the many small businesses that provide day-to-day flexibility in the market system through localized speculation and arbitrage. It is now widely recognized that large firms and small firms often have a symbiotic relationship with each other. Big firms that serve mass markets create demands for intermediate inputs that smaller firms can fulfil. Even where large and small firms compete, they often do not do so directly, because the large firm often supplies a standardized product delivered in a relatively impersonal way, while the small firm offers a customized product delivered in a more personal manner.

8.6   THE EVOLUTION OF THE INTERNATIONAL BUSINESS SYSTEM

The remainder of this chapter develops the theme of the flexible global economy introduced above. Following Schumpeter, it examines the evolution of the economy in long-term historical perspective. In line with both Schumpeter and the Austrians, it visualizes economic evolution as a process driven by the imaginative innovations of entrepreneurs. The entrepreneurs identify new opportunities for linking different parts of the global economy which have hitherto been isolated from one another on account of barriers created by high transport and communication costs. As transport and communication costs fall, and new linkages are created, new opportunities for specialization arise. The consequent increase in specialization advances the division of labour on a global scale.

The best way to explain the evolution of international business using a systems view is through a sequence of diagrams. These diagrams need to be kept as simple as possible without doing too much violence to the historical record. To this end, it is useful to adopt a number of conventions when setting up the diagrams. The first is that economic activities are indicated by boxes. The number of boxes in a figure indicates the extent of the division of labour. Since the evolution of the global economy is driven by the progressive advance of the division of labour, the number of boxes tends to increase as the economy evolves.

The division of labour has both a functional and a spatial dimension. The functional dimension is indicated by the labelling of the boxes; different letters correspond to different functions. The spatial dimension is captured by developing a simple, two-country representation of the global economy. The two countries chosen are assumed to be at different stages of development. Country 1 is an advanced economy, and country 2 is a less-advanced country that is in the process of catching up with it. The diagrams would take a rather different form if both the countries were at the same stage of development; in particular, the two countries would stand in a symmetric relationship to each other, rather than the asymmetric relationship portrayed below.

The asymmetry is chosen to reflect the localization of innovation in the advanced economy. The innovation of a new function is indicated by a black box. At most (though not all) of the stages of development a new function appears. Each new function appears first in the advanced country (country 1). This function may or may not get transferred to country 2 later on.

As new functions emerge, they need to be linked into the existing network of activities. Linkages involving material flows of products are indicated in the figures by thick lines. The arrows on these lines indicate the direction of material flow. Linkages involving flows of technology and expertise are indicated by thin lines. These lines typically originate with research activity, which is so important that it is specially denoted by a triangle instead of a square.

It is not just functions that can be innovated, but linkages too. It has already been noted that a new function necessarily generates new linkages, but new linkages can appear among existing functions as well. A sophisticated division of labour involves not just a large collection of specialized functions, but a dense set of linkages connecting these functions to each other. New linkages are indicated by black lines, while established linkages are shown in grey. Thus in each figure black denotes innovation: black boxes denote new functions, or new locations for existing functions, while black lines indicate new linkages between them.

There are eight figures altogether. Each is designed to illustrate a particular period in economic history. Periodization is, of course, an arbitrary exercise, and in some cases particular innovations have been allocated to a particular period mainly for expository purposes. Because the economic history of individual countries is so diverse, the diagrams focus on one specific advanced country: Britain (strictly speaking, England). This is warranted on the grounds that its history is well documented – in particular, convenient secondary sources are abundant – and also on the grounds that at crucial periods such as the Industrial Revolution Britain was the most advanced economy in the world. In discussing the British case, a colony that has since become industrialized is used to represent the other country.

The period of British history that is covered is very long – more than one thousand years. This is useful for expository reasons, as it emphasizes the tremendous historical continuity in international business activity. It is also necessary in order to take account of the long lags between major epochs of innovation, as well as the long lags that also used to characterize the diffusion of innovations. It is also historically accurate to trace the origins of the modern international economy back to the beginning of the second millennium. One of the first British entrepreneurs in international business for whom a reliable biography exists is Saint Godric of Finchale (near Durham) who was a pedlar, ship-owner, merchant and crusader 1085–1105 (Farmer, 1987). (Incidentally, he only became a saint because he retired from international business in order to do penance for his ill-gotten gains.) By the thirteenth century London merchants were heavily involved in international trade (Thrupp, 1948) and both the English and the Scots were making foreign direct investments in overseas ports soon after this time in order to support the export trade in wool (Davidson and Gray, 1909).

8.7   DIAGRAMMATIC ANALYSIS

The most basic economy is based on subsistence. Production of primary products, *P*, feeds directly into consumption, *C*, as indicated in Figure 8.1(a). Each household uses its holding of land to produce food for its own needs. Clothing is made from animal by-products and housing is constructed from timber or mud.

The first step in economic development is the emergence of local markets at strategic positions such as defensible hill-forts near river crossings. These sites may also be nascent religious and administrative centres. Peasants trade their household surpluses with each other in periodic markets. Products that

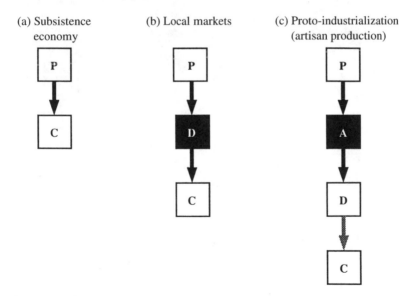

Figure 8.1   Early stages in the evolution of an economic system: the emergence of local markets

are not too perishable may be stored from one market day to the next. Eventually the growth of a nuclear settlement encourages the appearance of shopkeepers (such as butchers and bakers) who trade throughout the week. The settlement becomes a specialized distribution centre, *D*, as indicated in Figure 8.1 (b).

Increasing sophistication in the processing of animal by-products leads to the emergence of artisan production in textiles, pottery and jewellery. The artisans *A* agglomerate in the settlements, selling direct from their work-shops. Some of them may enjoy the regular patronage of the civil and religious authorities. In this way the villages integrate the functions *A* and *D*, as illustrated in Figure 8.1(c).

As village settlements expand into towns and cities, the rising urban de-mand for food promotes large-scale trade with the countryside. This in turn encourages better utilization of natural resources. Farmland is cultivated more intensively, marginal land is reclaimed and brought into production, fishing expands, and different regions begin to specialize in different types of agriculture: arable, dairy husbandry, sheep grazing, and so on. Surplus agri-cultural products are exchanged between different distribution centres. A network of trade develops, with centres at key locations – river junctions, estuaries, and the intersections of drovers' roads – emerging as nodes (Britnell, 1993; Britnell and Campbell, 1994). A hierarchy of towns develops, with the

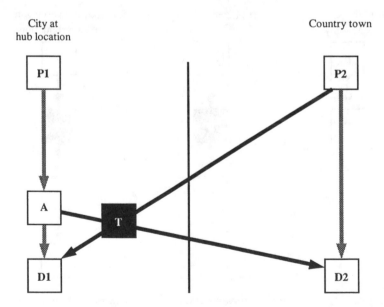

Figure 8.2   The development of inland commerce

trading hubs at the top, where specialist middlemen and supply contractors for the army, church and civil service are based. Artisan production is also concentrated in these centres because commercial wealth creates a large demand for luxury products. Figure 8.2 illustrates a typical link between a major trading centre on the left and a small town lower down the hierarchy on the right. The organization of inter-urban trade is indicated by *T*. It is based in the city. The city exports specialized high-value artisan products to the country town, and imports more homogeneous, surplus, agricultural products. The appearance in the country town's market of city merchants buying up food-stuffs in bulk may lead to charges of 'engrossing' by country consumers, who see the prices of their necessities being bid up. In some cases the merchants may bypass the marketplace, and go direct to the 'farm gates' of the larger farms, thereby 'forestalling' local consumer demand altogether.

International trade develops when the scope of inland trade extends across national borders. Because of the natural advantages of water transport over land transport – already apparent in the widespread use of rivers for inland trade – the cheapest mode of international trade is by sea. Sea transport raises new technological challenges, however. High winds and strong currents make oarsmen less efficient, and require greater use of sail, for which specialized rigging is required. Better navigation is needed when riverbanks and coastal landmarks are no longer visible. The threat of piracy makes armaments necessary. Longer journeys require more of the ship's accommodation to be used for the crew and their supplies. The trade-off between speed, size and security favours larger vessels, which in turn places increasing demands on construction technology. The seagoing sailing ship therefore emerges as the first piece of high-technology capital equipment required for the development of international business operations on a significant scale. This is illustrated in Figure 8.3. International trade, *T*, requires significant inputs of capital goods, *K*, in the form of ships. These ships make important demands on raw materials, *P* – notably timber. It has, indeed, been suggested that the ready availability of timber was an important factor in the development of major naval and commercial powers like seventeenth-century England. Many important maritime powers such as fifteenth-century Venice were noted for their skill in the design and construction of ships (Lane, 1973). They were also notable for the mastery of the geometrical principles underlying the design of navigational instruments. 'Trade follows the flag', it is said, and maritime technology is important not merely in developing trading opportunities but in planting the flag in foreign countries in the first place. Technological know-how of this kind is represented by the triangle *R* in the figure.

There are, of course, serious limits to what can be achieved using capital goods of wooden construction. Buildings are more durable when made of stone, and machinery is more durable when made of metal, but the availabil-

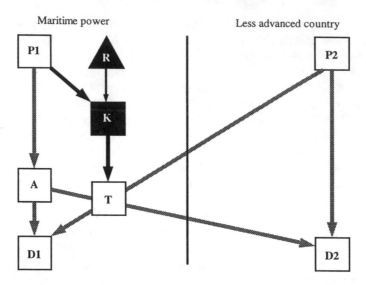

Figure 8.3   Long-distance maritime trade (1100–1350)

ity of stone depends on quarrying technique, and the availability of metals is a function of mining and smelting techniques. Stone replaced wood from an early period where prestigious buildings such as abbeys and churches were concerned. It was not until the beginning of the nineteenth century, however, that metals were widely adopted for machine-building. Nevertheless, an important step towards this goal was taken in the sixteenth and seventeenth centuries. Metals are of particular strategic significance for the manufacture of armaments. Metallurgy was a German speciality imported into England by immigrants. In an age of western European expansion, mining and metallurgical technologies provided colonizing countries like England with the military power they needed to defend their colonies and keep open their trans-oceanic supply lines (Nef, 1932, 1950).

This early military–industrial nexus is illustrated in Figure 8.4. Technology, *R*, now feeds into the primary sector, *P*, as well as the ship-building sector, *K*, boosting the productivity of the metal industries. Capital goods such as metal implements are supplied to the mineral industries, and the mineral industries supply metals to the capital goods industries for heavy guns and the like. This complex of industries benefited from strong demand in England in the seventeenth and eighteenth centuries because of the success of England in both organized piracy and settlement overseas (Parker, 1988). Chartered trading companies, organized on the joint stock principle, rose to prominence, providing consumers with exotic and fashionable imports such as tobacco, tea and beaver hats (Carlos and Nicholas, 1988), and providing

Home country   Colony

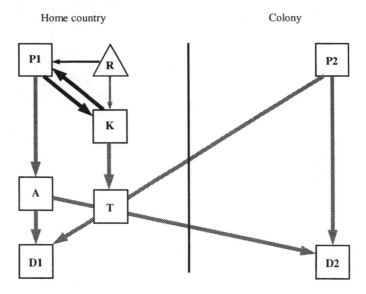

Figure 8.4   Mineral revolution (1560–1640) and oceanic revolution (1660–1760)

the sovereign who chartered them with a useful supply of revenue and soft loans.

Windmills harnessed wind-power in England from the late twelfth-century onwards, and water-wheels were available to harness water power for milling grain. But the bulk of energy supplied in production was still human and animal power. The breakthrough lay in the mining of coal, which became a significant energy source from the beginning of the seventeenth century. Coal was well adapted to raising steam, and steam is ideal as a regular source of stationary power to pump out mines and to power a factory. Although the factory system in the Lancashire cotton industry predates the use of steam power, it was the dependability and self-regulating property of steam power that allowed economies of scale and economies of continuous throughput to be fully realized in the factory system. The factory principle slowly diffused from the textile industry to the pottery industry and then to the engineering trades. Economies of long production runs encouraged firms to specialize in particular product lines, while economies of scale encouraged them to exploit export markets to the full. The modern manufacturing sector was born.

The situation is illustrated in Figure 8.5. The manufacturing sector exploits advances in the design of capital goods, which move at high speed in repeated cycles to perform their operations. The manufacturing sector has an increasing demand for coal and other raw materials from the primary sector.

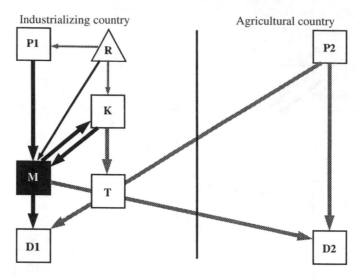

Figure 8.5   Industrial revolution (1780–1850)

It is also capable of achieving new levels of precision thanks to the use of machine tools such as high-speed lathes. The manufacturing sector can therefore contribute to the production of its own capital equipment, creating a virtuous circle in which better manufacturing methods lead to better equipment and better equipment leads to higher standards of production. This is indicated in the figure by the close links between *M* and *K*.

As the manufacturing sector expands its demand for minerals, so local supplies become exhausted (or the cost of extraction rises, which amounts to the same thing from an economic point of view). Raw materials need to be imported in order to sustain industrial growth. The technology of mineral extraction therefore needs to be exported overseas. Capital goods to work the mines need to be exported too. During the age of 'high imperialism' 1870–1914, Britain sent numerous mining and civil engineers abroad to open up new operations in Africa and South America (Cain and Hopkins, 1993). Technology was transferred abroad through the so-called 'free-standing firms' (Wilkins, 1988). These firms facilitated the export of capital equipment and promoted mineral exports from developing countries. As a result, there was a significant growth in intermediate product trade – capital goods were exported from Britain in exchange for raw material supplies. The growth of this trade was promoted by the advent of the steamship, and later by the cutting of new inter-oceanic canals at Panama and Suez (Davies, 1973). The development of new communication modes, such as the telegraph and telephone, also played an important role towards the end of the period.

Imperial power   Dependency, colony or dominion

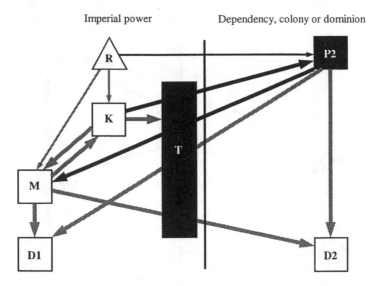

Figure 8.6   Imperialism (1870–1914)

These developments are illustrated in Figure 8.6. Mining technology is diffused from *R* to *P*2, and this is supported by an export of capital goods from *K*. Trade is significantly enlarged by the flow of capital goods and the returning flow of minerals from *P*2 to *M*.

With the imperial age the role of the British economy in promoting industrialization and the growth of trade reached its zenith. By the turn of the century Britain was already being overtaken by the US, and Germany was not far behind. European powers such as France and Sweden were also catching up. They employed the new electrical technologies which allowed them to harness their abundant supplies of hydro-power to overcome their comparative disadvantage in access to coal for raising steam. Britain, meanwhile, remained technologically dependent on its declining reserves of coal.

The first half of the twentieth century was the age of mass production and mass marketing, as Chandler (1977) has so notably emphasized. The emergence of specialized corporate research laboratories (pioneered in Germany) rendered the process of invention increasingly routine. Innovations in products and processes became tightly linked. Advertising became crucial in persuading consumers to accept highly standardized products. Strategies of superficial product differentiation through packaging and the use of colour became increasingly common. This is illustrated in Figure 8.7 by the very close connection between manufacturing, *M*, and distribution, *D*, in the mass-production system. Both draw equally on the stream of

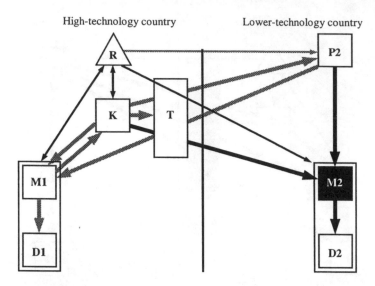

Figure 8.7   Mass production and manufacturing technology transfer (US 1918–1973; UK 1945–1973)

integrated product and process innovations emanating from the laboratory, *R*.

The technological and economic superiority of the US relative to Europe peaked in the early post-war period 1945–60. The 'dollar shortage' created by an enormous demand for US products pushed real wages in the US up to levels which encouraged the export of the simpler manufacturing processes (such as the final assembly of consumer durables) to 'cheap-labour' Europe. Technology transfer replaced trade (Dunning, 1958; Wilkins, 1974).

For the first time in world history, advanced technology had become a mainly proprietary product. The codification of the patent system in the late nineteenth century had been one of the factors encouraging the growth of entrepreneurial R&D in corporate laboratories, and the owners of new technologies wished to protect their intangible assets when they transferred them overseas. However, the contractual problems of licensing had not been fully resolved, and so FDI was the chosen mode. High-technology US firms invested directly in Europe. The European operation was essentially a replica of the US one, with one important exception, illustrated in Figure 8.7 – namely, that the capital goods embodying the process technology continued to be made in the US (as were some of the more sophisticated components too).

As Western Europe, and then Japan, narrowed the productivity gap with the US, the US once again became an economic base from which to export

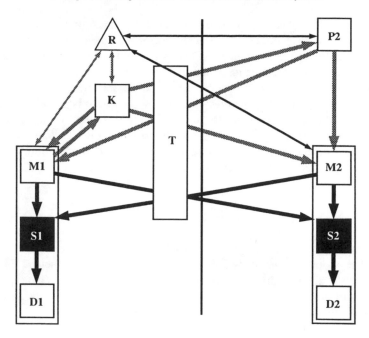

Figure 8.8   Globally rationalized production with global learning

ordinary manufactured products. The liberalization of trade under the auspices of UNCTAD had reduced tariffs, and the widespread adoption of containers as an inter-modal means of transport meant that international specialization of production could now be effected within the same manufacturing industry as well as between different manufacturing industries. Different countries began to specialize in different stages of production according to their natural resource endowments, their geographical position on international shipping routes and their structure of labour and management skills. Figure 8.8 shows how the sequence of production in a given industry can now be spread over different locations. It illustrates two relatively 'footloose' manufacturing operations, *M*1 and *M*2, each based in a different country, which feed complementary components into an assembly line. Each country has its own assembly operation which in turn feeds into its domestic distribution channel. These assembly operations, *S*1, *S*2, may combine the same mixture of components into slightly different configurations in order to adapt their final products to local consumer tastes in each country.

Another feature of the second half of the twentieth century was dramatic innovations in personal transportation and remote communication – the jet aircraft for business travel and the computer network for business communication. By reducing lags in information flow, these innovations allowed firms to learn from their operating experiences not only in their home environment but also in foreign environments. This is illustrated by the double-arrows which are attached to all the information flows in Figure 8.8. In Figure 8.7 the double-headed arrows applied only to domestic information flows in the home economy; the foreign country was still supposed to be a passive recipient of know-how (although in the case of countries such as Japan, where absorption of technology was very rapid, this supposition was clearly wrong). The double-headed arrows emphasize the importance to modern multinationals of learning from their operations throughout the world.

8.8   SOME 'LESSONS OF HISTORY'

The advantage of this schematic approach to the historical evolution of the global economy is that it demonstrates how a number of themes emerge repeatedly – albeit in different guises – at different epochs. This is in marked contrast to conventional histories of IB, which focus only on the last one hundred years or so.

IB history is often told simply in terms of the 'managerial revolution', which began with the US trust movement of the 1890s, spread domestically in the US until 1945, and internationally thereafter. This story emphasizes the development of mass-production technologies through corporate R&D, and their international diffusion through FDI. It is a story about the corporation rather than about the individual entrepreneurs who took the key decisions. It is about strategically-minded chief executives, supported by passive shareholders (the absentee financiers of the firm). Executives were successful, it is suggested, because they were professionally trained – they went to the right business schools, in other words – rather than because they were natural entrepreneurs.

This is a very specific story, which cannot be generalized over time. Indeed, it cannot be generalized over space either because, as the controversy over Chandler (1990) shows, the US experience does not really fit Britain, France, Germany or Japan. It is also a misleading story – this rather triumphalist account of the emergence of the modern corporation in the US may itself have contributed to the managerial complacency which became evident in the US towards the end of the 'golden age' of Western growth in 1973 (see Chapter 1). The evolution of the modern multinational, with its 'visible hand' of management replacing the 'invisible hand' of the market, may have looked like the culmination of economic evolution from the standpoint of the 1970s, but from the standpoint of the new millennium it looks just like any other transient historical episode – a brief spell of success which sowed the seeds of its own decline.

It is one of the strengths of the systems view that it embeds the developments of the last one hundred years within a general account of the advance of the international division of labour over the millennium. Taking the history back to earlier epochs strips away the legal cloak of incorporation, which disguises the true decision-makers in the firm, and focuses attention directly on the entrepreneur. As a result, it is possible to identify more clearly the fundamental sources of innovation. In terms of the scheme set out above, the conventional story is mainly a story about changes in research, R, and manufacturing, M, which has very little to say about changes in other functions such as primary production, P, capital goods production, K, or trade, T. It is true that distribution, D, also figures in the story, but only insofar as D is integrated with P. By taking a long-term perspective it is possible to identify important innovations in all of the functions included in the systems view.

- Technology, R, has a direct impact on the volume of trade, T, because of its influence on transport costs. The early development of international trade owed a great deal to advances in astronomy which improved navigation. Metallurgical technique improved the efficiency of naval guns and helped to keep piracy under control. The development of steam technology made scheduled liner shipping services viable, while jet aircraft now facilitate international just-in-time production of high-value/weight precision products like PCs.
- In explaining economic evolution it is important to distinguish between stocks and flows. Stocks are represented by capital. Stocks are necessary to support flows, because lags in the circulation of flows mean that flows cannot expand unless stocks increase at the same time. To permit flows to expand without a significant increase in stocks, the productivity of stocks must expand. Improving the productivity of the capital stock, K, in this manner is therefore crucial if long-run economic growth is to be financed at acceptable cost. This is why many of the most important technological advances are the ones that allow capital to be utilized more productively. Early advances in the design of textile equipment allowed machines to operate at high speed, increasing the throughput that could be achieved with a given amount of capital equipment, and giving an immediate boost to the industrial revolution. Sometimes advances in fixed capital afford economies in working capital. Thus advances in the design of ships and steam locomotives speeded up freight transport and reduced the amount of inventory and work in progress needed to support long-distance trade. More recently, advances in the design of computers have allowed a larger volume of information to be exchanged using a given quantity of computer hardware because the hardware can operate at higher speed.

- The technology of primary production, P, is just as important in the long run as the technology of manufacturing in raising global productivity. In the twentieth century, mining tends to be seen as a mature industry, even though allied activities such as oil exploration are obviously high-technology operations and are crucial for the cost-effectiveness of energy-intensive manufacturing industries. It is clear that advances in mining technologies prepared some of the foundations for the industrial revolution by improving the supply of coal; the low cost of British coal was undoubtedly a major stimulus to the adoption of steam-power in Britain, and this reinforced the mass-production tendencies of the factory system along the lines described above. Following Corley (1983) and Hennart (1983), more attention needs to be given to the primary sector in order to provide a balanced view of IB history.

- The distribution sector, D, also emerges as crucial. If there is a single image of the entrepreneur which fits all epochs of this millennium it is that of the merchant – someone who identifies market opportunities and places orders with producers in order to exploit them (Casson, 1997). It is the merchant who supplies much of the information on which the producer depends in order to determine an appropriate production mix. The role of the merchant was somewhat disguised in the twentieth century, though. In the era of mass production, when distribution was often vertically integrated with manufacturing, the role of the merchant was usually played by a manager – often the marketing director. The fact that the manager received a fixed salary should not disguise the fact that because of the highly judgemental nature of his decision-making, he was exposed to very considerable risks. A major risk related to his reputation in the industry, which meant that if he was dismissed for a spectacular failure he would never succeed in getting a similar job again. Following the recent trend towards the 'dis-integration' of firms, the role of internal entrepreneurs is becoming more visible again. Dis-integration, together with 'downsizing' and 'delayering', enhances the flexibility of the firm, as explained in Chapter 1, and gives more scope for the display of initiative by an internal entrepreneur. New information technology enhances entrepreneurial access to the knowledge base of the firm, as explained in Chapter 5. When the marketing department of a firm sells directly to consumers through a tele-sales department, and procures its product through competitive subcontracting, or even through simply 'badging' existing commodities – it is evident that the 'merchant' capability of the marketing manager is key to the firm's success. The emergence of entrepreneurship within the modern flexible firm may seem like a new development from the short-term perspective of the business strategy literature, but it is an enduring theme in business success as far as the historical record is concerned. The modern style of entrepreneurial management represents a return to a management style that first emerged in Western business many centuries ago.

8.9   FUTURE RESEARCH

There are two other points which, though not immediate consequences of the systems view, nevertheless merit further research.

It is worth noting that the 'product cycle' phenomenon applies not only to the international diffusion of manufacturing technologies, but to the diffusion of innovations in general. In particular, it applies to innovations of an institutional nature, such as the emergence of agricultural markets, and the large-scale financing of speculative exploration for minerals. In the case of Britain, these ideas were exploited domestically before being exported to other countries. It was mainly after London merchants had developed provincial sources of agricultural supply, and London capitalists had opened up mines in Cornwall and elsewhere, that they turned their attention to similar developments overseas. Many of the colonial exploits of the age of high imperialism were international versions of business ventures that had proved successful in the domestic sphere. Even today, in a 'post-colonial' world, general institutional innovations such as privatization and deregulation are very clearly following the traditional product cycle path of diffusion from advanced countries to developing ones. The product cycle may well have speeded up in manufacturing as global competition in that sector has intensified, but the cycle continues to work as steadily and as inexorably as ever in other fields.

The second point is that the diffusion of knowledge through licensing and FDI is a relatively recent phenomenon. Although an historical perspective often undermines the idea that recent developments are novel and unprecedented, it occasionally identifies developments which are truly novel. From this perspective, the extension of property rights to intangible assets such as knowledge during the nineteenth century was a key development. Up to this time, patents had only been awarded on a relatively *ad hoc* basis. There was no formal and systematic mechanism by which an ordinary citizen could acquire a patent to protect the exploitation of a new technology. Monarchs occasionally issued charters and patents to court favourites, but these were usually in connection with the collection of taxes and the working of mines rather than the exploitation of inventions. Even where patents for technology were issued, they were not normally recognized in other countries. It was not until the late nineteenth century that patent rights became internationally recognized, and that it became feasible to engage in international technology licensing as a means of transferring technology overseas.

Prior to the development of international licensing, migration was the major mechanism by which practical technological expertise diffused between countries. Skilled labour migration was strongly driven by market forces. Skilled workers protected their technological know-how through secrecy. They either kept their secrets to themselves, as 'tricks of the trade' to be passed on only to their apprentices, or as 'mysteries' to be shared among members of a guild (that is a craft trade union, or trade association). The Industrial Revolution witnessed significant labour mobility as mechanics moved about Britain, passing on their skills from one region to the next (Pollard, 1981). Later, the mechanics roved abroad, often going there as contractors to erect machinery and staying to set up a works of their own, or to work for expatriate entrepreneurs (Henderson, 1954). Indeed, before the Industrial Revolution an important element of 'mercantilist policy' in several European countries was to prevent emigrant workers from taking their trade secrets abroad, although generally the policy had little effect because it was so difficult to enforce. Indeed Britain, with its relatively stable and liberal political regime, was a major beneficiary of a continental 'brain drain' in the eighteenth century. Similarly, the US has benefited from a British 'brain drain' since 1945. Despite its contemporary relevance, however, migration of labour remains a neglected aspect of IB theory. Although migration is regularly discussed in the context of international human resource management, the focus is very narrowly upon the logistics of the relocation of employees within the firm. There has been little attempt to integrate discussion of this issue with wider aspects of IB, yet it is obvious, on reflection, that because of the 'tacit' nature of much technological knowledge, the transfer of technology and the migration of skilled labour are very tightly linked.

8.10   CONCLUSION

There are many other insights which can be derived from a detailed application of the systems view to the evolution of international business. The sample of results derived above should suffice to demonstrate the promise that is offered for further research. The systems view set out here is distinctively Viennese on account of its emphasis on the flexibility of the international business system, and on the importance of the entrepreneur in providing this flexibility.

The Schumpeterians and the Austrians ranged more widely, and displayed more intellectual curiosity, than most modern scholars would dare to do. Schumpeter, in particular, was not intimidated by the prospect of mastering the history of capitalism in many different countries over a long period of time – since the rise of negotiable credit instruments in the thirteenth century, in fact. It is ironic that despite the modern rhetoric of 'globalization' and 'evolution', modern IB scholars are in many respects more parochial than were the intellectual giants of Vienna one hundred years ago. International business scholars of today could derive a great deal of intellectual stimulus from re-reading classic authors such as Schumpeter, Menger and Bohm-Bawerk. It is hoped that this chapter will encourage them to engage with these writers for themselves.

REFERENCES

Audretsch, D.B. (1995) *Innovation and Industrial Evolution*, Cambridge: Cambridge University Press

Bohm-Bawerk, E. von (1884) *Capital and Interest*, authorized trans., London: Macmillan 1890

Britnell, R.H. (1993) *The Commercialisation of English Society, 1000–1500*, Cambridge: Cambridge University Press

Britnell, R.H. and B.M.S. Campbell (eds) (1994) *A Commercialising Economy: England 1086 to c.1300*, Manchester: Manchester University Press

Buckley, P.J. and M.C. Casson (1976) *The Future of the Multinational Enterprise*, London: Macmillan

Buckley, P.J. and M.C. Casson (1993) 'Economics as an imperialist social science', *Human Relations*, **46**(9), 1035–52

Cain, P.J. and A.G. Hopkins (1993) *British Imperialism: Innovation and Expansion 1688–1914*, London: Longman

Cantwell, J.A. (1989) *Technological Innovation and Multinational Corporations*, Oxford: Blackwell

Cantwell, J.A. (1995) 'The globalisation of technology: what remains of the product cycle?', *Cambridge Journal of Economics*, **19**(1), 155–74

Carlos, A. and S.J. Nicholas (1988) 'Giants of an earlier capitalism: the chartered trading companies as modern multinationals', *Business History Review*, **62**, 399–419

Casson, M.C. (1997) 'Entrepreneurial networks in international business', *Business and Economic History*, **26**(2), 811–23

Chandler, A.D., Jr (1977) *The Visible Hand: The Managerial Revolution in American Business*, Cambridge, MA: Belknap Press of Harvard University Press

Chandler, A.D., Jr (1990) *Scale and Scope*, Cambridge, MA: Belknap Press of Harvard University Press

Corley, T.A.B. (1983) *A History of the Burmah Oil Company, 1886–1924*, London: Heinemann

Davidson, J. and A. Gray (1909) *The Scottish Staple at Veere*, London: Longmans Green

Davies, P.N. (1973) *The Trade Makers: Elder Dempster in West Africa*, London: Allen & Unwin

Dunning, J.H. (1958) *American Investment in British Manufacturing Industry*, London: Allen & Unwin

Farmer, D.H. (1987) *Oxford Dictionary of Saints*, 2nd edn, Oxford: Oxford University Press

Hayek, F.A. von (1994) *Hayek on Hayek* (eds S. Kresge and L. Wenar), London: Routledge

Heertje, A. (1981) *Schumpeter's Vision*, New York: Praeger

Henderson, W.O. (1954) *Britain and Industrial Europe, 1750–1870*, Liverpool: Liverpool University Press

Hennart, J.-F. (1983) 'The tin industry', in M.C. Casson *et al.*, *Multinationals and World Trade*, London: Allen & Unwin, 225–73

Kirzner, I.M. (1997) 'Rationality, entrepreneurship and economic "imperialism"', in S.C. Dow and P.E. Earl (eds), *Conference to Celebrate Brian Loasby's Work at Stirling University, 1967–1997*, 1–21

Kogut, B. and U. Zander (1993) 'Knowledge of the firm and the evolutionary theory of the multinational corporation', *Journal of International Business Studies*, **24**(4), 625–45

Krugman, P.R. (1991) *Geography and Trade*, Cambridge, MA: MIT Press

Landes, D.S. (1969) *The Unbound Prometheus: Technological Change and Industrial Development in Western Europe from 1750 to the Present*, Cambridge: Cambridge University Press

Lane, F.C. (1973) *Venice: A Maritime Republic*, Baltimore: Johns Hopkins University Press

Menger, K. ([1871] 1971) *Principles of Economics* (eds J. Dingwall and B.F. Hoselitz), New York: New York University Press

Mensch, G. (1979) *Stalemate in Technology*, New York: Ballinger

Nef, J.U. (1932) *The Rise of the British Coal Industry*, London: Routledge

Nef, J.U. (1950) *War and Human Progress: An Essay on the Rise of Industrial Civilisation*, London: Routledge

Parker, G. (1988) *The Military Revolution: Military Innovation and the Rise of the West*, Cambridge: Cambridge University Press

Pavitt, K. (1989) 'International patterns of technological accumulation', in N. Hood and J.-E. Vahlne (eds), *Strategies in Global Competition*, London: Routledge

Pollard, S.J. (1981) *Peaceful Conquest: The Industrialization of Europe 1760–1970*, Oxford: Oxford University Press

Rosenberg, N. (1982) *Inside the Black Box: Technology and Economics*, Cambridge: Cambridge University Press

Schumpeter, J.A. (1934) *The Theory of Economic Development* (trans. R. Opie), Cambridge, MA: Harvard University Press

Schumpeter, J.A. (1939) *Business Cycles: A Theoretical, Historical and Statistical Analysis of the Capitalist Process*, New York: McGraw-Hill

Schumpeter, J.A. (1942) *Capitalism, Socialism and Democracy*, New York: Harper & Brothers

Schumpeter, J.A. (1953) *History of Economic Thought* (ed. Elizabeth Boody Schumpeter), London: Allen & Unwin

Teece, D.J. (1977) 'Technology transfer by multinational firms: the resource costs of transfering technological know-how', *Economic Journal*, **87**, 242–61

Thrupp, S.L. (1948) *The Merchant Class of Medieval London: 1300–1500*, Ann Arbor: University of Michigan Press

van Duijn, J.J. (1983) *The Long Wave in Economic Life*, London: Allen & Unwin

Vernon, R. (1966) 'International trade and investment in the product cycle', *Quarterly Journal of Economics*, **80**, 190–207

Wilkins, M. (1974) *The Maturing of the Multinational Enterprise: American Business Abroad from 1914 to 1970*, Cambridge, MA: Harvard University Press

Wilkins, M. (1988) 'The free-standing company, 1870–1914: an important type of British foreign direct investment', *Economic History Review*, 2nd series, **41**, 259–82

9. Networks in international business

9.1 INTRODUCTION

Entrepreneurship is widely recognized as a key factor in economic growth (Leibenstein, 1968). Historical studies of commercialization and industrialization suggest that the speed of 'take-off' is higher when entrepreneurs in related lines of activity work well together (Grassby, 1995). In the aggregate, entrepreneurs may work better as a co-operative network than as a collection of competitive individualists. Unfortunately, attempts to develop the idea of an 'entrepreneurial network' encounter the difficulty that both 'entrepreneur' and 'network' are somewhat nebulous concepts. Using economic theory, however, it is possible to define them in a more rigorous manner. This chapter elucidates the concept of an entrepreneurial network, distinguishes different levels of entrepreneurial network, and shows how these different levels have interacted historically to promote growth in the international economy.

The chapter is in three main parts. The first part analyses the concept of a network. The second discusses entrepreneurship, while the final part examines different types of entrepreneurial network, and considers the factors that influence their structure and their location.

9.2 AN ECONOMIC APPROACH TO NETWORKS

Until recently, economists assumed that competitive markets could handle information in a costless manner, failing to recognize that, whatever kind of institution is involved, information-processing incurs substantial costs. Moreover, to explain why people compete so readily, economists assumed that material greed was the dominant human motive. Recent research has sought to remedy these weaknesses (Casson, 1995). Information costs have been incorporated into decision-making using the theory of teams (Carter, 1995), and ethical constraints on greed have been introduced using theories of altruism (Collard, 1978) and 'self-control' (Thaler and Shefrin, 1981). In line with these trends, this chapter emphasizes information costs, and also stresses the social and ethical dimension of behaviour.

Within this new theoretical framework, networks emerge quite naturally as co-ordinating mechanisms. Co-ordination can also be effected through firms and markets. Networks have been commended as alternatives to firms on the grounds that their decision-making is more democratic and their outcomes more equitable. It has been said that networks are preferable to markets because they involve more social contact and encourage information to be shared; they are said to be more co-operative and less competitive, and to reinforce the sense of mutual obligation on which society depends (Best, 1990). The new theoretical perspective shows that networks are often more efficient too. Communication may be richer and more reliable within a network than within either a firm or a market. The question is no longer whether networks are required for co-ordination, but simply under what conditions they work best.

The choice between firm, market and network may be analysed using the principle that the most efficient arrangement will survive and less efficient arrangements will not. Individual members of a network face the alternatives of trading impersonally in a market or becoming ordinary employees of a firm. If the gains from belonging to the network are less than the gains they anticipate from these alternatives, then they will quit the network. If everyone behaves the same way then the network will disintegrate. Conversely, if people believe that they would be better off within a network than within a firm or market, then they will quit to join the network instead. In the long run the arrangement used under any given set of circumstances has a tendency to be the efficient one from the private individual's point of view.

What is efficient in one industry, or in one location, may not be efficient in another, however. Thus different institutional arrangements may coexist in different parts of the economy. The role of network theory is to identify the factors which govern which arrangement is used under which circumstances. As circumstances alter, the balance of advantages may change over time; thus a successful network may start to decline if a shift in technology or a change in the structure of demand creates new problems with which firms or markets can deal more easily.

Given that networks are widely used, it would be surprising if they all took the same form. Historical evidence clearly points to diversity. For example, the networks of the Northern Italian textile districts (Bull, Pitt and Szarka, 1993) have always been very different from the networks of the merchant community of a great metropolis like London (Brenner, 1993). There are differences across function (manufacturing, banking, scientific research), across industries (between mining and metal fabrication, for example), over space and over time. Within the general concept of a network, therefore, different types of network need to be identified. The failure, so far, to develop an adequate typology of networks is one of the major obstacles to further advance in the field. Without an adequate typology it is impossible to explain how the form of the network adapts to the specific co-ordination problems that it is used to solve.

The importance of distinguishing different kinds of network is underlined by the way that membership of different kinds of network overlaps. Some people belong only to local networks, based in small regions such as industrial districts or rural 'shires'. These people include self-employed artisans, leading farmers, local dealers, and so on. In each region, however, there will be a few people who belong to national networks too. These middle-level entrepreneurs include local wholesale merchants and other leading local employers. Within a national network there will be some who belong to an international network. These high-level entrepreneurs include major export and import merchants, managers of large industrial concerns, bankers, and so on.

A feature of entrepreneurial networks is that members of a high-level network specialize in belonging to several lower-level networks. Thus members of the international network will deliberately keep in contact with several national networks, while members of a national network will deliberately keep in contact with several local networks. The higher-level entrepreneurs maintain a presence in lower-level networks so that they can promote trade and investment between people in different lower-level networks. At each level they use their own network to share information that is surplus to their own requirements, and receive similar information in return. Each member may have knowledge of some local network that they cannot put to any further use themselves, but which may still be valuable to other people. Each member thereby derives advantage from information that others cannot use. Through the network they can also club together to advance their mutual interest in free trade, cheap transport and security of property.

9.3   BASIC CONCEPTS AND DEFINITIONS

An adequate definition of a network must be sufficiently general to accommodate the diversity noted above, yet specific enough to form the basis for rigorous analysis. For the purposes of this chapter a network may be defined as *a set of high-trust relationships which either directly or indirectly link together everyone in a social group*. A linkage is defined in terms of information flow between two people. It is a two-way flow in which individuals both send messages and receive them. The individual linkage is the basic element from which a network is built up. Different configurations of linkage create different kinds of network. In a dense network almost everyone can communicate directly with everybody else, whereas in a sparse network people often have to communicate indirectly through someone else instead. The geometry of the linkages is one of the dimensions on which a typology of networks can be based.

Networks play an important role in synthesizing information. Most economic decisions – in particular, investment decisions – are sufficiently complex that they cannot be taken using only information from a single source. It is necessary to pool information from several sources. Thus an employer seeking to expand production needs to know about product prices and raw material prices, as well as the cost of machinery and the latest technology embodied in it. While he could research these issues for himself, it is often cheaper to get information and advice from other people instead. 'Who you know' is often more important than 'what you know' because the *people* that you know can plug the gaps in *what* you know. This, of course, depends on knowing the *right* people. Sometimes the right people are those who know a lot of facts, but more often they are people who simply know a lot of other people who in turn know useful facts. These people can act as brokers, linking the decision-maker who demands the information to the person who ultimately knows the facts.

It is important to note that the flows of resources that the network is used to co-ordinate may also constitute a network, though not a network of the kind described above. They form a network in the sense that different factories within an industrial district may be connected to one another by intermediate product flows, as when leather soles and leather uppers are passed to an assembly line in which they are sewn together to make up shoes. Products may be transported over networks too; thus goods destined for export may be transported over a railway network, passing through various railway junctions (nodes) on their way to a port. Here they may be loaded onto liner ships, which follow a network of routes to different parts of the world. The difference between these networks and the type of network defined above is that the network defined above is concerned with information flow, and not with the flow of material products themselves. The material flows are the objects of co-ordination and the information flows are the means by which they are co-ordinated. The subject of this chapter is information flow, but to understand why different structures of information flow are used in different circumstances it is, of course, necessary to understand the structure of the product flow as well. This is illustrated by the modelling of international trade flows at the end of this chapter.

9.4   THE QUALITY OF INFORMATION

Considered as a commodity, information faces serious problems of quality control. Information may be false, and acting on false information can be very costly indeed. Information may be incorrect because of the *incompe-tence* of the person who supplies it – for example, his observations may not be correct. It may be due to a *failure of communication* – language difficulties or cultural differences may lead to a message being misconstrued. Finally, the error may be due to *dishonesty*. The source of the information may not bother to check it properly because he knows that someone else will suffer the consequences. More seriously, he may deliberately distort the information to influence the recipient's behaviour to his personal advantage. Networks can improve the quality of information by diffusing competence, in the form of best-practice techniques, by standardizing language and culture to reduce communication costs, and by encouraging honesty between members (Casson, 1997).

Dishonesty is a particular problem for information embodied in contracts. Contracts may be offered purely to lure people into situations where they can be taken advantage of. Dishonesty can be controlled in various ways. If there is a prospect of further trades, then enlightened self-interest may suggest to a potential cheat that the cheating should be postponed until further trades have taken place. If there is always a prospect of future trades, so that no-one is sure when the last trade will take place, then honesty may be sustained indefinitely. Repetition can be encouraged by breaking down one-off, large-value trades into recurrent low-value trades. This may also help to reduce inventory costs, though transport costs will almost certainly increase as a result. There are many instances, however, such as the supply of indivis-ible durable goods and infrastructure, where this is not practicable.

An alternative approach is to invest in reputation mechanisms. While peo-ple may not trade with the same person again, they may well expect to trade with people who are known to them. If they cheat one person then word may get around to other people and future trades will be lost as a result. This discourages cheating at the outset. Because networks facilitate such informa-tion flow, they can play an important role in strengthening reputation mechanisms.

The logic of this argument has a weakness, nonetheless. However enlight-ened, the logic of self-interest is that the decision to cheat represents a finely-tuned response to the circumstances that prevail at the time. The fact that a person cheated one trading partner does not necessarily mean that they will cheat another, because the material incentives may be different in the second case. To transfer experience from one encounter to another in a relevant form, the reputation mechanism must convey a large amount of information on the situation in which the cheating took place.

A further weakness of the reputation mechanism is that it only works if the cheat is caught. While it may discourage some people from cheating, it may simply encourage others to put more effort into devising more subtle forms of fraud. Finally, the assumption that reputation is of purely instrumental value has a number of counter-factual implications. For example, not only will businessmen start to defraud their customers shortly before they plan to retire, but they will maximize the value of their final transactions in order also to maximize their fraudulent gain. This is because, by assumption, they care nothing for their reputation in its own right.

This is where the high-trust nature of the network relationship becomes important. In a high-trust relationship both parties can trust each other even though they each face a material incentive to cheat. Because by definition a network is high-trust, the chances of being cheated are much lower when trading within a network than when trading outside it.

The basic idea behind a high-trust network is that people face emotional incentives as well as material ones, and that emotional incentives of an appropriate kind can outweigh material incentives that would otherwise induce people to cheat. If each person knows that the others face an emotional incentive of this kind, then each will believe that the others will not cheat. This belief is warranted because the supposition is correct. No-one cheats, predictions are borne out, and so a high-trust equilibrium is sustained.

9.5   EMOTIONAL MECHANISMS THAT ENGINEER NETWORK RELATIONS

What kind of emotional incentives are involved? One idea that will *not* be followed up here is that biologically-driven emotions, such as desire for revenge, help to sustain a climate of fear which discourages cheating. Victims will pursue cheats relentlessly, it is said, even at major material cost to themselves, just for the pleasure that 'getting even' affords. Potential cheats know this – even if they do not realize it to begin with, they may quickly offer reparation when they see that their victim's anger is being aroused. This incentive is particularly strong, it is claimed, because anger is difficult to fake (Frank, 1988).

The study of networks requires a rather different approach. The emphasis in this chapter is on social and ethical factors rather than biological ones. The contrast between humans and animals, and between a civilized society and an uncivilized one, is that in human civilizations natural biological emotions are controlled. The vengeance mechanism does not work well in a complex society with a sophisticated division of labour, because vengeance almost invariably generates negative externalities for innocent parties and thereby damages the system as a whole. A cult of vengeance represents a lack of self-control. A civilized society offers emotional benefits to those who exercise self-control. It rewards actions which confer positive exter-

nalities on other people, and penalizes those which confer negative externalities instead.

Respect is an important source of emotional reward and, conversely, guilt
and shame are emotional punishments. Conspicuous public service may be
rewarded with formal honours, while lesser action may simply elicit words of
praise. Respect is not only conferred by other people – it is something that a
person can also confer on themselves. Self-respect is, of course, a reflexive
concept. It is earned through recognition of one's own success.

The emotional reward from self-respect is typically generated during a
period of reflection. Reflection in turn requires relaxation, because only when
everyday decision-making has been temporarily suspended can the mind be
turned to focus on past performance instead. People differ in their capacity
for relaxation. Relaxation is a luxury for people who find it difficult to cope
with everyday decisions. In order to relax, they find it necessary to 'escape',
and in escaping they avoid reflection. By contrast, people who find it easy to
cope have more time to relax, and have less fear of reflecting on past mistakes
and omissions, because there are fewer of them. It follows that people who
are competent (in relation to the daily tasks that they perform) obtain the
greatest emotional benefit from self-respect, because they have the time to
spare for relaxation, and the incentive to spend it on reflection rather than
escape.

Providing time for relaxation is an important aspect of engineering network relationships. By alleviating the pressure of everyday decision-making,
it makes it possible for people to obtain rewards from self-respect. This in
turn strengthens the incentive to behave in a responsible way. Relaxation
strengthens network relationships in other ways as well. It is difficult for a
person to be dishonest when they are relaxed. Dishonesty normally gives rise
to tension because a liar has to concentrate on disguising the truth. This is
intuitively understood by many people. Social events often provide appropriate surroundings for negotiating important business deals because the relaxed
environment makes it more likely that all the parties are telling the truth.

Social events are important not only for their relaxing atmosphere, but for
the face-to-face contact they provide. Given that dishonesty arouses tension,
the symptoms of dishonesty tend to become visible when discussion is
face-to-face. Posture may be affected, and an inexperienced liar may even
blush. Symptoms of dishonesty could be apparent even in a letter, if the
handwriting is affected, or in a telephone conversation, if the voice and
intonation are not properly controlled. Notwithstanding this, the widest range
of symptoms, and the most revealing ones, are only available face-to-face.
This is one reason why face-to-face communication continues to be favoured
for many purposes, even though remote communication is usually much
cheaper.

Communal relaxation, combined with conversation, is important in creating affection too. It encourages people to share confidences. They realize that other people feel as vulnerable as they do. This recognition of mutual vulnerability stimulates empathy and altruism. The feeling of affection that results is another source of emotional reward. So too is the belief that this affection is reciprocated. While desire for respect encourages people to earn their reward through responsible behaviour, the desire to retain affection affords important incentives to loyalty. Providing opportunities to incubate affection is therefore another important strategy for strengthening network bonds.

Shared experiences are important in building up a sense of loyalty too. Strong emotions are aroused by danger, and facing a common source of danger also creates an emotional bond. The greater the danger, and the greater the mutual support in confronting it, the more intense the loyalty that people feel for each other afterwards. This form of bonding may be particularly important in a militaristic society. It has often been noted that many successful businessmen have a military background; this is often ascribed to the importance of strategy and organization, and the calculation of risk, in military service, but the importance of social bonding in facing common danger should not be overlooked. Military metaphors are frequently employed in motivation and team-building exercises, even when those involved have no direct experience of military service. Co-operation in the face of common danger is so important as a bonding mechanism that it is deliberately reproduced through competitive team sports. In some cases a leader of a group may deliberately exaggerate the dangers it faces in order to strengthen loyalties within the group. Internal factions are suppressed by focusing aggressive feelings on those outside the group.

Intense experiences stick in the memory and can be readily recalled in later life. Childhood experiences tend to be more intense than later ones, partly because vulnerability is greater at that time. The older people get, the more familiar are the situations that they face and the more experienced they are in dealing with them. The need to protect the child explains the emotional importance of parental ties. More generally, shared experiences in childhood are crucial in building trust that can be drawn upon in later life. This applies to siblings and to childhood friendships too. Investments in childhood bonding, made without any thought of material gain, can pay back many years later when people who have grown up together become involved in business deals. Even though they have left the environment in which they grew up, they may still be able to renew the bond when circumstances require it. Indeed, the further apart they have become in a geographical sense, the better placed they are to use their trust to set up international business deals.

It is not, therefore, only the family that incubates trust: school, university, the local church and the local sports team can all play their role. The ethnic ties that sustain trade-based diaspora depend not only on family (and therefore race) but also on religion, schooling and even shared enthusiasms.

More generally, this analysis implies that nurturing new members, and giving recruits the training that they need, is important in strengthening future attachment to any group. A network that supports new members is more likely to succeed in the long run than one that does not. It is the new members who will take over the leadership when the longer established members have retired. The more support they have been offered, the more competent they will be, and the more loyalty they will show to the traditions of the group.

9.6   FUNCTIONALLY USEFUL MORAL VALUES

If individuals are motivated by the desire for respect then their behaviour will reflect the basis on which respect is ascribed. If respect were conferred solely by birth, there would be little incentive to earn respect through good behaviour. It is because respect is conferred by good behaviour that people wish to behave in a decent way. What is good is determined by the system of moral values. It is certainly not the case that any set of moral values will do. The values that underpin trust are traditional ones such as honesty, loyalty and hard work. It is these values that give each member of the group the reassurance that the others will respect their interests.

It is important not merely that a majority of the group accepts these values, but that all the members do. If a significant minority were to subscribe to values that conflicted with these, then this reassurance would be undermined. People would hesitate to interact with other members of the group, and group activity would come to a stop. A successful group will therefore standardize on functionally useful values of the traditional kind, and defend these values against criticism from inside as well as from without.

How widely do the obligations to honesty, loyalty and hard work apply? Do they apply only to intimate friends with whom a confidence has been shared, or who have faced danger together? If so, then the network of trust is going to be so localized that little economic activity of any consequence can be supported. Do they apply only to people who identify themselves as members of the same group, and who have no connection with any other group? If so, then the economy will be split into independent segments which have no trade or investment links with one another. The most effective set of obligations, from an economic point of view, is an inclusive one, since this alone can integrate the entire economy into a single network.

There is, however, a problem in engendering the emotion required to make such universal moral values stick. It is difficult for a person to be committed to a purely intellectual argument for feeling obligations to people that they have never met. A group that wishes to enlarge its membership and widen its geographical scope must therefore invest in special mechanisms to strengthen its emotional life. Organized religion is the classic example of this. Moral values are personally endorsed by a supernatural authority to whom obedience is due. The reward for obedience may be immortality – a powerful incentive considering the length of time for which the rewards can be enjoyed. Imbued with religious convictions, individuals may continue to live by the moral values long after they have been separated from the parent group. Religious conviction has thus been very important in the colonization of distant territories, where pioneers have successfully transplanted their moral convictions and refused to compromise with conflicting local customs.

Sanctions based on the afterlife carry little weight with people who are impatient for their rewards, of course. However, insofar as the anticipation of the afterlife is a reward in itself, some of the reward can be enjoyed right away. Moreover, in societies with high rates of mortality, the afterlife arrives quite soon in any case. For medieval merchants who accompanied their goods at sea, it was liable to arrive at any time. The concept of the afterlife, moreover, suggests that network relationships themselves may endure. The network becomes like a family dynasty – it unites different generations, both the living and the dead.

In a secular society, personal authority may be vested in a leader. The wishes of the leader become the source of moral authority. This is potentially dangerous if the leader is a religious unbeliever, and therefore does not acknowledge any higher authority than himself.

Another solution is to inculcate respect for law within a formal framework such as that of a nation-state. Power is divided between legislators and the judiciary, and between civilian and military forces, in order to control its abuse. The great advantage of the law is that it is impersonal, so that its effectiveness does not decline with size as quickly as that of mechanisms based on personal bonds. Indeed, personal disinterest, in the form of impartiality, and tolerance of dissent, are both regarded as virtues in democratic legalistic systems. This strength of the law is also its greatest weakness, however, in the sense that people may be happy to behave quite badly to each other as long as they remain within the limits of the law. The system therefore depends critically on getting the fine detail of the legal system absolutely right. As the division of labour becomes more sophisticated, and the complexities of co-ordination increase, this becomes increasingly difficult. The law becomes increasingly bureaucratic, and so expensive to use that disorder begins to prevail instead.

Historically, different groups have used different mechanisms to build their business networks. The Quakers are perhaps the most striking example of a group which has deployed emotional mechanisms to sustain functionally useful values, and thereby to create prosperity for its members. In this context it is interesting to note that Quaker business groups achieved national prominence at a time when most other business groups were purely regional in their scope. The spread of religious ideas through travelling preachers, backed by the subsequent discipline of the yearly meeting, sustained high levels of commitment among the converts, even if there was some diminution of zeal in the more worldly later generations.

At the other extreme, the prosperity of London-based mercantile groups in the age of high imperialism owed a great deal to respect for the impartiality of the British legal system. This encouraged many continental Europeans to channel their speculative investment funds through London. Anonymous absentee owners provided capital for a faceless mass of workers in colonial territories around the world. In this antithesis of the face-to-face society, co-ordination was effected through a small group of merchant bankers, titled dignitaries, and other intermediaries, whose values were narrowly focused on providing reassurance for the private investor. Stewardship, confidentiality and respect for established institutions dominated concerns for personal welfare.

9.7   OVERLAPPING AND INTERLOCKING GROUPS

An alternative approach to the problem of size is to abandon the idea of a single large group, and to create a collection of smaller groups with overlapping memberships in its place. Each group is small enough to be personal, but has sufficient contact with other groups to constrain hostility towards them. It does not require charismatic leadership, nor does it need an expensive formal legal apparatus. It does, however, demand a moral code which not only promotes internal co-ordination but also creates respect for those outside the group.

Certain people may decide to specialize in membership of several groups. It becomes their responsibility to manage relations between them. Such people play a crucial role in co-ordinating economic systems. Successful economies co-ordinated on the network principle normally consist of overlapping regional and industrial groups, as indicated above. These groups would be of limited value if they had to function under autarky. On the other hand, they function extremely well when integrated into international and interregional trading systems. This integration is effected by a higher-level group of entrepreneurs, each of whom belongs to a number of regional or industrial groups.

Because it manages international trade, this high-level group is relatively dispersed but, because it is a group, its members share emotional commitments and a moral code. There are several such groups, sometimes associated with particular countries, or particular cities. Although the members themselves may travel widely because of the nature of their work, it is in these places that their families live, and that the institutions which they use for their transactions are based.

These high-level groups compete with each other for dominance in international trade and investment. There is competition within the groups as well, but this is regulated by mutual obligation in a way that competition between the groups is not. Members of each group share information with each other, picking up and using information that is superfluous to the others. The total amount of information circulating within the group at any time is a reflection of its collective expertise. This expertise can fluctuate as members of the group tap into new sources of information or their existing sources of information dry up. The external environment can change as well, sometimes making obsolete much of what a particular group may know. Groups that improve their access to sources of highly topical information improve their competitive position, and consequently bring prosperity to the countries and the cities in which they are based. Conversely, groups that lose control of relevant information sources fail to keep up to date with events. Their competitive position is undermined, and the nations and the cities in which they are based go into decline.

9.8 ENTREPRENEURSHIP: JUDGEMENTAL DECISION-MAKING IN A VOLATILE ENVIRONMENT

The key to understanding entrepreneurship is to recognize that decisions are taken in a volatile environment. This reflects the fact that the economy is in a constant state of flux. In the absence of volatility the economy would settle down into a permanent state of equilibrium. Most economists assume that the primary function of the entrepreneur is to organize production. This is a mistake. Schumpeter (1934) distinguished five types of innovation, of which only two have to do with production, yet self-styled Schumpeterians of today emphasize technological innovation in production to the exclusion of the other three forms. Two of the other three forms are concerned with developing new markets – for exports of finished goods, and for raw materials from new sources of supply.

Most markets are created because an entrepreneur – or in some cases a group of entrepreneurs – decided to set them up. Markets are institutions devised to overcome a series of obstacles to trade. To overcome these obstacles, markets tend to take a specific form. The entrepreneur acts as an intermediator, buying from sellers, reselling to buyers, and covering his costs by a margin between the buying and selling prices. Ordinary buyers and sellers are happy to pay this margin because the process of trade is greatly simplified for them.

There are four main obstacles to trade. The first is ignorance of whom to trade with, which is overcome by setting up a market at a convenient central place. The intermediators have a regular presence there. Sellers bringing their goods to market know therefore that there will always be someone willing to buy, while buyers know that there will always be someone willing to sell. To guarantee this situation, the intermediators need to hold stocks of goods to offer to the buyers, and stocks of money to offer to the sellers.

The mention of money brings us to the second obstacle to trade that intermediators help to overcome. This is the difficulty for the trader of specifying exactly what he wants to buy, and describing what he has to offer in return. This is overcome by inspecting goods that are on display – or at least examining a sample of them – and by holding money as a convenient means of payment to offer in exchange. The display consists of the goods that the intermediator holds in stock to satisfy immediate demand. Indeed, the intermediator may have notified the buyers in advance of the goods he has for sale by advertising them to the buyer in his home.

Next is the problem of negotiating price. This is simplified when there are several people to haggle with, since the presence of competitors encourages everyone to offer their best price at the outset. The presence of several intermediators dealing in the same good at the same place gives the buyers and the sellers confidence that the price quoted by each intermediator is a competitive one. The ease of searching for the best price ensures that all the prices are the best, and therefore obviates the actual need to shop around.

Finally, there is the problem of enforcement of contracts. Because of their constant presence in their market, intermediators quickly acquire a reputation. Once they have acquired a good reputation, it becomes a valuable asset which they have a strong incentive to maintain. It pays to be honest with everyone, because word of their default will quickly get around. This is the customer's guarantee of quality, and the supplier's guarantee that he will get paid. If the buyer and the seller were to try to deal with each other directly their sporadic appearance at the market and consequent lack of reputation would mean that neither could fully trust the other. The use of an intermediator therefore creates a chain of trust. The buyer pays in advance, and the seller in arrears. The intermediator thereby eliminates the risk from trading with people of no repute, while the people of no repute can trade because they both trust the intermediator.

9.9 ENTREPRENEURIAL NETWORKS AND THE GROWTH OF INTERNATIONAL TRADE

From an historical point of view the most dramatic impact of entrepreneurial networks has almost certainly been in the development of international trade. As far as Western European history is concerned, it is the Age of Discovery, and the subsequent Commercial Revolution, which testifies most vividly to their impact. However, the impact is so pervasive that it can be seen throughout the second millennium (Britnell, 1993; Snooks, 1995).

The obstacles to trade that were overcome were not simply those of transport costs, tariffs and the difficulty of operating in foreign jurisdictions. International relations were unstable. Where trade was possible, the interests of political leaders lay mainly in levying taxes and tolls. There was popular dislike of merchants who exported local foodstuffs, driving up the prices of necessities such as corn in local markets, or 'forestalled' local consumers altogether by buying wholesale at the farm gate (Chartres, 1985). There was also suspicion of import merchants, who were accused by the puritanical of creating a socially wasteful demand for novelties, and by the working classes of destroying local artisans' jobs.

The role of entrepreneurial networks in supporting international trade is illustrated schematically in Figure 9.1. It shows two industrial districts, located in different countries. In each industrial district there are three upstream plants connected to two downstream plants. Each plant is indicated by a square. Because the optimal size of plant is different at each stage, vertical integration is discouraged. It is therefore supposed that each plant is owned and managed by an independent, self-employed entrepreneur. Flows of intermediate product from an upstream plant to a downstream plant are indicated by thick black lines. The arrowhead indicates the direction of material flow. Any upstream plant can supply any downstream plant within the same district.

It is assumed that the two districts produce different variants of the same type of product. Both products are consumed in both countries. Some consumers prefer one variant, and others prefer another. The two variants may differ simply in design, having the same quality of workmanship and selling for roughly the same price. Alternatively, one product may be distinctly superior to the other in terms of quality, and sell for a premium price. Nevertheless, some consumers are always prepared to switch to the other variant if there is a significant fall in its price. To this extent the different varieties are substitutes for each other. Flows of the first variety are produced in country 1 and flows of the second variety are produced in country 2.

Goods for the home market are consigned directly to a domestic wholesale distributor, whereas goods for export are sent to the nearest port. This is also

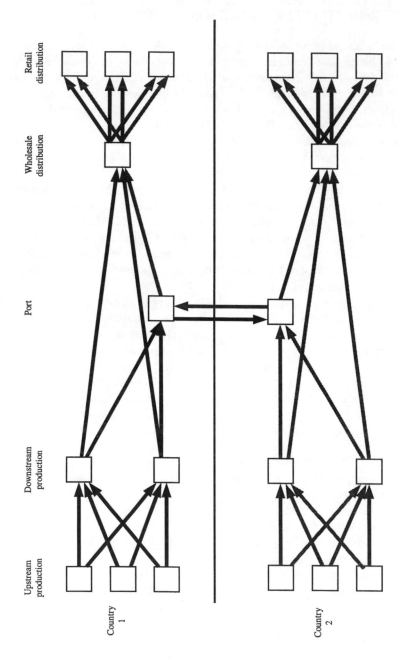

Figure 9.1   Product flow in an international trading system

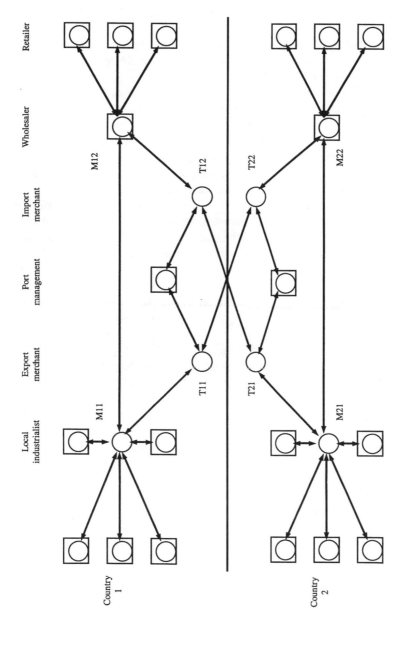

Figure 9.2   Information flows for the co-ordination of international trade

the port through which the other variety is imported. Goods are consigned from this port to the domestic wholesaler, who then combines the two varieties of good in the proportions requested by local retailers, and despatches them together.

Information flows are shown in Figure 9.2. They are indicated by thin black lines. Information flows between people – who are denoted by circles – rather than between plants. Information flow is a two-way affair, so there are arrowheads in both directions. In each district a merchant, M11, M21, specializes in handling information. He acts as an information hub. In contractual terms, he buys output from the upstream producers and 'puts it out' for downstream processing. He negotiates prices and quantities with the producers, using the information he has gathered from the upstream producers to inform his negotiations with the downstream producers, and vice versa. The information he processes is mostly encoded in price quotations.

Notice that information flows exhibit a different pattern from product flows. The information flows are intermediated by the merchant, whereas the product flows are not. The merchant handles the information and acts as a nexus of contracts between the producers, but he does not physically handle the product. The product is transported directly from the upstream producers to the downstream producers. The merchant simply gives instructions as to what product is to be delivered where. Because the merchant handles only information, the circle that represents him is not associated with any square.

The diagram shows only one merchant in each industrial district, and only one wholesaler in each domestic market. In practice there are likely to be several merchants of each type, and these merchants may constitute a group in their own right. Potentially they compete with one another, but in practice they can also collude. Thus the merchants within an industrial district may seek to impose customary prices for putting out when demand is buoyant, while reserving the right to cut prices further when times are bad. On the more positive side, they may organize an apprenticeship system in conjunction with a local college, and encourage 'on the job' training by collectively outlawing the 'poaching' of staff.

The figure shows four merchants specifically engaged in international trade. There are two in each country – one organizing exports and the other organizing imports. Like their domestic counterparts, these merchants do not handle the product whose flow they co-ordinate. Each export merchant buys from the merchant in his local industrial district and sells into the foreign distribution channel, setting a margin between his buying price and his selling price to cover his administrative costs. These costs comprise the charges levied at the ports, the cost of shipping, and of transport to and from the port. Thus in country 1 the export merchant T11 buys from the merchant M11 and sells to the merchant T22, who in turn sells on to the wholesaler M22. The import merchant T12 buys from the merchant T21 and resells to the wholesaler M12. Similarly, in country 2 the export merchant T21 buys from M21 and sells to T12, while the import merchant T22 buys from T11 and sells on to the wholesaler M22.

Note that intermediation by the merchants involves more than just a single stage. The domestic market involves two merchants, the putter-out and the wholesaler, while international marketing involves no less than four stages. Linking the putter-out to the wholesaler are the export merchant in the home country and the import merchant in the foreign country.

The justification for all these stages is that each intermediator overcomes some obstacle which the two adjoining intermediators would encounter if they tried to 'cut him out' and do business directly. In domestic markets it is the difficulty that ordinary people face in negotiating large deals, where fine judgement is required in fixing a suitable quantity and price. Collecting reputational information on quality of workmanship, and on reliability in payment and delivery, is also important. In the international context, combining knowledge of two different countries, and keeping this knowledge up-to-date, is the key advantage. Certainly, if critical information must be collected face-to-face, then a good deal of time-consuming travel may be involved. It could, of course, be something as simple as overcoming a language difference. The export merchant may speak the foreign language, for example, whereas the domestic merchant does not. This can only explain one additional stage of intermediation in an international context, though. There must be another factor too, such as a special knowledge of local customs and laws needed to enforce contracts.

The structure of networks that supports international trade is shown in Figure 9.3. There is a hierarchy of networks with interlocking membership. Each network is indicated by a box, enclosing the individual members of the group. The highest-level network comprises the international merchants. The figure illustrates additional horizontal and vertical links within this group. These links will tend to arise naturally from chance meetings at conferences and international trade fairs. Such events are a traditional method of setting up business deals in foreign markets. The fairs allow export merchants from different countries to share their experiences of other countries with merchants in non-competing lines. They also allow export and import merchants from the same country to share information relating to the prospects for the domestic industry as a whole. More generally, everyone can form an assessment of how well everyone else is doing, and therefore benchmark their own performance against that of their competitors with greater accuracy.

There are two middle-level networks, comprising the merchants of each country. Half the members of each network belong to the high-level international network, and the remainder to low-level domestic networks. The figure

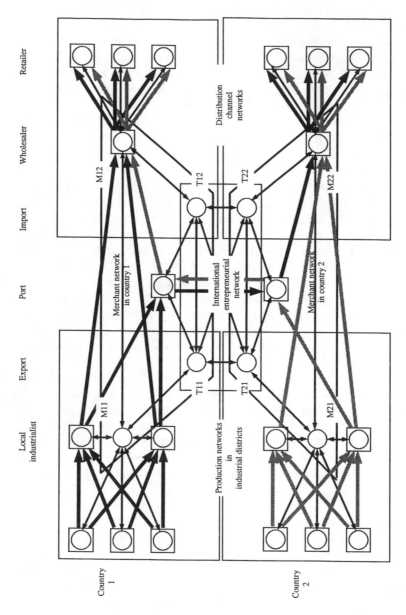

Figure 9.3   International trade: entrepreneurial networks

272

shows that there are two main types of low-level network: one concerned with production and the other with distribution. Within the production network the role of the putter-out is dominant. As indicated earlier, there will normally be a group of putters-out. They will form a local business elite, and will socialize with each other. They also form the dominant group within the wider network that includes the artisan entrepreneurs. The self-employed artisans are the lowest level of entrepreneur in the system in terms of the overall significance of the strategies they pursue. There is a similar distinction between the wholesalers and the retailers within the distribution network. The wholesalers are essentially the 'channel leaders', dictating terms to the retailers because of their superior access to information through their backward links into production.

It should be emphasized that from an economic point of view the links between entrepreneurs at different levels are maintained largely on the initiative of the higher-level entrepreneurs, who find the high-trust network links a cost-effective way of maintaining control. If the international merchants did not socialize with the domestic merchants, then they might have to integrate backwards into production, or integrate forward into distribution, to achieve the control they require. Similarly, if the putters-out did not socialize with the artisans, then they would have to integrate into production themselves and take on the artisans as employees. This would require a detailed knowledge of craft production methods, which they do not have. Again, if the wholesalers did not socialize with the retailers, then they might have to integrate forwards into retailing themselves, and take on the retailers as their employees. The costs of employee supervision are such that it is cheaper to invest in a few 'handshakes' and some friendly hospitality instead.

9.10   THE GEOMETRY OF NETWORKS

It is worth noting that the geometry of the network at each level is different. In the low-level network the local merchant is the hub of communications. Co-ordination is effected by communication between merchant and artisan, and not between one artisan and another. The artisans may need to communicate to arrange delivery of the upstream output to the downstream producer, but it is the merchant who has decided who the upstream producer and the downstream producer will be. The existence of a hub creates a hierarchy in the network. This is not a hierarchy of authority and control, as exists inside the typical firm, but a hierarchy of influence. The effect may still be much the same, in the sense that the artisans defer to the judgement of the merchant in setting the price because he has a wider view of the situation than they have.

The high-level network is not hierarchical at all, since all the members can communicate directly with each other. By contrast with the low-level network, the high-level network is democratic and collegial. This reflects the dispersion of expertise within the group. Everyone knows something which could conceivably be important to any of the others. This provides a strong incentive to maintain direct channels of communication, even though the cost, in terms of the time that is devoted to socializing, may be very high.

The middle-level network resembles the rim of a wheel, rather than its hub. Members communicate directly with adjacent members. Putters-out are in touch with wholesalers and export merchants; wholesalers are in touch with putters-out and import merchants, and so on. This structure reflects the fact that the linkages are focused on maintaining channels of distribution for both domestic and imported products. Direct linkages that do not support this function, such as those between the export merchants and the domestic wholesaler, and the import merchants and the putter-out, are not maintained at all. The link between the export merchants and the import merchants exists only because of their common membership of the high-level group.

This analysis demonstrates the connection between the geometry of the group and the function it performs. In general, the lower the level of the group, the greater the focus on supporting routine operations and the stronger the hub effect.

9.11   THE LOCATION OF HIGH-LEVEL ENTREPRENEURIAL NETWORKS

Entrepreneurs tend to be relatively footloose. The higher the level at which they operate, the more footloose they seem to be. Many entrepreneurs seem to grow up in relatively open societies where immigration is common, outside influences are strong, and the force of purely local custom and tradition is relatively weak. They are communities in which newcomers are welcome and status is ascribed on the basis of competence and contribution to community rather than place or family of birth. The strong commercial links of these communities with the outside world make ambitious young people aware of the opportunities that exist elsewhere.

High-level entrepreneurs are willing to pursue profit opportunities wherever they may lead. As people who have already achieved some success in their local economy, they have the means to 'buy themselves in' to social networks elsewhere – however exclusive these networks may be. Indeed, in many cases the entrepreneur has a footloose background before he achieves success. His entrepreneurial ideas may have been generated through his experience of travel. Historically, this experience could be military service, diplomatic service, scientific survey work or engineering work. It could be connected with the itinerant trade of the pedlar, drover or the latter-day sales representative (Pirenne, 1925; Fontaine, 1996).

In discussing entrepreneurial mobility, the most appropriate unit of analysis is probably the region, though smaller units, such as towns and cities, and larger units, such as nation-states, may also be appropriate. For the early modern period, when transport was relatively costly and communication was slow, the town is the appropriate unit of analysis but, as transport and communication costs have fallen over time, so larger units have become more appropriate. Even now, however, the typical nation-state remains too populous, and its population too widely dispersed, to function effectively as a networking unit, except for the elite functions connected with government and finance. Apart from compact city states such as Singapore, therefore, it is most appropriate to make the region rather than the nation the unit of analysis.

Given that entrepreneurs are mobile, the regions that are most successful in the long run will be those that are most attractive to entrepreneurs. The most obvious attraction is that the region is an information hub. It is here that the kind of wide-ranging synthesis of information that is required for major innovations can most readily be effected. Since a large amount of commercial information is encoded in the form of prices, and prices are set in markets, the range of markets is a crucial factor.

Furthermore, an existing market centre is the obvious place for an entrepreneur to develop a new market for an innovative product. By creating a new market where existing markets can be found, the entrepreneur simplifies the shopping process, since on a single visit an ordinary customer can accomplish several trades. This agglomeration economy is reinforced by other economies too. In any given market, the intensity of competition and the degree of liquidity are both important in guaranteeing customers reasonable prices when trading at short notice. By simply joining an existing market an entrepreneur can give that market greater 'depth'. By reducing customers' information costs, this greater depth makes the market centre an even more attractive place to trade. In aggregate terms, this generates increasing returns to market size, as measured by the volume of trade. As customers switch their trade from one market centre to another, so the centre to which they switch becomes marginally more attractive to other customers, while the centre from which they switch becomes less attractive at the same time. This encourages strategic rivalry between different market centres, in which each centre attempts to subsidize the marginal customer, so that intra-marginal customers receive better service, and become willing to pay slightly more (Krugman, 1991). It is the centres that play this strategy to best effect that in the long run become most attractive to new entrepreneurs.

When intermediators have a poor reputation for integrity, goods have to be inspected before purchase. This means that the marketplace must be at a freight transport hub, but where standards of integrity are high, goods can be traded by sample instead. Inter-modal specialization becomes possible. Rail and shipping specialize in moving freight, while jet travel and telecommunications are used for the communication of information. As a result, major ports and railway junctions where break-bulk and make-bulk operations are carried on, and processing of raw materials is carried out, are no longer attractive as market centres and information hubs. Airports and telecommunications infrastructure become more important instead.

Another effect of trading by sample is that itinerant selling becomes easier. If customers are not too concerned about comparing prices, because the alternatives are few, then the market may effectively be dispersed to customers' premises. This diminishes the centralizing attraction of the hub, but does not eliminate it altogether. For, while it discourages people from visiting the hub, it still leaves the hub as a strategic location where sales representatives reside.

Agglomeration in the market system is strongest when customers value price comparisons, and like to inspect the goods and receive quotations face-to-face. It is also strong when market-making entrepreneurs require support from specialized professional services. The availability of space around the hub is important too – for exhibition centres, conference facilities and hotels. Population density cannot be too high if it is to offer an acceptable quality of life to wealthy entrepreneurs and their families – even if the quality of life for those who provide them with unskilled manual services is very bad.

It goes without saying that, to facilitate the enforcement of contracts, a market centre requires an efficient and honest legal system which is well adapted to resolving potentially complex legal disputes. People must be free to enter markets, and to incorporate companies. Business and government must network effectively, and obviously taxation and the risk of expropriation must be low. The local culture should be welcoming to entrepreneurial immigrants, and conducive to networking. Networking among entrepreneurs not only improves their overall quality of service to the customer, but also facilitates the collective financing of strategic investments designed to increase the volume of trade. A highly competitive and impersonal culture is not appropriate, because it presumes too much self-interest and breeds distrust in matters that inevitably remain inadequately covered by the law. In the long run the most successful central places are those whose culture engineers high levels of trust among entrepreneurs.

REFERENCES

Best, M.H. (1990) *The New Competition: Institutions of Industrial Restructuring*, Oxford: Polity Press

Brenner, R. (1993) *Merchants and Revolution: Commercial Change, Political Conflict and London's Overseas Traders, 1550–1653*, Cambridge: Cambridge University Press

Britnell, R.H. (1993) *The Commercialisation of English Society, 1000–1500*, Cambridge: Cambridge University Press

Bull, A., M. Pitt and J. Szarka (1993) *Entrepreneurial Textile Communities: A Comparative Study of Small Textile and Clothing Firms*, London: Chapman and Hall

Carter, M.J. (1995) 'Information and the division of labour: implications for the firm's choice of organisation', *Economic Journal*, **105**, 385–97

Casson, M.C. (1995) *Studies in the Economics of Trust*, Aldershot: Edward Elgar

Casson, M.C. (1997) *Information and Organisation: A New Perspective on the Theory of the Firm*, Oxford: Clarendon Press

Chartres, J.A. (1985) 'The marketing of agricultural produce', in J. Thirsk (ed.), *The Agrarian History of England and Wales V: 1640–1750, II Agrarian Change*, Cambridge: Cambridge University Press, 406–502

Collard, D.A. (1978) *Altruism and Economy*, Oxford: Martin Robertson

Fontaine, L. (1996) *History of Pedlars in Europe* (trans. V. Whittaker), Oxford: Polity Press

Frank, R.H. (1988) *Passions within Reason: The Strategic Role of the Emotions*, New York: W.W. Norton

Grassby, R. (1995) *The Business Community of Seventeenth Century England*, Cambridge: Cambridge University Press

Krugman, P.R. (1991) *Geography and Trade*, Cambridge, MA: MIT Press

Leibenstein, H. (1968) 'Entrepreneurship and development', *American Economic Review*, **58**, 72–83

Pirenne, H. (1925) *Medieval Cities: Their Origins and the Revival of Trade* (trans. F.D. Halsey), Princeton, NJ: Princeton University Press

Schumpeter, J.A. (1934) *The Theory of Economic Development* (trans. R. Opie), Cambridge, MA: Harvard University Press

Snooks, G.D. (1995) 'The dynamic role of the market in the Anglo-Norman economy and beyond, 1086–1300', in R.H. Britnell and B.M.S. Campbell (eds), *A Commercialising Economy: England 1086 to c.1300*, Manchester: Manchester University Press, 27–54

Thaler, R.H. and H.M. Shefrin (1981) 'An economic theory of self-control', *Journal of Political Economy*, **89**(2), 392–406

10. Conclusion: methodological issues in international business

with Sarianna M. Lundan

10.1 INTRODUCTION

This book has outlined a new research agenda for international business studies. It has focused on economic aspects of the subject, although its implications are more far-reaching than that. Quite how far-reaching they are is one of the issues addressed in this chapter.

The new research agenda is radical in the sense that it involves four major changes in approach. These changes were outlined in Chapter 1 and are explained in more detail below (Section 10.2). They involve switching from a relatively static, partial, deterministic and narrowly economic view of IB to a more dynamic systems-oriented view in which the impact of volatility is fully recognized. The new approach shows how entrepreneurial activity generates flexibility within the global system, and explains how social as well as economic factors govern the way in which the system evolves.

The global systems view set out in this book is not the only way of approaching the modelling of IB, however. For example, Whitley (1992a, b) has articulated a competing view of IB using his theory of national business systems. Similarly, Porter (1990, 1991) has set out his views on IB by extending his ideas on competitive strategy. Thus there is strong competition between rival models.

A long-standing source of competition in IB modelling derives from the different disciplines represented in the subject. The approach adopted in this book builds on the foundations of economic theory. In many cases, rival approaches are based on other disciplines. Thus Whitley draws on sociology and social anthropology for his inspiration. In other cases the discipline is the same, but the method of application is different. Thus while Porter also grounds his work in economics, he proposes to use 'frameworks' rather than models to apply economic insights to practical problems. The nature of interdisciplinary competition in IB is examined in Section 10.3. Alternative perspectives are evaluated in Sections 10.4 and 10.5, and the conclusions are summarized in Section 10.6.

10.2 THE GLOBAL SYSTEMS VIEW – A SUMMARY AND RESTATEMENT

As explained above, there are four distinctive aspects to the global systems view in comparison with traditional economic theories of IB.

From a Partial to a Systems View

In the 1970s the main focus of theoretical interest was the nature of the multinational enterprise (MNE). The global systems view seeks to put the MNE in context by examining the MNE's environment as well. This is part of a switch away from a purely firm-centred view of IB. Future advances in IB depend upon having as good a model of the global economic system as a whole as currently exists for the MNE as a firm. The old research agenda recognized the importance of the firm's environment, of course, because changes in the environment were an important stimulus to changes in the behaviour of the firm. Thus according to the product cycle theory (Vernon, 1966), the growth of a foreign market was likely to lead to a switch from exporting to FDI. Changes in the environment were usually taken as given – the environment was exogenous, in other words. For the sake of simplicity, interest focused on explaining the impact of given changes on the behaviour of the firm. The fact that the collective responses of firms to systematic changes in their environment would feed back to induce further changes was recognized in principle, but excluded from the analysis. It is not that the original approach was wrong, therefore, but simply that it was deliberately partial in its view of the problem.

Introducing Volatility and Information Cost

Systems thinking is not a new phenomenon. The 'cybernetic' models formulated by engineers in the 1960s were important examples of systems thinking. These models featured interdependencies between subsystems which are a hallmark of the systems view. They also featured feedback loops which made the models dynamic. The nature of the feedback – whether it was positive or negative – governed the stability of the systems over time. This type of modelling was applied to the global economy by Forrester (1971). Writing in the final years of the 'golden age' of growth, systems theorists controversially identified 'limits to growth' arising from the exhaustion of raw material inputs to industry (Meadows *et al.*, 1974). A widespread criticism of these models was that they were inflexible. They were typical of the 'hard-wired' models favoured by engineers, which assume that the structure and the parameters of the system remain fixed over time. Unstable models simply 'explode' or crash, because the individual agents within them – firms and households, for example – are too rigid in their behaviour to make an intelligent response to problems.

The natural response to increasing resource scarcity, for example, is to develop substitute products. In a market economy this process of substitution is guided by changes in relative prices. Resources that are nearly exhausted increase in price, and producers are encouraged to economize on their use by switching to alternative inputs, or by producing different types of output instead. This form of flexible response is elegantly captured by the Walrasian model of neoclassical economics, in which price adjustments maintain all markets for goods and services in perpetual equilibrium.

The Walrasian model has problems of its own, however. According to the model, all adjustments are costlessly effected by the Walrasian auctioneer, whereas in practice, of course, information is extremely costly to collect. Indeed, much information is prohibitively costly, which means that most decisions are taken under uncertainty. The Walrasian auctioneer could cope with this problem by introducing contingent forward contracts, were it not for the fact that the communication of information is costly too. To co-ordinate all the efforts of individual agents in responding to uncertainty would incur formidable communication costs. In practice, the negotiations involved in pricing all the contingent forward claims involved would be quite prohibitive. The Walrasian model is therefore inadequate for the proper articulation of a systems view.

The problem with rejecting the Walrasian model is that an attitude of 'anything goes in a world of uncertainty' tends to develop if nothing is put in its place. An important step forward in developing an alternative to the Walrasian model is to recognize that, while uncertainty is widespread, the form that uncertainty takes often remains invariant over time. This is because there are systematic causes of volatility in economic systems. By incorporating the drivers of volatility into a model of the system, it is possible to make some definite statements about how the system will behave. If some part of a system is repeatedly subjected to random shocks, it is possible to calculate the probability that a shock of a given type will occur during any given period of time. Rational individuals can use this probability, together with the cost of information, to evaluate alternative decision-making strategies, and to select the best. One strategy is to delay a decision until it is known whether some relevant shock has occurred. Another is to take a measurement which will show in advance whether or not the shock is going to occur. Given the cost of delay, and the cost of measurement, the probability of the shock can be used to determine whether the decision should go ahead, with or without a measurement being made.

Different parts of the system may be subjected to different types of shock. Each part of the system can adopt decision-making procedures that deal most effectively with the types of shock to which they are most heavily prone. Once the types of shocks impinging on each and every part of the system have been identified, it is possible, in principle, to determine how far the different parts of the system need to be in communication with each other, and what sort of things they need to communicate about. The more that shocks originating in one part of the system are transmitted to other parts of the system, the more important it is that different parts of the system remain in regular contact with each other. These principles, and others like them, provide important predictions about the way that intelligent agents will establish systems to minimize the inconvenience caused by the uncertainties that they face.

In the context of the modern global economy, each country, and each market, faces its own distinct sources of volatility. Firms that operate in these countries, and these markets, are part of the institutional response to volatility. It is their managerial procedures which determine how uncertainties are handled on a day-to-day basis. By spanning national boundaries, MNEs have the capacity to co-ordinate responses to different shocks at different locations. The same type of co-ordination could also be effected by external market forces, without the intervention of MNEs. The advantage of the MNE over the market lies in its superior ability, in certain circumstances, to synthesize such information from different sources, and to develop a co-ordinated response.

Entrepreneurship and the Evolution of Flexible Systems

The Walrasian model has another defect, which is shared by the alternative model set out above. Both models assume that in the long run the structure of the global economy is basically fixed. This assumption rules out, therefore, the innovation of new products. In the Walrasian model this restriction is evident from the assumption that the number of markets is fixed. It is somewhat less evident in the case of the model of volatility. The problem with the model as set out above is that it assumes that all shocks are essentially transitory, and that the probabilities governing the incidence of the shocks remain stable over time.

A satisfactory alternative model must allow for a change in the number of product markets in the global system. This requirement can only be met, in a simple fashion at least, by a sleight of hand. The alternative model is specified in such a way that it includes from the outset all the product markets that could conceivably be required. Within the framework of this model, an innovation occurs when a product which was previously not produced begins production. The product may not have been produced previously because it was too costly, or simply because the technology had not been invented to manufacture it – it all depends on the initial parameters of the model. The introduction of new products generally renders others obsolete, and so these cease production. The essence of innovation, as Schumpeter (1934) noted, is structural change through 'creative destruction'. The mix of products produced in the economy changes. This process of structural change is modelled by incorporating all of the products into the model at the outset, and allowing production of some to become positive, while at the same time the production of others declines to zero.

It might be objected that this approach is highly artificial, because most people do not actively consider whether products that are not produced should really be produced. The reason why they do not do so is readily explained within the terms of the model, however. The explanation is that information is so costly that decisions of this kind cannot be taken on a regular basis.

Within any economic system, however, there are certain individuals for whom information costs are much lower than for the average person. Such people may positively enjoy speculating about 'what if' scenarios – and, in particular, about what would happen if products not yet available were to be produced. Because they enjoy such speculation, their curiosity may drive them to collect information that will help them to decide whether the product really would sell if it were actually produced. Indeed, a market economy encourages such speculators to go even further, and calculate whether they could make a profit from commencing production on a trial basis at their own expense. Although they face uncertainty, they can invoke decision-making procedures of the kind described above to assess whether they should innovate right away, or wait to see how the situation develops. These people specialize in taking judgemental decisions of this kind, because their low information costs give them a personal comparative advantage in this sort of activity. They are the entrepreneurs within the system, and it is their decisions which are vital in determining how the structure of the system evolves over time.

Once an entrepreneur has successfully established a market for a new product, he needs to ensure that the market is properly organized. As explained in Chapter 5, he needs to structure the flow of information through the market so that overall cost of carrying out transactions is as low as possible. This is not just a question of minimizing transaction costs, as these costs are conventionally defined, because the conventional approach places too much emphasis on problems created by opportunism. It is, rather, an exercise in minimizing overall information costs, where information costs include both those that stem from opportunism and those that do not – such as the costs of making contact with customers and communicating the specification of the product to them. The entrepreneur will normally minimize information costs by setting up a specific organization – a market-making firm – for this purpose.

Marketing rather than production is the core activity of the market-making firm. The firm may well engage in production too, but only if economies of vertical integration encourage it. The firm may also integrate into R&D if the product requires continuous improvement in order to keep ahead of the competition. This ongoing R&D may spin off ideas which lead the firm to diversify into other product lines. In this way, maintaining entrepreneurial drive through internal R&D not only sustains the evolution of the economic system, but powers the evolution of the firm as well.

There is, however, still a limit to what a formal model of this kind can achieve. It is unrealistic to claim that a manageable model can include every conceivable product that might ever be produced. It is clearly absurd to pretend that an economic modeller, however good at their job, can anticipate the judgements that will be made by many thousands or millions of competing entrepreneurs in a global system. For this reason, the model has limited value as a forecasting tool.

The situation with historical explanation is significantly different, however. Where history is concerned, the range of products that were actually produced within a given epoch is known. Obviously, the longer the time span involved, the wider the range of products that will have been produced. But the total number of products that has ever been produced remains finite.

The formal modelling of entrepreneurial innovation is extremely valuable in charting the history of the global system. Early configurations of the global economy can be interpreted as highly constrained analogues of the global economy of today. They were highly constrained because technology was not so far advanced, hence transport and communication costs were much higher than they are today. Thus the further back in time the modeller moves, the less advanced the division of labour tends to have been, and the fewer products there were in circulation at the time. In the very earliest economies for which evidence exists, the number of traded products was, by contemporary standards, extremely small. There are, of course, historical cycles to contend with, connected with the rise and decline of empires, but the overall trend is still very clear.

The reason why this trend is so clear is that technological progress in the global economy is cumulative. Each successive civilization 'stands on the shoulders' of its predecessors as far as the accumulation of technical knowledge is concerned. Some technologies are of much greater significance than others, however. As demonstrated in Chapter 8, improvements in transport technology are vital in driving down transport costs. From a global systems perspective, transport costs determine the extent to which local varieties of a given product, each produced and sold in a local market, are replaced by standardized global products which are produced in just a few locations for sale throughout the world. Similarly, advances in communication technology drive down communication cost – especially over long distances. IB scholars are already aware of the importance of long-distance communication costs for the management of international business operations. What may not be so familiar to them, though, is the way that falling long-distance communications costs cause office activities to become increasingly centralized in locations where clerical labour is cheap. The same trend also encourages the relocation of entrepreneurial activities to specialized communications hubs, where information from all over the world is collected and synthesized to guide innovation decisions respecting globally standardized products.

Integrating Social Factors into Economic Motivation

There is a long tradition which asserts that entrepreneurial innovation is driven by more than merely the pursuit of profit. Likewise, there is a good deal of evidence that managers and workers in MNEs are motivated by more than just a desire for wage or salary income, and an easy life of shirking on the job. This suggests that material motivation explains only a limited aspect of behaviour within an economic system. Moral and social factors also need to be taken account of. Such factors have important implications for the theory of IB. As explained in Chapter 5, for example, the role of opportunism in transactions can be overstated, because there is no incentive for transactors to be dishonest about certain types of information; it might have been added that, even where an incentive to cheat exists, transactors may resist the temptation because of moral or social constraints on their behaviour. This has significant implications for the long-standing issue addressed by internalization theory about where the boundaries of the firm are drawn. In a society where social and moral norms are high, and people are strongly committed to respecting these norms – a 'high-trust' society, that is – the tendency to cheat in arm's-length transactions will be low. The absence of opportunism means that the incentive to internalize intermediate product markets will also be low. At the same time, however, internal markets will tend to operate in a highly efficient way. This is because the managers who administer these markets will be honest and hard-working. Thus both internal and external markets will exhibit low transaction costs, and the internalization decision will be of little strategic consequence. On the other hand, in a society where norms are low, and commitment to respect these norms is weak – a 'low-trust' society, in other words – opportunism will be a serious problem. As a result, transaction costs in external markets will be high. At the same time, transaction cost will be high in internal markets too, as managers seek to deceive their employers and to shirk on the job. With the cost of both arrangements being so high, making the right choice between them is very important. In a low-trust society, therefore, the internalization decision acquires a strategic importance that it lacks in a high-trust society.

Indeed, one of the reasons why internalization decisions are so important in IB is that trust between transactors tends to be much lower in international transactions than in purely domestic ones. Another reason is that many IB transactions involve technology transfer, and technology affords exceptional opportunities for cheating. Thus international technology transfer is an area where the internalization decision really is an important one. The converse of this is that transaction costs tend to be much lower in domestic markets and in markets for ordinary tangible commodities whose quality is easy to inspect, such as the ordinary intermediate products passed on from upstream production to downstream production in a manufacturing industry. The dangers of overemphasising opportunism are therefore somewhat less in the international technology transfer arena emphasized by Buckley and Casson (1976) than in the context of domestic multi-stage production emphasized by Williamson (1975).

Where opportunism is an important problem, moral and social techniques for reducing it are of considerable significance to the firm. In a low-trust society it may pay the owners of a firm to invest in creating a distinctive corporate culture of their own. This culture can be reinforced by suitable recruitment strategies, based on hiring people from the small number of families or educational institutions that inculcate traditional work-related values such as honesty. The owners of the firm need to be careful in the way they promote their corporate culture to the employees, however. An argument to the effect that 'You should work hard so that we can make more profit' is unlikely to be persuasive. However, appointing a charismatic chief executive, who believes in the intrinsic social value of the firm's product, and who articulates this belief not only in what he says but in what he does, may well have the desired effect. The owners of the firm must recognize, however, that in making such an appointment they are incurring extra costs, because they must allow the chief executive to pursue his own agenda alongside their own. The executive may sell the product at a loss to poorer customers, in fulfilment of his social mission. It may be necessary for the owners to permit this in order that the chief executive can gain credibility for the values that he espouses. Without some sacrifice of profit by the owners, they will not reap the larger gains arising from the better motivation of their employees.

Different kinds of profit sacrifice may be relevant to motivating different categories of employee. Subsidies for poor consumers may appeal mainly to wage-earning employees, corporate contributions to educational and medical charities may have greater salience for salaried managers, while setting aside a proportion of the R&D budget for 'blue skies' research may have a major impact on scientists and engineers, and so on.

The ability to enhance employee motivation in this way is a potential source of competitive advantage to the firm. Better-motivated workers will have higher productivity, better-motivated managers will utilize the firm's resources more efficiently, and better-motivated R&D staff will be more innovative. The weaker the culture of the country, the greater the value to be derived from a corporate culture of this kind.

10.3 INTERDISCIPLINARY COMPETITION IN MODELLING

The systems view set out in this book has so far been advocated mainly as a device for gaining new insights into the behaviour of the MNE. The systems view helps to explain why the environment of international business has changed in the way it has – not just since the end of the 'golden age', but since international business relations first rose to prominence centuries ago. It therefore helps to deepen understanding of why firms engaged in international business have transformed themselves in the way that they have. There is, however, another even bigger pay-off from the systems view. This pay-off arises from placing the explanation of the behaviour of firms on the same footing as the explanation of the behaviour of all the other institutions in the global system of which they form a part. The principle that organizations emerge to cope with volatility applies not only to firms, but to all other forms of organization. Similarly, the notion that moral and social forces underpin spontaneous co-operation explains many other aspects of social order besides the maintenance of order within the firm.

The systems view therefore encompasses the whole of the environment within which international business operates. With suitable modification, the same principles that explain the behaviour of firms will explain the behaviour of governments, trades unions, employers' associations, schools, universities, and so on. All of these institutions allocate resources that they own and control by processing information in order to arrive at decisions. They all need to communicate with other organizations in order to co-ordinate their own decisions with those being made in the rest of the system.

Consider, for example, the location decision made by an MNE which is investing in some country for the first time. The traditional approach would rightly emphasize the importance of local labour costs in the investment decision, and the saving in transport costs and tariffs would be recognized too. Against these savings would be set any additional costs due to a loss of scale economies caused by investing abroad instead of expanding production at home. More recent literature on foreign investment has tended to emphasize other factors in the location decision, however. The increased volatility of global markets during the 1990s encouraged many firms to divest their operations in small markets. This sharpened the focus of host country policy-makers onto those factors that are most likely to make firms stay. The thrust of policy has shifted from the attraction of foreign investment to its retention, and this has been reflected in the IB literature. Long-term relationships between local institutions have been identified as one of the keys to encouraging firms to 'embed' themselves in particular locations.

The advantages of local 'embeddedness' are manifest in many ways. The quality of relations between foreign firms and the host government is important in safeguarding the firm against any hikes in taxes that could be imposed once it has committed itself to the investment. The quality of relations between local trades unions and local employers' associations is important in ensuring that industrial relations are good. Bad industrial relations can push up labour costs both by increasing wages through strike threats, and by reducing productivity through restrictive working practices. The quality of relations between government, professional associations and schools is important in ensuring a good local supply of suitably qualified employees, and so on. The existence of these relationships is likely to prove particularly significant in the long term. However, modelling the long-term impact of these relationships on the performance of the firm is difficult if these other sorts of organization cannot be modelled within the same framework that is used to model the firm.

An approach to global systems which encompasses institutions of almost every conceivable kind represents a specific form of integrated social science. It involves two distinct forms of intellectual integration. On the one hand, it integrates a range of different theoretical insights into the nature of social systems, and on the other it integrates the study of different nations and regions into a study of a single global unit. To accept the claims advanced for the global systems approach set out in this book is therefore equivalent to accepting that the theory of institutions that underpins it can form the basis of an integrated social science.

This claim may be too strong for many readers to accept. Objections are likely to centre on the prominence given to economic concepts within this book. For many IB scholars, economics – considered as a social science discipline – is an 'outlier'. Economists tend to pursue the development of their discipline in isolation from other social sciences. They usually ignore the work of sociologists, political scientists and the like, and regard any proposition in social science as firmly established only when it has been proved as a theorem in economics. This arrogant attitude provides the grounds on which other social scientists feel justified in ignoring what goes on in economics.

Both these attitudes are mistaken. If the aim of social science is to explain how various types of institution work, then it should, in principle, be open to any social science to put forward ideas on how any given institution works. It is a mistake for any social science to claim a monopoly of explanation of certain types of institution. The idea that one set of principles – such as economic ones – apply in one sphere of social science, say, where markets are concerned – and another set of principles – say political ones – apply in another sphere, say, where governments are concerned, makes it virtually impossible to analyse the two sets of phenomena – governments and markets – in a mutually consistent way. It is far better for scholars who have developed principles that explain markets to modify and generalize those principles to explain government behaviour as well, while at the same time scholars who have developed principles that explain government behaviour set out to modify and extend their principles to explain market behaviour too. Competition between these two approaches will, it is hoped, establish a creative tension out of which an integrated set of principles can emerge. These integrated principles will explain both sets of phenomena – government behaviour and market behaviour – on equal terms.

This does not imply, however, that the two initial approaches will be equally represented in the final theoretical synthesis. Indeed, this is most unlikely to be the case. The need for internal consistency means that the synthesis is likely to be achieved by elevating one set of principles to a rather abstract plane – turning them into very general axioms – while the other set of principles is turned into a set of qualifying and contingent principles which indicate how these general axioms are to be interpreted in any particular case. This is what has happened in the case of this particular book. The principles of economics have been reduced to a tiny core of very general and abstract principles – most notably, the principle of instrumental rationality – and then combined with a range of principles taken from other social science disciplines. These other principles include the costliness of information processing – which Simon (1959) took from cognitive science and psychology – and the idea that individuals have moral and social, as well as material and selfish objectives – which is taken from sociology and anthropology.

The process of competition described here is sometimes condemned as social science 'imperialism'. Economists, in particular, stand accused of imperialism because of the way that they have taken their core economic principles and applied them to politics – in 'constitutional economics', for example (Buchanan *et al.*, 1978), and law – the economics of law (Posner, 1981). Instead of condemning such imperialism, however, some social scientists have resolved to take the fight to economics. Building on the work of Etzioni (1988) and others, socioeconomists have begun to apply sociological principles to that key institution of the economy – the market (for a survey see Smelser and Swedberg, 1994). They have correctly pointed out that markets are social institutions in the sense that they have their own customs, procedures and codes of conduct. Markets, in other words, are 'socially embedded', just like any other economic institution, including the firm (Granovetter, 1985). By taking competition from economics seriously, these writers have been able to reformulate conventional sociological principles in more practical and relevant terms. Furthermore, by stimulating economists to re-examine the foundations on which their own discipline is based, this development can help to promote further refinements in economics too.

It should also be noted that conflicts between economics and sociology are not always as sharp as the protagonists on either side proclaim. Some propositions, such as 'mutual benefit sustains co-operation', are common to both disciplines. As present, these similarities are disguised by the different terminologies employed by the different disciplines; the same proposition may sound quite different when expressed in different professional jargon. Another advantage of an integrated social science is that such duplication is avoided: in the spirit of Occam's Razor, each proposition is stated only once.

The concept of a competition between different disciplines to build an integrated social science is only workable if there are some criteria by which the 'winner' can be determined. If each discipline has its own criteria for measuring success, then these criteria may be manipulated to ensure that each discipline wins according to its own criterion. It must be admitted that there are serious disagreements between the social sciences about how the performance of different theories should be assessed. Positivists, for example, believe that objective evidence alone should discriminate between rival theories, while other scholars, who are more sceptical of objectivity or accuracy, tend to emphasize introspective validity instead, or even just intuitive appeal. Economists incline to positivism, believing that prices and quantities are the main things that need to be explained, while sociologists are more interested in explaining qualitative evidence, and tend to attach greater weight to introspective validity. Sociological theory normally fails the economists' test, because it fails to offer quantitative predictions, while economic theory fails the sociologists' test because it often lacks introspective validity. Relativists argue that theories should be assessed on a local and contingent rather than a universal and absolute basis. Relativism is a very convenient refuge for people who like to assert that their own theory is best, without wishing to engage directly with rivals who claim that some other theory is the best one instead. Extreme relativism is quite nihilistic, therefore, as far as the competitive evaluation of theories is concerned.

Agreement on evaluation is therefore necessary if sustained progress in the construction of an integrated social science is to be achieved. Once some such agreement has been attained, each discipline can set out to generalize from the specific principles on which it was originally based. In seeking to generalize, some of the more narrow and specific principles will have to be

discarded, and be replaced by more general ones. These more general principles are likely to be imported from other disciplines, since the scope for the
discovery of wholly new principles is small. The process of competition, therefore, tends to have a transformational effect on the individual disciplines that
are engaged in the competition. Each discipline plays to its strengths by assuming a particular role in the emergent theoretical synthesis. This is the role to
which it is best suited – that is the role in which its comparative advantage lies.

A distinctive pattern of specialization is suggested by the emergent synthesis set out in this book. The strength of economics lies in its internal
consistency, which it achieves through its axiomatic method; the strength of
psychology lies in its understanding of mental processes for handling information; while the strength of sociology plays to its expertise in emotional
interactions, and so on. When each discipline plays to its strength, the outcome is the one described above. The principle of rational action, drawn from
economics, is elevated to an abstract level, and then qualified by the principle
of information costs, drawn from psychology, and by the principle of moral
and social motivation drawn from sociology. These two sets of qualifications
are very important. They mean that the principle of rational action has very
different implications for behaviour within the global systems view set out
here than it does within the context of a conventional economics textbook.

If it is accepted that theoretical progress is most likely to come from
competition, then the question arises as to who the main competitors are, and
how their theoretical constructs perform. Which social disciplines are the
main competitors to the global systems view set out in this book? As already
indicated, the following sections discuss two main rivals. The first is the
business strategy approach of Michael Porter (1980, 1990). Although this
approach has limited impact on the social sciences as a whole, it is widely
used as a pedagogic framework in business schools, and it has made a
significant impact on the IB literature – for example, through the work of
Hamel and Prahalad (1994). The second approach is the 'national business
systems' approach to the global economy set out by Richard Whitley (1992a,
b). Whitley's approach exemplifies the anti-Positivist theoretical stance common to many sociologists and social anthropologists who have written on IB
issues. Other competitors could have been discussed, but two case studies are
sufficient to bring out the main points. In particular, the New Institutional
Economics (Droback and Nye, 1997) promoted by Williamson (1985) and
North (1990) is too close to the approach set out in this book to justify
separate discussion. Although there are some important differences, most of
these are of a technical nature and would take a considerable amount of space
to explain.

A final judgement on the relative merits of these approaches would be
premature, because none of them is fully articulated as yet. Furthermore, no

single approach is likely to perform best according to all the criteria used in the different disciplines, and some diversity of approach is likely to remain. It will come as no surprise to the reader to learn, however, that the approach set out in this book is judged to have the greatest potential for further development. If this judgement is correct, it means that the global systems view should become the dominant approach in IB within the foreseeable future.

10.4 PORTER'S FRAMEWORKS

Porter's approach is similar to the one in the book, in the sense that it transplants concepts from the firm to other types of institution, rather than the other way round. Thus Porter followed up his study of the competitive advantages of firms (Porter, 1980) with a study of the competitive advantages of nation-states (Porter, 1990) in which he applied to the nation-state some of the same concepts of strategy that he had previously developed to analyse the strategies of firms. This parsimonious use of concepts affords Porter's exposition significant economies of scope. It reduces the intellectual investment required of the reader, who no longer has to master two different sets of concepts and then attempt to relate the two.

Porter's approach is also similar in that it is grounded in economics. Porter's language is much vaguer, however, and his arguments less formal, than those employed in this book. Porter contrasts 'models' and 'frameworks'. He sees the traditional method of economics as model-building which 'abstracts the complexity of competition to isolate a few key variables whose interactions are examined in depth' (Porter, 1991, p. 97). 'The applicability of any model's findings are almost inevitably restricted to a small subgroup of firms or industries whose characteristics fit the model's assumptions' (1991, p. 98). Porter identifies the progress of strategic management with its ability to construct frameworks. 'Instead of models, however, the approach was to build frameworks. A framework, such as the competitive forces approach to analysing industry structure, encompasses many variables and seeks to capture much of the complexity of actual competition' (1991, p. 98). Frameworks are analogous to systems which are tailored to particular industries or companies. 'My own frameworks embody the notion of optimisation, but no equilibrium in the normal sense of the word. Instead, there is a continually evolving environment in which a perpetual competitive interaction between rivals takes place. In addition, all the interactions among the many variables in the frameworks cannot be rigorously drawn'.

It is important to note that many of Porter's remarks relate to the modelling of industries rather than firms. An industry consists of a number of firms, all producing rather similar products, so that the cross-price elasticities of substitution between them are reasonably high. If the industry consists of a small number of firms, then formal modelling of oligopolistic interactions can be extremely complex, so the case for frameworks is reasonably strong. Porter tends to focus his own analysis at the industry level, but many of his followers apply it instead mainly at the firm level. The case for using frameworks rather than models at the firm level is much weaker, though.

The models of rational strategic choice presented in Chapters 2, 3 and 6 address many of the issues raised by strategic management theory in connection with an individual firm. Their results demonstrate that, while some of the precepts of the strategic management literature are sound, many are not. The strategic management approach often fails to examine all the alternative strategies in a given situation, concentrating on pair-wise comparisons of alternative strategies that seem intuitively plausible in some particular situation. Conclusions derived from strategic management theory can therefore be misleading compared to those obtained from a rigorous economic approach.

A major strength of economic modelling, as indicated above, is its axiomatic method. Assumptions are always made explicit. In the context of IB, this entails specifying fully all the strategies available to each firm and spelling out their details. Strict assumptions are used in order to simplify the analysis as much as possible. Simplicity provides logical transparency, and ensures that the results can be easily understood. Porter, by contrast, does not always make his assumptions explicit. It is easy for those who leave their assumptions implicit to criticize those who make their assumptions explicit, because they can point to the counter-intuitive nature of some of the assumptions that are made. The possibility that the main conclusions may remain quite robust when some of these explicit assumptions are relaxed is often ignored. It is difficult, however, for those who make their assumptions explicit to criticize those who leave them implicit, because they cannot be really sure what their assumptions are. Implicit assumptions leave the modeller free to deny that any specific assumption has been made, and therefore free also to claim that their implicit model is more realistic than the explicit alternative. In fact the implicit alternative is not really a viable alternative at all, since as long as key assumptions remain implicit there is no check that the model is logically sound.

As emphasized throughout this book, instrumental rationality has a distinctive role in economic methodology. Its role in IB theory is to predict the circumstances under which firms will choose a given strategy. The assumption of rationality is not a piece of misguided psychology, but a response to the practical need for simplicity (Buckley and Casson, 1993). When the firm's objective is profit maximization, the choice of strategy is driven by the firm's structure of revenues and costs. This is determined by the firm's environment. The identification of the key characteristics of this environment enables the firm's behaviour to be modelled in a very parsimonious way. The predictions of the model emerge jointly from the profit-maximization hypothesis and the restrictions imposed by the modeller on the structure of revenues and costs. Predictive failure of the model is addressed by re-examining these restrictions and not by discarding the maximization principle that is at the core of the theory.

The variables entering into an economic theory of rational choice do not have to be of a strictly economic nature. The criterion for inclusion is that they are analysed from a rational action point of view. A good illustration here is the analysis of international joint ventures (IJVs) in Chapter 6, where economic factors such as market size are supplemented by technological, legal, cultural and psychological factors to generate a satisfactory model.

Economics is a far more versatile discipline than many strategic management theorists seem to believe. The versatility of economic theory is reflected in the way that it continually evolves. Economics is a 'moving target' as far as its critics are concerned. In many cases, the critics fail to keep up with its advances. For example, recent developments in the subject mean that it is now much easier to analyse industry dynamics than it was when Porter first developed his frameworks twenty years ago. In particular, the non-co-operative theory of games is now widely used in studies of industrial organization. It addresses many (though not all) of the issues raised by Porter's analysis of oligopoly. Indeed, it can be argued that the concept of oligopolistic rivalry cannot really be formally articulated outside the context of the theory of games. In this sense, the conclusions that Porter derives from his framework must remain provisional until formal game-theoretical analysis has determined whether they are logically sound or not.

The dynamics of industrial evolution can now be formally addressed by exploiting the theory of real options set out in Chapter 7. Real option theory explains why managers are often much more cautious than simple static economic models suggest that they ought to be. Indeed, it could be said that an intuitive understanding of the principles of real options is a key source of competitive advantage to the firm. A chief executive who is willing to consider the 'downside' as well as the 'upside' when making an investment decision is likely to acquire a far better long-term track record for making profits than one who always takes an optimistic view – even though the optimist tends to conform to many people's intuitive idea of a good entrepreneur. The theory of strategic management can hardly be complete, therefore, until the principles of real options have been fully taken into account. Since the principles of real options have already been formalized, the easiest way to take account of them is within the context of a formal theory of strategic management. As far as individual firms are concerned, this formal theory will resemble the theory set out in this book, although as far as oligopolistic industries are concerned, the formal theory will include elements of the theory of non-co-operative games as well.

Overall, it may be suggested that strategic management theorists have been unduly sceptical about the scope for formal modelling in addressing strategic issues within a systems view. This criticism applies much more to Porter's followers, however, than it does to Porter himself. Economic models do much more than rationalize what everyone already knows. The way in which they are constructed means that they do not merely explain the facts which they were designed to deal with, but also have a capacity to generate novel predictions. Testing these predictions leads to new results, which in turn provide a further stimulus to theoretical development. The ability of economic models to draw attention to phenomena that have not been noticed, and to integrate the explanation of these phenomena with explanations of already known phenomena, is the true measure of their success. By contrast, the predictions of strategic management theory are often too vague or ambiguous to stimulate new empirical work, and as a result, progress in theory development since its inception has been relatively slow.

10.5   WHITLEY'S 'NATIONAL BUSINESS SYSTEMS' APPROACH TO THE GLOBAL ECONOMY

This book began by noting the shock to Western countries caused by the emergent competition from newly-industrializing Asian countries in the 1970s. Popular explanations of these national 'economic miracles' were often couched in terms of national culture. Some commentators went even further, and attributed the rise of the Asian economies in general to 'Asian values' which were common to all these countries. Morishima (1982), for example, focusing on Japan, identified the root of these values with the Confucian ethic.

From a policy perspective, it is obviously important to understand in what ways the national business systems of Asian countries differ from their Western counterparts. Both managers and politicians have tried to isolate a 'winning formula' underpinning Asian success (Zysman and Tyson, 1983). It is also important to know whether such a winning formula (if it exists) could be transferred to other countries (Gerlach, 1992). The transfer of cultural values, and the institutional forms that embody them, is well documented in history, and is strongly supported by artistic and archaeological evidence. Furthermore, many Americans still believe that their own traditional values, such as 'freedom under law', and their associated democratic institutions can, in principle, be transferred to every country. Notwithstanding this, it has been argued that Asian values are different. It is said that they reflect the distinctive psychology of certain ethnic groups, and cannot be transferred to Western peoples. Alternatively, they are held to reflect a naive belief in the wisdom of those in authority, and so are unsustainable in more 'realistic', or cynical, Western countries. If these objections were correct, they would have profound implications for the stability of international relations in the new millennium.

There exists, therefore, a social demand for a conceptual framework that will facilitate analysis of these issues. The most direct approach is based on simple stereotyping. This approach employs concepts such as the 'Anglo-Saxon firm', the 'Asian business system', 'Mediterranean culture', the 'spirit of Chinese capitalism' and so on (see for example Laurent, 1983; Redding, 1991). An extreme example is the concept of the J-type firm, which is said to lie behind Japan's success in the 1970s. Sometimes the approach is backed up by quite sophisticated analysis (Aoki, 1984), but this is the exception rather than the rule. When carried to its logical conclusion, this approach suggests, for example, that economic behaviour in China can be explained by its C-type business system, and that differences between Korea and China can be explained by the fact that Korea has a K-type business system instead. Such explanations are, of course, devoid of substance, because they are mere tautology.

To properly satisfy the demand for explanation it is necessary to develop a set of concepts and definitions within which mutually consistent propositions can be advanced. Contributions in this vein range from the informal comparisons offered by Vogel (1991), to the more formal comparative approach adopted by Hamilton and Biggart (1988), and the theoretical arguments of Jones (1995, 1997) and Foss (1997).

One of the most sophisticated treatments of culture is provided by Whitley (1992a, b). His two books focus on Europe and Asia respectively. The following critique focuses on his analysis of Asia, because this is most relevant to the theme of this book. Whitley views the global economy as a collection of different cultural units, each pursuing its own historically-rooted path towards economic development. In contrast to Porter, and to the approach adopted in this book, the individual decision-maker has only a limited place in Whitley's analysis. When firms are deeply influenced by their national culture, they do not perceive all the alternatives open to them, but only those that their culture legitimates as being reasonable ones. In similar situations, therefore, different firms will act very differently if they come from different cultures.

Whitley focuses his discussion on 'national business systems' (NBSs), which he regards as embodiments of national culture. Many of the shared beliefs within a culture relate to fundamental issues, such as what forms of institution are most natural for the organization of economic activity. These beliefs are reflected in the structure of a country's NBS, and a study of an

NBS can therefore reveal a great deal about the national culture that underpins it. Whitley does not offer a single simple definition of a national business system (NBS). He defines it indirectly by describing three principal dimensions along which these systems vary, namely:

1. the predominant type of firm;
2. the strength of high-trust network-type relationships between firms, as opposed to impersonal market relations; and
3. the sources and nature of authority within organizations – in particular, the nature of managerial authority and worker subordination.

Each of these dimensions is partitioned into a number of discrete categories. This approach allows Whitley to provide a compendium of facts about each country, which locates each country in a particular region of a three-dimensional cultural space. Some regions of the culture space are viable, and others are not. Each viable region offers a distinctive path of development, but no region is obviously superior to the others. Each country is locked into its particular region and predestined to follow the path associated with it.

By identifying just three key dimensions, Whitley avoids the gross oversimplification of one-dimensional analysis – such as a distinction between Confucian and non-Confucian countries. At the other extreme, he also avoids the proliferation of dimensions that occurs when every country is held to be specific in a different way from every other country.

Whitley emphasizes the differences between national cultures within Asia, as well as their similarities. He does not talk about 'Asian values', but about national values. He correctly emphasizes the importance of disaggregation in combating the superficial kind of stereotyping mentioned earlier on. Yet his own disaggregation does not go any further than the national level. There are a number of different ways in which a national economy can be disaggregated (Räsänen and Whipp, 1992; Storper and Scott, 1995), but none of them figure prominently in Whitley's analysis.

In most countries there is a substantial cultural difference between the metropolis on the one hand, and outlying rural areas on the other. Differences between rural areas also emerge from past settlement patterns of immigrant groups, and from the influence of geography on the type of agriculture and the nature of village life. These cultural differences may be quite significant as far as economic performance is concerned. Face-to-face communication is much easier at the regional level than it is at the national one, and a good deal of 'networking' will take place at this level. This was mentioned in the discussion of industrial districts in Chapter 9. Regional culture may influence the form that networking takes. Some networks may be open and outward-looking, and serve to promote competitiveness, while others may be closed and inward-looking, and serve to inhibit it. The global systems view suggests that the impact of culture is more readily seen at the regional level than at the national one (see also Casson, 2000, Ch. 7).

Immigration patterns are highly relevant to the present as well as the past. Some of the Asian countries studied by Whitley have suffered from major ethnic tensions – in particular between 'overseas Chinese' business communities and the indigenous groups. While the overseas Chinese own a great deal of wealth, the indigenous groups often wield the greatest political power. Indeed, it is striking how many countries have suffered from cultural conflicts at one time or another during the twentieth century – from the class conflicts that have troubled the UK, and the racial conflicts that afflict the US, to political conflicts that have led to revolutions and civil wars in various European countries.

It should not be forgotten that the primary responsibilities of the nation-state relate to defence and law and order. Cultural factors are undoubtedly an important influence on domestic legislation and foreign policy, but this does not mean that culture itself is fashioned exclusively by the nation-state. The formation of culture is usually distributed around a variety of different social groups, rather than concentrated on the state. A democratic state will attempt to reflect this diversity, by legislating for mutual toleration, and universal respect for individual rights. It is the totalitarian state that typically attempts to manipulate culture, and to promote the interests of one cultural group, which holds power, at the expense of others, which do not. Beliefs about the desirability of alternative political systems are therefore key aspects of culture as far as political stability is concerned. These beliefs are not necessarily part of some national consciousness, however, but rather beliefs about national politics that are held by disparate groups.

An even more serious problem concerns differences between industries. The global systems view suggests that cultures will vary between groups of people attached to different industries. Insofar as a national culture exists, therefore, it reflects, in part, the industrial composition of the economy. This industry-specific approach denies that there is anything fundamental about C-type, K-type and J-type entities. The fundamentals relate instead to the forms of organization that are most appropriate for particular industries at particular stages of technological development. Each industry has its own particular functional logic, which determines the best-practice style of management, and the most appropriate pattern of ownership. Thus economies of scale mean that the steel industry in each country is dominated by a small number of very large firms, while diseconomies of scale mean that the printing industry normally consists of a large number of small firms. In general, each industry has its own distinctive 'recipe' (Spender, 1989). Managers are aware of this recipe, and willingly conform to it because they accept that it is appropriate for their conditions. The comparative advantage of the country, as determined by natural resource endowments, labour skills, and so on, governs which type of industry dominates the country, and therefore governs which form of organization is typical of that country (Gray and Lundan, 1993).

Whitley makes no attempt to integrate this industry-specific view into his analysis. In fact, he goes out of his way to rebut the industry-specific approach, by arguing that the same industries are organized differently in different countries, and that different industries are organized in a similar way in the same country. Thus international variation always dominates inter-industry variation in Whitley's view. The nature of the country's firms, and of inter-firm arrangements and authority structures, has nothing to do with industry recipes in this view. It is explained, he seems to suggest, by the history of the country instead. The overall result is that Whitley significantly understates the cultural diversity within the countries that he studies.

Another serious problem for Whitley's country-centred approach is that NBSs change over time. This is a crucial issue as far as Asian economics are concerned, because change is obviously a major feature of the fast-growing countries featured in Whitley's book. Whitley recognizes the problem, and responds by postulating that each country has its own particular dynamics of change. Thus, while certain superficial aspects of the country's economy may change, the fundamental aspects do not – these fundamental aspects are invariant, and keep each country locked into its own trajectory of growth. Furthermore, when countries grow, they do not grow together in Whitley's view. They remain equidistant in cultural terms, or they may even grow apart, but there is certainly no tendency towards convergence. This is a very strong conclusion in the light of the way that Asian business systems have altered during the 1990s. Although change in Asia has been slower than many Western commentators would have wished, changes have definitely occurred. Convergence between Asian and Western systems, however slow, is difficult to accommodate within Whitley's approach.

What is supposed to be the mechanism that keeps each country on its distinctive path of development? Whitley argues that it is normally most efficient to carry on conducting business in the same way that you conducted it in the past. New institutions are extremely costly to innovate – especially if the innovation is of a radical nature. Incremental change is much cheaper, and much less risky, while no change at all is the cheapest strategy of all. But this is only a partial answer to the question. It does not explain how the initial conditions came about, and Whitley does not address this issue head-on. There seem to be two main possibilities, however.

The first is that institutions are set at some 'defining moment' in a country's past. This defining moment – a crisis, for example – may have temporarily freed up the normally rigid institutional framework of the country, and allowed a new set of institutions to take their place. For example, military defeat at the hands of invaders may have led to traditional rulers being deposed, and a new elite coming to power. The moment of change passed quickly, though – just long enough for the new elite to consolidate their position. The new leaders rewrite history to legitimate their rise to power, and may even erase the record of the previous regime, so as to portray themselves as the founders of the nation-state. If this is Whitley's view, then the defining moment must have occurred a long time ago in the countries that he studies, for he writes as though the national cultures in which Asian business systems are embedded originated long before their economic contact with the West.

The other possibility is that the business system evolves slowly in response to numerous incremental changes, too small and too infrequent to be reconstructed from later evidence. While the system remains primitive, it is quite flexible, and adjusts in response to unrecorded random change. However, as it becomes more complex it also becomes more rigid. Social organization evolves into a 'civilization' with a distinctive set of values and beliefs. This civilization has a sort of logic to it – it facilitates the co-ordination of individual action. But the civilization exists to maintain not only values and beliefs of functional value, but those of a quite arbitrary nature as well. In this view, culture represents the 'legacy of the past', but the past is too inscrutable to be subjected to rigorous analysis.

By contrast, the analysis of change is easily effected within the industry-specific view favoured by the global systems approach. According to this view, the origins of post-war Asian growth lie in a massive shift of population from the countryside to the towns, which transferred labour out of agriculture and into manufacturing. Trade liberalization and falling international transport costs, when superimposed on the change in labour supply, caused a major shift in international comparative advantage (see Chapter 1). This was recognized by foreign multinationals, which invested in offshore processing in Asian countries. High rates of domestic saving, coupled with progressive financial deregulation and increased capital mobility, allowed these investments to be financed at low interest rates. This investment was a major stimulus to the growth of labour-intensive assembly operations in high-technology manufacturing industries, and further boosted export performance.

While shifts in comparative advantage connect a country's economic environment to its industrial structure, the logic of information costs, as explained in Chapters 4 and 5, connects industrial structure to organizational form. Each industry faces a distinctive pattern of volatility, and evolves a distinctive set of procedures in response to this. These procedures are in turn supported by a distinctive organizational structure. Any change in the pattern of volatility, or in the level of information costs, induces a change in organizational structure. As the new organizational forms prove their worth, so cultural beliefs are updated – with a lag – to reflect the new reality. The shorter the lag, the better the industry will perform.

Economic principles, not national culture, are the constants in the analysis, and they effect a mapping from the fundamental drivers of comparative advantage and information costs into institutional forms. The roots of change are located in the present, rather than in the past. The business system in each country continually adjusts to changing circumstances, and the speed and direction of this adjustment are only weakly affected by the initial position from which the adjustment process began.

In the industry-specific view, the principal constraint on the speed of adjustment is the very considerable cost of setting up new institutions, and the consequent incentive for the citizens of a country to make the best possible use of the institutions that they already have. An institution is an indivisible entity, and as such incurs fixed costs when it is set up, and quite possibly when it is closed down as well. Indivisibilities and irreversibilities are very significant in the case of an interdependent set of institutions such as an NBS. Any single change in the environment is unlikely to warrant change. As successive changes occur, however, and problems with existing institutions accumulate, there comes a point where the benefits of change outweigh the costs, so significant institutional change is ready to occur. This shows that the lags that are so evident in institutional change do not have to be viewed as the consequence of mere inertia, sustained by social rather than economic forces, but can be viewed instead as the result of rational calculation based upon adjustment costs.

It was noted earlier that, although the concept of an NBS is fundamental to Whitley's analysis, he never defines it in formal terms. He specifies the dimensions of variation, but not the functions that an NBS performs. This shortcoming is another consequence of his rejection of the industry-specific approach. Because he plays down differences between industries, he tends to treat each industry, and by implication each firm, as a miniature replica of the 'typical' industry or 'typical' firm. He fails to emphasize that the division of labour within a country is not a mere fragmentation of a large unit – the nation – into many smaller units – individual firms. In fact, the division of labour resolves the national economy into a set of distinct specialized units – separate firms and industries – each with their own particular characteristics: patented technologies, individual brand names, distinctive management practices, and so on. Different industries complement one another, and are connected by substantial intermediate product flows. A key aspect of the co-ordination effected by an NBS is the maintenance of these linkages. By keeping transaction costs low in intermediate product markets, the overall efficiency of the national economy is secured. Because Whitley fails to appreciate the heterogeneity of the industrial base, he fails to recognize the role of the NBS in co-ordinating inter-industry relations.

The international environment in which a national economy operates is in a constant state of flux, as emphasized throughout this book. The more open the economy, the more vulnerable it is to external economic shocks. In the long run, the success of an economy depends upon its ability to restructure its internal division of labour in the light of changes in its environment. In an increasingly global, and therefore interdependent, world economy, the need for change is continual. Because of the complexity of the division of labour, changing it is a difficult task. It calls for special expertise.

In mixed economies, such as those of Asia, responsibility for restructuring is shared between government and entrepreneurs in varying proportions. Government specializes in setting the general 'rules of the game' – determining the balance between competition and co-operation, for example, and providing intelligence on export markets as a public good – while entrepreneurs specialize in more specific issues connected with pricing, output and investment in their firms. One of the most crucial functions of an NBS is to provide an efficient framework in which these entrepreneurial activities can be carried out. It is unfortunate that because of his rather limited analysis of the division of labour, and his emphasis on stasis rather than change, Whitley never really gets to grips with this crucial aspect of an NBS.

Whitley's rejection of the industry perspective, and his refusal to set out his theoretical principles, appear to have a single common cause, which is an ideological commitment to anti-rationalism in social science research (in this respect, see also Whitley, 1984). This commitment requires him to reject the industry-specific view because of its rationalist pedigree, as reflected in its efficiency-driven logic. It also requires him to deny that his arguments are based on rational action principles, even when they lead him, as they sometimes do, to the same conclusions as the rational action arguments of the global systems approach.

Whitley clearly believes in the superiority of sociological theory over economic theory, and attempts to use his book to demonstrate this point. Like many sociologists, he also wishes to emphasize the organic nature of societies. He rejects the atomistic model of society which underpins traditional neoclassical economics. He stresses the value of co-operation, as opposed to competition. He admires Asian societies, because he sees in their culture the kind of organic thinking to which he is sympathetic, and he sees in their institutions the commitment to co-operation which he considers to be so lacking in capitalist Western countries. He wishes to take economists 'down a peg' by showing that economic performance has sociological roots, and that organic societies, like the Asian countries in his study, can outperform Western ones based on atomistic principles.

In his darker moments, he seems to see the discipline of economics as a kind of pseudo-scientific apology for atomistic social structures. He believes that the root of this problem lies in its postulate of rationality. Unfortunately, he is quite wrong about this. Some principles akin to rationality, and the allied concept of efficiency, are indispensable for rigorous social scientific modelling. Modern institutional economics demonstrates quite clearly that rational action does not imply social atomism; indeed, rational action in a world of transaction costs leads directly to the creation of the very kinds of social institution which Whitley so admires.

It is a pity that Whitley denies himself the use of rational action modelling because, if he had used it, he could have expressed his arguments in a much more direct and parsimonious way. It is an even greater pity when it is realized that his rejection is based on an outsider's misunderstanding of what the use of the rational action principle involves.

The way forward for research on NBS is for change – and for entrepreneurs as agents of change – to be given a much more prominent role in the analysis of business systems. This can be readily achieved using a rational action approach, simply by recognizing that change is continuous, that adaptation to change requires information to be constantly updated, and that entrepreneurial institutions are required to update information in an efficient way. Ignoring change can never lead to an adequate theory of institutions, because handling information, and allocating the freedom to use it, is what institutions are all about. It is only by placing change centre-stage, but at the same time recognizing that response to change is a costly process, that an adequate theory of NBS can be developed.

10.6   CONCLUSION

This chapter has evaluated two alternatives to the global systems view expounded in this book. The results of the evaluation process are summarized in Table 10.1. The table identifies six desirable properties of a theory of IB, which are listed in the left-hand column of the table.

Four of these properties have already been highlighted in discussions of the systems view in previous chapters. The first is that the theory should be formalized. This means that it can be articulated in a rigorous way. The assumptions of the theory should be explicit, and hypotheses should be derived from these assumptions by a totally transparent logical process. Ideally, it should be possible to examine special cases of the theory with the aid of mathematical models – even though the entire theory may be too general to be summarized conveniently in mathematical terms. The global systems view satisfies this criterion completely; Porter's competitive strat-

Table 10.1   *Summary evaluation of three alternative approaches to
analysing international business behaviour in a global context*

	Global systems	Strategic management	National business systems
Formalization	Strong	Moderate	Weak
Emphasis on volatility	Strong	Strong	Weak
Entrepreneurship	Strong	Moderate	Weak
Social and economic factors integrated	Strong	Moderate	Moderate
Industry competition	Weak	Strong	Weak
Culture	Moderate	Weak	Strong

egy theory satisfies it only partially, and Whitley's theory of NBSs not at
all.

The second requirement is that the theory should take explicit account of
volatility. It is impossible to provide a full account of organizations without
recognizing that they exist primarily as a response to volatility. Members of
organizations collaborate in pooling information in order to update the allocation of resources under their control in response to continually changing
circumstances. This point applies to firms, governments, trade associations –
indeed, to every type of organization within the global economic system.
Despite his extensive discussion of different varieties of organization, this
fundamental point is never made explicit by Whitley. He seems to regard the
existence of organizations as self-evident, and to assume that their organizational structures are determined by historical legacy, rather than by the
functional requirements that they need to fulfil. In consequence, the NBS
approach must be judged weak in its treatment of volatility. While Porter is
mainly concerned with the implications of volatility for the competitive strategies of the firm, there is no doubt that he also appreciates its wider significance
for the organizational structure of the firm. Like the global systems view,
therefore, Porter's approach must be deemed successful in addressing the
volatility issue.

Organizations are best adapted to handling a particular type of volatility:
namely, a stream of transitory shocks driven by a continuing random process. They are not as well adapted to handling changes that affect the type of
volatility they face. This was the problem that confronted Western business
in the 1970s, as described in Chapter 1. A persistent change in the type of
volatility calls for a change in organizational forms. Existing organizations
must either adapt, or gradually fail and die. Firms, for example, need to be

restructured if they are to survive. New firms must be set up to replace those firms that are too rigid to change their ways. Competitive markets provide the incentive to make these changes, but it is entrepreneurs who respond to the incentives that the markets create. Entrepreneurs are people with the vision to recognize the need for change. Explicit recognition of entrepreneurship is the third requirement of an adequate theory, and it is here that the global systems view demonstrates perhaps its greatest strength. It draws a clear distinction between routine responses to volatility within an organization, and the improvised responses which lead organizations themselves to change.

Porter's approach to entrepreneurship is ambivalent. On the one hand, much of what he writes about competitive strategy – especially about the dynamics of industry entry and exit – could be thought of as a sort of 'primer' for practising entrepreneurs. On the other hand, by reducing competitive strategy to a set of precepts which, in principle, anyone can follow, he denies the all-important aspect of improvisation which is at the core of entrepreneurship as described above. If every firm in an industry followed Porter's precepts literally, then some very bizarre outcomes would result. It is only because some business leaders have the wit to improvise that these outcomes are avoided. As a result, it must be judged that Porter achieves only moderate success in analysing the role of the entrepreneur.

Whitley achieves no success in this field whatsoever. His view of systems and organizations emphasizes stasis rather than change. The 'dead hand of the past' lies heavily throughout Whitley's work. This is directly connected with his neglect of the entrepreneur. As noted above, a major paradox of Whitley's work on the Asian economies is that he explains the tremendous economic changes that they have achieved by stressing how little has actually changed. He fails to identify the role of Asian entrepreneurship in economic success, because his static vision of an NBS leaves no room for the entrepreneur.

The fourth desirable characteristic of a theory is the integration of social and economic factors. Because Porter relies heavily on the tool-kit of traditional economics, he places only limited emphasis on the social dimensions of corporate behaviour. However, the flexibility of his framework means that others have been able to incorporate insights from organizational behaviour into his approach. Because the resultant theory has not been formalized, however, it remains an uneasy mix of economic and sociological theory. Thus some recent accounts of strategic management suggest that managers who are highly rational in their attitudes to competitors may be highly irrational in dealings with their own colleagues. There may be some useful insights embodied in this view, but it cannot claim to be a proper theory of management behaviour until the boundaries between the rational and irrational have been properly explored, and the nature of the switch between the two modes of behaviour explained more fully. Strategic management theory therefore scores only moderately well on this criterion.

Whitley too achieves only moderate success, but for a rather different reason. He bases himself on sociology rather than economics. Since he applies himself to the study of economic phenomena, he is obliged to adapt his sociological insights for this purpose. The problem with Whitley is he does not adapt them enough. The reason, rather oddly, is that he does not accept the legitimacy of economic theory even for the analysis of economic phenomena. He tries to extend his sociological theory single-handedly into the economic domain. This means that in some cases he simply 're-invents the wheel' – an outcome that is sometimes disguised by expressing his results in unfamiliar jargon. If his execution were successful, he would finish up reinventing the whole of economics. This would have the advantage of expressing all the insights of economics and sociology in a single integrated form. In fact, however, he reinvents only a small amount of the subject. Key concepts like comparative advantage and information costs never get to be reinvented at all. As a result, they are just ignored, and important aspects of Asian economic growth remain unexplained. Although Whitley achieves some moderate success in his enterprise, therefore, his sociological theory of economics remains far from complete. Even if it were to be completed, it is doubtful if it would be as parsimonious as an economic theory, because of its rejection of rational action. But a final judgement on this issue cannot be made until both research agendas are complete.

Some readers may object that, up to this point, the evaluation has been weighted in favour of the global systems view, and its economics-based approach. This is because the four criteria so far used to evaluate the theories coincide with the qualities that the global systems view sets out to achieve. It could he said, with good reason, that neither Porter nor Whitley set out specifically to construct a theory of the global economic system, so they are bound to appear inferior on these criteria. A fair evaluation would take account of what the alternative theories themselves set out to achieve. The remaining two criteria in the table attempt to address this issue.

The fifth criterion reflects the main strengths of Porter's theory – its analysis of industry dynamics. It must be admitted right away that the global systems view is weak in its analysis of industrial dynamics. The formal models presented in Chapters 2, 3, 6 and 7 all focus primarily on the individual firm. Where interactions with other firms are involved, they are mainly of a co-operative rather than competitive nature – for example, the other firms are all joint venture partners, subcontractors or licensees.

The sixth criterion reflects the main strength of Whitley's theory – its focus on culture. Culture is certainly included in the global systems view, but only to a limited extent. The significance of corporate culture in motivating employees has been alluded to in several chapters, but not in any systematic way. Whitley seems to take the view that a full analysis of culture is impossible within the rational action framework of economics. However, it has been demonstrated elsewhere (Casson, 1991; 2000, Ch. 1) that this is wrong. Culture can be analysed from a rational action perspective in terms of the interaction between leaders and followers – leaders who fashion and articulate values and beliefs, and followers who share these beliefs. This interaction can generate efficiency gains because it exploits the 'public good' properties of values and beliefs. However, to apply such insights systematically, it is necessary to consider their implications, not only for firms, but also for regions and nation-states – indeed, for every type of institution that makes up the global system.

It is clear, therefore, that development of the global systems view remains incomplete. That is why this book is subtitled 'a new research agenda' rather than 'a new theory'. There remains a good deal of work to be done. Some of this is very ambitious work, moving from firm dynamics to industry dynamics, and from corporate culture to national culture. This is high-risk research, pushing forward the frontiers through conceptual advances. Other work is of a more technical nature – refining the models set out in this book by relaxing their more restrictive assumptions, such as increasing the number of countries, or number of firms. This work is somewhat less risky, but no less demanding in its own way. To add to the excitement, there is the continuing competitive challenge from alternative research agendas, both inside the IB field and outside it. The competing theories identified above are already established competitors, but new entrants are also likely to emerge. How long will it be, for example, before someone will propose a model of chaotic global dynamics as a basis for IB research?

There is a need for a new agenda, because the old agenda has already done its job. The theory of IB has proved to be one of the most successful fields of applied economics, in terms of its power to explain key facts, and its relevance for management and for public policy. These strengths need to be maintained by the new agenda. The old agenda is an excellent 'launch pad' for the new one. Progress in IB is most likely to come from building on existing foundations, rather than rejecting them in favour of something entirely new. This book has set out to show how this can be done.

REFERENCES

Aoki, M. (ed.) (1984) *The Economic Analysis of the Japanese Firm*, Amsterdam: North-Holland

Buchanan, J.M. *et al.* (1978) *The Economics of Politics*, London: Institute of Economic Affairs

Buckley, P.J. and M. Casson (1976) *The Future of the Multinational Enterprise*, London: Macmillan

Buckley, P.J. and M. Casson (1993) 'Economics as an imperialist social science', *Human Relations*, **46**(9), 1035–52

Casson, M. (1991) *Economics of Business Culture: Game Theory, Transaction Costs and Economic Performance*, Oxford: Clarendon Press

Casson, M. (2000) *Enterprise and Leadership: Studies on Firms, Markets and Networks*, Cheltenham: Edward Elgar

Drobak, J.N. and J.C. Nye (eds) (1997) *The Frontiers of the New Institutional Economics*, San Diego: Academic Press

Etzioni, A. (1988) *The Moral Dimension: Towards a New Economics*, New York: Free Press

Forrester, J.W. (1971) *World Dynamics*, Cambridge, MA: Wright-Allen Press

Foss, N.J. (1997) 'Understanding Business Systems: An Essay on the Economics and Sociology of Organisation', Copenhagen Business School, Mimeo

Gerlach, M.L. (1992) *Alliance Capitalism: The Social Organisation of Japanese Business*, Berkeley, CA: University of California Press

Granovetter, M. (1985) 'Economic action and social structure: the problem of embeddedness', *American Journal of Sociology*, **91**, 481–510

Gray, H.P. and S.M. Lundan (1993) 'Japanese multinationals and the stability of the GATT system', *International Trade Journal*, **7**(6), 635–53

Hamel, G. and C.K. Prahalad (1994) *Competing for the Future*, Boston, MA: Harvard University Press

Hamilton, G.C. and N. Woolsey Biggart (1988) 'Market, culture, and authority: a comparative analysis of management and organisation in the Far East', *American Journal of Sociology*, **94** (supplement), S52–S94

Jones, E.L. (1995) 'Culture and its relationship to economic change', *Journal of Institutional and Theoretical Economics*, **151**(2), 269–85

Jones, E.L. (1997) 'China's strategic preferences', *Agenda*, **4**(4), 495–504

Laurent, A. (1983) 'The cultural diversity of Western conceptions of management', *International Studies of Management and Organisation*, **13**(1–2), 75–96

Meadows, D. *et al.* (1974) *The Limits to Growth: A Report for the Club of Rome's Project on the Predicament of Mankind*, 2nd edn, New York: Universe Books

Morishima, M. (1982) *Why has Japan Succeeded?: Western Technology and the Japanese Ethos*, Cambridge: Cambridge University Press

North, D.C. (1990) *Institutions, Institutional Change and Economic Performance*, Cambridge: Cambridge University Press

Porter, M.E. (1980) *Competitive Strategy*, New York: Free Press

Porter, M.E. (1990) *The Competitive Advantage of Nations*, London: Macmillan

Porter, M.E. (1991) 'Towards a dynamic theory of strategy', *Strategic Management Journal*, **12** (special issue), 95–117

Posner, R.A. (1981) *The Economics of Justice*, Cambridge, MA: Harvard University Press

Räsänen, K. and R. Whipp (1992) 'National business recipes: a sector perspective', in R. Whitley (ed.), *European Business Systems: Firms and Markets in Their National Contexts*, London: Sage Publications

Redding, S.G. (1991) *The Spirit of Chinese Capitalism*, Berlin: de Gruyter

Schumpeter, J.A. (1934) *Theory of Economic Development* (trans. R. Opie), Cambridge, MA: Harvard University Press

Simon, H.A. (1959) 'Theories of decision-making in economics and behavioural sciences', *American Economic Review*, **49**, 253–83

Smelser, N.J. and R. Swedberg (eds) (1994) *The Handbook of Economic Sociology*, Princeton, NJ: Princeton University Press for the Russell Sage Foundation

Spender, L.C. (1989) *Industry Recipes: The Nature and Sources of Managerial Judgement*, Oxford: Basil Blackwell

Storper, M. and A.J. Scott (1995) 'The wealth of regions: market forces and policy imperatives in local and global context', *Futures*, **27**(5), 505–26

Vernon, R. (1966) 'International investment and international trade in the product cycle', *Quarterly Journal of Economics*, **80**, 190–207

Vogel, E.F. (1991) *The Four Little Dragons: The Spread of Industrialization in East Asia*, Cambridge, MA: Harvard University Press

Whitley, R. (1984) *The Intellectual and Social Organisation of the Sciences*, Oxford: Clarendon Press

Whitley, R. (ed.) (1992a) *European Business Systems: Firms and Markets in their National Contexts*, London: Sage

Whitley, R. (1992b) *Business Systems in East Asia: Firms, Markets and Societies*, London: Sage

Williamson, O.E. (1975) *Markets and Hierarchies: Analysis and Anti-trust Applications*, New York: Free Press

Williamson, O.E. (1985) *The Economic Institutions of Capitalism*, New York: Basic Books

Zysman, J. and L. Tyson (1983) *American Industry in International Competition – Government Policies and Corporate Strategies*, Ithaca, NY: Cornell University Press

Index